Permanent Evolution

Selected Essays on Literature, Theory and Film

Cultural Syllabus

Series Editor: Mark Lipovetsky (Columbia University)

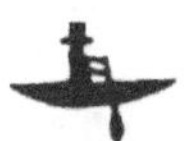

Permanent Evolution

Selected Essays on Literature, Theory and Film

YURI TYNIANOV

Translated and Edited
by AINSLEY MORSE
and PHILIP REDKO

Boston
2019

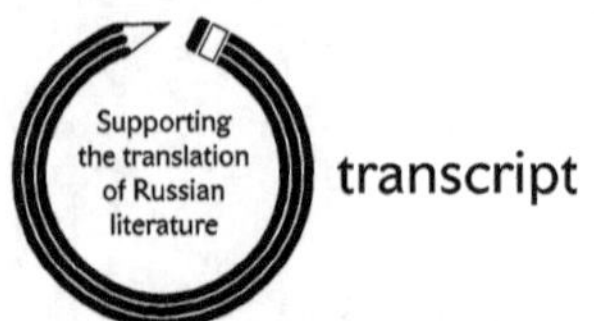

The publication of this book is supported by TRANSKRIPT: The Program for the Support of Translation of Russian Fiction, Poetry, and Non-fiction.

Library of Congress Cataloging-in-Publication Data

Names: Tyni͡anov, I͡U. N. (I͡Uriĭ Nikolaevich), 1894–1943, author. | Morse, Ainsley, translator, editor. | Redko, Philip, translator, editor. | Tyni͡anov, I͡U. N. (I͡Uriĭ Nikolaevich), 1894–1943. Arkhaisty i novatory. Selections. English. | Tyni͡anov, I͡U. N. (I͡Uriĭ Nikolaevich), 1894–1943. Poėtika, istorii͡a literatury, kino. Selections. English.

Title: Permanent evolution : selected essays on literature, theory and film / Yuri Tynianov; translated and edited by Ainsley Morse and Philip Redko.

Other titles: Cultural syllabus.

Description: Boston: Academic Studies Press, 2019. | Series: Cultural syllabus | Includes selected works from the author's "Arkhaisty i novatory" and "Poėtika, istorii͡a literatury, kino". | Includes bibliographical references and index.

Identifiers: LCCN 2019022646 (print) | LCCN 2019022647 (ebook) | ISBN 9781644690628 (hardback) | ISBN 9781618118417 (paperback) | ISBN 9781644690635 (adobe pdf)

Subjects: LCSH: Russian literature--History and criticism--Theory, etc. | Motion pictures--History. Classification: LCC PG2948 .T9613 2019 (print) | LCC PG2948 (ebook) | DDC 891.709/0042--dc23

LC record available at https://lccn.loc.gov/2019022646
LC ebook record available at https://lccn.loc.gov/2019022647

ISBN 9781644690628 (hardcover)
ISBN 9781644690635 (ebook)
ISBN 9781618118417 (paper)

Book design by PHi Business Solution.
Cover design by Ivan Grave.
On the cover: artwork by Pavel Zaltsman, *Habitat*, 1934. P., ink; *Gulliver*, 1930's. P., ink, pen. Courtesy of Lotta Zaltsman and Maria Zusmanovich.

Published by Academic Studies Press.
1577 Beacon Street
Brookline, MA 02446 USA
press@academicstudiespress.com
www.academicstudiespress.com

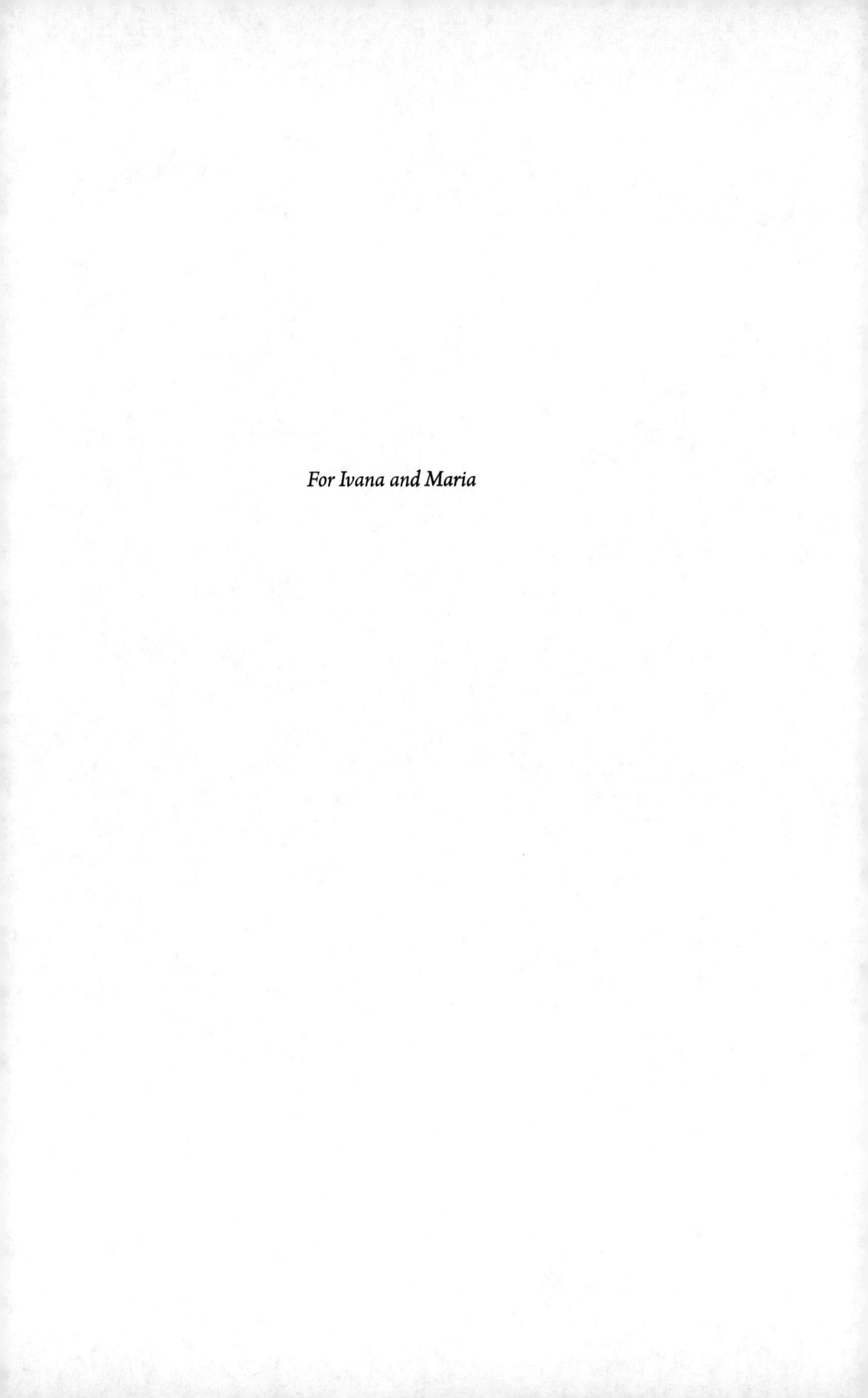

For Ivana and Maria

Contents

Acknowledgements

The following people provided hugely generous support as editors, readers and consultants on the texts: Polina Barskova, Alexandra Berlina, Caroline Lemak Brickman, Daniel Brooks, Marietta Chudakova, Luba Golburt, Daniel Green, Daria Khitrova, Vera Koshkina, Andrei Kostin, Ilya Kukulin, Mark Lipovetsky, Basil Lvoff, Alexander Markov, Carl Mautner, Tatiana Neshumova, Sergei Oushakine, Andrei Ustinov, Maria P. Vassileva, Sarah Vitali, and Michael Weinstein.

Special thanks to the editors at Academic Studies Press who supported and shepherded the project through its various stages: Oleh Kotsyuba, Igor Nemirovsky, Faith Stein, Ekaterina Yanduganova, Kira Nemirovsky, and Stuart Allen.

The article "Interlude" was published, in an earlier draft, in the journal *Common Knowledge* 24, no. 3 (2018): 498–542. Thanks to editors Aden Bar-Tura, Jeffrey Perl, and Kevin M. F. Platt.

Acknowledgments

A Note from the Editors-Translators

Compared to many pre-revolutionary literary critics and their Marxist successors, the Russian Formalist critics are mostly straightforward and accessible writers—Viktor Shklovsky, for instance, has been extensively translated, and comes across clearly in English. Tynianov is a somewhat stranger bird. Though rarely dry and never pedantic, his style can swing wildly between chatty, lapidary, and downright opaque. In his introduction to the 1929 collection *Archaists and Innovators,* Tynianov acknowledged that his language was sometimes difficult and even unclear, but that "language does not merely transmit concepts, … it is also a means of their construction."[1] As translators, we have strived to let Tynianov be Tynianov, which meant maintaining a mostly layperson's register of language in conjunction with sudden bursts of inventive terminology.

This book is the first comprehensive collection of Tynianov's theoretical work in English, as well as the first time that more than two essays appear translated in one consistent voice: prior publications of his theoretical essays have been translated at different times and by different people and scattered throughout anthologies.[2] Tynianov's sense of the complex interconnectedness of literary processes is mirrored in his own compact, sometimes strikingly poetic writing: the same metaphors, phrases, and literary examples keep turning up in

1 Iurii Tynianov, *Arkhaisty i novatory* [Permanent Evolution] (Leningrad: Priboi, 1929) includes "Literary Fact," "On Literary Evolution," "The Ode as Oratorical Genre," "Tyutchev and Heine," "Dostoevskii and Gogol (Toward a Theory of Parody)," "Interlude," and "On Khlebnikov."

2 Some of Tynianov's historical novels have been translated into English: Yuri Tynianov, *Death of the Vazir-Mukhtar,* trans. Susan Causey and Vera Tsareva-Brauner (London: LookMedia, 2018); *Lieutenant Kijé; Young Vitushishnikov: two novellas,* trans. Mirra Ginsburg (1990); *Young Pushkin,* trans. Anna Kurkina Rush and Christopher Rush (2007).

unexpected corners, simultaneously exhibiting new facets and reminding the reader of their previous uses. A further motivation for translating these essays as a group was to demonstrate the remarkable coherence and consistency of Tynianov's thought (notwithstanding his occasionally slapdash terminology) over a wide range of material.

Tynianov's terminology invites further explanation. Certain terms—many of them rather unremarkable words with ordinary dictionary meanings, like *shift* or *plan*—acquire specific meanings in Tynianov's theoretical constructions. These terms pop up in different articles, in application to different material, throughout the collection—and the frequency of these recurrences was, again, a major motivation for undertaking a large-scale translation of Tynianov's work. To take one example: the concept of "shift" (covered by the noun *smena*—meaning both a change or alteration and a length of time, for example "the night shift"—and the related verb *smeshchat'/smestit'*) can also mean to "displace" or "supplant"; the idea of "succession" is also present. Of the available options, "shift" is the most open-ended and capacious; we occasionally substitute one of the other options for clarity's sake. Recurring terms like these, along with less familiar Russian literary terms, have been marked in the texts and are defined in the Terms appendix at the end of the volume.

Just as he returns again and again to concepts like that of "shift" or "orientation," Tynianov makes frequent reference to a wide array of figures stretching across three centuries of Russian literature. The first part of the appendix ("Names and Terms") identifies writers and other figures who appear in multiple articles; if a name or term is not identified in a footnote, it will be marked with a superscript N or T and found in this section.

While we felt it crucial to give Tynianov a recognizable and consistent English voice, the copious quotations in his articles (primarily of poetry) were another matter. Wherever possible, we gratefully made use of excellent existing translations: James Falen's masterful, rhymed *Eugene Onegin*, Jesse Zeldin's rendition of Gogol's *Selected Passages from Correspondence with Friends*, or Clarence Brown and W. S. Merwin's classic translations of early Mandelstam. When left to our own devices with the poetry, we tended to prioritize Tynianov's theoretical aims; our goal was to demonstrate Tynianov's points about the function of poetic devices rather than to create freestanding poetic translations.

While this collection reproduces about half of the articles included in *Archaists and Innovators*, the main source for original texts was the exhaustively annotated *Poetics. Literary History. Film* (1977).[3] Edited by Alexander and Marietta Chudakov, and Evgeny Toddes, this seminal volume remains the most comprehensive Russian edition of Tynianov's work and represents a truly heroic effort on the editors' part. As Marietta Chudakova recalls, they spent two years in the archives composing and assembling the notes (over 250 pages' worth), and another four years pushing the volume past the formidable, multitiered behemoth of Soviet censorship. While Tynianov was not himself subject to state repression, many of his contemporary subjects (Akhmatova, Mandelstam, Pasternak, and others) had become unprintable in the years following the initial publication of his articles. For example, Chudakova reminisced about an editor telling her to reduce the number of times Mandelstam was mentioned in the notes from seventeen to two, resulting in some peculiarly convoluted formulations ("compare a different assessment of these same features of the Serapions' prose by the author of 'A Conversation about Dante' [...]").[4] Despite these compulsory verbal acrobatics, the notes to the 1977 edition are a priceless resource; we relied on them extensively in our work as translators and have gratefully translated some of them as notes to the English text of the articles.

The articles in this collection present Tynianov's "greatest hits" (his most frequently anthologized foundational theoretical statements like "Literary Fact" and "On Literary Evolution"), in company with denser, thornier works like "The Ode as an Oratorical Genre" and "On the Composition of *Eugene Onegin*," and lesser-known pieces that seem to address narrowly specialized topics: "Tyutchev and Heine" or "On the Screenplay." As its title indicates, *Poetics. Literary History. Film* groups the articles by discipline; by contrast, this collection is organized for the most part in chronological order, in an attempt to demonstrate the continuity of Tynianov's thought as it crisscrosses thematic, generic, and disciplinary boundaries. As each article shows, Tynianov never really wrote "just" about Tyutchev, or screenplays, or odes: while discussing concrete material, often in exacting and illuminating detail, Tynianov always has a larger theoretical point to make, using whatever material is closest at hand

---

3 Iurii Tynianov, *Poetika. Istoriia literatury. Kino*, eds. M. O. Chudakova, A. P. Chudakov, and E. A. Toddes (Moscow: Nauka, 1977), or *PILK* (as this volume is affectionately known in Russian), is the source for all of the articles translated here except for "On Khlebnikov." Henceforth, the volume will be referred to as *PILK*. Selected notes in this publication are by A. P. Chudakov [*AC*]; additional notes are by Yuri Tynianov [*YT*] and the translators [unmarked].

4 See "The Serapion Brothers. Almanac 1" [Serapionovy brat'ia. Almanakh I], in ibid., 449 n8.

(see Daria Khitrova's introduction for an extended discussion of Tynianov's theoretical practice).

This collection aims to show Tynianov's place in the history of literary theory, while also pointing to the practical relevance of his thinking for literary analysis today. The literary scholar Lydia Ginzburg, who studied with Tynianov in the 1920s, later described the distinctive nature of Tynianov's thinking and its surprisingly broad applicability:

> Tynianov's ideas, rather than being incontestable or irrevocable (that never happens), were applicable in a very enduring and tenable way. There are ideas, indeed very substantial ones, which function exactly as intended and move in a straight line from teacher to student. Then there are thoughts that spread out in circles: they can be influential in various contexts and at great distances from the article or book in which they are first suggested. This is how it worked with Tynianov's ideas. They generated new concepts, were applied and tested in practice. Using material, meanwhile, that Tynianov himself had not studied. Transplanted into a new environment, his conceptions continued working and bringing in new results.[5]

We hope very much that this most recent translation will take root and continue to bring in new results for students of literature all over the English-speaking world.

Ainsley Morse
Riverside, CA

Philip Redko
Cambridge, MA

August, 2018

---

5 Lidiia Ginzburg, "Tynianov—literaturoved," in *Zapisnye knizhki* (St. Petersburg: Iskusstvo-SPb, 2012), 447.

Introduction

DARIA KHITROVA

At present, the knowledge of Russian Formalist thought within Anglo-American academic circles is often limited to Viktor Shklovsky's[N] notion of defamiliarization and his distinction between fabula[T] [story or storyline] and *siuzhet*[T] [plot]. Illuminating as they are, both concepts come from the early period of Formalism (which is also the source of many popular misconceptions about the Formalists and their work). At the same time, a whole range of seminal theoretical discoveries by Formalist scholars, Yuri Tynianov in particular, remains largely overlooked or unknowingly reinvented by scholars of different disciplines, from English to Comparative Literature to Film Studies. Tynianov's entrance onto the international stage is an important step in advancing modern literary theory—and recovering its history.

This volume does not offer a complete edition of Tynianov's scholarly works. More translations will hopefully follow. And English-speaking readers have yet to discover Tynianov's historical fiction, which is still widely read in Russia and is among the masterpieces of Modernist prose. That being said, this volume is a groundbreaking step towards rediscovering Tynianov—not just for the sake of historical justice, but for the future of literary studies.

***

In his foreword to a 1928 volume by Velimir Khlebnikov[N] (another thinker who defied categorization—see "On Khlebnikov" in the present collection),[1] Tynianov offers an assessment that applies equally well to his own aesthetic and literary-theoretical sensibilities: "Standing before the judgment of Khlebnikov's

1 Others have noted the parallel between Tynianov and Khlebnikov. Veniamin Kaverin and Vladimir Novikov's volume on Tynianov—*Novoe zrenie* (Moscow: Kniga, 1988)—is partially built around this analogy.

new framework, literary traditions find themselves flung wide open. The result is an enormous shift[T] in traditions.[2] 'The [twelfth-century] Igor Tale' is suddenly more modern than [contemporary poet Valery] Briusov."[3] (227) Six years earlier, Osip Mandelstam had likewise linked Khlebnikov and "The Igor Tale": "When the vivid and complex language of 'The Igor Tale' was first heard—secular, worldly, and Russian through and through—this was the beginning of Russian literature. And as long as Velimir Khlebnikov, a contemporary Russian writer, is immersed in the thick of Russian etymology, in the darkness of its night, which is so dear to the clever reader, Russian literature is kept alive […]."[4]

Just as Mandelstam considered "The Igor Tale" the origin of Russian literature, we can consider Formalism a kind of point of origin for Russian (and not only Russian) literary theory. But the Formalists showed that historical time is not linear: the distant past can live in the future; the future can be buried under a mountain of cultural layers. "Nothing repeats itself in history," Boris Eikhenbaum[N] wrote, "because nothing ever disappears, it only undergoes various transformations."[5] The same can be said of literary studies: Formalism today "is suddenly more modern" than poststructuralism or postmodernism.[6] Like Khlebnikov, it "burrowed enough pathways in the ground

2 Tynianov's notion of the "shift" is central to his thinking in virtually all of the articles in this collection. See, in particular, "On Literary Evolution" (267–282).

3 "The Igor Tale" (also known as "The Tale of Igor's Campaign" or "The Lay of the Host of Igor") is a late twelfth-century epic poem by an anonymous author. The sophistication of its language and style set it apart from other early Russian writing.

4 Osip Mandel'shtam, *Slovo i kul'tura* (Moscow: Sovetskii pisatel', 1987), 58.

5 Boris Eikhenbaum, *Lermontov: Opyt istoriko-literaturnoi otsenki* (Leningrad: Gosudarstvennoe izdatel'stvo, 1924), 9.

6 I want to state from the outset that I understand "Formalism" to mean the work of the scholars who comprised the core of Petrograd's "Society for the Study of Poetic Language" [OPOYAZ]: Shklovsky, Tynianov, Eikhenbaum, Jakobson, and, up to a certain point, [Boris] Tomashevsky. One of the main reasons that the Formalist method is often misunderstood has to do with the utterly chaotic way its members were counted (something inherited from the literary journal polemics of the 1920s): the ranks of Formalism often include Viktor Zhirmunsky, members of the Moscow Linguistics Circle, members of the Left Front of Art (LEF), and even, in some publications, the Constructivists and Dziga Vertov's "kino-eyes" [kinoks]. While all of these groups and individuals had more or less direct links to the Formalists, trying to assemble a coherent scholarly system from the sum of their works would be to act, as Roman Jakobson put it, like the "police who, when ordered to arrest a certain person, would bring in everybody and everything they happened to find in the suspect's apartment as well as all passersby encountered in the street, just to make sure" (see Viktor Erlich, *Russian Formalism: History—Doctrine* [The Hague: Mouton, 1955], 71). The Moscow Linguistics Circle had one link in common with the core members of OPOYAZ—Jakobson; for LEF, the link was Shklovsky (Osip Brik, who had been a key figure in early

to last into the next century." A hundred years have almost passed; Tynianov has yet to be discovered.

To this day, surveys of literary theory often judge Formalism by its name: Formalism privileges form, they claim, and analyzes texts without considering historical context. Both of these assumptions are incorrect. "Without naming Khlebnikov and sometimes without even having heard of him, poets are using him; he is present as a framework, a tendency" (192); the same can be said about Tynianov's legacy as a scholar. "Khlebnikov's language theory was hurriedly declared *zaum*[T], and everyone settled happily for the notion that he had invented a kind of meaningless sound-speech. But the point of Khlebnikov's theory lay elsewhere. He shifted poetry's center of gravity from questions of sound to the question of meaning." (225) That same tendency to simplify led scholars to file away Formalism as a matter of schoolboy excesses, the raging puberty of literary theory, even though the question of meaning—not in terms of fabula or form, but as function—had been raised by none other than the Formalists.

The two culprits behind this mishandling of the Formalist legacy are Stalinism and the persistent appeal of a simplified narrative, whose causal logic is so entrenched that we barely notice how its explanations have not changed in a hundred years. In scholarship, causality can be deadly—mostly because of how dismally predictable its results are, how it can only lead to redundancy. If we already know that industrialization or capitalism is the cause, and everything else the effect, why bother reading to the end? Any study becomes, as Eikhenbaum said, "a trip to a known destination with a ticket purchased well in advance."[7] The algebra of literary processes is replaced by finger counting, a neat sequencing of literary epochs, all similarly characterized by social upheavals (and often by the very same ones: in literary history, Romanticism, Realism, Naturalism, and Modernism all get to share industrialization like it's some kind of communal apartment). The way to tell that this periodization is, at best, only good enough for a high school cheat sheet is to try to determine the main intellectual currents of our present moment (cf. Hegel's *Zeitgeist*). For every current

OPOYAZ, had become the leader of LEF and moved away from Formalist theory in the early 1920s). Eikhenbaum and Tynianov treated both of these groups with caution, and sometimes with skepticism or even disdain. They parted ways with Zhirmunsky in the early 1920s; Tomashevsky publicly declared Formalism to be dead in 1927—*DK.*

7 B. M. Eikhenbaum, *Lev Tolstoi: Issledovaniia. Stat'i.* (St. Petersburg: Fakul'tet filologii i iskusstv Sankt-Peterburgskogo Gosudarstvennogo Universiteta, 2009), 149. The text is dated July 14, 1928.

there is a countercurrent, as well as countless competitors to both; all of these are constantly changing, and they exist only in dynamic relation to each other. We cannot predict which of them will, in hindsight, turn out to be more prominent than the rest and contribute to our understanding of the period (and give it its name), and which one will seem to us secondary and only attract attention later on—we will find out only after the fact. The present, like any other period of time, is like a soup that is still on the stove. Or, as Tynianov and Roman Jakobson[N] put it: "Pure synchronism is now revealed to be an illusion: each synchronic system has its own past and future as integral structural elements of the system." (287)

The Formalists struggled as best they could to free scholarship from primitive causality—but certainly not from historical context. Tynianov does not mince words in summing up the issue: "Studying phenomena cannot be reduced to studying their [genesis], or else the entirety of the study of mankind would be reduced to studying the only causal act that led to its creation."[8] Historical phenomena, both literary and otherwise, coexist, though not always at the same time: they work separately or in unison. These interactions are a productive area of inquiry; by contrast, the prefabricated hierarchy of factors that assigns one "series"[T] of phenomena (economic, political, social) a leading role as causes, and another (literary, cultural) a subordinate role as effects, is both unproductive and unfair. Literature and art risk being relegated to the role of distant colonies, occasionally reached by the echoes of political and economic events in the capital. History is more complex than that.

A hundred years later, Eikhenbaum's ominous warning still holds true—or has become true again: "Literary scholarship did not expend tremendous effort to liberate itself from serving the history of culture, philosophy, psychology, etc., just to become a servant of the judiciary and economic sciences and to live the sad life of cheap journalism."[9] The rapid transformation of the humanities into a province of the social sciences makes us hope that Formalism is still in our future.

Another victim of the simplified narrative is the very history of Formalism. Viktor Erlich, whose otherwise insightful *Russian Formalism: History—Doctrine* (The Hague: Mouton, 1955) set the tone for Formalism's reception by English language scholarship, decided to organize it around a narrative

---

8 Quoted in D. Ustinov, "Materialy disputa 'Marksizm i formal'nyi metod' 6 marta 1927," *Novoe Literaturnoe Obozrenie* 50 (2001): 259. Note that Ustinov gives the word "illegible" in brackets, while there is every reason to assume Tynianov means "genesis" (as given in the text)—*DK.*

9 Eikhenbaum, *O literature* (Moscow: Sovetskii pisatel', 1987), 436.

arc of rise and fall. As a result, Formalism was reduced to the earliest concepts (and not even all of them) introduced by Shklovsky and Jakobson: literariness, device, defamiliarization, and the distinction between fabula and *siuzhet*. The later work of the Formalists is presented as a search for compromise and a gradual retreat from their positions, which, we are told, were not worth defending in the first place because they were too radical. It reads like Erlich is trying to convince the Formalists, now grown up and mature at the end of the 1920s, to be less stubborn, to drop their youthful rambunctiousness, and accept the sober triumph of common sense; this recalls parents of recent college grads talking their children into getting a haircut and buying a nice suit.

Erlich's indefatigable belief in the social ("real life") foundation of literature only proves that science is counterintuitive: to come to the conclusion that the Earth revolves around the sun, and not the other way around, one must overcome everyday habits of perception. What's even more important is that the narrative he proposes, which has taken hold in English language scholarship, is inaccurate: Formalism did not start declining, and then, besieged by crisis and internal disagreements, fall off entirely, only managing to pass its sputtering torch to Prague structuralism, as Erlich (a student of Jakobson, who had moved to Prague) would have it. Toward the end of the 1920s, as a result of disagreements and battles, Formalism settled on two main plans of attack: a collectively authored history of Russian literature and a radical reestablishing of OPOYAZ.[10] There were, of course, disagreements among the core members of the Formalists (Shklovsky, Tynianov, and Eikhenbaum), but these were considered productive. They could not conceive of scholarship without arguments or doubts. Tynianov said of their "dogma-free world": "We are on the way. I don't know where we'll end up."[11]

The opportunity to move freely ahead, without knowing where they would end up—further indication of the Formalists' resistance to causal determinism—was harshly blocked by political dogma.[12] In February 1929,

10 On the reestablishing of OPOYAZ, see A. Galushkin, "'I tak, stavshi na kostiakh, budem trubit' sbor …,' K istorii nesostoiavshegosia vozrozhdeniia Opoiaza v 1928–1930 gg.," *Novoe Literaturnoe Obozrenie* 44 (2000): 136–153. On the collectively authored history of Russian literature, see Tynianov, *PILK*, 570–571.

11 Quoted in Ustinov, "Materialy disputa," 259.

12 It is hard to imagine that, if an opportunity presented itself for OPOYAZ and its collective work to be revived, they would not have taken advantage of it because of scholarly disagreements or personal grievances (they had fought and reconciled many times before). At the

Eikhenbaum responded to Shklovsky's suggestion that they hold a new debate: "Everywhere you look it's all politics and no scholarship. They will pester us with 'causality,' and rejecting causality will be considered heresy, a deviation, etc."[13] This "deviation" [uklon] referred to the mortally dangerous accusation of Trotskyism (Leon Trotsky had been exiled from the USSR that very same February of 1929). Soon enough Tynianov and Eikhenbaum were fired from the State Institute of Art History for "ideological unfitness"; any new public associations (including literary ones) were virtually banned; censorship and attacks in the press grew to a feverish pitch (the very word "formalism" became a slur and has retained that connotation to the present day). Under these circumstances it was pointless to hold a debate, not because it had already been won or lost, but because at that point any form of discussion was impossible.

Formalism didn't die of natural causes; on the contrary, its life was cut short just when it was getting started. What we are left with is just the preliminary work. That realization makes it even more impressive how many "pathways" the Formalists left behind for future work—especially Tynianov, who was allotted all of ten years from the beginning of his doctoral work to the completion of his last theoretical article. Let us try to reconstruct these pathways.

***

It is difficult to summarize Formalist theory because the Formalists never really bothered to formulate it—it was never their goal to do so. They thought of theory as a process, rather than a starting point or a specific destination to which you can buy a train ticket. Theory was useful to them not as a legend explaining a map, but as a means of doing actual work. Their theory

---

time they had been planning a conceptual volume that would have contained responses to the theses of Tynianov and Jakobson (see Galushkin, "'I tak'": 136–153). This format assumed the existence of internal polemics. The frequently repeated explanation that "external and internal reasons" brought about the decline of Formalism was convincingly refuted by M. O. Chudakova thirty years ago (M. O. Chudakova, "Sotsial'naia praktika, filologicheskaia refleksiia i literatura v nauchnoi biografii Tynianova i Eikhenbauma," in *Tynianovskii sbornik: Vtorye Tynianovskie Chteniia* [Riga: Zinatne, 1986], 103). To take her thought even further, these reasons were really "external and external": the powerful ideological and repressive pressure of the late 1920s created the reasons which we have come to call "internal," such as Tynianov's and Eikhenbaum's pessimism about their ability to "work," Jakobson's inability to participate, Shklovsky's rising fear of repression due to his dubious political past (which, as Galushkin points out, led to his disingenuous repentance and acceptance of Marxism; neither Tynianov nor Eikhenbaum were then repentant). On the contrary, in their letters of 1928–1929, these scholars discussed their work with overwhelming enthusiasm and energy.

13 Quoted in Ustinov, "Materialy disputa," 278.

grew, became more precise, more complex, and took on new shapes; it was not defined and then applied. In our academic work, the verb "to use" determines our relationship to theory: "you may want to use this or that theorist," a professor will advise their students. Thus theory works less as a question that gets asked than as a predetermined answer, a ready-made dress: you can try it on and see if it suits you. The Formalists would not have recognized this ready-made object as theory; once something had been completed, they considered it over and done with. This is why we cannot "use" formalist theory—but we can continue its work.

Jakobson talked about Tynianov's "faith in the coexistence of the present and the past, [...] the continuity between yesterday's memories, and prototypes and portents from the distant past."[14] This observation holds the key to Tynianov's scholarship. The present and the past, the contemporary and the historical, do not follow each other like marks etched on a ruler; they coexist, they live side by side. Grandmothers wear the fashions of their youth, their daughters find them outmoded, their granddaughters don't notice, but their great-granddaughters copy their style—and all the while, the original dress is still there. They are all contemporary. The contemporary person does not know what will happen tomorrow, but neither does history. "We don't know where we'll end up." We still don't know where they would have ended up. And if any given day has its tomorrow, then history is just a muddle of contemporaneities, none of them ready or resolved.

Tynianov sees the history of literature not as a history of results pinned down in time, but a history of processes, unfinished and unresolved. The opening chapter in his novel about Alexander Griboedov[N] [*The Death of the Vazir-Mukhtar*] concludes with the words: "Nothing had been decided yet."[15] This is also the starting point for Tynianov the scholar: it describes the nature of contemporary literature as well as its history. In Tynianov's view of history, a writer like Shakespeare or Pushkin[N] is not yet a monument. His is not a history of finished results, but a dynamic system of possibilities, a history of what happened and what did not happen. It is a history of doubts and choices, of what was decided and what was rejected or did not come to pass. "There are roads we have lost, rivers that dried up or changed course."[16]

---

14 R. O. Jakobson, "Iurii Tynianov v Prage," in *Selected Writings*, vol. 5 (The Hague, 1979), 561.

15 Iurii Tynianov, *Sobranie sochinenii v trekh tomakh* (Moscow/Leningrad: GIKhL, 1959). 2:12.

16 Iurii Tynianov, "Predislovie," in *Dnevnik V. K. Kiukhel'bekera* (Leningrad: Priboi, 1929), 3.

We can draw two conclusions from this. First: Tynianov's method is to examine the literary text as a process.[17] He is interested in drafts, preliminary work, crossed out sections, typos, misattributions, misunderstandings, mishandlings, and everything else that happens to a text in the course of its creation and subsequent life—and not out of some archaeological curiosity. A text does not emerge fully formed from its author, like Athena from the head of Zeus. The many doubts surrounding a text—the structure of the plot, the choice of meter, stylistic changes—are proof of the broad spectrum of possibilities inherent in the literary system. But even when the text is printed and becomes a finished material object, the text itself is more than just a sum total of its parts; it remains a process—a dynamic and often contradictory system of relations and interactions. Formalism is not interested in form, but in *formation*—the deformations and transformations that occur as part of the ongoing process of the text, which, counterintuitively, never comes to an end.

The second conclusion is that what is possible does not always come to be. Choices are not always successful. Elements of a text can be in conflict, sticking out or jostling with each other. Things that have been cast aside (by the author, or by history as written by the victors) can turn out to be more productive. Mistakes and accidents can be systemic. The periphery, the place where the system ceases to operate, can tell us more about its workings than the center. This is Tynianov's chosen material. His favorite characters are misfits, both people and texts; not the finished results of history but its rough drafts and lost roads. The poets Wilhelm Küchelbecker[N] and Pavel Katenin[N] were written out of literary history in the 1820s, and that action seemed irreversible at the time. However, when literature is seen as a process, "nothing has been decided yet" and the "outcasts" have every right to become heroes.[18] "Woe from Wit," the comedy that cemented Griboedov's[N] legacy, was the successful side effect of his unsuccessful work on a tragedy; as Tynianov demonstrates, the pathos of high tragedy is still in the text, peeking out from under its comic surface.

The most salient feature of Tynianov's critical legacy is his ability to theorize literary history while historicizing literary theory. Tynianov's theory of

17 Tynianov's student at the State Institute of Art History, Tamara Khmel'nitskaya, has a very insightful article about this, "Emkost' slova" [The capacious word], in *Vospominaniia o Iu. N. Tynianove. Portrety i vstrechi*, ed. V. A. Kaverin (Moscow: Sovetskii pisatel', 1983), 121–137.

18 *Otverzhennye* [The Outcasts] is the standard Russian translation of Hugo's *Les Misérables*, and Tynianov wanted to use this title for a publishing project that remained unrealized—an anthology of Russian poets who were mocked or became critical failures in their lifetimes in spite of the evolutionary significance of their experiments. See Tynianov, *PILK*, 431, 538.

literature is always a theory of history; literary history requires its own theory because it is the least beholden to temporal laws. Shklovsky understood Tynianov's work in the following way: "Literature exists outside of time; i.e., its sound is that of an organ, not a grand piano: it keeps resonating."[19] Rather than being discarded, its objects pile up, so they can eventually be reintroduced as new possibilities. Literary history is thus free from any kind of external determinism, not just causal, but also temporal. Dates are linked to results, but processes are ongoing and "don't know where [they'll] end up." Literature does not move forward along a timeline, but in all possible directions. Shklovsky suggested that Tynianov's book *Archaists and Innovators* (cited in the Translators' Preface) should have been called *Archaists-Innovators*;[20] its argument traces how, again and again, a marginal literary trend built around archaic language and intentionally difficult poetic speech brought fresh air into Russian literature, along with new possibilities for its development. It is often the case that you have to go backwards to move forward.

In 1930, the volume *How We Write* [Kak my pishem] was published in Leningrad. In it, famous contemporary writers, from Andrei Bely[N] to Mikhail Zoshchenko, were asked to answer sixteen questions about their work habits ("When do you work: morning, evening, night?"; "Do you use substances, and in what amounts?"; and so forth).[21] The book's introduction stated that "the organization of labor is, in fact, the leitmotif of everything that has happened in our country over the last few years."[22] Tynianov ignored virtually all the guidelines, instead submitting sixteen numbered examples of Modernist theoretical microprose. For question ten, "What do you find more difficult: the beginning, end, or middle of a work?" Tynianov wrote the following:

> I like rough-edged, unpolished, unfinished things.
>
> I respect the rough, unpolished misfits, the mutterers, whose sentences you have to finish yourself. I love the provincials in whom history lies piled in awkwardly uneven layers, and who therefore tend to take the sharpest turns." There are quiet rebellions that have been hiding in a crate for a hundred or two hundred years. When the house is set to be demolished or rebuilt, the crate is found and broken open.

19 Ibid., 568.

20 Ibid.

21 Ibid., 6.

22 *Kak my pishem* (Moscow: Kniga, 1989), 5. In the afterword to this latest edition, M. O. Chudakova contends that this statement about labor was Zamiatin's.

"Oh," they say, "look at him! So ugly."
"Friend, call me by my name."[23]

***

The tenets of early Formalism, which Shklovsky was calling "antediluvian" by the late 1920s, are well known; the development of Formalist theory over the course of the 1920s is less widely known.[24] It is often described as either a concession or a kind of sobering up; as if the Formalists admitted, of their own free will (or maybe not), that literature cannot exist "separate from life." This reading is incorrect. The pathos of early Formalism lies in its specificity, in the right of literary study to focus on literature, rather than serve other related fields. The social sciences, psychology, history, etc., use literature as a resource, as raw material; for literary studies, literature is the end rather than the means. Theirs was the pathos of a war for independence, a declaration of autonomy. After independence has been won and new borders drawn, negotiations with neighboring countries can commence.

In 1925, in response to ideological attacks on Formalism by prominent state figures (including Trotsky and State Commissar of Enlightenment Anatoly Lunacharsky), Eikhenbaum felt compelled to summarize Formalist theory. Hoping to show that its opponents had entirely misunderstood what it was, he decided not to provide a list of tenets, but to trace Formalism as a process, starting with the first OPOYAZ publications.[25] Three years later, when putting together a volume of his own theoretical works, Tynianov rejected this approach out of a kind of authorial humility:

> I should have presented the works in the order they were written: then the contradictions found among them could be explained as a gradual reworking of conclusions, in response to the broader material being discussed; so the theoretical articles at the beginning of the volume would be seen as

---

23 Ibid., 144.

24 This is not to discount the scholarly work dedicated to Formalism, from the fundamental monograph by Aage Hansen-Loeve to recent works by Arkady Bliumbaum, Ilya Kalinin, Yan Levchenko, Ilona Svetlikova, and others who engage deeply and thoroughly with Formalist theory, as well as the serial *Tynianov Collections* of essays and materials, edited since 1984 by Chudakova, Chudakov and Toddes (editors of *PILK*).

25 Eikhenbaum, *O literature*, 375–408. An English version is available: Boris Eikhenbaum, "The Theory of the 'Formal Method,'" in *Russian Formalist Criticism: Four Essays*, ed. and trans. Lee T. Lemon and Marion J. Reis (Lincoln, NE: University of Nebraska Press, 1965), 99–139.

> conclusions drawn from a specific set of materials, and as a set of assumptions based on these conclusions, rather than a collection of theses. ...
> ... It seems immodest to force the reader to take the same route through topics and conclusions that I walked, since the subject of this book is the evolution of literature, rather than that of the author.[26]

The editors of the present volume have no reason to indulge Tynianov's modesty: his works are given here in more or less chronological order, and the reader is given the opportunity to "take the same route through topics and conclusions" and to observe Tynianov's theoretical process.

"Dostoevsky and Gogol. Toward a Theory of Parody" (written in 1919, published in 1921) was Tynianov's first published article. He had joined OPOYAZ only a year earlier, and he was already building on their previous work. Shklovsky had analyzed parody as a device based on examples from Boccaccio and Sterne in articles from 1918–1919. Tynianov looks at one example—the mean-spirited parody of Nikolai Gogol[N] in Fyodor Dostoevsky's *The Village of Stepanchikovo* (the simplified narrative of high school textbooks usually shows Gogol and Dostoevsky as peaceful neighbors in the portrait gallery of eternal glory).[27] Tynianov shows that parody is not just a device operating within the text, but a force shifting the order of values in a literary system, and thus an evolutionary mechanism. What is more, Dostoevsky parodies Gogol using Gogol's own devices, which Tynianov traces from early, "comic" Gogol to the later Gogol-as-prophet, demonstrating their immutability. The "moral revolution" that Gogol envisioned was supposed to come about in accordance with the laws of his fiction, "marvelously and simply." Devices change their function, in this case, from literary to moral; and Tynianov shows that literature advances not by immanent development, but by pushing off from existing phenomena.

The three essays that follow "Dostoevsky and Gogol" in this volume—"Tyutchev and Heine," "The Ode as an Oratorical Genre," and "On the Composition of *Eugene Onegin*"—were all written in the early 1920s, and all serve as both independent historical-theoretical works, as well as historical-theoretical satellites of Tynianov's purely theoretical work, his 1924 book *The Problem of Verse Language* [Problema stikhotvornogo iazyka] (Leningrad: Academia, 1924). Tynianov summarized the findings of this book in the article "Interlude" (also 1924): "Poetry is speech transformed; it is

26 Tynianov, *PILK*, 395.

27 For more on Gogol, see "Dostoevsky and Gogol" (27–63).

human speech that has outgrown itself. Language in poetry has thousands of unexpected shades of meaning; poetry gives language a new dimension. New poetry is new vision." (175)

At first, Tynianov suggested *The Problem of Verse Semantics* as a title for the work, but this was rejected by the editor, who disliked the unpoetic sound of "semantics." The starting point of his argument is a straightforward observation: verse does not merely sound different from prose; the sound aspect and rhythm of poetry are what makes it poetry. But Tynianov further demonstrates that rhythm does not merely shape meaning—it *forms* meaning within verse. The meaning of a word in a poem is different from the meaning of the same word in prose or in nonliterary speech, not least in terms of quantity. In everyday life, we strive toward economy, specificity, narrowness of meaning, in order to be best understood by our interlocutors; we pick one meaning from among the many possible dictionary definitions of a word; we converse in meanings and don't pay much attention to sound. Verse operates in the opposite, wholly uneconomical, way; it actualizes rather than rejects the other existing (or even just potential) meanings of a word. Sound has a direct influence on meaning—it becomes a *semantic* factor. Moreover, in poetry each word drags its many poetry-specific meanings and associations along like a long bridal veil: a rose in a line of verse will evoke not a florist's stall but "that which we call a rose ..."; "uncle" will refer not to your own relative but to [Eugene] Onegin's.

In the three articles on the language of poetry, Tynianov analyzes verse semantics with reference to another theoretical question—that of literary evolution, which undermines the established historical narrative at every step. The well-mannered classicism of the eighteenth century is shown to be the arena of an epic battle over the priorities of verse: Mikhail Lomonosov[N] insisted on difficulty, Alexander Sumarokov[N] on clarity. Fyodor Tyutchev,[N] who to this day is taught to schoolchildren as a "Romantic," is actually an inheritor of the tradition of eighteenth century rhetoric. Pushkin's *Eugene Onegin* turns out to be not the story of the "superfluous" Onegin and faithful Tatyana, but a grand verse experiment, whose main character is merely a semantic unit used to link the different parts of the work.

In 1924, Tynianov published "Literary Fact," the first manifesto of his theory of history, which starts out by asking outright "What is literature?" The answer: it depends; "the fact of evolution sweeps away all firm and static definitions." The same principle applies to all literary terms, genres, and even texts. The word "evolution" brings to mind a kind of organic continuity, so Tynianov specifies: "Not gradual evolution, but a leap; not development, but shift." (154) This is an evolution that does not move along the axis of time; it is a redistribution of values, a geographic approach to history: "As it turns out, it's not just the borders of literature—its periphery and frontiers—that are fluid: the center itself is fluid as well. Instead of one primordial, regular stream of succession flowing and evolving at the center of literature, with new phenomena congregating around its edges, it is these new phenomena that come to occupy the center, while what was previously in the center is in turn relegated to the periphery." (156) This is not a history of progress—and that is one of the principal tenets of Formalism.

Tynianov uses "literary fact" to mean any verbal construct that is perceived as literature. The novel is surely one, but a literary fact can also be an anecdote, a memoir, a radio or film screenplay, or any other verbal genre. The makeup of literature changes with each historical period: in one literary system the letter is a literary fact, in another it is not. The border between literature and *byt*[T] [everyday life] is often traversed, and, as Tynianov shows, the movement mostly originates from the side of literature, which invades everyday life whenever it runs out of material. Literature, which we often describe in passive terms like "reflection" is, in fact, active and even aggressive. Literature is not a mirror but an invader.

Tynianov applies the laws of literary evolution to the contemporary moment—and also uses the contemporary to illuminate the laws of literary evolution. This is how the article "Interlude" works; its cast of characters are not only Tynianov's contemporaries but also his interlocutors. Here, another one of Tynianov's central ideas appears for the first time—the fact that themes are of secondary importance in a text. A theme arises from the text, from the friction between words; it is inherent to, rather than precedes, the text. Themes, as commonly understood, are not a part of a literary system; Tynianov describes the relationship between theme and author using metaphors of colonization and autonomy. Pushkin seized one theme after another, and was never dependent on any one of them; meanwhile, when a theme seizes its author (which, Tynianov claims, is what happened to Anna Akhmatova[N] and Vladimir Mayakovsky[N] around 1924), they face the danger of dependence and automation.[28] In fact, it is the random, unpremeditated themes and objects that forge new connections between words and, thereby, new meanings—we see this in the works of Khlebnikov, Mandelstam, and

28 For more on Mayakovsky, see also "On Mayakovsky" (293) and "Interlude." (173–216).

Boris Pasternak. Rather than originality or individuality, this is a question of the inevitability of what has been said: "The connection between objects that he proffers is unknown to you—it is incidental—but once he has laid it out, you seem to recall it, as though it had already happened. And the image becomes inevitable" (Tynianov on Pasternak in "Interlude"). That is also what Tynianov calls a "new way of seeing," which, once adopted, cannot be "unseen."

Tynianov continued his work on Khlebnikov's poetry in a separate essay, "On Khlebnikov" (1928). The genre of this essay is neither article nor introduction; Tynianov is working on a new mode of writing—we could call it theoretical prose. Its closest models were Mandelstam's articles from the volume *On Poetry*, as well as Khlebnikov's own theoretical prose. "On Khlebnikov" is both a summary of Tynianov's theory of evolution, and a moving portrait of a fearless poet and scholar. "In its methods, poetry is close to science—this is what Khlebnikov teaches us. Like science, it should be opened up to encounters with all kinds of phenomena." (228) After reading Tynianov's second novel, *The Death of the Vazir-Mukhtar*, Mayakovsky greeted him with the words, "So, Tynianov, shall we talk, nation to nation?"[29] In his introduction to Khlebnikov's work, Tynianov addresses him—and himself—scholar to scholar. "The new framework wields a compelling power and strives for expansion. [...] This is why Khlebnikov could bring about a revolution in literature: because his framework was not exclusively literary, because he used it to make sense of both the language of verse and the language of numbers, incidental street conversations, and world-historical events." (227) Literature lives by means of expansion into neighboring as well as distant spheres. Khlebnikov, a vagrant and a poet-theorist, had the audacity to incorporate into poetry spheres that were quite distant from it, like the language of numbers. This was also the scholarly ethos of the Formalists—to go beyond their own usual borders. And so they ventured into the world of cinema.

Throughout the twenties, Tynianov's—and his family's—financial and social standing remained precarious. The usual scholarly path—a doctorate followed by a teaching position—did not quite happen for him as planned. Tynianov was affiliated with the university, but that did not grant him any kind of status or income. It was practically impossible for him to get a more permanent position because of his divergence from both more traditional academic scholarship and the incoming Marxist dogma. Until the State Institute of Art

29 Kaverin and Novikov, *Novoe zrenie*, 11.

History was shut down in 1930, Tynianov taught there, but the institute (barely tolerated by the authorities, even in the 1920s) had very limited funding.[30] He worked many side jobs: teaching high school literature, translating Comintern correspondence, copyediting at a publishing house, editing a magazine. His perpetual lack of money is what first led him to take up the historical prose that would bring him great acclaim.[31]

Cinema held a special place among Tynianov's many day jobs, and it immediately became part of his theoretical interests. He wrote his first article on cinema, "Film—Word—Music" (1924), before he started working at a film studio—from the position of a literary critic. The ideas in the text are thoroughly surprising for something written in 1924: "Cinema is an abstract art." (231) To begin with, Soviet montage cinema was in its infancy and there was little talk of abstraction in cinema. Furthermore, Shklovsky had already tackled the subject of cinema and had interpreted it in quite the opposite way: "Film poetics is a poetics of pure plot."[32] Tynianov uses the word "abstract" quite loosely—he is interested in the analytical technique of cinema, that of fragmentation. In contrast with the unified stage of the theater, cinematic montage fragments space, time, and even the body of the actor into distinct parts. Moreover, the "silence" of cinema is not silence, not the absence of speech: "film uses speech, but it is abstracted speech, broken down into its component parts." (232) The actor's gestures tell us that they are saying something; the titles announce what exactly is being said; the music provides a sound dimension to this speech. Tynianov the literary theorist saw another mode of language in silent cinema—analytical and minimalist. Naturally, the next step for him was working on screenplays.

Tynianov's love affair with cinema unfolded at breakneck speed. In the fall of 1925, he began working on his first script; early in the following year he was appointed as a consultant at the script division of Sevzapkino (later to be renamed Lenfilm), and in the summer he became head of the newly established film department at the Institute of Art History (he left both jobs in the fall of 1927). Tynianov approached film scripts from every possible angle—as

---

30 See K. A. Kumpan, "Institut istorii iskusstv na rubezhe 1920–1930-kh gg," in *Konets institutsii kul'tury dvadtsatykh godov v Leningrade* (Moscow: Novoe Literaturnoe Obozrenie, 2014), 8–129.

31 A complete biography of Tynianov has yet to be written. The main sources about his life are the commentaries by Chudakova, Chudakov, and Toddes in their edition of *PILK*; Kaverin's memoirs; and V. F. Shubin, ed., *Yuri Tynianov. Bio-bibliographic Chronicle* (St. Petersburg: Arsis, 1994).

32 Viktor Shklovskii, *Literatura i kinematograf* (Berlin, 1923), 26.

practitioner, critic, and theorist. For his first script—*The Overcoat* (1926)—he also wore the hat of a literary historian.

Tynianov's approach to film, like his approach to literature, is grounded in specificity. In his article "On the Screenplay" (1926)—which was based both on his own experiences writing screenplays and on his work as a reader in the screenplay division at the studio—he laments the literariness of film, its unproductive reliance on literary fabula. This is especially obvious where the two genres meet—in the staging of literary classics. Tynianov sets out to solve this problem. He describes his work on *The Overcoat* (see the article "On FEX" [289–292]) as an attempt not to stage Gogol, but to translate him into the language of film. Gogol's love of detail is translated into disproportionately sized props (such as a giant decorated teapot); the scene where the overcoat is stolen is shot almost entirely from above, making the beleaguered "little man" quite literally small. The most radical intervention, however, lay in the changes made to the plot: viewers could barely recognize the classic story—and were outraged because of it. The film included plotlines from other Gogol stories, including variants from his drafts, as well as Gogolian motifs inspired by the writer and borrowed from Dostoevsky and Saltykov-Shchedrin.[33] The film showed Gogol as part of literary evolution, at the intersection of what was written, unfinished, or copied by others. *The Overcoat* was a parody of Gogol, but a parody in Tynianov's sense of the word—a changing of the function of a device.

The question of how to write was central to the work of the Formalists, and they never stopped experimenting with the form of their historical-theoretical writings, especially after OPOYAZ stopped publishing their collective volumes (because of Shklovsky's persecution by the Soviet authorities and his escape from Russia in 1922), which was the genre that felt most natural to them. The conventional format of a scholarly article, with its stiff language and rigorous structure, had no room for theory or history (the fact that Formalists did not generally get along with academic circles did not make publication any easier). The language of literary criticism and scholarship in the middle of the 1920s was in an interlude, just like the poetry of the period, as Tynianov observed.

Hence the Formalists' experiments with language and the search for new forms or genres. Shklovsky was first to break that ground with the genre-bending

33 See Iu. Tsiv'ian, *"Na podstupakh k karpalistike," Dvizhenie i zhest v literature, iskusstve i kino* (Moscow: NLO, 2010), 236–244.

Zoo, or Letters not about Love,[34] and Tynianov immediately praised his friend's radical invention: "We are not used to reading a novel that is also a work of scholarship. We are not used to scholarship in 'letters about love' or in 'letters not about love.' Our culture is founded on the prim and proper differentiation between scholarship and art."[35] In 1929, Eikhenbaum published *My Annals,* a quasi-journal made up of memoirs, juvenile poetry, theoretical articles, criticism, and literary history.[36] In the mid-1920s, Shklovsky was writing books where similar elements (including travelogues and production sketches, a favorite early Soviet genre) appear side by side, separated only paragraph by paragraph, rather than given in different sections. Tynianov also experimented with different intonations: "Literary Fact" was written almost as a manifesto and published in the aggressive *LEF* journal, while the film articles (except for "The Foundations of Film") appeared as feuilletons in the newspaper *Kino;* the essay "On Khlebnikov" functions as theoretical prose as well as emotional obituary.

For Tynianov, novels and film scripts thus became a genre of literary-historical work (which is not to say that they did not contain elements of fiction). They were necessary because, paradoxically, they provided a way out of historical causality. Shklovsky wrote: "Film does not require any kind of motivation. My explanation for this is, maybe, too simple: in film, things are not told, but shown."[37] The Formalists countered causality with the much more complex "interrelation"[T] of phenomena, both literary and historical. Montage—which is the primary device of Tynianov's scripts, novels, and short fiction—is well suited to show these interrelations.

In his theoretical work "The Foundations of Film" (1927), which was written after a year of professional experience in the film industry, Tynianov did what early Formalism had not been ready to do. *The Problem of Verse Language* proves that sound forms the meaning of verse, and, in a similar manner, "The Foundations of Film" shows that the formal, stylistic features of cinema (angle, lighting, shot length) are in fact semantic signs, bearers of meaning, and the plot of a film grows out of them. "Cinema does not convey the visible world per se, but in terms of its semantic interrelations; otherwise, cinema would be just a living (and lifeless) photograph. The visible man and visible object only become

34 Viktor Shklovsky, *Zoo, or Letters not about Love* (Leningrad: Atenei, 1924).

35 Tynianov, *PILK,* 166.

36 Boris Eikhenbaum, *My Annals* [Moi vremennik (Leningrad: Izdatel'stvo pisatelei v Leningrade, 1929)].

37 Shklovskii, *Literatura i kinematograf,* 50.

elements of cinematic art when they are given, and function, as a semantic sign. This first premise gives rise to the concept of film style; the second to the concept of film construction. The semantic interrelations of the visible world are conveyed through its stylistic transformation. Meanwhile, the relations between people in a shot, between people and things, and between the part and the whole (what is usually called "the composition of a shot"), the camera angle and perspective from which they are filmed, and the lighting—all these take on tremendous significance." (248) This same article also contains the most coherent explanation of Shklovsky's distinction between fabula and plot.

Montage plays a crucial role in establishing the interrelations of meaning. "Montage is not the linking together of shots, it is their differentiated *succession* [smena]—this is exactly why any shots that are interrelated in at least some way can displace one another. ... They displace one another in the same way a single line of verse, one metrical unit, is succeeded by another: at a precise boundary. Cinema *jumps* from shot to shot, just as a poem jumps from line to line. ... The 'jumpy' nature of cinema, the role played in it by the unity of the shot, the semantic transformation of ordinary objects (the word in poetry, the object in cinema)—these are what cinema and poetry have in common." (258) Tynianov has in mind "new montage" (and not mere continuity, which subjects film to the laws of real time): "'film time' is not real duration, but duration as a matter of convention, based on the interdependence of shots or of visual elements within a shot." (251)

We see here a theory of montage that is simultaneously a theory of *literary evolution*. Tynianov had already demonstrated the "jumpy" nature of evolution in his article "Literary Fact": "Not gradual evolution, but a leap; not development, but shift"—the same applies to how montage organizes shots. In the article "On Literary Evolution," which was written in the same year as "The Foundations of Film" (1927), the concept of interrelation[N] is used to describe, in order, the relationships between elements within a text, between a text and literature as a whole, between literature and speech as well as other related fields, including social phenomena. "Jumpy" evolution already coexists with other kinds of evolution, which are potentially "slower," but for Tynianov it is more important to stress the lack of coincidence, the independence and distance between the movement of literary evolution and that of historical time ("real duration"). This autonomous temporality allowed for the inclusion of specific historical moments in the history of literature, as neither Eikhenbaum nor Tynianov wanted them entirely left out ("[A]ttempts to construct a closed literary series, and to examine evolution within it, are constantly running up against neighboring cultural, social and "real-life" series, and are therefore doomed to remain incomplete." (267), but it also avoided the notion of evolutionary stages, or the inertia of the portrait gallery (Pushkin, Lermontov, Gogol). Most importantly, it bypassed the otherwise inevitable determinism inherent to any dogma (in this case—historical determinism).

The fight for an autonomous historical timeline was a fight for an autonomous way of seeing. The picture becomes clearer if we follow Tynianov's method and look at the speech series, wedged between the social and the literary series. In the Soviet Union, the ostensibly neutral word "time" became weighed down by massive deterministic connotations over the course of the 1920s. Critics, party members, and workers all swore by "our time" ("our day and age"); "our time" was supposed to finally put everything properly into place, once and for all. "Time" meant the Soviet state, its projects, and the labor that went into them. Time tossed aside what was considered superfluous and demanded sacrifices. Shklovsky, engaged in painful negotiations of compromise with the Soviet system, wrote: "Time does not make mistakes; time cannot be guilty before me."[38] The concept of "our time" took on a connotation of loyalty; time determined everything—and everything, present or past, had to be determined by time. Needless to say, this determinism was suffocating for scholarship or any other form of thought.

In Shklovsky's early formulations, evolution was imagined as a cycle: the youngest branch makes its way to the center—there it becomes automatized (worn out and faded by use)—and then a new branch comes to the fore. This pattern works well when literary evolution is isolated from extra-literary phenomena. In the article "On Literary Evolution," Tynianov poses the question of the interrelation of literary phenomena with extra-literary ones and introduces a new *historical* parameter—function. "Having analyzed individual elements of a work, such as the plot or style, rhythm, and syntax in prose, rhythm and semantics in poetry, etc., we are convinced that these elements can be abstracted to a certain extent *as a working hypothesis*, but that they are all *interrelated with one another* and exist in interaction." (269). This interrelation is what Tynianov calls "function" (borrowing the mathematical use of the word). The function of formal elements changes from system to system, and it makes no sense to examine form as separate from function. Form, or any formal element, has no meaning if you look at it in isolation. We often make our freshman students learn, for example, to recognize the basic poetic meters. But if you've

38 Viktor Shklovskii, *Gamburgskii schet: Stat'i, vospominaniia, esse* (Moscow: Sovetskii pisatel', 1990), 309.

established that a poem is written in iambic trimeter, you've established nothing. You have to look and see how this particular meter is, first of all, interrelated with the metric expectations of the period (keeping in mind earlier periods as well). How often do poets use it? For what genres? Is it a fairly standard choice or does it send a specific signal to a reader? Secondly, how it is interrelated with other formal choices (genre, rhyme, vocabulary style, theme, etc.). Unlike American New Critics, Russian Formalists never called for the immanent study of a literary *text.* A text is never autonomous; literature is.

Thus, literary evolution is not the evolution of literary form, but the history of the "evolutionary interaction of forms and functions." (282) "We currently see the novel as interrelated with 'the novel' according to its size, or the way the plot is developed, while at one time it was defined according to the presence of a love story." (276) When we fail to account for how form functions, we risk missing its meaning and significance. Tynianov thus reexamines the concept of "tradition": "'Tradition,' the fundamental concept of the old literary history, proves to be an unjustified abstraction of one or more literary elements from a specific system—in which they play a specific role and are typecast in a certain way—which are then converged with identical elements of another system in which they play a different role, to make a falsely unified and seemingly cohesive series" (269). For Tynianov, history is constructed by montage, analytically, resisting continuity.

It stands to reason that Tynianov uses examples from linguistics. In "On Literary Evolution," he conclusively demonstrates what he had already noted in "Literary Fact": the role of the speech series as the inevitable mediator between the literary and the social series. No detail of economic or social reality can determine or explain *Eugene Onegin,* but the genres and elements of literature are correlated with everyday verbal phenomena, which, in turn, can be directly or indirectly interrelated with social phenomena. Literature stays alive by acquiring new verbal material (dialectisms, jargon, political, social, scholarly terminology, etc.). Tynianov's examples—Lomonosov's odes built on oratorical speech, Nikolai Karamzin's[N] literary systems built on the habitual speech of the (imaginary) salon—show a relatively indirect interrelation with the social series.[39] Eikhenbaum, in his work on Tolstoy, demonstrated more obvious and direct connections: thus the dialogue around the "woman question" in *Anna Karenina* quotes almost verbatim from contemporary

39 For more on Karamzin, see both "On Literary Evolution" (267–282) and "The Ode as an Oratorical Genre" (77–113).

writing on the matter, as well as from Tolstoy's own opinions expressed in letters (and strategically assigned to female characters in the novel). Still, this connection between the literary and the social is presented through the filter of speech, and the fact of Tolstoy's assigning his own words to female characters is no less important than the words themselves.

The functionality of form and the interrelation of literature with the speech series (what Tynianov called the "orientation"[T] [*ustanovka*] of a text or genre toward the speech genre closest at hand) are scholarly tools of immense value.[40] A hundred years after the fact, literary studies has barely begun to approach them. Tynianov has yet to be discovered.

The Formalists started working on their collective literary history in the mid-1920s. In 1928, Tynianov travelled to Germany for medical treatment and then to Prague to visit Jakobson and present "On Literary Evolution." The results of this visit are their collective theses, which summarize their most recent theoretical findings for the purpose of subsequent work, and which close with a call to reestablish OPOYAZ under Shklovsky's leadership. Shklovsky energetically set about making this happen in early 1929, but quickly realized that the external resistance was insurmountable. The theses, which had been written as a prologue, became an epilogue instead. Jakobson wisely remained in Prague. Undeterred, Tynianov wrote to Shklovsky in November about their plans to collaborate on a literary history, and even began negotiating with a publisher.[41] Two months later, at the end of January 1930, Shklovsky (who feared repression more than the others due to his political past), published "A Monument to a Scholarly Mistake"—conceived as a strategic retreat, the article ultimately became an act of renunciation as well as the end of Formalism.[42]

In April 1930, Mayakovsky committed suicide. Tynianov had always been skeptical of the poet's attempts to write poems according to what the "newspapers" (i.e. the Party) wanted, and to pledge himself to serving his "day and age"; in early 1931 he wrote to Shklovsky: "What terrible deaths befell all the people who died this year and last: no one paid any notice, and they all died of natural causes, they blurred and lost firm edges; Mayakovsky died the same way."[43]

40 For more on Tynianov's concept of "orientation [*ustanovka*]," see both "On Literary Evolution" (267–282) and "The Ode as Oratorical Genre" (77–113).

41 See Tynianov, *PILK*, 570.

42 See Galushkin, "'I tak'": 136–153.

43 "'Razzhimaiu ladoni, vypuskaiu Vazira': iz pisem Iu. N. Tynianova V. B. Shklovskomu," *Soglasie* 30 (1995): 206.

Mayakovsky had shot himself in the heart, but to Tynianov, this death was terrible because it was *natural*. Formalism died the same kind of violently natural death. "A Monument to a Scholarly Mistake" was the gunshot; the natural cause of the "blurring" was the ceaseless, dull, everyday, *humiliating inability to work*—because of censorship, attacks in the press, dismissals from teaching appointments, rejections from print publications, lack of freedom, official dogma, fear of repression, lack of money, and even the debt accrued to the tax inspector, to whom writers, ironically, owed high taxes as members of the "professional class."

This is all described in *Kiukhlia* [Tynianov's novel about Küchelbecker[N]]: "There was no money, no status, but, most importantly, there was no air."[44] Formalism did not "come to an end"; it was suffocated, the air stolen from its lungs. Paradoxically, Tynianov managed to take back some stolen air for himself in historical fiction, despite all the risks—of which there were many. As Lydia Chukovskaya said: "even setting aside his grave, chronic, terminal illness, it was not easy to be Yuri Tynianov in Russia in the twenties and thirties of our century."[45] Tynianov died in 1943 of multiple sclerosis; two suicide notes were found in his papers, at least one of them from 1937.[46]

***

Tynianov is not an easy read, nor does he conform to the standards of academic writing. His explanations of terms are cursory at best, even when they are his own invention; he is careless with his references (what is the reader to do with a note that just says "see Eikhenbaum"?); he gets carried away with quotations; and he is in too much of a hurry to finish his own thoughts. There is no way his (or, for that matter, Shklovsky's) works could pass modern-day academic peer review. Academic outcasts from the outset, the Formalists never bothered to master proper academese.

This "rough-edged, unfinished" writing has ideas moving so fast it makes your head spin, and it leaves behind a multitude of "pathways [burrowed] in the ground." Tomashevsky said about Tynianov's works that "they are difficult because there is an unusual quantity of material behind every phrase, every paragraph. [This material] is a condensed clot, so to speak, of thoughts about

44 Tynianov, *Sobranie sochinenii*, 1:177.

45 L. K. Chukovskaia, *Dom poeta* (Moscow: Vremia, 2012), 89.

46 V. A. Kaverin, *Epilog* (Moscow: Vagrius, 2006), 235–237.

the history of literature."[47] Tynianov's articles could be expanded into whole books, his paragraphs into articles. This tendency toward concise, condensed theoretical speech, which is not always easy on the reader, reveals an acute awareness of the future (and the haste of a man conscious of his advancing illness). Every article is like a pile of notes, an outline or rough draft of a future book or a chapter in a collectively authored literary history.

One colleague joked that Tynianov published not articles but drafts of articles. That's also almost true. For the Formalists, scholarship was a process: it is more important to understand than to write. One of Tynianov's main theoretical works—the article "On Literary Evolution"—was written in an almost algebraic language. This is, in fact, what saved it: Eikhenbaum was certain that the journal that published it (*Eyes on Literature* [Na literaturnom postu]), which was notorious for its ideological stiffness) only did so because its editors did not understand it.[48] In the introduction to *Archaists and Innovators*, Tynianov wrote:

> Every article is written in order to make something clear; when it becomes clear, the article is cancelled out and appears unsatisfactory.
>
> This has partly to do with the difficult and often unclear language that many [of my] articles are written in, which the critics, if they wish, could describe as augurial language, i.e. an intentional obscuring of the meaning of one's own words. That's what one critic recently did. I would like to register my dissent.
>
> The thing is that language does not merely transmit concepts but is also a means of their construction. Thus, for example, the summary of someone else's thoughts is usually clearer than the telling of one's own. Sometimes an aphoristic way of thinking comes to one's aid. Unfortunately, I lack that ability: instead, there is the restlessness of concepts.[49]

Language is not the form but the instrument of thought. Its lack of clarity and its restlessness are a search for new meaning—and when everything becomes clear, scholarship comes to an end. Eikhenbaum concludes his "Theory of the 'Formal Method'" (1925) with the following: "When the time comes when we

47 Tomashevskii, "Darovanie literaturoveda," 226.

48 See Tyniavov, *PILK*, 519.

49 Ibid., 396.

can admit that we have a theory that is all-encompassing, appropriate for all examples of the past and future, and thus not in need of or incapable of evolution, we must also then admit that the formal method has ceased to be—that the spirit of scholarly inquiry has left it. This has not happened yet."[50] And, in spite of nearly a century of thought about Formalism, this has still not happened.

Translated by Maria Vassileva, with Ainsley Morse and Philip Redko

50 Eikhenbaum, *O literature*, 408.

Part One

THEORY THROUGH HISTORY—THEN

Dostoevsky and Gogol (Toward a Theory of Parody) (1919/21)[1]

1

Discussions of "literary tradition" or "succession" usually assume a more or less straight line linking the youngest representative of a given branch of literature with the eldest. However, things are actually much more complicated. Instead of a continuation of the straight line, there is something more like a departure, a reaction against something—a struggle. But representatives of other branches or other traditions do not provoke this kind of struggle: they are just given a wide berth; they can be either rejected or venerated, and are struggled with through the mere existence [of other traditions]. This was the nature of the silent struggle of virtually all of nineteenth-century Russian literature with Pushkin,[N] passing him by even as he was publicly venerated. Proceeding from the "senior," "Derzhavin"[N] line, Tyutchev[N] did not mention his predecessor in any way, while eagerly and officially glorifying Pushkin.[2] Dostoevsky venerated Pushkin in the same way. He wasn't even averse to calling Pushkin his forebear; openly ignoring the facts well established by contemporary criticism, he contended that the "pléiade" of writers in the 1860s came directly out of Pushkin.[3]

At the same time, Dostoevsky's contemporaries were eager to see him as a direct descendent of Gogol.[N] Nekrasov[N] talked to Belinsky[N] about a "new

---

1 "Dostoevskii i Gogol. K teorii parodii," written in 1919, appeared as a book (brochure) in the "Theory of Poetic Language" series published by OPOYAZ[T] in Petrograd in 1921. It was Tynianov's first publication. The translation is based on Iurii Tynianov, "Dostoevskii i Gogol (k teorii parodii)," *PILK*, 483–489. Selected notes to this publication are by A. P. Chudakov [*AC*]; additional notes by Yuri Tynianov [*YT*]; and the translators [unmarked].

2 For Tynianov on Pushkin, see "On the Composition of *Eugene Onegin*" (114–150); for Tynianov on Tyutchev, see also "Tyutchev and Heine" (64–76). Also see "On Parody" (294–328), as well as "Dostoevsky and Gogol" (27–63), for a continuation of Tynianov's thinking on the subject.

3 Fyodor Dostoyevsky, July/August 1877, *A Writer's Diary* [Dnevnik pisatelia]—*YT*. Where possible, the translators have replaced Tynianov's citations from Russian sources with existing English translations. Here, refer to Dostoyevsky, *Writer's Diary*, vol. 1, trans. Kenneth Lantz (Evanston, IL: Northwestern University Press, 1993), 1068–1069.

Gogol," Belinsky called Gogol "Dostoevsky's father"; the news about a "new Gogol" even made it all the way out to Ivan Aksakov[N] in Kaluga. A shift[T] was called for, and it was imagined as a direct, "linear" succession.[4]

There were only a few mentions of struggle. (Pletnyov:[N] "he's chasing down Gogol"; "he wanted to destroy Gogol's 'Notes of a Madman' with his 'Double'").

And it was only in the 1880s that Strakhov decided to say something about how Dostoevsky had from the very beginning "offered a corrective to Gogol." The first to speak openly about Dostoevsky's struggle with Gogol was Rozanov. [5] Every literary succession is first and foremost a struggle, the destruction of an older whole and the reconfiguration of old elements.

2

Dostoevsky openly takes his lead from Gogol; he emphasizes this. "The Overcoat" is mentioned in *Poor Folk,* and the characters in "Mr. Prokharchin" discuss the plot of "The Nose" ("'You, you, you're stupid!' Semyon Ivanovich muttered. 'You could have your nose eaten off, but you'd eat it yourself with bread and never notice ...").[6] The Gogolian tradition is reflected erratically in Dostoevsky's early works. "The Double" is immeasurably closer to Gogol than *Poor Folk,* as is "The Landlady" in comparison to "The Double." This erratic quality is particularly visible in "The Landlady," which was written after *Poor Folk,* "The Double," "Mr. Prokharchin" and the "Novel in Nine Letters." The characters in "The Landlady" are close to those of [Gogol's] "A Terrible Vengeance"; the style, with its hyperbole and parallelisms (although the second part of the parallel being developed in great detail and acquiring a sort of independent meaning is a feature inherent to Gogol and uncharacteristic of Dostoevsky. We can compare the parallel of the black tailcoats at the gubernatorial ball and the flies on the lump sugar, which has an overdeveloped second component (in *Dead Souls*), with the parallel of Ordynov's seizure and the thunderstorm ("The Landlady,"

---

4 Tynianov's notion of the "shift" is central to his thinking in virtual all of the articles in this collection. See, in particular, "On Literary Evolution" (267–282).

5 Vasily Rozanov[N] first published his study of Dostoyevsky in 1906. See Vasily Rozanov, *Dostoyevsky and the Legend of the Grand Inquisitor* [Legenda o velikom inkvizitore F. M. Dostoevskogo], trans. Spencer E. Roberts (Ithaca, NY: Cornell University Press, 1972).

6 Fyodor Dostoevsky, *Poor Folk and Other Stories,* trans. David McDuff (New York: Penguin, 1988), 237.

chapter one),[7] the second component of which is equally independent); the complicated syntax and Church Slavonicisms (inverse pronouns) and accentuated rhythm of the periods that close with dactylic clausulas—all of this points to an apprenticeship that has suddenly come into its own.

At this point it had yet to be determined what exactly in Gogol was essential for Dostoevsky; it's as though Dostoevsky was trying out different Gogolian devices, combining them. This is where we get the general resemblance of his early pieces to Gogol's work. It's not just that "The Double" is close to "The Nose" and "Netochka Nezvanova" to "The Portrait": certain episodes from "Netochka" can be traced to "The Portrait"[8] and others to "A Terrible Vengeance,"[9] while many of the images in "The Nose" are close to those found in *Dead Souls*.[10]

For instance, compare the following to "The Nose": "A fine thing it would be if there was something wrong with me today [...] A fine thing if something untoward had happened, and a strange pimple had come up, or *something equally unpleasant*" (Golyadkin at the mirror).[11]

Dostoevsky's style so obviously repeats, varies and combines Gogol's that the former's contemporaries could hardly ignore it (Belinsky wrote about Dostoevsky's Gogolian "turns of phrase," and Grigorovich wrote of "the influence of Gogol on [Dostoevsky 's] phrase constructions").[12] At first, Dostoevsky reflected both levels of Gogol's style: the high style and the comic. Compare, for instance, the repetition of names in "The Double": "Mr. Golyadkin clearly

---

7 Tynianov has in mind chapter one in part two, with the triple repetition of the "storm situation" in Katerina's story—*AC*.

8 See chapter 7: "It suddenly seemed to me as though the eyes of the portrait were, in confusion, turning away from my searching, questioning gaze, that they were trying to avoid it, and that there was a duplicity in those eyes; it appeared that I had been right [...]"—*YT*. Fyodor Dostoevsky, *Netochka Nezvanova*, trans. Jane Kentish (New York/London: Penguin, 1985), 147.

9 Cf. chapter 7 (Pyotr Aleksandrovich at the mirror): "It seemed to me as if he were making up his face [...] his face had changed completely. The smile on his lips had disappeared as if at a word of command [...] His eyes had been deeply concealed behind his spectacles [...]" (Dostoevsky, *Netochka*, 153). See the magician's transformation in "A Terrible Vengeance"—*YT.*

10 Compare Golyadkin Jr.'s (the younger Golyadkin's) gestures with Chichikov's (*Dead Souls*, vol. 2, chapter 1): Golyadkin "jerked his stumpy little legs into life and darted off [...]"; Chichikov "bent down deftly [...] and leapt back with the legerity of a rubber ball"—*YT.* See F. M. Dostoevsky, *The Double*, trans. George Bird (Bloomington, IN: Indiana University Press, 1958), 131.

11 Ibid., 12.

12 Dmitri Grigorovich (1822–1899) was a writer, critic, and friend of Dostoevsky.

perceived that the hour for a bold stroke and the humiliation of his enemies was at hand. Mr. Golyadkin was agitated. Mr. Golyadkin felt a kind of sudden inspiration [...],"[13] with the beginning of Gogol's "The Tale of How Ivan Ivanovich Quarreled with Ivan Nikiforovich" and others.[14] The other aspect of Gogol's style is evident in "The Landlady" and "Netochka Nezvanova" ("My soul failed to recognize yours, although it found new light beside its beautiful sister soul").[15] Later on, Dostoevsky would drop Gogol's high style and use the low style nearly everywhere, sometimes stripping it of its comic motivation.

Another testament to this is found in Dostoevsky 's letters, which he considered to be works ofliterature. ("I wrote him such a letter! In a word, a model of polemics. How I dressed him down. My letters are a chef d'oeuvre of *lettristics*.").[16] These letters are full of Gogolian words, phrases, and names: "You're such a lazybones, Fetyuk, simply a Fetyuk!;"[17] "A letter is nonsense, letters are written by pharmacists."[18] Dostoevsky seems to play at Gogolian style in the letters: "I retired because I retired [...]" (1844);[19] "Provincial laziness is destroying you in the flower of your years, dear brother, and that's all there is to it. [...] There's unbelievable admiration everywhere, terrible curiosity about me. I've met a heap of the most respectable people" (1845);[20] "The overcoat has its virtues and its inconveniences. The virtue is that it is unusually full, in fact double, and the color is good, just what you need for a uniform, gray [...]" (1846).[21]

This is stylization: rather than adhering to the style, this is playing with it. And if we recall how eager Dostoevsky was to draw attention to Gogol (in *Poor Folk*, "Mr. Prokharchin"), how he so openly and obviously derived from him, it becomes clear that we should really be talking about stylization rather than "imitation," "influence," etc.

Yet another feature: even as Dostoevsky was constantly mentioning the names of Khlestakov, Chichikov and Poprishchin in his letters and articles,

---

13 Dostoevsky, *The Double*, 67. Translation modified.

14 See I. Mandel'shtam, *O kharaktere gogolevskogo stilia* (Helsingfors: Novaia tip. Guvudstadsbladet, 1902), 161—*YT*.

15 Dostoevsky, *Netochka*, 140.

16 Letter to M. Dostoyevsky, 30 September 1844—*YT*. See F. M. Dostoevsky, *Complete Letters of Fyodor Dostoyevsky*, 5 vols., ed. and trans. David Lowe and Ronald Meyer (Ann Arbor, MI: Ardis, 1988), 1:98. Translation slightly modified.

17 Ibid., 1:116—*YT*. Letter to M. Dostoyevsky, 8 October 1845. Gogol's Nozdrev (*Dead Souls*) uses the word "Fetyuk" to refer to people he does not like.

18 Ibid., 1:124—*YT*. Dostoyevsky refers to Gogol's "Poprischchin" ("Notes of a Madman") in this letter to his brother, 1 April 1846.

19 Ibid., 1:97. 30 September 1844.

20 Ibid., 1:117. 16 November 1845.

21 Ibid., 1:132. 17 September 1846,

he maintained Gogolian names in his own works as well. The heroine of "The Landlady" is Katerina, just like in "A Terrible Vengeance"; Golyadkin's lackey and Chichikov's lackey share the same name, Petrushka. The last names "Pseldonimov" [a play on "pseudonym"—*trans.*] "Mlekopitayev" [mammal] (in "A Nasty Story") and "Vidopliasov" [dancing] (in *The Village of Stepanchikovo*) represent a typical Gogolian device, introduced in order to be played with. Dostoevsky would hang onto his Gogolian last names for all time (cf. "Ferdyshchenko," which recalls Gogol's "Krutotryshchenko"). Even Raskolnikov's mother's name, *Pulcheria* Aleksandrovna, comes across as a stylized name if we remember Gogol's *Pulcheria* Ivanovna.

Stylization is close to parody. Both of them live a double life: behind the one level of the work there is a second level that is stylized or parodied. But parody requires a discrepancy between the two levels, that they be shifted; the parody of a tragedy will be a comedy (either by accentuating the tragic notes or by substituting comic elements—it can work either way), and the parody of a comedy can be a tragedy. This discrepancy is not present in a stylization: there, both levels correspond to each other—the stylizing level and the stylized one showing through it. And yet parody is very close to stylization; a stylization that is comically motivated or accentuated becomes a parody.

But Gogol had one feature that consistently prodded Dostoevsky to struggle, all the more so since this quality was extremely important to him: Gogol's "characters" or "types." Strakhov recalled (in the late 1850s): "I remember how Fyodor Mikhailovich made some very subtle observations regarding the *consistency of various characters* in Gogol, the vividness of all of his figures: Khlestakov, Podkolyosin, Kochkaryov, et al."[22] In 1858, Dostoevsky criticized Pisemsky's[N] *One Thousand Souls* in the following way: "Is there even one *new character, any original creation*, which had never appeared before? All of this is old stuff invented long ago in our writer-innovators, especially Gogol" [emphasis *YT*].[23]

In 1871, Dostoevsky was delighted by the types in Leskov's[N] novel: "The nihilists are distorted to the point of indolence, but on the other hand, the individual characters! How's *Vanskok* for you! Gogol never had anything more typical or accurate."[24] And in the same year he wrote of Belinsky: "He treated *Gogol's types* [emphasis *YT*] with hideous superficiality and disregard and was

22 F. M. Dostoevskii, *Polnoe sobranie sochinenii* [Complete Works], vol. 1 (St. Petersburg: Tip. A. S. Suvorina, 1883), 176—*YT*. Khlestakov is a major character in Gogol's play *The Government Inspector*; Podkolyosin and Kochkaryov are characters in another play, *The Wedding*.

23 Dostoevsky, *Complete Letters*, 1:346. 31 May 1858. Translation slightly modified.

24 Ibid., 3:310. 30 January 1871. Nikolai Leskov's novel *At Daggers Drawn* [Na nozhakh] was published in 1870.

just ecstatically happy that Gogol *had exposed* things" [Dostoevsky's emphasis].[25] These Gogolian "types" are thus one of the important points in Dostoevsky's struggle with Gogol.

3

Gogol saw things in an unusual way; there are many individual examples of this, including his descriptions of Mirgorod, Rome, Pliushkin's dwelling with its famous junk-pile, the singing doors in "Old World Landowners," or Nozdrev's hurdy-gurdy.[26] The latter example points to another aspect of the vivid description of these objects: Gogol had an eye for the comic quality inherent to *things*. "Old World Landowners" begins with a parallel between the ancient houses and their ancient inhabitants, and goes on to develop this parallel for the whole duration of the story. "Nevsky Prospekt" is built around the effect of complete identification between costumes and their parts with the body parts of people out strolling: "One displays a smart overcoat with the best beaver, another a nose of exquisite Grecian beauty [...] a fourth a pair of most ravishing eyes, and a perfectly marvelous hat [...]."[27] The humor here is achieved through the listing one after another, with unchanging intonation, objects that are not compatible with one another. Gogol uses the same device when comparing the overcoat "with a charming life companion": "and this sweet helpmate was no other than the selfsame overcoat with its thick padding of cotton wool and its strong lining that would last a lifetime."[28] Here, too, the humor lies in the discrepancy between the two images, the living and the material. The device of the material metaphor is canonical for comic descriptions; cf. Heine[N]: "the universe has been repainted [...] the old gentlemen councilors have donned new faces";[29] also cf. Marlinsky's "The Frigate Hope," where the naval officer writes about love using naval terminology; this is another variant of the

25 Ibid., 1:361. (30) May 1871.

26 Tynianov refers to Gogol's "Mirgorod" cycle of short stories (1835); the tale "Rome" (1842); the characters Pliushkin and Nozdrev from *Dead Souls* (1842); and a story from the *Evenings on a Farm near Dikanka* cycle (1832).

27 Nikolai V. Gogol, *The Overcoat and Other Tales of Good and Evil*, trans. David Magarshack (New York: Norton, 1965), 166.

28 Ibid., 249.

29 H. Heine, *Ideen. Das Buch Le Grand* (1826), ch. 6, in H. Heine, *Werke und Briefe*, vol. 3 (Berlin: Akademie Verlag, 1961), 142—*AC*. For more on Heine, see "Tyutchev and Heine" (64–76).

device.[30] What is emphasized here is precisely the imperfection of the connection, the mismatch between two images.

This is why the object is so important for comic descriptions.

And this is why Gogol raises lifeless nature to an idiosyncratic principle of literary theory: "He would say that all that a tale—or really any story—needed to succeed was for the author to describe a room or a street that were familiar to him. 'He who has the capacity to convey his own living quarters in vivid images can subsequently turn out to be a truly remarkable author,' he would say" (Annenkov).[31] In this situation, the object takes on the significance of a theme.

Gogol's primary device for describing people is the mask.

The mask appears most often as clothing or costumes (note the great significance of clothing in Gogol's descriptions of physical appearance), but a grossly accentuated appearance can also act as a mask.

Here is an example of a geometric mask:

> A face in which one could not find a single corner, but meanwhile, one not marked by light, rounded features. The forehead did not drop straight to the nose but was rather entirely sloping, like an icy hill for sledding. The nose was an extension of it—great and blunt. And the lips, though the upper one stuck out further. There was absolutely no chin. A diagonal line ran from the nose all the way to the neck. This was a triangle whose apex was located at the nose [...] ("The Streetlamp was Dying").[32]

More often, however, there is a mask "coated in flesh"; this is emphasized by intimate nicknames like "muzzlekins [*mordash*], little capon [*kaplunchik*]" (the ones Chichikov uses for himself). Moving on, we see simple linguistic metaphors being realized and transforming into verbal masks; consider the following gradations of the device: 1) the smoking brewer turns into the chimney of the brewing house, a steamship, and a cannon ("May Night");[33] 2) the hands in

30 Alexander Bestuzhev (1797–1837), a Romantic writer and member of the Decembrist movement, wrote under the pseudonym Marlinsky.

31 Pavel Annenkov (1813–1887) was a literary critic known as Gogol's biographer. He also wrote on Pushkin.

32 N. V. Gogol, *Complete Works* [Polnoe sobranie sochinenii], vols. 1–14 (Moscow: Izd. Akademii nauk, 1937–1959), 3:331.

33 See later: "[...] The brewer's *squat little structure* shook again with loud laughter" [ibid., 3:166]—*YT*.

"A Terrible Vengeance" and the monsters in the first version of "Vyi" (masks as parts); 3) "The Nose," where the metaphor is realized as a mask (this is the effect of a broken mask); 4) "Korobochka," where the material metaphor becomes a verbal mask;[34] 5) "Akaky Akakievich" [of "The Overcoat"—*trans.*] where the verbal mask has lost its link to semantics and anchored itself to sound, becoming a sonic or phonic mask.

A material mask can be broken—this is the general contour of the plot (in "The Nose"). A verbal mask can split: Bobchinsky and Dobchinsky, Big Foma and Smaller Foma, Uncle Mityai and Uncle Minyai; this is also where the paired and inverted names belong: 1) *Ivan* Ivanovich and *Ivan* Nikiforovich; Afanasy *Ivanovich* and Pulcheria *Ivanovna* (paired); 2) Kifa Mokievich and Mokii Kifovich (inverted).[35] In this connection, sound repetitions play a decisive role: first in terms of articulation,[36] and later in terms of composition as well: 1) nonsense words—*pul'pul'tik, mon'munia* (in "The Carriage"); 2) [the last names of characters] *Lyulyukov, Bubunitsyn, Tentetnikov, Chichikov*; 3) [first and last names] *Ivan Ivanovich, Pythagoras Pythagorovich* (*Chertokutskoy*); 4) [first and last name plus patronymic] *Pyotr Petrovich Petukh*; 5) [paired and inverted names] *Ivan Ivanovich—Ivan Nikiforovich, Uncle Mityai and Uncle Minyai, Kifa Mokievich and Mokii Kifovich.*

Masks can be equally material and spectral: Akaky Akakievich is easily and naturally replaced by a ghost, and the mask of the Cossack in the red *zhupan* is replaced by the mask of the wizard ["A Terrible Vengeance"—*trans.*]. It is the movement of the masks that is almost always spectral, but this movement is what gives the impression of action.

The hyperbolic quality typical of Gogol's images across the board is also typical of his images of physical movement. Just as he could not bear to see

---

34 Last names like *Zemlyanika* [Wild Strawberry] and *Yayichnitsa* [Fried Egg] represent a more complicated development of the device: a verbal mask that does not coincide in terms of grammatical gender, which creates a significantly more comic effect. The formal aspect of these names is crucial—*YT*. Nastasia Petrovna Korobochka (her last name means "little box") is a character in *Dead Souls* whose household reflects her well-organized, fundamentally mercantile spirit.

35 Big Foma and Smaller Foma, Uncle Mityai and Uncle Minyai, and Kifa Mokievich and Mokii Kifovich are all characters in *Dead Souls*; Afanasy Ivanovich and Pulcheria Ivanovna are the heroes of "Old World Landowners"; Bobchinsky and Dobchinsky are characters in the play "The Government Inspector."

36 See Boris Eikhenbaum,[N] "How Gogol's 'Overcoat' is Made" [Kak sdelana "Shinel'" Gogolia, in *Poetika* (Petrograd: OPOYAZ, 1919)], in *Gogol From the Twentieth Century: Eleven Essays*, ed. Robert Maguire (Princeton, NJ: Princeton University Press, 1974), 269–291.

fast-moving traffic on the street because he would immediately start imagining crushed pedestrians, he created a story about a chopped-off nose. Objects in motion are demonic: the rising corpse, the dumplings flying of their own accord into Patsyuk's mouth, the backwards-running horse in "A Terrible Vengeance," the troika that is Old Russia. For Gogol it was enough to know the verbal mask in order to immediately determine its movements. Prince D. A. Obolensky related how Gogol created a mask and its movements according to a verbal sign:

> At the train station, I found a comments book and read a pretty funny complaint written by a certain gentleman. Upon hearing the complaint, Gogol asked me, "Tell me, who do you think this gentleman is? What are the qualities and characteristics of this man?" "I have no idea," I answered. "Well, I will tell you." And he began to describe in the most hilarious and original way *first the outward appearance* of this gentleman, *and then told me the entire history of his career,* even *acting out* certain episodes from his life. I remember that I guffawed like a madman, but he *played out* the whole thing perfectly seriously" (emphasis *YT*).[37]

Naturally, the complaint had been signed by the man who wrote it; Gogol took this last name and, like a verbal mask, transformed it first into a material mask (the man's appearance), and then methodically created its movements ("played out") and sketched out a plot (the "history of his career" and "episodes"). In this way, both gestures and plot are predetermined by the masks themselves.[38]

---

37 *Russkaia starina* (1873), vol. 8, 942–943—*AC.*

38 This is precisely in line with the idea that Gogol's plots are traditional or anecdotal (see Eikhenbaum, "How Gogol's 'Overcoat' is Made"—*YT*). Even the plot of "The Nose," so shocking at first glance, was not so at the time of its appearance, when "noseology" was a prevailing plot phenomenon: See Sterne's *Tristram Shandy*, Marlinsky's "Mulla-Nur," and entertaining articles on rhinoplasty (for instance, on the organic reconstruction of a nose in *Son of the Fatherland* [Syn otechestva] part 65, no. 35 (1820): 95–96 and part 75, no. 3 (1822): 133–137). What was conspicuous and new in "The Nose" was, evidently, not the plot, but the unmotivated shift of two masks: 1) the "chopped-off and baked *nose*"—See what has been said about the hyperbole of Gogol's images of physical movement, as in his "Nevsky Prospekt," where Hoffmann wants to chop off Schiller's nose; and 2) the "breakaway, independent *Nose*"—a realized metaphor; this metaphor shows up in Gogol (in his letters) in various degrees of realization: "*My Nose can smell* even the tail end of the Sirocco" (Letter to A. P. Elagina, 28 June 1840, in Gogol, *Complete Works*, 11:294); "Believe me, I am often visited by the frenzied desire to turn into *just a nose, such that there would be nothing else—no eyes or arms or legs, nothing but one enormous nose,* with nostrils like good-sized buckets, such that

"The Tale of How Ivan Ivanovich Quarreled with Ivan Nikiforovich" is entirely a product of the resemblance and non-resemblance of *names*. Ivan Ivanovich's name is repeated fourteen times in the beginning of chapter one; Ivan Nikiforovich's is repeated almost as many times; furthermore, there are sixteen mentions of their names in conjunctions and comparisons. Projecting the non-resemblance of verbal masks onto material ones results in the complete opposition of both: "Ivan Ivanovich is tall and lean. Ivan Nikiforovich is a little shorter, but makes up for it in corpulence. Ivan Ivanovich's head is like a horseradish, tail downwards; Ivan Nikiforovich's head is like a radish, tail upwards,"[39] and so on. Or the projection of the *resemblance* of names onto the *resemblance* of masks: "Both Ivan Ivanovich and Ivan Nikiforovich greatly dislike fleas [...] Still, in spite of certain dissimilarities, both Ivan Ivanovich and Ivan Nikiforovich are excellent fellows" (226). Projecting the *non-resemblance* of masks onto the plot results in the quarrel between Ivan Ivanovich and Ivan Nikiforovich; projecting their *resemblance* results in their equivalence in the context of "boring life."

Similarly, the non-resemblance of the names of Uncle Mityai and Uncle Minyai projected onto a material mask results in their great and slight height, their thinness and fatness. Gogol's "characters" or "types" are, essentially, masks, sharply defined and not subject to any "breakthroughs" or "developments." One and the same motif runs through all of the protagonist's movements and actions—Gogol's art is full of leitmotifs. The masks can be immobile, "bloated," as with Pliushkin, Manilov, and Sobakevich in *Dead Souls*; they can also be revealed through gestures, as with Chichikov.

Masks can be either comic or tragic—Gogol works on two levels, the high tragic level and the low comic one. The two usually go together, taking turns at regular intervals. One of Gogol's early critical articles ("Boris Godunov. Pushkin's Poem"), in which he talks about the "two warring natures of man," already demonstrates the particular features of both levels—in the speech of Pollior (the high level) and in the conversations of the "cheery cube" and "coffee-colored overcoat" (the low level). The difference in masks corresponds to the difference

---

I could breathe in as much as possible of the fragrance of spring" (Gogol to M. P. Balabina, April 1838, in Gogol, *Complete Works*, 11:145. Emphasis *YT*). Gogol plays with this unmotivated shift of masks, baring the device toward the end of the tale: "[...] no, that I cannot understand, I simply cannot understand it!" [Gogol, *The Overcoat*, 231]. This shift, rather than the plot per se, is why the story is felt as comic—*YT.*

39 Nikolai Gogol, *Mirgorod*, trans. David Magarshack (New York: Farrar, Straus, and Cudahy, 1962), 225.

in styles (the high style entails amplification, tautology, isocolon, neologisms, archaisms, etc., while the low style entails irrationality, barbarisms, dialectal features, etc.). The two levels are differentiated primarily through lexicon and can be traced to different linguistic spheres: the high style to that of Old Church Slavonic and the low style to the dialectal.[40] The levels are also usually attached to specific literary genres, which can be traced to different traditions: that of Gogolian comedy and that of his selected correspondence; the latter style harks back to eighteenth-century sermons.

But Gogol's principal device—his system of material metaphors and masks—can be applied equally well at both of these levels. When addressing moral and religious topics, Gogol brings in his entire system of images, sometimes stretching metaphors to the limits of allegory. This is evidenced in his *Selected Passages from Correspondence with Friends* (1847):[41] cf. the repetitions of expressions like "encumbered [our souls] with all kinds of rubbish" (133); "you are cluttering up [your own intelligence] with alien muck" (171); "spiritual property" (received from the "Heavenly Landlord," and which one should either pay interest on or relinquish); Karamzin had a "well-organized soul" (72); ten years hence Europe will no longer be "coming to us only to acquire skins and lard, but to acquire [...] wisdom" (169); "To organize roads,

40 The dialectal features in Gogol's language are not at all limited to the particularities of Little Russian [an old-fashioned designation for Ukrainian—*trans.*] and Southern Russian. His notebook contains words from Simbirsk governorate, which he copied down from [Nikolai] Yazykov,[N] "Words from Vladimir Governorate" and "Words of a Volga Boatman." Alongside these are many technical words (relating to fishing, hunting, husbandry, etc.). His interest in intimate domestic language is also evident: he noted the word *Pikot'*, the family nickname of Praskovya Mikhailovna Yazykova. He also noted foreign words with parodic, shifted semantics, and false folk etymologies (*moshinal'nyi* as an adjective recalling "machinery," but derived from *moshennik*, a swindler; or "proletariat" being derived from *proletat'*, to fly over), which anticipated the language of [Nikolai] Leskov. *Dead Souls* contains Northern/Great Russian words (like *shanishki*, a kind of pancake, *razmychet* meaning "scatters" and others). Note that Gogol wrote down these words (in his notebook) very precisely, but made semantic mistakes fairly often (for instance, he mixed up the words *podvalka* and *podvoloka*, which have different meanings). It would appear that he was less interested in semantics than in phonetics.

The introduction of dialectal features (which in *Dead Souls* is not strongly motivated) was a conscious artistic device for Gogol, which would be further developed in subsequent literature. The selection of dialectal expressions and technical terms (see, in particular, the names for dogs: *murugie* for russet, *chistopsovye* for purebred, *gustopsovye* for thick-haired, etc.) reveals the articulatory principle—*YT*.

41 Nikolai Gogol, *Selected Passages from Correspondence with Friends* [Vybrannye mesta iz perepiski s druz'iami], trans. Jesse Zeldin (Nashville, TN: Vanderbilt University Press, 1969). Tynianov's quotations from *Selected Passages* will be cited by page numbers from this edition.

bridges, and communications [...] is truly necessary; but to make smooth the many inner roads [...] is still more necessary" (178); god is the "heavenly sovereign."[42]

In this way, making only lexical adjustments, Gogol brought all these images into the realm of morality.

But the different applications of the device served different ends: at the comic level, the point of the material metaphors was in the conspicuous discrepancy between two images; meanwhile, [at the serious level of morality] their aim was to give a sense of the connection between the images. This is evidently what Gogol had in mind when he wrote: "How to bring all the idleness of the world, in all its forms, down to a resemblance with the simple idleness of town life? And how can this town idleness be elevated to a transfiguration of the world's idleness? For this one must *include all the similarities* and introduce a graduated progression."[43] Meanwhile, the strength of the *material* metaphors lies in the discrepancy, in the non-resemblance of what is being brought together; this is why something that had been an acceptable device in the realm of art was felt as unacceptable in the realm of morality and politics.

Perhaps this provides a partial explanation for the impression the *Selected Passages* made even on those of Gogol's friends who agreed with his position; Gogol himself considered the primary reason for the book's failure to be its "means of expression." But his contemporaries were inclined to see the reason for its failure in the fact that Gogol had changed his devices.

In fact, there is a complete overlap of devices.

Having set as his aim this time to "get acquainted with the soul," Gogol proceeded according to the laws of his art. Consider his request for responses to the *Selected Passages*: "What would it cost you to keep a kind of journal in which every day you would write down something like the following: 'Today I heard such-and-such an opinion; it was expressed by such-and-such a person; [...] I don't know his way of life, but I think he's such-and-such; he has a proper and decent (or indecent) appearance; he holds his head like this; blows his nose like this [...]'; in other words, without omitting anything that meets the eye, from large to small."[44] This is the same thing we saw in the scene at the station, but

42 Translation slightly modified.

43 Gogol, *PSS* [*Complete Works*], 6:693—*YT.* This passage comes from Gogol's notes for *Dead Souls.*

44 Letter to Rosset, 15 April 1847—*YT*. Excerpt published in Nikolai Gogol, *Dead Souls*, ed. Suzanne Fusso, trans. Bernard Guilbert Geurney (New Haven, CT: Yale University Press, 1996), 284.

a slightly different move; Gogol wishes to draw conclusions about character through movements and outward appearance.

Similarly, the transfiguration of life was also meant to take place according to the laws of his art (the shifting of masks). Everything will be transformed by Yazykov's[N] poetry, or *The Odyssey* in Zhukovsky's[N] translation; but it can be still simpler to transform a Russian person: just call him an ignorant peasant woman or a greedy hamster; just say that, look, the German says the Russian is good-for-nothing—and he will instantly be made into a different person. There are also snippets of plot constructions. One can produce a moral revolution in the simplest, thriftiest way imaginable—all one need do is travel around Russia: "In the course of your voyage you can introduce [people—*YT*] to each other and have mutually beneficial exchanges of information, like an efficient merchant: the information you acquire in one town you can sell in another at a profit, enriching everyone, and at the same time enriching yourself most of all."[45] This "trade in information" faintly recalls the "purchase of dead souls." Chichikov must rise again, and reforms are to be carried out in his Chichikovian manner.

Just as the mask of the Cossack in the red *zhupan* is changed into the mask of the wizard (in "A Terrible Vengeance"), even Pliushkin was meant to be transfigured, simply and magically.

4

The question of characters is where Dostoevsky comes up against Gogol.

Dostoevsky started out with epistolary and memoiristic form. Both of these, especially the first, are poorly equipped for the development of a complex plot; but Dostoevsky 's primary task at first (as I've indicated already to some extent) was to create and develop characters, and this task only gradually became more complicated (the unification of a complex plot with complex characters). As early as *Poor Folk*, Makar is the vehicle for an attack against this aspect of "The Overcoat": "Why, it's simply not true to life, for such a civil servant could not possibly have existed."[46] This is Makar speaking ("I didn't show my ugly mug,"

45 Gogol, *Selected Passages*, 121, translation slightly modified. The title of this chapter in the *Selected Passages* is "It is Necessary to Travel Through Russia."

46 Fyodor Dostoevsky, *Poor Folk & A Little Hero*, trans. David Magarshack (New York: Doubleday, 1968), 91.

says Dostoevsky),[47] and the introduction of literature into the purview of his cast of characters is one of Dostoevsky 's felicitous and time-tested devices. But Dostoevsky himself, throwing off the mask of a character, very pointedly says the same thing in the beginning of part four of *The Idiot*. Having analyzed Podkolyosin and George Dandin as *types*, Dostoevsky states his opposition to types in art:[48] "Filling novels with *human types only*, or simply with odd and fantastic people, would be impossible, indeed, *uninteresting*. In our view, a writer should try to seek out interesting and instructive nuances even among commonplace elements." He indicates the nuances of "certain ordinary individuals": "an ordinariness which steadfastly refuses to accept what it is, and desperately desires to become original and independent."[49] These nuances are created through contrast; Dostoevsky's characters are, above all else, contrastive. We find contrasts in the characters' speeches, in which the finale necessarily contrasts with the beginning, and not only through unexpected shifts to new topics (the idiosyncratic "destruction of illusions" in Dostoyevskian conversations), but also in terms of intonation: characters' speeches begin calmly and end in frenzy, and vice versa. Dostoevsky himself was fond of contrast in conversations; he was known to end serious discussions with a joke (A. N. Maikov), and would furthermore construct his readings around a contrast of intonations:

> *Until the poet is summoned*
> *To sacrifice by great Apollo ...*
>
> with *quiet* pathos, he would begin *slowly* in a *low crooning* voice; but when he would get to the line:
>
> *But when the divine Word*
> *Touches on that subtle ear,—*
>
> his voice would ring out now with *intense*, throaty, and *high* notes, and all the while he would *sway his hand steadily* through the air, *as if portraying* to himself and to me these waves of poetry.[50]

---

47 The full quotation, from a 1 February 1846 letter to Mikhail Dostoyevsky, reads: "[The public has] gotten used to seeing the author's mug in everything; I didn't show mine, however" (Dostoevsky, *Complete Letters*, 1:122).

48 Ivan Podkolyosin is the protagonist of Gogol's play "The Wedding" (1842). Georges Dandin is the eponymous protagonist of a play by Molière (1668).

49 Fyodor Dostoevsky, *The Idiot*, trans. Alan Myers (Oxford: Oxford University Press, 1992), 486.

50 V. V. Timofeeva [O. Pochinkovskaia], "A Year of Working with a Famous Writer" [God raboty s znamenitym pisatelem], *Historical Herald* [*Istoricheskii vestnik*] 2 (1904): 506—

Strakhov says the same thing about his manner of reading: "His right hand, drawn spasmodically down to his side, was obviously restraining itself from making the desired *gesture;* his voice was *amplified to a scream.*"[51] This special role of contrastive intonations must be what made it possible for Dostoevsky to *dictate* his novels.[52]

The fact that Dostoevsky initially chose the epistolary form is thus telling: not only *must* each letter be called forth by the previous one through *contrast,* but in its very nature this form naturally contains the contrastive shift of questioning, exclamatory, and exhortative intonations. Dostoevsky would subsequently carry these qualities of epistolary form over into the contrastive organization of his novels' chapters and dialogues. Both the epistolary and memoir forms were traditional for plot-poor constructions. Dostoevsky gives us pure epistolary form in *Poor Folk* and pure memoir form in *Notes from the House of the Dead*; the *Novel in Nine Letters* represents an attempt at combining epistolary form with a more developed plot, and *The Insulted and Injured* is the same sort of attempt using the memoir.

In *Crime and Punishment,* the contrast between the plot and the characters already shows literary organization: the frame of a crime plot is peopled with characters that contrast with it (the murderer, the prostitute, and the police inspector of the plot outline are replaced by a revolutionary, a saint, and a wise man). The plot in *The Idiot* unfolds in a contrastive manner, which coincides with the contrastive exposure of the characters; the zenith of plot tension is simultaneously the greatest exposure of the characters.

It is curious, however, that, while openly dissociating himself from Gogol's "types," Dostoevsky uses the latter's verbal and material masks. I have given some examples of this; here are a few more: names with inversions (Pyotr Ivanovich and Ivan Petrovich in the *Novel in Nine Letters*); and we find the device of sound repetition even in *The Idiot*: Alexandra, Adelaida, Aglaya.

In their outward appearance, Svidrigailov, Stavrogin, and Lambert are pointedly masks.[53] Perhaps there is yet another contrast here: a verbal *mask*

YT. Dostoyevsky reads from Alexander Pushkin's famous poem "The Poet" [Poet] (1827). Emphasis *YT*.

51 F. M. Dostoevsky, *Complete Works* [Polnoe sobranie sochinenii] (1883), 1:312—*YT*. Emphasis *YT*.

52 Beginning with the novella *The Gambler* [*Igrok*] (1866), Dostoevsky "wrote" by dictating his work to a secretary and then working with her to correct the typed-up manuscripts.

53 Svidrigailov is the main villain in Dostoyevsky's *Crime and Punishment*, Stavrogin is the antihero of *Demons* [*Besy*], and Lambert is a villainous figure in *A Raw Youth* [Podrostok].

that covers a contrastive *character*.[54] Thus a device organic to Gogol, when introduced by Dostoevsky, acquires new significance—through contrast. Similarly, further study must determine how Dostoevsky uses Gogol's syntactic-intonational figures; perhaps it will prove that one and the same "turns of phrase" are arranged in a more contrastive order in Dostoevsky than in Gogol. Dostoevsky uses Gogol's devices, but they are not, in and of themselves, crucial for him. This helps to explain the workings of Dostoevsky 's parody of Gogol: a stylization undertaken in order to achieve a specific set of aims turns into a parody when these aims are no longer there.

5

Dostoevsky insistently weaves literature into his works: it is rare for his characters *not* to talk about literature. This presents, of course, a highly convenient parodic device:[55] when a given character expresses a literary opinion, it becomes colored with *his* opinion; if this is a comic character, then his opinion will also be comic.

Netochka Nezvanova contains a parody of "Jacopo Sannazaro";[56] it is declaimed by a hapless German, Karl Fyodorovich, who commences to dancing after the reading (he is also a bad dancer): "The drama concerned the misfortunes of a certain great painter called Gennaro or Jacopo, who cried out on one page, 'No one recognizes me!' or on another, 'I am famous!' or 'I have no talent!' and a

54 For example, the reader's very acquaintance with the Yepanchin sisters [the aforementioned Alexandra, Adelaida, Aglaya—*Trans.*] also takes place, as it were, through contrast. Besides the comic repetition of "A" in their names, the initial mention of them prepares the reader for a comic impression, which will subsequently be completely destroyed: "*All three Yepanchin girls* were sturdy young ladies, tall and blooming, with magnificent shoulders, powerful bosoms, and *strong, almost masculine arms*; as a consequence of their health and strength they naturally *enjoyed eating well on occasions* […]. Besides tea, coffee, cheese, honey, butter, cutlets, and Madam Yepanchina's favorite special fritters, and so on, a rich hot broth might also be served" (Dostoevsky, *The Idiot*, 39). Here we see a complete overlap of verbal masks with the expression "all three girls"; the verbal mask thus has the proper surroundings for subsequent contrast—*YT*.

55 In the later (1929) essay "On Parody" (294–328), Tynianov introduces a distinction between the terms "functionally parodic" [*parodiinyi*] and "formally parodic" [*parodicheskii*]. In this, significantly earlier, essay, however, he does not point out a distinction between the terms.

56 Jacopo Sannazaro was a fifteenth- to sixteenth-century Italian poet noted for introducing the theme of Arcadia to European literature. The play was by Nestor Kukolnik (1809–1868), a prolific writer of Gogol's generation; Tynianov mistakenly refers to the author as "[Alexei] Timofeev," another minor dramatist of the late Romantic period.

few lines later 'I am talented!' It all ended most pathetically."[57] In *The Insulted and Injured,* old man Ikhmenev criticizes *Poor Folk* (parodying a review in *The Northern Bee*) and talks at length about Belinsky.[58] *Demons* contains parodies of Ogaryov's[N] poems, Turgenev's[N] "Enough," and Granovsky's letters; in its polemics it parodies Senkovsky,[N] and General Ivolgin's reminiscences parody war memoirs.[59] But Gogol is parodied as early as in *Poor Folk*; among the several parodies that serve as minor episodes, there is a parody of "The Story of How Ivan Ivanovich Quarreled with Ivan Nikiforovich": "Do you know Ivan Prokofyevich Zholtopuz? I mean the man who bit the leg of Prokofy Ivanovich. Ivan Prokofyevich is a man of a violent temper, but of rare virtues; Prokofy Ivanovich, on the other hand, is extremely fond of radishes and honey. It all happened at the time Pelageya Antonovna knew him. Do you know Pelageya Antonovna? I mean, the woman who always puts on her skirts inside out ...."[60]

Cf. "The Story of How Ivan Ivanovich Quarreled with Ivan Nikiforovich": 1) Anton Prokofyevich Golopuz (*Mirgorod,* 264), 2) "You know Agafya Fedoseyevna, don't you? I mean the lady who bit the assessor's ear, of course" (221); 3) "Ivan Ivanovich is of a somewhat timid disposition. Ivan Nikiforovich, on the other hand, wears trousers with such wide folds [...]" (225–226); 4). "He had it made a long time ago before Agafya [Fedoseyevna] had gone to Kiev. You know Agafya Fedoseyevna, don't you?" (221).

The parody is so obvious that it can be established through a simple side-by-side comparison. All the minor details have been preserved: the paired names of Ivan Ivanovich and Ivan Nikiforovich are replaced by inverted names, the device of logical syntax in conjunction with nonsense is evident, and the characters' last names have been parodied.

The essence of parody lies in the mechanization of a given device. This mechanization will be felt, of course, only when the device being mechanized is known. Parody thus attains a double objective: 1) it mechanizes the device; 2) it organizes new material, and this new material will moreover be the old mechanized device.

---

57 Dostoevsky, *Netochka,* 42.

58 The *Northern Bee* [Severnaia pchela] was a literary and political journal published in St. Petersburg during the first half of the nineteenth century, edited by the notorious Faddei Bulgarin, a writer, editor, and eager informant of the imperial secret police.

59 Timofei Granovsky (1813–1855) was a medievalist and close friend of Ogaryov and Herzen. He was one of the leaders of the "Westernizer" movement. For Senkovsky, see also "On Parody" (171).

60 Dostoevsky [Magarshack], *Poor Folk,* 73.

A verbal device can be mechanized through repetition, when that repetition does not fit into the compositional plan; also through a rearrangement of parts (a familiar parody is reading a poem from the bottom up); through pun-like shifts of meaning (schoolboy parodies of classical poems); through the addition of ambiguous refrains (the parodic refrain to Euripides' poem in Aristophanes' "The Frogs": "... lost his little flask of oil,"—this is a particularly popular device for jokes); finally, through isolating the device from similar devices and joining it to contradictory ones.

In Dostoevsky's parody discussed earlier [in *Poor Folk*], the device is not emphasized at all: it is felt as parody only against the background of a text that clashes with it completely in terms of style.

This parody is not motivated by the epistolary form, since it is an episodic insertion; but this form *is* what motivates the following reference to its style: "it may be a little bit too ingenious and certainly too playful, but quite innocent, without the slightest hint of freethinking or liberal ideas."[61] The parody of contemporary criticism is also motivated by its belonging to Makar: "Literature is such an excellent thing, Barbara, such an excellent thing. I found that out from him the other day. A profound thing! It fortifies the hearts of men, it's instructive and—all sorts of things of a similar nature are written about in his book. Beautifully written! Literature is a picture, I mean, a certain sort of picture, and a mirror. A medium for the expression of passions, for the most subtle criticism, a lesson in morals, and a document."[62]

But the parody in "Uncle's Dream" is already completely unmotivated: "Marya Aleksandrovna Moskaleva is, of course, Mordasov's leading lady—of that there can be no doubt whatsoever. She deports herself as though she had no need of anyone, and as though, on the contrary, everyone had need of her. [...] Such a requirement is, after all, a sign of very considerable diplomatic skill [...] About some of the inhabitants of Mordasov, for example, she knows such capitally important and scandalous things that were she to relate them on some convenient occasion and prove them to be true as she alone knows how, Mordasov would suffer something akin to the Lisbon earthquake [...] She knows, for example, how to slay, tear to pieces, and annihilate [...] And of course, as everyone knows, such a characteristic is proper to the very highest society [...] Marya Aleksandrovna has even been compared, in a certain respect, to Napoleon. This was, needless to say, something done in jest by her enemies—more by way of

61 Ibid., 73.

62 Ibid., 69.

caricature than with any pretension to truth. [...] Do you recall that infamous episode that brewed up in our midst about a year and a half ago [...]? [...] How well the embarrassing, scandalous incident was hushed up and suppressed!"[63]

This is from the beginning of "Uncle's Dream" (excerpted). All of the devices here are Gogolian: adjacent clauses are bookended by one and the same word ("had no need"—"had need"); hyperbole; synonyms in order of importance (compare "to slay, tear to pieces, annihilate," "hushed up and suppressed" with Gogol: "cheered and refreshed," "murky and unclear," etc.); foreign words as a comic device (compare Dostoevsky's "capitally important and scandalous" [Russian: *kapital'nye, skandaleznye—trans.*] with Gogol's "his behavior was becoming far too scandalous [*skandalezno*]"), etc.

We thus have no reason not to take this excerpt for a stylization. Toward the end of the chapter, however, Dostoevsky himself reveals its parodic nature, by partially tearing off the parodic mask (but only halfway, because the act of revealing itself is carried out through the same parodic style): "All that the well-disposed reader has just read was written by me some five months ago, out of sheer tender emotion. [...] I had intended to write something in the manner of a eulogy for that magnificent lady and to represent the whole business in the form of a playful letter to a friend, in the style of the letters that used to appear in the halcyon days of yore (which will thankfully never return) in *The Northern Bee* and other periodical publications."[64]

Dostoevsky gives the wrong address: although *The Northern Bee* did publish "letters to a friend," they weren't written in a Gogolian style. The epithet "playful" in relation to Gogol's style is used similarly in the parody of "Ivan Ivanovich & Ivan Nikiforovich."

In this easy and inconspicuous fashion, stylization crosses over into parody. And who can say how many of these undetected parodies (because he himself did not reveal them) we might find in Dostoevsky? Isn't the quotation about the three Yepanchin girls parodic?[65] Perhaps this subtle web of stylization-parody overlaying a tragic, developed plot is what constitutes Dostoevsky's grotesque

---

63 Fyodor Dostoevsky, *Uncle's Dream and Other Stories*, trans. David McDuff (New York/London: Penguin, 1989), 122–125. Translation slightly modified.

64 Ibid., 126.

65 Also compare the beginning of *Notes from the House of the Dead* [Zapiski iz mertvogo doma]: "They [cities—*YT*] are generally very well provided with district police inspectors, assessors, and all the other minor-ranking officials. In general, a government post in Siberia is an uncommonly snug one, in spite of the cold"—*YT.* Fyodor Dostoevsky, *The House of the Dead*, trans. David McDuff (New York/London: Penguin, 1985), 21.

singularity.

Parody exists to the extent that the second, parodied layer remains visible, peeking through the rest of the work. The more narrow, specific, and limited this second layer is, and the more all the details of the work are colored with this duality and perceived from a dual perspective—the stronger the work's parodic quality.

If the second layer blurs into the general concept of "style," then parody becomes one of the elements of a dialectical shift of schools and comes close to stylization, as in "Uncle's Dream." But what if there is a second layer, even a specific one, but one that has not entered into literary consciousness, that has not been detected or has been forgotten? In such a case, the parody is naturally perceived on a single plane, exclusively with regard to its organization, i.e., like any other work of literature.

The aim of this article is, among other things, to indicate the previously undetected second level of one of Dostoevsky 's novels, to indicate the parodic nature of his *The Village of Stepanchikovo*. This is a case of specific parody: the second level is limited to a single work, and by type is close to the simple parody of "Ivan Ivanovich & Ivan Nikiforovich." What follows will serve as illustrative material for this specific type.

6

The Village of Stepanchikovo [*Selo Stepanchikovo i ego obitateli*] appeared in 1859. Dostoevsky worked on the novel for a long time and held it in high regard; in terms of reception, however, it was little noticed by the public. In 1859 Dostoevsky wrote to his brother: "The novel, of course, has great shortcomings and the main one, perhaps, is long-windedness; but what I'm just as certain of as I am of an axiom is that at the same time it has great merits and that it is my *best work*. I spent two years writing it (with a *break in the middle* for 'Uncle's Dream').[66] The beginning and middle have been polished, the end was written hastily. But I put my soul, my flesh and blood into it [...] there are two enormous *typical characters* that I *have been creating and writing down* for five years, polished beyond reproach (in my opinion)—characters that are completely Russian and which until now have been poorly represented by Russian literature" [emphasis *YT*].[67] The full title of the novel (in letters, Dostoevsky referred to it as either a "comic

66 See the above statement about the parodic nature of "Uncle's Dream"—*YT.*

67 Dostoevsky, *Complete Letters*, 1:363–364. 9 May 1859,

novel" or a tale) is *The Village of Stepanchikovo and its Inhabitants. From the Notes of an Unknown.* As is evident from the title, the novel was written in the form of a memoir; its main aim (as we can see in the letters) was the depiction of two new characters. These were Foma Opiskin and "Uncle" Rostanev. Opiskin is a parodic character: the material for parody came from Gogol's personality, and Foma's speeches parody Gogol's *Selected Passages.*[68]

At this point I must remark, regarding my own commentary: Dostoev-

---

68 Dostoyevsky's relationship to Gogol is complicated, and particularly his relationship to Gogol's personality. When the news of Gogol's death came in 1846, Dostoyevsky appended a typical postscript to a long letter: "I wish you all happiness, my friends. Gogol died in Florence two months ago" (ibid.). In literature, Gogol is evidently something that Dostoevsky has to overcome, something he must necessarily surpass. See what he writes, in a letter to his brother, about "The Double": "You'll like it even better than *Dead Souls*" (ibid., 122); and about the *Novel in Nine Letters*: "It'll be better than Gogol's 'Lawsuit'" (also in a letter to his brother). Dostoyevsky's last known statements on Gogol differ significantly from the traditional view of criticism (see "Gogol's laughing mask," "the demon of laughter," and the polemics in *Demons* against Gogol's self-definition: "visible laughter through invisible tears," etc.) and compel us to see in him a predecessor of later critics like Rozanov and Briusov, et al. Dostoevsky's attitude toward the *Selected Passages* is well known: upon first hearing about it he wrote his brother: "I haven't been telling you anything about Gogol, but here's a fact for you. In next month's issue of *The Contemporary* a piece by Gogol will be published—his will, in which he disavows all his works and declares them useless and even more than that" (ibid., 131—letter of 5 September 1846, translation slightly modified). As is also well known, reading and aiding in the reproduction of Belinsky's letter to Gogol was the primary accusation leveled at Dostoyevsky during the Petrashevsky Circle trial. Later, having broken off ties with Belinsky's circle, Dostoyevsky evidently drew on vivid memories of it with regard to the *Selected Passages.* Nearly all of the quotations from Gogol given below for comparison are cited in Belinsky's review of the *Selected Passages.* Clearly, Dostoyevsky's relationship to the *Selected Passages* did not change over time. He wrote in 1876: "Gogol may be weak in his *Selected Passages*, yet he is characteristic" (Dostoevsky, *A Writer's Diary*, 1:431); in late 1880: "To drape yourself in clouds of magnificence (Gogol's tone, for instance, in the *Correspondence with Friends*) is insincerity, and even the most inexperienced reader senses insincerity. It's the first thing that gives you away" (letter to Ivan Aksakov, 4 November 1880, 5:289–290). Upon his release from prison, Dostoyevsky periodically reread Gogol, for instance while working on *The Village of Stepanchikovo* and "Uncle's Dream" (see Baron A. E. Vrangel', *Vospominaniia o F. M. Dostoevskom v Sibiri 1854–56* [St. Petersburg, 1912], 30–32). 1857 saw Kulish's publication including two volumes of Gogol's letters, which meanwhile provoked a reassessment of the *Selected Passages* question (Chernyshevsky's article). Dostoyevsky kept working on his novel right up until sending it off to print, rewriting parts, etc. (See his 29 October 1859 (1:412) letter to his brother from Tver). For this reason, I will refer occasionally to Gogol's letters (from Kulish's edition) as material that was well known to Dostoyevsky. Textual comparisons here are, however, less important than a comparison of the actual devices, since for the purpose of parody other phrasal material could also be used (V. Shklovsky). Of course, this is not true for cases in which the object of parody is the actual lexicon—*YT*.

sky's animosity toward the *Selected Passages from Correspondence with Friends* does not suggest an explanation for his parody of it, just as his relationship to Gogol will not clarify any parodies of the latter's character. These two elements happened to overlap, but they could just as easily not have; anything can be material for parody; no psychological backstory is necessary. Parodies of the Bible are popular among Orthodox Jews; Pushkin, while admiring Karamzin's *History*, parodies it in his "Chronicle of the Village of Goriukhino"; he also parodies the style of the *Iliad* and his own well-known couplet: "I hear the silenced sound of divine Hellenic speech"—"Gnedich the one-eyed poet, who did translate blind Homer";[69] the many parodies of the *Aeneid* go hand-in-hand with great appreciation for it. The point is that the very essence of parody, its two levels, constitutes a specific and valuable device.[70] This is why we will not be surprised to find that, alongside Dostoevsky's ill-disposed relationship to the *Selected Passages*, alongside his parody of it (which, however, we have yet to prove), he used the very same *Selected Passages* in "A Little Hero" (a work written in prison)—but as the material for stylization rather than for parody.

Compare: "There are women who are like *sisters of mercy in life*. One need hide nothing from them, at least nothing *that is hurt and vulnerable in the soul*. Whoever may be suffering, *go to them* boldly and hopefully without fear of being a burden, *because* few of us know how much infinite patience and love, compassion and forgiveness might be found in some woman's heart. Inexhaustible treasures of sympathy, consolation, and hope are to be found in these pure hearts, which are also often hurt, for a heart that loves much,

---

69 The quotes are from, respectively, "On the Translation of the *Iliad*" and "Toward the Translation of the *Iliad*" (both 1830), two-line poems which refer to Nikolai Gnedich (1784–1833), a poet best known for his work translating Homer.

70 There are people who claim that in our time, parodying is "mocking," "antipathy," and even "hatred" toward the object of parody. If this was actually the case, there would be no way to understand the cheerful reaction of the objects of parody to the parodies themselves. For instance, A. P. Kern told the following story about [Alexander] Pushkin: "One time [...] he was in a terrible mood, standing in the living room by the fireplace with his hands behind his back... Illichevsky walked up to him and said:

У печки, погружен в молчанье,	By the stove, in silence smothered,
Поднявши фрак, он спину грел	His collar high, he warmed his back
И никого во всей компанье	And every soul of all those gathered
Благословить он не хотел.	He would not deign to bless, alack.

This cheered Pushkin up and he became quite good-humored" (D. N. Maikov, *Pushkin* [St. Petersburg, 1899], 265)—*YT*. The poem parodies Pushkin's well-known poem "Demon" (1823).

grieves much, but its *wounds are carefully hidden* from inquisitive eyes. For deep sorrow is most often silent and hidden. They are not aghast at the depth of the wound, nor at *its suppuration*, nor at *its stench*; anyone who comes to them is by that very fact worthy of them. They seem, indeed, to be born for great, heroic deeds [...]."[71]

In its theme (cf. Gogol's "Woman in the World"), individual expressions ("sisters of mercy in life," "suppuration and stench"), and syntactic framework ("go to them," "nothing that is hurt and vulnerable"), as well as the noticeable accretion of Church Slavonicisms, this passage might have been found in the *Selected Passages.* And Dostoevsky worked quite eagerly with both historical and contemporary material relating to Gogol's personality. Granovsky and Turgenev served as material for parodic characters in *Demons*; in the *The Life of a Great Sinner*, Belinsky, Granovsky and Pushkin were meant to visit Chaadaev in his monastery. In this connection Dostoevsky stipulates: "After all, it's not Chaadaev I have; I'm just taking that *type* for the novel" [emphasis *YT*].[72] And we cannot be sure that there was no parodic tinge to his sketch of Pushkin. After all, Dostoevsky is very interested in the emotional reshuffling of his characters: it's no accident when one of the other characters in *The Idiot* calls Ippolit "Nozdrev in a tragedy," and Dostoevsky himself was delighted by Strakhov's description of the protagonists of *Demons*: "These are *Turgenev's heroes in their old age*" [emphasis *YT*].[73] We find anecdotal tidbits from Gogol's life in the novel; Dostoevsky generally loved to bring in tidbits like this (such as the names of streets and doctors; Ippolit consults with "Mr. B"—Botkin [in *The Idiot—trans.*]). Here are two examples. In 1844, Dostoevsky wrote his brother: "In his last letter Karepin, apropos of nothing, advised me not to amuse myself with Shakespeare. He says that Shakespeare and a soap bubble are the same thing. I wanted you to understand this comical trait, the irritation with Shakespeare. But what does Shakespeare have to do with anything?"[74] Later, in "Uncle's Dream," this rancor toward Shakespeare would be incorporated as a comic feature in Marya Aleksandrovna's conversations.

But Dostoevsky carried over the tragic features of real life into his works as well, sometimes sharply changing their emotional coloring from tragic to

71 "A Little Hero," in Dostoevsky, *Poor Folk*, 185 (translation modified). Emphasis *YT*.

72 Dostoevsky *Complete Letters*, 3:248. 25 March (6 April) 1870.

73 Dostoevsky quotes Strakhov in a letter to Apollon Maikov. See *Complete Letters*, 3:324. 2 (14) March 1871.

74 Ibid., 1:98. 30 September 1844,

comic. I apologize for the morbid example, but it is extremely convincing:

Andrei Dostoevsky [the writer's brother—*trans.*] recalled the tombstone at their mother's grave: "Our father left it to my brothers [Fyodor and Mikhail] to choose the inscription on the tombstone. They both decided that it should indicate only the name and dates of birth and death. For the back side, however, they selected an inscription from Karamzin: 'Rest in peace, dear ashes, until the joyous dawn. ...' And this exquisite inscription was carried out."

In *The Idiot,* General Ivolgin tells the tale of Lebedev, who claims to have lost his left leg; the general says "he picked up the leg and took it home and later buried it in the Vagankov Cemetery, and says he erected a memorial over it with an inscription on one side: 'Here lies the leg of Collegiate Secretary Lebedev,' and on the other 'Rest in peace, beloved ashes, till resurrection's joyous dawn."[75]

Thus, Gogol's character is parodied by inserting the *Selected Passages*-era Gogol into the character of an unsuccessful writer and "hanger-on."[76]

Foma Opiskin is first and foremost a man of literature, a missionary, a teacher of morals—his influence rests on these qualities. The narrator's uncle "[had supreme belief] in the genius and erudition of Foma [...] the very words 'science' and 'literature' inspired my uncle with the most naive and artless awe [...]"; Foma has suffered for the truth.[77] This was a new phenomenon noted down and tested by Gogol, cf.: "Among us, even a simple scribbler, who is not a writer and not only has no beauty of soul but is even at times quite scoundrelly, in the depths of Russia will by no means be taken as such. On the contrary, among everyone in general, even among those who hardly ever hear anything about writers, there is the conviction that a writer is something superior, that he certainly should be someone noble [...]" ("On the Lyricism of our Poets," 63–64) [translation slightly modified].

The name of Foma Opiskin became pejorative ("a successful type") to such an extent that it was taken as a pseudonym by a comic writer from *Satirikon.*[78]

---

75 Dostoevsky, *The Idiot,* 522–523. Dostoyevsky would go on to use the same phrase in his 1873 fantastic tale "Bobok," where it also appears in a grotesque, humorous setting.

76 Interestingly, Dostoyevsky has another parodic character who is a hanger-on—Stepan Trofimovich [Verkhovensky], who demonstrates the same sort of "wandering" and even the same satchel. This parodic shift of the characters in *Demons* [Besy] corresponds to the overall shift [from] Russia > Petersburg > a provincial city (the action of *Demons* takes place in a provincial city)—*YT.*

77 Fyodor Dostoevsky, *The Village of Stepanchikovo and its Inhabitants,* trans. Ignat Avsey (Ithaca, NY: Cornell University Press, 1987), 39.

78 The writer was Arkady Averchenko. *Satirikon* was a Russian weekly magazine of satire and humor published between 1908–1913.

But Foma's critics did not scrutinize him enough. He is not only a rogue, a Tartuffe, a hypocrite, and an impostor: "He is a most impractical person, a poet you could say, in his way" (144, translation slightly modified), as Mizinchikov puts it.

Dostoevsky remained true to himself in his contrastive depiction of Foma. This rogue subjects his enemies to his influence (Bakhcheyev); also under his influence, "Nastenka is fond of reading the lives of the saints, and maintains with remorse that good deeds alone are not enough, that really they ought to distribute everything to the destitute and seek happiness in poverty" [243].

Foma's vanity is also literary: "Who knows but that such warped vanity might perhaps merely be a deceptive manifestation of initially corrupted personal dignity, dignity which might have sustained its first reverses perhaps in childhood, in circumstances of oppression, poverty, filth [...]?[79] But [...] Foma Fomich was an exception to the general rule. [...] He had once tried his hand at literature, and had suffered disappointment and rejection; but, of course, *literature has ruined mightier men than Foma Fomich*—especially rejected literature" [34, emphasis *YT*]. Gogol's everyday experience is sustained in all of its tiny details. There were few memoirs about him at that time, but those features of Gogol's that would later be mentioned in memoirs were, of course, known at the time. Berg recalls:

> It is difficult to imagine a more pampered writer or one with greater pretensions than was Gogol at that time. [...] Gogol's Moscow friends, or more precisely, his *servitors* (it would seem that Gogol did not have a single true friend his whole life long), surrounded him with unparalleled, reverential attention. Every time he came to Moscow he would find, with one of them, everything he needed for the most peaceful and comfortable life imaginable: a table laid with the dishes he loved best, a quiet, secluded space and servants ready to answer to his tiniest whimsy. [...] Even the close acquaintances of Gogol's hosts were required to know how to properly conduct themselves, were they to suddenly meet him and speak with him.[80]

All of this is kept up in Dostoevsky 's novel. Foma is wined and dined: "Tea, tea,

79 See Gogol: "[...] my attitude toward people has always been quite unpleasant and repellent [...] And in part it is the result of a trivial vanity, peculiar to those among us who have made our own way from the gutter into society and esteem that they have the right to regard others arrogantly" (Gogol, *Selected Passages*, 5)—*YT*.

80 I. V. Berg, "Vospominaniia o Gogole 1848–1852," in *Russkaia starina*, no. 1 (1872): 118.

sister darling! Plenty of sugar, dearest! Foma likes his tea sweet after his sleep" [106]; his quiet and seclusion are jealously guarded: "'He's writing an essay!' he would say, on tiptoe, though Foma's study was two rooms away" [38]; Gavrila is assigned specially to attend to Foma's caprices; the uncle instructs his nephew on how to behave "should they meet."

Also cf. the description of Foma's rooms: "The great man resided in splendid comfort" [193]. Foma conducts himself in the Rostanev household like Gogol did at the Aksakovs'.

Foma's appearance also seems to have been copied from Gogol. "Gavrila was quite right in referring to him as a *shabby* little man. Foma Fomich was *short of stature,* with greying *fair hair,*[81] a *hooked nose* and face densely lined with tiny wrinkles. [...] To my surprise he appeared in a *dressing gown*—of foreign cut, true [...]" [105, emphasis *YT*]. "Foma Fomich was sitting in a comfortable armchair, in *an ankle-length frock coat,* but without a tie" [194, emphasis *YT*]. Hints are sprinkled all over the place that create a sort of Gogolian background: Yegor Ilyich once met a certain writer in Petersburg: "the one with the funny nose" (200); in one of his sermons Foma mentions Gogol directly; Foma suffered for the truth "in forty-something or other" (54). Obvious hints start on page ten of the novel: "I can clearly recollect [Foma's] words when he spoke to us in my uncle's house at Stepanchikovo after becoming virtual lord and master: 'I'm no lodger in this house,' he announced mysteriously, 'I'm no lodger here! Just give me a little time to arrange everything, to show you the way of things, and then adieu: to Moscow, to publish a journal! *Thirty thousand people will throng every month to attend my lectures.* My fame will spread far and wide, and then—woe betide my enemies!" [35, emphasis *YT*]. Thirty thousand people at lectures is, of course, Khlestakov's thirty-five thousand couriers (though this could also perhaps be a reference to Gogol's unsuccessful run as a professor).

"But his genius, even before it had established itself, insisted upon immediate reward. The prospect of being paid in advance is always alluring, and in his case especially so. I know he had seriously convinced my uncle that he, Foma, was destined one day to perform a great feat, a feat for which he had been expressly summoned into this world, and that a winged creature or something of that kind was providing him with the necessary encouragement. Namely,

81 Gogol described himself as "stocky and plain." Letter to A.S. Danilevsky, 11 April 1838 (N. V. Gogol, *Writings and Letters* [Sochineniia i pis'ma], vol. 5 (St. Petersburg: P. A. Kulish, 1857), 306 [11:132]; "Gogol was fair-haired," S. Aksakov,[N] et al.—*YT.* See S. Aksakov on Gogol's clothing: "a frock coat rather like an overcoat" (*Istoriia moego znakomstva s Gogolem* [Moscow: Tip. Volchaninova]), 16. Compare A. Slonimsky's objection, ibid., 30—*YT.*

he was to compose *a profoundly searching* magnum opus *of a spiritually edifying nature that would shake the earth* and stun all Russia. And then, after all Russia had been stunned, he, Foma, scorning glory, *would withdraw to a monastery, spend the rest of his days and nights praying in the caverns of Kiev for the salvation of his fatherland*" [35–36, translation modified, emphasis *YT*].

It is known how significant Gogol considered his *Selected Passages* and what kind of a response he expected they would elicit. "The time will soon come," he wrote, "when all will become clear" [8:85]; the publication of this book "is much needed, both for me and for others; in a word, it is needed for the common good. My heart tells me this and also the unusual mercy of God" [8:112]. "Withdrawing to a monastery" hints at Gogol's journey to Jerusalem; cf. "Before the Tomb of Our Lord will I pray for all my compatriots, not excepting one among them [...]."[82] Dostoevsky had already written to his brother regarding this testament in 1846: "He says he will not take up the pen for the rest of his life because his business is praying."[83] The "earth-shaking" may be parodying Gogol's article about Yazykov's poem "The Earthquake": "You will find the words, expressions will be found; *fire*, not words, will fly from your lips, as they did from the lips of the ancient prophets [...] The true Russian you will lead to inveigh against discouragement, you *will raise him above* the terrors and *shakings of earth*, as you raised the poet in your 'Earthquake'" [88, 87, emphasis *YT*].[84]

Foma Fomich is deeply concerned with the peasant question. Significantly, his posthumous papers include "an absurd discourse on the *significance and character of the Russian muzhik and how to handle him*" [194]; he also writes "about the forces of production": "[...] first he spoke to the peasants about farm management, although he could not tell oats from wheat, then in suave tones explained the *sacred duties of the peasant to his master*, touching in passing upon the subject of electricity and the *division of labor*, of which, of course, he understood not a jot, went on to explain the revolution of the earth around the sun, and finally, in a state of euphoria at his own eloquence, turned to discussing the ministers of the crown. I understood this. [...] The peasants, as always,

---

82 Gogol, *Selected Passages*, 6.

83 5 September 1846—*YT*. See Dostoyevsky, *Complete Letters*, 1:131.

84 See, moreover, the beginning of this passage with the following excerpt from "The Historical Painter Ivanov": "I am working along on something which will soon astonish you, but which I cannot now tell you about, because much of it is still not comprehensible even to me. So while I am at work, wait patiently and give me money for my support"—a statement attributed to the painter [151]—*YT*.

listened submissively to Foma Fomich" [39–40, emphasis *YT*].

But this is the program of two articles in the *Selected Passages*, "The Russian Landowner" and "To One Who Occupies an Important Position"; cf. particularly the part about the ministers: "'The governor-general is a minister of internal affairs pausing on the road.' [...] The governor-general is sent out in order [...] to give a push to everything, by his authority to ease the difficulty of many places in their dealings with more distant ministries [...]" (177–178, translation slightly modified). And subsequently, on the "division of labor": "First, establish the legal limits of every position, and every official of the province in a full knowledge of his position. [...] To restore every position to its legal circle has now become so difficult [...]" [179–180]. Foma's farewell sermon goes even further in developing the position of "The Russian Landowner": "You're a landowner; you should sparkle like a diamond on your estates [...]":

> "And so remember that you are a landowner," continued Foma [...] "Do not imagine that ease and lust are the privileges of the landed gentry. Perish the thought! *It's not ease that's needed, but zeal toward God, Tsar and country! The landowner must toil, toil and toil again, like the meanest of his peasants!"*
> "What! Must I go and *plough the fields for the laborers,* is that what you mean?" Bakhcheyev grumbled. [...]
> "And now you of the household staff," Foma Fomich continued [...] "Love your masters and be obedient to their will, be humble and meek. Your masters' love will be your ample reward. And you, Colonel, practice justice and compassion toward your servants. Behold, they are of the human kind—molded in the image of God, *children, so to speak, entrusted to your care by the Tsar and the land that he rules.* Heavy lies the burden of duty upon you, but your reward will be great! [204, emphasis *YT*].

Compare Gogol: "Take up the business of the landowner as it should be taken up, in the proper and lawful sense. [...] *God will make you answer* if you should change this rank for another, because everyone must *serve God* in his place [...]" [137–138, translation modified, emphasis *YT*].

"And you, who have not hitherto served zealously in any special career, will deliver such *service to the Tsar* in your rank of landowner as no other great official has delivered" [145, translation slightly modified, emphasis *YT*]. "[...] be a patriarch, the inceptor of everything, the vanguard of all things [...] and you should dine together with [the peasants], and *go out to work with them, and in the work you should be the vanguard,* inciting everyone to work robustly [...]" [141, emphasis *YT*].

"Use powerful words: 'Now let's get to it, lads, all together!' *Take an axe or scythe in your hands;* this will be good for you [...]" ("The Russian Landowner") [141, emphasis *YT*]. Tentetnikov develops the same line of thought: "I [...] am a landowner; and this is no trifling title, either. If I take the time to *care for, cherish and improve the lot of the people entrusted to me* [...] then how will my service be any worse than the service of a head of some department or other [...]?" [7:17; emphasis *YT*].

Foma's reflections on literature, which directly follow his reflections on the "dances of the Russian people," parody Gogol's article "Subjects for the Lyric Poets [...]," as well as part of "On the Theater, on the One-sided View towards the Theater [...]."

> "I'm astounded, Pavel Semyonych," he continued. "What do our modern men of letters do—our poets, scholars, and thinkers? Why do they pay no attention to what songs the people of Russia sing, what songs the Russian people dance to? What have all these *Pushkins, Lermontovs, Borozdnas* been doing up to now? I am astonished! People are dancing the komarinsky, this apotheosis of drunkenness, and all we get from them are the *praises they sing to forget-me-nots*! Why don't they compose *more edifying songs* for the use of the people, and give up their forget-me-nots? Here we have a social problem! Let them portray a peasant, but an *ennobled peasant,* a settled and responsible villager and not simply a *peasant* [Russ: *muzhik*]. Let them portray a *rural sage in all his simplicity,* wearing bast shoes if need be—I'll accept even that—but enhanced by virtues, which—I say this without fear—may even be the envy of some greatly overrated Alexander the Great. I know Russia and Mother Russia knows me: that's precisely why I'm saying this. Let them portray this peasant, if they like, burdened by family responsibilities, advancing old age, cooped up in a stuffy hut and maybe starving too, yet perfectly content and uncomplaining, *glorifying his poverty* and indifferent to the gold of the wealthy. Now let the rich man, his heart moved to tenderness, bring his gold to him; let there even be a merging between the peasant's virtues and the virtues of his lord and maybe master. The rustic and the lord, placed so far apart on the ladder of society, are finally united in their virtues—there's an elevated thought!" [109–110, emphasis *YT*].

Compare Gogol: "Only separate the properly named higher theater from those capering ballets, vaudevilles [...] which pander to depraved tastes or depraved hearts [...]" [74].

Compare the "forget-me-nots" with Gogol's reference to "poetic playthings" [81]. Also compare to Gogol Foma's episode with the lord and poor peasant: "In a triumphal hymn, exalt the unknown toiler who, to the honor of the lofty Russian race, although among grafters [...] Exalt him and his family, his noble wife who would rather wear her old, unfashionable bonnet and be the object of others' laughter than permit her husband to be unjust and mean. Put forward their *fine poverty*, so that, like a holy thing, it may strike everyone's eyes and so that *each of us may wish to be poor himself*" ("Subjects for Lyric Poets of Present Time") [88].

When Foma preaches of suffering as the path to good deeds, he refers directly to Gogol: "As for myself, let it be said that misfortune may be the mother of virtue—Gogol's words, if I'm not mistaken—that frivolous author sometimes not devoid of a grain of sense. Exile is misfortune! I shall now go out into the world, a wanderer leaning on my staff, and who knows, through my misfortunes I may yet attain new pinnacles of virtue! This thought is the last comfort left to me!" [226].

Compare Gogol: "[...] misfortune softens a man; his nature then becomes more sensitive and more accessible to the understanding of subjects beyond the conception of a man in his habitual, daily situation [...]" ("Help the Poor"); and in the same article: "the holy and profound purport of misfortune" [31].

7

The examples of Foma's speech given above are notable in terms of style, and Foma himself comments on his style. Thus the uncle repeats Foma's own statement that "there is something melodious in his turns of phrase" [112, translation modified]; one of the peculiar features of this solemn phrasing is, however, expressions like "clodhopper," "pug," "boor," "shilly-shally," "Dutch-faced moron," and so on.

This is deliberate and constitutes a system. "'I called him a Dutch-faced moron deliberately, Pavel Semyonych,' he remarked [...] I find it quite unnecessary ever to mince words. *Truth must out.* No matter how you cover up filth, filth it will remain. So why go to the trouble of deceiving oneself and others" [106–107, emphasis *YT*]. "You have about as much appreciation of beauty and refinement, if I may say so, Colonel, as a bull has of good beef! That was rude and cruel, I admit; but at least it was *honest and just*. None of your toadies will ever tell you anything like that, Colonel" [117, emphasis *YT*]. "Why didn't you wring my neck like a farmyard cockerel's in the very beginning, because ... well, because, for instance, it couldn't lay eggs. Yes, that's right! I stand by this comparison, Colonel, even though it has a *provincial flavor* about it and is reminiscent of the *trivial tone of our contemporary literature* [...]" [132, emphasis *YT*].

The *Selected Passages* combine high style with expressions like "unwashed mug," "scoundrel," "the scribbler scribbled, and like a dog he dribbled." This mélange was deliberate. Gogol himself explained it in a letter to Rosset: "[...] I almost intentionally left in all sorts of places capable of cutting to the quick through their cocksureness"[85] [8:278].

The high style is maintained with equal rigor.

In Foma's farewell sermon (as in Gogol's sermons), instructions related to farm management coincide, in terms of style, with moral exhortations: "[...] you still haven't cut the grass on that patch of wasteland in Kharinskaya. Don't leave it too late: have it cut and have it cut quickly. Such is my advice ... [...] I know you wanted to clear that strip of Zaryanovo woodland; leave the trees alone—that is my second piece of advice. Forests must be preserved: for they retain moisture on the earth's surface. ... What a pity you put in your spring crops so late; really, it is surprising how late you have sowed your spring crops!" [205]; cf. Gogol's well-known letter to Danilevsky: "But listen, now you must heed my word, for my word is doubly powerful over you, and woe unto anyone who does not heed my word. [...] Buckle under and occupy yourself with your estate for a year, for one year only. Don't start anything new, don't try to improve anything, don't even offer support, but look into everything, keep an eye on the muzhiks, the steward [...] So then, carry out this my entreaty in all humility and full obedience!"[86]

Individual devices of Gogol's style are also parodied.

"'What sort of person were you before I arrived? But I have kindled a spark of the divine fire in you, and it will glow in your soul forever. Have I kindled a divine spark in you or not? Answer me: have I, or have I not, kindled a spark in you?" and so on [40–41].

---

85 Vissarion Belinsky paid particular attention to this aspect of Gogol's style. See his review of *Selected Passages*, where he lists the expressions "foolish society noddle," "rushes into nonsense," "unwashed mug," et al.—*YT*.

86 Gogol, *Sochineniia*, 5:447 [11:342–343]—*YT*.

"'Well, don't you feel,' the tormentor continued, 'that you've now been spiritually uplifted as though an angel had been sent to lull your heart? Do you feel the presence of this angel? Answer me!'" [137].

"Why did he not come running to me earlier, joyful and beautiful—for indeed, love does beautify the features—why did he not then fly into my arms, weep tears of infinite joy on my bosom, and reveal to me all, all? Or am I a crocodile who would rather devour you than give you worthy counsel? Or am I some kind of vile bug? [...]" [3:148].

Compare Gogol: "Have I really gone entirely out of my mind? [...] And what led you to the conclusion that a second volume is necessary right now? Have you really stolen into my head? Have you sensed the existence of a second volume? [...] Which of us is right? He who already has the second volume in his head or he who does not even know of what the second volume will consist?" ("Third Letter Apropos *Dead Souls*") [107].

"Who told you that their illnesses are incurable? [...] So are you really an omniscient doctor? Why did you not request help of someone else? Is it really in vain that I asked you to report everything in your town to me [...]? Why have you not done this, especially since you yourself [...] have attributed to me an understanding which is not common to all people? Do you really think that I would not be able to help your incurably ill people [...]?" ("The Wife of a Provincial Governor") [124].

In this case Dostoevsky 's parody works through varying combinations of *images:* images like "the spark of heavenly fire" or "a fallen angel" are close to images in Gogol's *Selected Passages* (cf., at the very least, the "electric spark [...] of that poetic fire"—"On the Essence of Russian Poetry and on its Originality" [214]) but in Gogol they do not combine with the syntactic form of the escalating questions; the comedy here lies in the discrepancy between syntax and semantics.

Dostoevsky also parodies Gogol's exaggerated escalations, through the repetition of single words: "You are proud, inordinately proud! [...] You are an egoist, and a sordid egoist at that ... [...] You're a boor, you're a trespasser upon the hearts of men of goodwill, you're so selfishly eager to draw attention to yourself [...]" [137, translation slightly modified].

Compare Gogol: "And you are proud: already you do not want to see anything; you are self-confident: you think that you already know everything; you think that all the circumstances of Russia have been disclosed to you; you think that no one can teach you anything [...]" ("To a Myopic Friend") [172].

Two more extremely important features in Gogol are parodied in this way:

1) "'I shall give away this secret,' screeched Foma Fomich, 'and it will be the noblest deed that ever was! The *Good Lord Himself has sent me to expose the world in its iniquity*! I'm ready to proclaim your sordid misdeed from the thatched rooftop of a peasant's hut for the benefit of every landowner who lives here and everyone who passes through here!'" [206].

Compare Gogol: "Do not be troubled by abominations, serve every abomination up to me! I find nothing unusual in abomination: I have enough abomination of my own. So long as I was not myself sunk in abominations, each abomination troubled me [...] since then, as I began to observe abomination more closely, my soul became more lucid [...] And now above all I thank God for having honored me, be it only partially, with a knowledge of abomination [...]" ("The Wife of a Provincial Governor") [135].

Also cf. "[...] no other writer has the gift of representing the banality of life so clearly, of knowing how to depict the banality of a banal man with such force that all the *petty details* which escape the eyes *gleam large* in the eyes of all" ("Third Letter Apropos *Dead Souls*") [103, translation slightly modified, emphasis *YT*].

2) "'... I want to love mankind, to love mankind,' yelled Foma Fomich, 'but people are being kept away from me, I am forbidden to love, they force people away from me! Give me, give me a man so that I may love him! Where is this man? Where has this man hidden himself? Like Diogenes with his lantern, I've been yearning to find one true soul all my life long, but in vain, and I can't even begin to love anybody until I find that person. Woe to him who has turned me into a misanthropist! "Give me a man," I cry, "that I may love him!"—and I'm fobbed off with a Falaley! Should I love Falaley? Would I wish to love Falaley? Could I love Falaley even if I wanted to? No! Why not? Because he is Falaley. Why do I hate mankind? Because mankind is made up of Falaleys, or beings like Falaley! I don't want Falaley, I detest Falaley, I spit upon Falaley, I'll make mincemeat of Falaley—and if you ask me to choose, I'd rather love the evil spirit Asmodeus than Falaley!'" [227].

Compare Gogol: "'I cannot embrace this man: he is vile, he is a debased spirit, he has soiled himself by innumerable actions; I will not allow this man even into my presence; I do not even want to breathe the same air as he; I will make a detour in order to go round him and not meet him. I cannot live with base and contemptible people—can I really embrace such a man as a brother?" ("Easter Sunday") [253].

Also cf: "I love the good, and I search for it and burn with it; but I do not love my abominations and I do not hold their hands, as my heroes do; I do not love those meannesses of mine which separate me from the good. I struggle, and will struggle with them, and with the help of God I will expel them" ("Third Letter Apropos *Dead Souls*") [107]. "But how can we love our brothers, how can we love men? The soul desires only to love the beautiful, and poor men are so imperfect, there is so little beauty in them! How shall we do it?" ("It is Necessary to Love Russia") [111].

The repetition of the name is also a device used often by Gogol; cf., for instance: "[…] it is necessary, like Ivanov, to die to all the enticements of life; like Ivanov, to instruct oneself […] like Ivanov, to wear a simple pleated jacket […] like Ivanov, to endure all […]" ("The Historical Painter Ivanov") [155].

In both of the excerpts given, the parody achieves ultimate precision by emphasizing Gogol's tautology; the very name "Falaley" is a typical, semantically denotative verbal mask ("Falaley" sounds like *rotozei* [dimwit or yoyo]). The question of the "perfectly beautiful man" is also raised here, and Gogol's ideal mask elicits Dostoevsky 's usual response: the imperfect man is beautiful.

8

In *The Village of Stepanchikovo*, Dostoevsky made use of all the possible means of *verbal* parody. The very lexicon of the *Selected Passages* is parodied.

"'Erect no monument for me!' Foma shouted, 'erect none for me! I need no monuments of stone! Set me up a monument in your hearts, and nothing more, nothing, nothing!'" [216].

Compare Gogol: "I will that no memorial [*pamiatnik*] be raised to me, that such trifles not be thought of, for they are unworthy of a Christian. Let the one of my friends to whom I have really been dear erect a different monument to me: let him erect it in his inner conscience by his steadfastness in the vicissitudes of life, by the courage and freshness he gives to everyone around him. Whoever, after my death, achieves a loftier soul than the one he had during my lifetime will show that he really loved me and was my friend; only in this way will he erect a memorial to me" ("Testament") [7–8, translation modified].

The verbal parody here is extremely simple: instead of the Russian word *pamiatnik*, we get the foreign word *monument*. The comic effect of foreign words embedded into texts is the basis, of course, for macaronic poetry; Heine makes broad use of this kind of poetry.[87] In Russian prose, Gogol uses this device for comic effect: "The ladies of the town of N—were what is called

---

87 See "Tyutchev and Heine" (64–76).

présentable"; "a slight *incommodité,* as she put it, which had befallen her, in the form of a pea-shaped growth on her right foot."[88] Dostoevsky diversifies this device to an extraordinary degree: we find examples of it completely devoid of comic coloring, perhaps as a rudiment of Karamzin's linguistic influence: "the mephitic air" (*Notes from the House of the Dead*), "infernal," etc. The "Winter Notes on Summer Impressions" are written almost completely in parodic jargon, whereby either Russian words are written in French transcription and pronunciation: *un outchitel, la baboulinka* [cf. Russian *uchitel'*—teacher, *babulen'ka*—version of "grandmother"], or French words in Russian: *epuzy* [French: *les époux,* spouses—*trans.*].

Dostoevsky is especially fond of using this device of masked words in his parodies; thus Turgenev's "Enough" becomes Karmazinov's "*Merci*" in *Demons.*[89]

We should also note the increased comic effect that results from using the plural: "I need no *monuments*!"

The next device of verbal parody is that of disengaging an epithet from its target and attaching it to a different word.

Foma: "Gogol [...] that frivolous author sometimes not devoid of a grain of sense" [226].

Compare Gogol: "You will marvel at the jewels in our language: its sonority is already a gift: everything is *grained* and as large as *pearls,* and really, sometimes the name is still more jewel-like than the thing itself" ("Subjects for the Lyric Poets [...]") [86, translation modified, emphasis *YT*].

The "grainy pearl of language"—"grainy language"—"a grainy thought"—this is the path of separation: an epithet that only relates to one image in an association of images ("a pearl of language") is related directly to the second, while this second image is replaced by another, similar one. This kind of disengagement is one of the mechanizing devices.

We have already seen mechanization through repetition in the "spark of heavenly fire" example. The device becomes even more powerful if the repetition comes from another one of the characters.

"'I say this with a bleeding heart and not, as you may perhaps suspect, to exult and elevate myself above you in triumph.'

88 Gogol, *Dead Souls,* 154, 164. Note that in Russian the French words are given in Cyrillic transliteration.

89 Dostoyevsky's farcical and affected writer Karmazinov writes "Merci," a self-satisfied summing-up of his writing career; Turgenev's "Enough (Notes of a Deceased Artist)" was seen by his contemporaries as a culminating gesture and was, moreover, written while Turgenev was living in Paris.

'My heart bleeds too, Foma, I assure you ... '" (the uncle) [133–134].

Compare Gogol: "Who can know, perhaps these woes and sufferings that have been bestowed upon you have been bestowed precisely in order to produce in you that wail of the spirit that would not out but for these sufferings. Perhaps it is this very wail of the spirit that is meant to be the crucible of your poetry. [...] Here all is wailing of the heart and an unfeigned rapturizement to God" (letter to N.M. Yazykov, 15 February 1844).[90]

Dostoevsky 's protagonists often parody one another, much as Sancho Panza parodies Don Quixote in their conversations (V. Shklovsky).[91] But the statements of Dostoevsky 's characters are enclosed in their author's quotation marks, and become metaphorical parodic commonplaces. Thus, Foma's phrase: "I know Russia and Mother Russia knows me" reappears without any context in "Winter Notes on Summer Impressions"; the invalid's phrase in "Winter Notes" regarding Rousseau, "*L'homme de la nature et de la verité*" [French: a man of nature and truth—*YT*], is carried over, without any connection to Rousseau, into *Notes from the Underground*.

But sometimes Dostoevsky simply replicates entire expressions from the *Selected Passages*; for instance, Foma's statement regarding "decorum in expression": "*Only a foolish society noddle* could conceive of such senseless niceties" [107, translation modified] repeats word-for-word a phrase from the "Third Letter Apropos *Dead Souls*": "[...] such a foolish idea could only be formed in a *foolish society noddle*" [107, translation modified, emphasis *YT*]. The expression given here in italics was also, incidentally, highlighted by Belinsky in his review of the *Selected Passages*.

9

The fact that the parodic nature of *The Village of Stepanchikovo* did not register in the wider literary consciousness is curious, but not exceptional. Parodies of plot models are deeply hidden in this way: it is unlikely anyone would have figured out the parodic nature of "Count Nulin" if Pushkin himself had not left

---

90 The lexicon of *Selected Passages* was etched into Dostoyevsky's memory. He was already parodying the phrase "pour out in song" in *Demons*: when Captain Lebyadkin declaims his poems to Stavrogin, he says that they "poured out in song" from inside him, as in Gogol's "Farewell Tale"—*YT*.

91 Tynianov refers to Shklovsky's article "How Don Quixote is Made" [Kak sdelan Don-Kikhot]. See V. Shklovskii, *O teorii prozy* (Moscow: Federatsiia, 1929).

evidence of the fact.[92] How many other undetected parodies are out there? As long as the parody remains undetected, the work changes; that is, this is how every work of literature changes once it has been disengaged from the level at which it made its mark. But even a parody founded primarily on stylistic particulars, when disengaged from its second level (which might simply be forgotten), naturally begins to lose its parodic nature. This resolves to a significant degree the question of parody as a comic genre. The comic is a connotation that ordinarily accompanies parody, but it is in no way a connotation of the parodic per se. When the parodic nature of a work becomes elided, the connotation remains. Parody lies entirely in the dialectical play of the device. If the parody of a tragedy is a comedy, then the parody of a comedy can be a tragedy.

92 Tynianov refers to Pushkin's 1830 "Note on Count Nulin" [Zametka o poeme "Graf Nulin"], in which the poet (five years after the fact) explains his motivation for writing the poem and refers specifically to parodying "both history and Shakespeare" (Alexander Pushkin, *Sobranie sochinenii v 10 tomakh* [Moscow: GIKhL, 1959–1962], 6:368).

Tyutchev and Heine (1921)[1]

1

There are two areas of inquiry within literary history that lack clear demarcation: the study of the *genesis* of literary phenomena, and of their *traditions*. These areas, which are also pertinent to the study of how these phenomena relate to one another, are antithetical both in their criteria and their value vis-à-vis one another.

The genesis of literary phenomena belongs to the transient realm of crossings between languages and between literatures, whereas tradition is rule-bound and circumscribed by a given national literature. Thus, while Lomonosov's[N] poetry can be traced back genetically to *German* models, it also advances certain metrical innovations for *Russian* poetry; the proof, in this case, is the very vitality of the poetry. It is impossible to reconstruct a genetic literary history, but there is a certain negative value in establishing the genesis of a literary phenomenon: it demonstrates for the umpteenth time the unique nature of verbal art, which proceeds from the extraordinary complexity and intricacy of its material—the word.[2]

In poetry the word is, above all, a meaning that has been determined by its sound (an external sign). However, this meaning is also largely determined by the extent to which the material has been *previously used*. The word does not exist in a vacuum, but as part of a familiar series[T] with its own particular coloring; it is a *lexical element*. Seen this way, the words "winged" and "wingèd" have nothing in common as poetic elements.[3]

This also resolves the question of foreign "traditions" and "influences" in literature. The point here is not how a given phenomenon represents the historical continuation or endpoint of certain phenomena; we are interested how the

---

1 First published in the journal *Books and Revolution* [Kniga i revoliutsiia] 4 (1922): 13–16; dated 1921 by Tynianov. Translation based on "Tiutchev i Geine," *PILK*, 29–37. Note that this work is derived from a book-length project that was never completed; the surviving manuscript for that project is also published in ibid., 350–394. Selected notes by A. Chudakov [*AC*], 407–409. Additional notes by Yuri Tynianov [*YT*] and the translators [unmarked].

2 Tynianov further develops his ideas about genesis (and evolution) in literature in the later article "On Literary Evolution" (267–282).

3 In Russian, the examples are *изнуренный* and *изнурённый*, both of which mean "exhausted"; the first spelling, without the diacritical marks over the "e," is markedly archaic.

latter *serve as the occasion for* the new phenomenon. One and the same phenomenon can be genetically traced to a foreign model, and at the same time develop a new tradition within its own national literature, one that is at odds with, even hostile to, that model.

2

An analysis of Tyutchev's[N] work shows that he took the "Archaist"[T] branch of Russian poetry (which harks back to Lomonosov and Derzhavin[N]) and made it canonical.[4] He is the link between the "flowery" oratorical odes of the eighteenth century and the lyric poetry of the Symbolists.[T] Taking Derzhavin's lexicon as a starting point, he did a great deal to soften the archaic contours of the solemn and philosophical ode, blending them with certain elements of Zhukovsky's[N] style.

Given how important these traditions were for Tyutchev, it is especially interesting to note the encounter between his work and the work done in the 1820s by Heinrich Heine,[N] who brought German *Lieder* into the canon.

The first instance of this contact goes back to the beginning of Tyutchev's career: in 1827, *The Northern Lyre* published his translation of Heine's "From Foreign Parts" ("In the gloomy North ...").[5] Most of his other translations of Heine also date back to the late 1820s and early 1830s.

The personal encounter between the two poets (in Munich, spring and summer of 1828)[6] allows us to establish two facts. In his 1828 article on Wolfgang Menzel's "German literature," Heine gives us what appears to be an example of "Tyutcheviana."[7] Writing on Goethe in his youth and old age, Heine notes: "A certain witty foreigner very aptly compared our Goethe to

4 For more on Lomonosov and Derzhavin, see "The Ode as an Oratorical Genre" (75).

5 The *Northern Lyre* [Severnaia lira] (1827) was a Moscow almanac noted for its Romantic aesthetic orientation and emphasis on translation.

6 See Heine's letter of 1 April 1828 to Varnhagen in *Heinrich Heines Briefwechsel*, Bd. 1 (Munich and Berlin: Fridrich Hirth, 1914), 507–509; of 1 October 1828 to Tyutchev (ibid., 529–531); of 11 June 1838 to Farnhagen (ibid., 627); of the end of 1832 to Hiller (*Heines Briefe*, vol. 2 [Berlin: H. Daffis, 1906], 16; and to Ad. Stahr, *Zwei Monate in Paris* (Oldenburg: Schnellpressendruck und Verlag der Schulzeschen Buchhandlung, 1851), 338. See also G. Kerpeles, *H. Heine. Aus seinem Leben und seiner Zeit* (Leipzig: A. Titze, 1899), 114–115—*YT*.

7 Wolfgang Menzel (1798–1873) was a conservative German poet and critic. The term "Tyutcheviana" refers to extra-literary anecdotes, tales and quasi-scholarly gossip, etc. pertaining to Tyutchev.

an old robber chief, who has left his trade to lead a respectable middle-class life among the notables of a provincial town, tries scrupulously to practice all the philistine virtues, and becomes hideously embarrassed when he happens to meet some disreputable fellow from Calabria who wants to renew their old comradeship."[8]

"Tyutcheviana" is a curious phenomenon that underscores the transpersonal and *involuntary* nature of art. *For a number of reasons,* the comic genre *remained foreign to the archaist trend* in lyric poetry with which Tyutchev was affiliated. Despite being pithy and well-aimed, his epigrams lack the comic touch so abundant in Pushkin's[N] epigrams.[9] As a result, alongside his more high-style *literary* work, Tyutchev produced comic *oral* material, which did not find expression in literature proper. Tyutchev's comic style harks back to French wordplay and old-fashioned anecdotes; in the latter (of which the anecdote quoted above is an example), the central role is played less by the words than by facial expressions and gestures. The following quip by Tyutchev is similar to the one by Heine quoted earlier:[10] "A certain very worldly man was, by virtue of his employment, closely acquainted with a minister who was far from worldly. Because of his position, he was obliged to make appearances from time to time at his dinners and soirees." "Well, and how did he hold up?" Tyutchev was asked. "He behaved very respectably," replied the poet, "like a countrified marquis in an old French operetta who finds himself at a village feast: he was affable to all, said a kind word to everyone there, and at the first opportunity did a pirouette and disappeared."[11]

The second fact related to the poets' personal encounter concerns a passage in part 3, chapter thirty of "Travel Pictures" ("Italy. I"), which has long baffled Heine scholars. This passage was written immediately following Heine's departure from Munich, and is partly based on the notes he wrote while in that city. In the passage, Heine speaks of Russia and Napoleon in the same breath: "[...] in the wonderful change of watchwords and of representatives in the great battle, it has come to such a pitch that the most enthusiastic friend of revolution can only see the safety of the world in the victory of Russia, and must

8 *H. Heines sämtliche Werke,* Bd. 7 (Leipzig and Vienna: Prof. E. Elster, 1890), 256; G. Geine, *Polnoe sobranie sochinenii,* vol. 4 (St. Petersburg: Izd. A. F. Marksa, 1904), 462—*YT*.

9 For Pushkin, see also "On the Composition of *Eugene Onegin*" (114–150).

10 Heine's witticism comes immediately after the Tyutchev-like phrase: "Goethe's creations ... which will continue to live long even after the German language itself lies dead ..."—*YT.*

11 F. I. Tiutchev, *Complete Works* [*Polnoe sobranie sochinenii*] (St. Petersburg: Izd. A. F. Marksa, 1913), 601—*YT*. Subsequent references will be to this edition and given in brackets.

regard Czar Nicholas as the gonfalonier of freedom […] Russia is a democratic state—I would gladly say, a Christian state—if I might be permitted to use this so often misused word in its sweetest and most cosmopolite sense, for the Russians, by the very extent of their realm, are freed from the narrow-mindedness of a heathenish national vanity."[12]

With this formulation, so bewildering to Strodtman, Geert, and others, Heine seemed to transform Tyutchev's conception of Russia into a poetically justified merging of contradictions, according to the laws of his art.

3

Tyutchev's poem "Napoleon," written in the 1830s, begins with the following lines:

Два демона ему служили,	Two demons served his every whim,
Две силы чудно в нем слились:	Two forces wondrously fused in him:
В его главе — орлы парили,	In his mind—eagles winged,
В его груди — змии вились …	In his breast—serpents writhed …
Ширококрылых вдохновений	The aquiline, audacious flight
Орлиный, дерзостный полет,	Of his broad-winged inspirations,
И в самом буйстве дерзновений	And, in the very frenzy of audacity,
Змииной мудрости расчет [285][13]	His serpentine wisdom's calculation.

Ivan Aksakov[N] produced a thematic comparison between this poem and poems by Khomyakov,[14] but another comparison suggests itself as well. In his "French Affairs" (1832), Heine compares Lafayette to Napoleon: "Freilich! er ist kein Genie, wie Napoleon war, in dessen Haupte die Adler der Begeisterung horsteten, während in seinem Herzen die Schlangen des Kalküls sich ringelten" ["He is indeed no genius, as was Napoleon, in whose head the eagles of inspiration built their nests, while the serpents' calculation entwined in his heart"].[15]

12 *H. Heines sämtliche Werke,* 3:277–280; Heine, *Polnoe sobranie sochinenii,* 1:319, 1:321—*YT.* English translation from Heinrich Heine, *The Works of Heinrich Heine,* trans. Charles Godfrey Leland, vol. 3 (London: William Heinemann, 1891), 108–112.

13 Tynianov footnotes the non-standard spelling of "serpentine" [*zmiinoi* in place of the expected *zmeinoi*].

14 Both Aksakov and the poet and philosopher Aleksei Khomyakov (1804–1860) were prominent Slavophiles.

15 *H. Heines samtliche Werke,* 5:40; Heine, *Polnoe sobranie,* 6:37—*YT*. English translation from Heine, *Works of Heine,* 7:65.

Here we seem to have more or less the same thing, in different languages, the one expressed in prose and the other in poetry. And so it would be, if the deciding factor in verbal art was the *definition* of a word, rather than its *connotative coloring*; its material rather than its verbal image. (Of course the very word "image" has by now lost all meaning, and perhaps we should go back to Lomonosov's term "aversion" [*otvrashchenie*], or the term "perversion" [*izvrashchenie*] favored by Shishkov's circle, which so effectively underscores the fractured semantic line of literary tropes.)[16] But while the overlap of two phrases ("eagle of inspiration," "serpent of calculation") suggests a kind of purely verbal trait, the *word* takes on a crucial role as a lexical element, whose form is recast by poetry or prose. In Tyutchev's work, this role is played by archaic style:

> В его *главе* — орлы *парили,*
> В его груди — *змии вились.* [81]

> In his *mind*—eagles *winged,*
> In his breast—*serpents writhed.*

The epithet "*broad-winged* inspirations" (what Lomonosov called allumination [*priluchenie*]) likewise belongs to Tyutchev's flowery mode. Compared to Tyutchev, Heine's "Kalkül" seems deliberately prosaic, even mercantile. Furthermore, the *tradition* Tyutchev follows in his handling of the Napoleonic theme comes not from Heine, but from Derzhavin (cf. his 1812 "A Lyrico-Epic Hymn on the Routing of the French"):

Дракон, иль демон змиевидный [100]	A dragon or a serpentine demon
-------	------
Змей—исполин [101]	Serpent—titan
-------	------
И Бог сорвал с него свой луч [105]	And God tore off his ray of light
-------	------
Упала демонская сила. [109][17]	The demonic power dwindled.

16 For more on these terms see "On the Composition of *Eugene Onegin*" (note 9) and "The Ode as an Oratorical Genre" (75).

17 Gavrila Derzhavin, *Works* [*Sochineniia*], vol. 3, ed. Ia. Grot (Moscow: Tip. Imperatorskoi Akademii nauk, 1866), 110–117.

Seen in relation to Derzhavin, Tyutchev's imagery takes on an archaic, odic tone; while in Heine's work, the same image recalls the much-used device (usually comic) of the verbal elaboration of the image, which mostly serves to fill out the line [lyric period].

4

The first volume of Heine's *The Salon,* published in 1834, contained, among other things, a trilogy of lyric poems titled "In der Fremde" [Abroad]. Heine took great care in arranging the poems in his collections, turning them into little chapters, as it were, of fragmentary novels (in this, perhaps, he was echoing the theories of Schlegel, who thought of Petrarch's poetry collections as fragmentary lyric novels).[18] Heine was perhaps all the more eager to group his poems into "trilogies"[19] given that the miniscule size of these poems contrasted parodically with Goethe's gargantuan "Trilogie der Leidenschaft" [Trilogy of Passion].[20] The subject matter and poetic texture (the syntactic and phonetic construction) of the first poem in Heine's trilogy, "Es treibt dich fort" [It drives you forth] corresponds to that of Tyutchev's poem "From land to land ..." (published in *Russian Archive* in 1879).

Here is Heine's poem:

Es treibt dich fort von Ort zu Ort, Du weiβt nicht mal warum; Im Winde klingt ein sanftes Wort, Schaust dich verwundert um.	Driven from place to place, You haven't any idea why; The wind carries over a gentle word,— You look round wonderingly.
Die Liebe, die dahinten blieb, Sie ruft dich sanft zurück: «O komm zurück, ich hab' dich lieb, Du bist mein einz'ges Glück!»	Beloved one, who's stayed behind, Now calls you softly back: "Come back to me, I love you so, You are my only joy!"

18 A. W. Schlegel, *Vorlesungen über schöne Literatur und Kunst*, Bd. 3 (Heilbronn: K. Gerolds Sohn, 1884), 204, 208–209—*AC*. August Schlegel (1767–1845) was a prominent figure in German Romanticism. For more of Tynianov's thoughts on the fragment, see "Literary Fact" (155–166) and "On the Composition of *Eugene Onegin*" (125–128; 147).

19 See "Tragodie" in F. I. Tiutchev, *Polnoe sobranie sochinenii* (St. Petersburg: A.F. Marks, 1913), 4:37—*YT*.

20 Goethe's "Trilogy of Passion" (1824) includes the poems "To Werther," "Elegy" and "Reconciliation."

Doch weiter, weiter, sonder Rast,	But onward, onward without rest,
Du darfst nicht stillestehn;	You never may stand still;
Was du so sehr geliebet hast	What you once did love the best,
Sollst du nicht wiedersehn.[21]	You never again will see.

And here is Tyutchev's:

Из края в край, из града в град	From land to land, from town to town,
Судьба, как вихрь, людей метет,	Fate, like a gale, sweeps people on.
И рад ли ты, или не рад,	Whether you are glad or not,
Что нужды ей?… Вперед, вперед!	What does she care? Onward, on!
Знакомый звук нам ветр принес:	A familiar sound brings us the wind:
Любви последнее прости …	Farewell, the last of love …
За нами много, много слез,	Countless tears do lie behind;
Туман, безвестность впереди! …	Ahead lie fog and the unknown!
«О, оглянися, о, постой,	"O look back, o wait a while,
Куда бежать, зачем бежать? …	Where can you run, why do you run?
Любовь осталась за тобой,	Love has stayed behind you,
Где ж в мире лучшего сыскать?	Where can anything better be found?
Любовь осталась за тобой,	Love has stayed behind you,
В слезах, с отчаяньем в груди …	In tears, despairing in its heart …
О, сжалься над своей тоской,	O, take pity on your sorrow,
Свое блаженство пощади!	Keep your own bliss from harm!
Блаженство стольких, стольких дней	The bliss of many, many days
Себе на память приведи …	Recall to your mind …
Все милое душе твоей	Everything your soul holds dear
Ты покидаешь на пути! … »	You leave by the side of the road! …"
Не время выкликать теней:	The time has passed to summon shadows:
И так уж мрачен этот час.	The hour is somber anyway.
Усопших образ тем страшней,	The image of the dead is the more horrifying
Чем в жизни был милей для нас.	The dearer they were to us in life.

21 Heine, *Heines sämtliche Werke*, 1:262. Subsequent quotations from this volume will be given in brackets following the poem.

Из края в край, из града в град	From land to land, from town to town,
Могучий вихрь людей метет,	A mighty gale sweeps people on,
И рад ли ты, или не рад,	Whether you're glad or not glad,
Не спросит он … Вперед, вперед! [81–82]	It will not ask … Onward, on!

The two poems overlap in their subject matter as well as in certain metrical and even sonic features:

1) Our attention is drawn to the first line because of the caesura, which is itself set off through sonic repetitions—

Es treibt dich fort
Из края в край [From land to land]
von Ort zu Ort
Из града в град [From town to town][22]

—here, even the sounds that are repeated are essentially the same;[23]

2) the overall metrical and semantic pattern

Die Leibe, die dahinten blieb
Все милое душе твоей [Everything your soul holds dear]
Im Winde klingt ein sanftes Wort
Знакомый звук нам ветр принес [A familiar sound brings us the wind]

(in the latter example, the sounds repeated are also the same).

As for the meter, here we have a strong similarity to another poem by Heine, "Anno 1829":

Daβ ich bequem verbluten kann,	So that I might bleed out comfortably
Gebt mir ein edles, weites Feld!	Give me a wide and noble field!
Oh, laβt mich nicht ersticken hier	O let me not be smothered here
In dieser engen Krämerwelt! (1:271)	In this cramped shopkeepers' world![24]

22 Tyutchev repeats the structure of this line in the third stanza: "Where can you run, why do you run?"—*YT.*

23 Among the many instances of sound coincidence in Tyutchev's poem vis-à-vis Heine's, we can point to the similarity between the German phrase "*es treibt*" and the Russian "*iz kraia*"; the two phrases mean different things, but they are in the same position within their respective lines. Furthermore, the vowel sounds are dipthongs in both instances, and the devoiced "z" in "iz" sounds like the German "s" in "es." Also cf. *von Ort zu Ort* and the end-words *metyot, vperyod.*

24 Heine, *Poems of Heine*, 125.

The penultimate stanza of this poem is particularly interesting, as it is metrically similar to the first (and last) stanza of Tyutchev's poem.

Ihr Wolken droben, nehmt mich mit,	Oh clouds up there, take me along,
Gleichviel nach welchem fernen Ort!	To some place, any place, far away!
Nach Lappland oder Afrika,	To Lapland or to Africa,
Und sei's nach Pommern—fort! nur fort! (1:272)	Even Pomerania—gone! Just gone! (Ibid.)

The genesis of Tyutchev's poem can thus be traced back to Heine's poem. But even here we can see two different artists at work. Heine expresses the motif of the "familiar sound" ("sanftes Wort") with concision:

O komm zurück, ich hab dich lieb,
Du bist mein einz'ges Glück.

[Return, I love thee, O be kind, / My only joy art thou!]

Tyutchev, meanwhile, develops this motif over three stanzas, which are central to the poem as a whole and linked to one another through things grabbed and carried over from stanza to stanza, e.g. "Love has stayed behind you" (stanza 3, line 3, and stanza 4, line 1). Tyutchev has turned Heine's romance into a march, down to such characteristic features as a chorus (the "*we*": "A familiar sound brings *us* the wind"; "The dearer they were to *us* in life") and dialogue. The distinctive features of Heine's poem are the conversational brevity of its periods and the simplicity of its lexicon. In Tyutchev's poem, these features are pathos, the rhetorical elaboration of the periods and the archaic lexicon:

O komm zurück, ich hab dich lieb,
Du bist mein einz'ges Glück

О, оглянися, о, постой.	O, look back, o, wait a while.
Куда бежать, зачем бежать?	Whither run, wherefore run?
Любовь осталась за тобой,	Love has stayed behind you,
Где ж в мире лучшего сыскать? [82]	*Where can anything better be found?*

Tyutchev's analytical syntax is also worth noting:

Усопших образ *тем страшней,*
Чем в жизни был милей для нас.

> The image of the dead *is the more horrifying*
> *The dearer they were to us in life.*

5

The same question of *genesis and tradition* applies equally well to Tyutchev's *translations.*

Tyutchev rarely—and with reluctance—marked poems as translations (which is why editors are hardly justified when they group his translations together in a separate section). He had every right to do so, and not because he showed little concern for fidelity in translation. On the contrary, his translations of Heine all attest to his scrupulousness and his desire to preserve the features of the original. To achieve this, Tyutchev took a remarkable approach: he provided Russian analogues for the devices of the German poem, while always staying true to his own verbal tradition. The first thing we notice about his translations of Heine is the selection. The chosen poems are not so much thematically similar to Tyutchev's work as they are representative of Heine's own manner. They include such un-Tyutchev-like poems as "Liebste, sollst mir heute sagen" ["My love, you should tell me today"] and "In welche soll ich mich verlieben" ["Which one should I fall in love with"], the second of which is from the cycle *Lieder der niederer Minne* [Songs of the Lower Minne].[25]

Tyutchev added a title to his first translation [from Heine], which begins "In the gloomy North ...": he called it "From Foreign Parts." By doing so, he imbued the poem with a suggestion of his own lyric theme. The poem contains lines written in a version of the *pauznik*[T] (based on amphibrachs). This was common practice in Russian poetry of the time,[26] and Tyutchev apparently wanted to provide an analogue for the meter of the original (a "pauznik" based on iambic trimeter).

In the poem "Shipwreck," Tyutchev also tried to provide an analogue for the meter of the original, conveying its free rhythm by alternating iambic pentameter, tetrameter, and trimeter. The ending of Heine's poem is disrupted by a metrical surprise: the short, striking line, "In feuchten Sand."

25 "Liebste, sollst mir heute sagen," in Heinrich Heine, *Buch der Lieder, Lyrisches Intermezzo* (Hamburg: Hoffmann und Campe, 1827), 124. Tyutchev's translation, "Drug, otkroisia predo mnoiu ..." in *Polnoe sobranie,* 410. "In welche soll ich mich verlieben," in *Buch der Lieder,* 101. Tyutchev's translation, "V kotoruiu iz dvukh vliubit'sia ..." in *Polnoe sobranie,* 411.

26 See the article by D. Dubensky in *Athenaeum,* 1828, part r, p. 149—*YT.*

In its stead, Tyutchev gives us something resembling a monologue from a classical drama:

Молчите, птицы, не шумите, волны,	Keep quiet, birds; don't clamor, waves,
Все, все погибло — счастье и надежда,	All, all is lost—happiness and hope,
Надежда и любовь! ... Я здесь один, —	Hope and love! ... I am here alone—
На дикий брег заброшенный грозою,	Tossed on this wild shore by a storm,
Лежу простерт — и рдеющим лицом	I lie stretched out, digging my ruddy face
Сырой песок морской пучины рою! [408]	Into the damp sand of the sea so deep!

Tyutchev's translation of this poem testifies to the complete victory of tradition over genesis. Not only does Tyutchev meticulously translate every one of Heine's complex epithets, he adds to them as well. In doing so, however, he gives them an archaic spin:

И из умильно-бледного лица	And from the touchingly pale face
Отверсто-пламенное око	The open'd flaming eye
Как черное сияет солнце! ...	Shines like a black sun! ...
О черно-пламенное солнце.	O blackly flaming sun.

In these lines, Heine resembles no one so much as Derzhavin (in "To a Lover of the Arts"): "Blackly flaming, open gaze."[27]

Finally, Tyutchev's translations of "Liebste, sollst mir heute sagen" [My love, you should tell me today] and "Das Leben ist der schwüle Tag" [Life is a humid day] are heroic attempts to convey a foreign mode. In the first of these, Tyutchev gets across Heine's humorous tone by using eighteenth-century Russian humor, imbuing a high-style lexicon with an antiquated conversational style:

Василиски и вампиры,	Basilisks and vampires,
Конь *крылат* и *змий зубаст* —	*Winged* horse and *toothed serpent*—
Вот мечты его кумиры, —	These are the idols of his fancy—
Их *творить* поэт *горазд.*	The poet knows how to *create* them.
Но тебя, твой стан *эфирный,*	But you,—your *airy* figure,
Сих ланит волшебный цвет.	The bewitching color of *those cheeks,*
Этот взор лукаво-смирный —	That slyly submissive gaze—
Не создаст сего поэт. [410]	The poet cannot call these to life.

27 Derzhavin, "To the Lover of the Arts" [*Liubiteliu khudozhestv*] (1791), in *Poems* [*Stikhotvoreniia*] (Leningrad: Sovetskii pisatel', 1957), 167.

In the second of these translations, Tyutchev encountered another tradition that was just as foreign to him: that of the German *Lieder*. He tried to convey its singsong tone, but even here his characteristic analytical syntax utterly transforms the entire framework of the poem:

> *Если* смерть *есть* ночь, *если* жизнь *есть* день —
> Ах, умаял он, пестрый день меня! ... [412]

> *If* death *be* night, *if* life *be* day—
> Then, oh, dappled day has done me in!

Foreign material thus provided Tyutchev with a pretext, an occasion for creating works which, in terms of the Russian tradition, can be traced back to the eighteenth century.

6

Tyutchev is a Romantic: this has seemed like an unshakeable position, despite the muddle around the question of Russian romanticism. This position must be reevaluated.[28]

Granted, philosophical and political thought made up the prosaic bedrock of his poetry, and many of his poems seem like illustrations of, or even polemical speeches on, various key issues of romanticism. But it is precisely in relation to Derzhavin that Tyutchev—a successor of Derzhavin, a protégé of Rayich,[N] and a student of Merzlyakov[N]—emerges as the heir to the eighteenth century philosophical and political ode and intimate lyric poem. Consequently, Tyutchev's romantic manifesto, "Nature is not what you think," can be seen as a new phase of the ode:

Они не видят и не слышат,	They do not see and do not hear,
Живут в сем мире, как впотьмах,	But live in this world as if in darkness,
Для них и солнцы, знать, не дышат,	To them, it seems, suns do not breathe
И жизни нет в морских волнах. [94]	And there is no life beneath the waves.

28 Tynianov refers to his own (and the other Formalist critics') insistence on a critical reevaluation of labels like Romantic and Classicist, which were staples of literary criticism of the nineteenth and early twentieth century (that is, their direct predecessors). Despite their efforts, this "stadial" model of literary history became de rigeur by the 1930s: according to this model, Romanticism was seen as a crucial stage on the path to realism (and onward to Socialist Realism).

Similarly, Tyutchev's other, more intimate mode is, in fact, a stylization of the eighteenth century idyllic "song":

Так мило-благодатна,	So sweetly gracious,
Воздушна и светла	Aerial and bright
Душе моей стократно	A hundred times over
Любовь твоя была. [190]	Was your love to my soul.

Just as the romantic figure Victor Hugo revived the old tradition of Ronsard in France, Tyutchev—who was *genetically* rooted in German romanticism—stylized Derzhavin's old forms and gave them new life in the post-Pushkin context.

The Ode as an Oratorical Genre (1922)[1]

Among the multivalent terms that help to define a literary work, the concept of *orientation*[T] deserves special attention.[2]

What does orientation mean for a particular literary work, genre, or movement?

We can no longer describe a literary work as the "sum total" of its various parts: plot,[T] style, etc. These abstractions have long been obsolete; plot, style, etc. all exist in interaction, the same way that rhythm and semantics interact and are interrelated[T] in poetry. A work of literature is a system of interrelated factors. The interrelation of a given factor with all the others is its *function* vis-à-vis the system as a whole.[3] It is plainly evident that each literary system is formed not through the peaceful interaction of all its factors, but rather through the priority—the foregrounding—of one factor (or a group of them) that functionally subordinates and colors the rest. In Russian scholarship, this factor has come to be called the "dominant"[T] (Broder Christiansen, Boris Eikhenbaum[N]).[4] This does not mean, however, that the subordinated factors are unimportant and can be ignored. On the contrary, this subordination, indeed transformation, of all the other factors by the principal one is what reveals to us the action of that principal factor—the dominant.

It is also obvious that there is no such thing as an *individual* work in literature: an individual work is part of a system of literature, with which it is interrelated in terms of genre and style (while becoming differentiated within the system), and a given work has a function within the literary system of a specific period. If a literary work is torn from the context of one literary system

1 First published in the journal of the literature department of State Institute of the Art History [Vremennik otdela slovesnogo iskusstva G3]—*Poetika* 3 (1927): 102–128; dated 1922 by Tynianov. Translation based on "Oda kak oratorskii zhanr," *PILK*, 227–252. Selected notes to this publication by E. A. Toddes [*ET*], 490–501. Additional notes by Yuri Tynianov [*YT*] and the translators [unmarked].

2 For more on "orientation [*ustanovka*]," see also "On Literary Evolution" (especially 273–280).

3 In "On Literary Evolution" (284–285), this relation is termed the "syn-function"—*ET.*

4 Broder Christiansen (1869–1958) was a German philosopher and linguist.

and moved to another, it will take on a different coloring, accumulate different traits, become part of a different genre, and lose its own genre; in other words, its function will migrate.

This, in turn, leads to a migration of functions within the work; in a given time period, a factor that was once subordinated can end up becoming the dominant.

This is how the concepts of "high" and "low" change from era to era. This is how Pushkin's[N] prose, which in its own literary system was considered "difficult" (Shevyryov[N]), is now a model of "light" prose;[5] this is how Lermontov,[N] whose contemporaries saw him as an eclectic poet (B. Eikhenbaum), by Ogaryov's[N] time was seen as radically original.[6] This is how works of literature that are transplanted from their national system into a foreign one acquire an entirely different function.

Literary systems are interrelated with the extra-literary series closest at hand—speech; this includes both the material from neighboring forms of verbal art and everyday speech. Interrelated in what sense? In other words, where might we find the closest social function of the literary series? This is where the term *orientation* comes into play.[7] Orientation refers not just to the dominant of a literary work (or genre), which functionally colors the subordinated factors, but also to the function of a work (or genre) vis-à-vis the closest extra-literary series.[8]

---

5 For Pushkin, see also "On the Composition of *Eugene Onegin*".

6 For Lermontov, see also "Interlude" (179; 201–202); "Literary Evolution" (269–272); "On Parody" (299–302).

7 The term "orientation" needs to be purged of its goal-oriented connotation. The concept of a function precludes the concept of teleology. A teleological view of literature assumes "creative intent," and whatever isn't covered by the latter is deemed incidental or simply left out of the analysis. Meanwhile, the concept of "the incidental" in relation to "creative intent" turns out to be anything but incidental within the literary system—*YT*. See Tynianov's reprisal of this position in "On Literary Evolution" (273–280).

8 I proposed a detailed theory of literary interrelations (between constructive, literary, and speech functions) in a lecture series on the history of Russian poetry, which I gave at the Advanced State Courses of the Institute of Art History in 1924 and 1925. I have summarized it both in my article on literary evolution and here, where I deal specifically with the speech function (the orientation). In one of his articles, V. V. Vinogradov claimed that the "speech function" was "unscientific." ["Zoshchenko's Language (Notes on Lexicon)" [Iazyk Zoshchenki. (Zametki o leksike)], in *Mikhail Zoshchenko, Stat'i i materialy* (Leningrad: Academia, 1928), 53, 56–58—*ET*.] There are some scholars who are used to "speaking on behalf of scholarship as a whole, as if they (or a certain someone understood to be them) had been specially entrusted with defending its honor from time to time; as if scholarship were their aunt, or sister, or some other close relative of the weaker sex." Moreover, these scholars "try to convince themselves and others alike that

This is why the speech orientation is so tremendously important in literature.

1

The literary struggle of the first half of the eighteenth century concerned the functions of poetic speech. It was clear to all involved that the pressing issue was the proper constructive application of both the phonic and semantic elements of verse, and that future directions for poetry depended on the proper approach to the functional connection between these elements. This historical moment, in the wake of the recent metrical revolution,[9] when the foundations of poetry were still fresh, enabled an especially clear perception of the specific nature of *slovo*[T] ["language" or "word"] in poetry.

The fiercest struggle was waged in *lyric poetry*, a form that represented the essence of poetic language most clearly, where the play of its powers was on full display.

The central issue was most clearly felt in the struggle around the ode. It was here that the two opposing tendencies, each resolving the issue of poetic language in its own way, took shape.

In section one of his *Rhetoric* (1748), Lomonosov[N] writes: "Rhetoric [*krasnorechie*] is the art of speaking beautifully on any subject, and thereby *inclining* others to one's own opinion [...] Language [*slovo*] can be expressed in two ways, as prose or as poetry. [...] The former is used to write homiletics, histories, and

---

they have the interests of all of humanity, of catholicity, in their pockets" (A. A. Potebnya,[N] *Thought and Language* [*Mysl' i iazyk*] [Kharkov: Zhurnal ministerstva narodnogo prosveshcheniia, 1913], 212); and "From Notes on Russian Grammar" [Iz zapisok po russkoi grammatike], part 3 (Kharkov: D. N. Poluekhtov, 1899), 6. Meanwhile, in another article, Vinogradov writes: "The question of 'orientation' toward the interdependence of certain types of 'everyday' monologue, and of the 'signs' of this interdependence—its devices and aspects—as well as its reflection in the semantics of literary speech can, of course, only be gestured toward at this time" (*Chronicle of the State Institute of Art History* [Vremennik gosudarstvennogo instituta istorii iskusstva], 3 [Leningrad, 1927]: 15). It is hard to say what makes this "more scientific" than the "speech function" to which, apart from the term itself, it is identical—*YT* (1928). The text of this article (in *PILK*) is taken from the definitive 1929 edition (Iurii Tynianov, *Arkhaisty i novatory* [Leningrad: Priboi, 1929]); when preparing this edition, Tynianov added this note to his 1922 text. Viktor Vinogradov (1895–1969) was a Soviet linguist and scholar of literature.

9 The "metrical revolution" refers to the adoption of the syllabotonic system (instead of purely syllabic, which does not count stresses), starting in the mid-seventeenth century.

books of instruction; the latter for composing hymns, odes, comedies, satires, and other kinds of poems."[10] Here, we should note the emendation that Lomonosov made to the first edition of his treatise on rhetoric (*A Short Guide to Rhetoric for the Benefit of Lovers of Eloquence* [Kratkoe rukovodstvo k ritorike na pol'zu liubitelei sladkorechiia], 1744). There, Lomonosov wrote that a given subject should be "depicted with appropriate words, in order to *prove* to listeners and readers that it is right."[11] The "incline" of the second edition is altogether different from the "prove" of the first. Here, rhetoric's power to convince is contrasted with its capacity to "influence"; the point is to "speak beautifully" and "incline the listener," rather than prove that something is right, or "depict with appropriate words." That this is a crucial distinction for rhetoric was argued persuasively by Longinus in his description of two types of lofty oratory, which Lomonosov most likely knew: "Grandeur does not persuade the listener, but, rather, astonishes him. That which genuinely astounds always takes the upper hand over the persuasive and agreeable."[12] It was unsurprising, then, that Lomonosov pressed the issue in the second edition, where the logically persuasive use of oratorical language was cast aside in favor of the emotionally affecting. Moreover, Lomonosov emphasized the difference between poetic language and logical verbal constructions, which can be seen in his very definition of the tasks of poetry. At the end of the chapter titled "On the Invention of Arguments," Lomonosov cautions: "In accordance with the rules of this chapter, the examples contained herein are depicted logically in order that they be more clearly understood. But authors who are skilled in rhetoric favor arguments that are appropriately embellished, and these have an altogether different appearance" (section ninety-three) [3:165]. And, as though in contrast to Trediakovsky's[N] concept of lofty oratory, which the latter associated with "wisdom,"[13]

---

10 The second and third sentences in this quotation are from section eight of the 1748 *Rhetoric* in M. V. Lomonosov, *Complete Works* [Polnoe sobranie sochinenii, henceforth—*PSS*] (Moscow: Izd. Akademii nauk SSSR, 1952), 7:91, 96–97. Tynianov proceeds from the premise that Lomonosov's poetry carries out the principles of his rhetoric—*ET.* Note that this and subsequent citations are given from a more recent edition of Lomonosov than the one used by *YT*: M. V. Lomonosov, *Works (8 vols.)* [*Sochineniia: v 8–mi tomakh*], vol. 3 (St. Petersburg: Akademiia nauk, 1895). In-text citations from *PSS* are in square brackets.

11 Lomonosov, *Rhetoric*, Section 1 (*PSS*, 7:23)—*ET*.

12 From "On the Sublime," attributed to Pseudo-Longinus. The treatise was originally attributed to Cassius Longinus, a third-century writer, and canonized by Boileau in the seventeenth century; Lomonosov read it in Boileau's translation (1674)—*ET*.

13 In his "Discourse on Rich, Variable, Artful and Diverse Oratory" [Slovo o bogatom, razlichnom, iskusnom i neskhodstvennom vitiistve] (1744)—*ET*.

Lomonosov writes (in the chapter "On the Excitation, Satisfaction, and Representation of the Passions"): "Some might think that the rules proposed in this chapter for the excitation, satisfaction, and representation of the passions do not originate in the common source of invention, e.g, in rhetorical loci, as do the doctrines treated in other chapters. And indeed, they are founded on philosophical doctrines regarding morals; however, the causes responsible for exciting the passions should stem from the aforementioned rhetorical loci" (section 128) [3:204].

All this had an impact on the rhetorical organization of *the ode,* a poetic genre that was oriented toward an extra-poetic speech series (lofty oratory).

In the ode, the elements of poetic language were utilized—structured—through the lens of oratorical practice.

In this sense, "oratorical practice" can and must be treated as a unique principle of construction, a dominant that revealed new aspects of poetic language and that was simultaneously an orientation toward the extra-literary series closest at hand.

2

The ode as a genre of lofty oratory was formed out of two reciprocal principles: the principle of maximum impact at any given moment, and the principle of verbal development and elaboration. The former was responsible for the ode's style; the latter, for its lyric plot. The lyric plot, meanwhile, was formed as the result of a compromise between the sequential logical construction (the "syllogistic" construction) and the associative progression of interlinking verbal masses. In Lomonosov's poetry, the richness of every verse group or stanza distracts us from the schematic skeleton of its "logical" construction. Subsequently, the ode split along these two main lines: among Lomonosov's successors and imitators, some eclectically unified his theory with opposing ones, opting for the plot-based skeleton of the ode; in the struggle between opposite trends, this gave rise to the term "dry ode." Others opted for the associative interlinking of images, and this gave rise to the term "senseless ode."

The principle of maximum impact at any given moment took the upper hand in Lomonosov's lyric: the more obvious the oratorical purpose of the verse, and the more the poem was felt as something to be recited out loud, the more significance was attached to the successive, delaying element, to the value of each stanza, of each verse group in and of itself.[14] On the oratorical and emotional level at which the impact of this language was conceived, a different model for the elaboration of this language took hold: in place of the logical, syllogistic skeleton, there was an irregular alternation of tension and resolution, with maximum tension and maximum discharge. Moreover, under these conditions favoring the greatest possible impact of each verse line, the ode expanded quantitatively: the number of stanzas was determined not (or not only) by the development and exhaustion of a theme, but primarily by the exhaustion of oratorical effect. In Lomonosov's odes, the number of stanzas ranged from twelve to thirty-two, the average being twenty-three to twenty-four.[15] For Vasily Petrov, who took the elements of Lomonosov's style to their "decadent" extreme, this number goes up to fifty.[16]

At the same time, the oratorical principle of the ode powerfully foregrounded its intonational organization. Oratorical poetic language, oriented towards recitation, had to be organized according to the principle of maximum intonational richness. And the ode's ten-line stanza proved a complex and obliging canvas for this unique syntactical and intonational framework.[17]

The crucial factor here was the distribution of syntactic units between the four-line substanza—which formed part of the large stanza—and the two three-line units. In this context, two organizational factors come into view: the pause factor and the intonation factor.

In the *Rhetoric* (sections forty-three and forty-four), Lomonosov touches on the distribution of syntactic units in his description of different periods. He distinguishes three types of periods: *round and measured*;

---

14 In *The Problem of Verse Language*, Tynianov closely examines the "successive [*suktsessivnyi*] nature of speech material in verse" as aesthetically significant, part of the intentionally obstructed or impeded quality of poetic language. In contrast to this "successivity" (indeed, as its opposite), Tynianov points to the simultaneity of practical speech. See Iurii Tynianov, *Problema stikhotvornogo iazyka* (Leningrad: Sovetskii pisatel', 1965), 68–76, 169–170, etc.—*ET.*

15 The smallest number of stanzas in Lomonsov's odes is fourteen (in his trochaic translation of Fénelon, 1738); the largest is forty-four (the ode commemorating Empress Elizaveta's arrival from Moscow to St Petersburg, 1742)—*ET.*

16 Vasily Petrov (1736–1799) was a court poet and translator known primarily for his odes.

17 The earliest and most canonical stanzaic pattern was aAaA + bbB + ccB (feminine rhymes in a, b, and c; masculine rhymes in A and B). Lomonosov and Sumarokov[N] were already varying and modifying this pattern—*YT.* Note that Tynianov uses lowercase letters for feminine rhymes and capital letters for masculine, while more recent scholarship uses the opposite notation. For more on Sumarokov, see section three.

fluctuating; and *segmented*.[18] In round and measured periods the "members, as well as subjects and predicates, do not differ greatly in size"; in *fluctuating* periods "the parts within the periods, that is, the members, or the subjects and predicates within the clauses, are very unequal"; in segmented periods "[the] discourse is made up of very short periods, each, for the most part, consisting of just one member; long periods may be turned into segmented ones by removing conjunctions." (It is telling that Lomonosov himself does not provide *verse* examples of round periods, evidently because he considered them a neutral ground against which the intonational pattern should stand out.)[19]

The following stanza can serve as an example of a round and measured period:

Я слышу Нимф поющих гласы,	I hear the voices of singing Nymphs
Носящих сладкия плоды,	Bearing sweet fruit;
Там в гумнах чистят тучны класы,	On threshing-floors they clean fat ears of wheat,
Шумят огромныя скирды.	Huge haystacks murmur.
Среди охотничей тревоги	In the commotion of the hunt
Лесами раздаются роги,	The woods fill with the sound of horns,
В покое представляя брань.	A quarrelsome note where peace prevails.
Сию богине несравненной	Hence to this incomparable goddess
В избыток принесут осенной	Earth, water, woods, and air bring
Земля, вода, лес, воздух дань. [7, 793]	Autumn's lavish bounty as tribute.

18 In this section, Tynianov refers to a number of concepts from classical rhetoric, which made their way into Russian rhetorical discourse thanks to Lomonosov; in addition to classical authors like Aristotle and Cicero, he drew on intermediaries including Nicolas Boileau, Nicolas Caussin, Johann Gottsched, and Francis Pomey. It was from the latter's *Candidatus rhetoricae* (1714) that Lomonsov borrowed the descriptions of the three types of "period." Here, "member" corresponds to the Greek *colon*, a clause that is grammatically but not logically complete; a "period" refers to a complete sentence (or thought) composed of several clauses.

19 Of the following three quotations, the second and third are given by Lomonosov himself as examples of fluctuating and segmented periods (in his 1748 *Rhetoric*, sections forty-three to forty-four 44 [*PSS*, 7:123–125]). In the interest of greater clarity, Tynianov arranges the lines differently from Lomonosov, separating the periods within the stanzas—*ET*.

An example of a fluctuating period:

Как лютый мраз она прогнавши,	As when, chasing out the bitter cold,
Замерзлым жизнь дает водам,	She gives life to the frozen waters,
Туманы, бури, снег поправши,	Trampling mists, blizzards, and snows,
Являет ясны дни странам,	She shows bright days to all the lands,
Вселенну паки воскрешает,	Once more resurrects the universe,
Натуру нам возобновляет,	Renews nature for our benefit,
Поля цветами красит вновь:	And strews the fields with flowers;
Так ныне милость и любовь	Just so, the graciousness and love
И светлый Дщери взор Петровой	And clear gaze of Peter's Daughter
Нас жизнью оживляет новой. [8, 96]	Revives us with new life.

An example of a segmented period:

Уже врата отверзло лето,	Summer has already flung open its gates,
Натура ставит общий пир,	Nature spreads a banquet for all,
Земля и сердце в нас нагрето.	Earth and the heart within us are warmed.
Колеблет ветьви тих зефир,	Mild Zephyrus sways the branches,
Объемлет мягкий луг крилами,	Encloses the soft meadow in his wings,
Крутится чистый ток полями,	A pure stream circles through fields,
Брега питает тучный ил,	Rich silt nourishes the riverbanks,
Листы и цвет покрылись медом,	Leaves and flowers drip with honey,
Ведет своим довольство следом	The beauteous lord of luminaries hurries
Поспешно красный вождь светил. [8, 103].	To bring contentment in his footsteps.

Thus the round and measured mode consists of three syntactic units distributed across the three divisions within the stanza; the substanza and two three-line units: 4+3+3. The ideally "round mode" should have total syntactic parallelism between 1) the two halves of the substanza, and 2) the two three-line units.

The second, fluctuating mode is characterized by an uneven distribution of syntactic units across the three divisions. This results in the most complex intonational pattern. Every uneven distribution turns the last, [ostensibly] terminal line—the line marking the division after the short stanza (or after the first three-line unit)—into a line followed by an intra-stanzaic enjambment. This significantly deforms both the line of the division and the ones that follow. Moreover, the size of the syntactic unit determines whether this intonational deformation will be distributed over the entire three-line unit that follows, or only part of it. In the former case—where it is distributed over the entire three-line unit—we get a broken intonational line. The greatest intonational escalation comes when the intonational resolution of the whole stanza occurs only in the last line (or part of it).

Finally, the third, segmented mode is characterized by the distribution of syntactic units across verse series, or verse lines. This is the mode that most accentuates pauses.

The following passage demonstrates the importance Lomonosov attached to the principle of the distribution of syntactic units in a stanza, as well as the extent to which he made the structure of an ode dependent on its intonational line: "The order and transformation of periods in the flow of discourse is the most important thing; it is effected through the placement of units and the transference of their parts and members. The placement of whole periods depends on the measured combination of long and short periods, fluctuating and segmented, so that they are pleasing in their variety and do not become tedious with their monotonous flow, which, like a nearly entirely unchanging note played on a single string, is unpleasant to the ear" (section 177) [3:243–244].

The first stanza thus took on particular significance, since it established the intonational mode. In the other stanzas, this mode would go through gradual variations; these would accumulate, and, by the end, the intonational line would either go back to what it was in the beginning, or reach an equilibrium. Cf. the typical "measured" intonational progression in the ode, "On the Name Day of His Imperial Highness, the Grand Prince Peter Fyodorovich" (its opening stanza was quoted above in the example of segmented periods).

The stanzaic distribution of syntactic units in this ode is as follows: segmented, segmented-fluctuating, fluctuating, fluctuating-segmented, round, round-fluctuating, round-fluctuating, round, round-segmented, round-segmented, round-segmented, round, round, round. Starting with a segmented stanza, the intonational mode progresses through variations of round and fluctuating periods before settling on round periods. The absence of strong tension typical of fluctuating periods, whose presence here is weak and partial, as well as the overall prevalence of the round mode, make this an example of a "measured" ode.

The ode to Elizaveta Petrovna is something else entirely.[20] Here, we see a transition from a fluctuating to a round mode. Moreover, both the syntactic units and their corresponding graphemes were, for Lomonosov, perfectly

20 "Ode to Elizaveta Petrovna (Ode on the Arrival of Her Majesty Great Empress Elizaveta from Moscow to St. Petersburg in 1742 for the Coronation)." Lomonosov, *PSS*, 8:82–102—*YT*.

clear-cut declamatory features. "Every period," he wrote, "should be spoken *distinctly* from every other; that is, having finished one, the speaker should pause for a bit; the parts separated by colons and commas should be set off with a slight *change in voice* and a barely perceptible *pause*" (1744 *Rhetoric*, 7:78, section 137).

Lomonosov was well aware of the intonational connotations of "interrogative" and "exclamatory" sentences: "For questions, exclamations, and other strong figures, the speaker should *raise* his voice with a certain purposeful direction and abrupt stops. For exposition as well as for gentle figures, he should speak in a steadier manner, and in a somewhat lower voice" (ibid., section 136).

This union of two principles—that of the shift between interrogative, exclamatory, and declarative intonations, and that of the intonational use of complex stanzas—is the source of the uniquely declamatory quality of the ode. The following stanza from Lomonosov's translation of Jean-Baptiste Rousseau's "Ode à la Fortune" shows just how unconstrained Lomonosov was in his use of interrogative intonations:

Quoi! Rome et l'Italie en cendre	Почтить ли токи те кровавы,
Me feront honorer *Sylla?*	Что в Риме Сулла проливал?
J'admirerai dans Alexandre	*Достойно ль* в Александре славы,
Ce que j'abhorre en *Attila?*	Что в Атилле всяк злом признал?
J'appellerai Vertu guerriere	За добродетель и геройство
Une Vaillance meurtriere	*Хвалить ли* зверско неспокойство
Qui dans mon sang trempe *ses mains?*	И власть окровавленных рук?
Et je pourrai forcer ma bouche	И принужденными устами
A louer un Heros farouche,	*Могу ли* возносить хвалами
Ne pour le malheur *des Humains?*	Начальника толиких мук?
	[8, 662–663, 1100]

What! That Rome and Italy in ashes	Shall I honor the bloody founts
Would cause me to honor *Sylla*?	That Sulla set gushing in Rome?
That I would admire in Alexander	*Should* Alexander bask in glory
That which I abhor in *Atilla*?	For that which all revile in Attila?
That I would call martial Virtue	*Should I praise* as virtuous and heroic
A murderous Valor	This beastly turmoil
That dips *its hands* in my blood?	And the reign of bloodied hands?
And could I force my mouth	And with forced lips
To praise a savage Hero,	*Can I* praise to the skies
And this not bring misfortune to *all Mankind*?	The originator of such suffering?

Here, Lomonosov has set out, in perfect symmetry, words that convey "ascension and abrupt stop": these are the first words of both couplets in the substanza, and they appear in the second line of both three-line units. In this way, the intonational pattern in the three-line units is uniformly intensified, while remaining perfectly symmetrical.

Characteristically, when Sumarokov[N] also translated this ode, he not only refrained from emphasizing the intonations of this stanza—he did not even end it on a *question.*

We must also call attention to the special intonational function of the verse lines that conclude both the substanza and the three-line units (lines four, seven, and ten). These "lines of division" are quite naturally foregrounded; for this reason, they frequently stand apart syntactically in Lomonosov's poetry. They were later used similarly in Petrov's poetry, and subsequently adopted by Derzhavin for use in aphorisms and maxims.

The oratorical functions of lyric poetry foregrounded the declamatory nature of the ode with remarkable force. A unique oratorical system of sounds and metrical patterns took shape. In sections 172 and 173 of the *Rhetoric* (1748), Lomonosov asserts:

> It seems to me that in the Russian language, the frequent repetition of the letter *a* can aid in the depiction of splendor, vast spaces, depths, and heights, as well as sudden fear. Frequent use of the letters *e, i, iat'* [ѣ], and *iu* [ю] can be used to depict tenderness, affection, and mournful or minor things. With *ia* [я], one can show pleasant things, mirth, softness and sympathy; with *o, u,* and *y* [ы], terrible and powerful things: wrath, envy, fear, and sadness [section 173]: The hard consonants *k, p, t,* and soft consonants *b, g,* and *d* have a dull pronunciation. They have neither sweetness nor power unless another consonant is attached to them; therefore, they can only be used to portray actions and activities that are dull, lazy, and possess a hollow sound, such as the hammering of cities and houses being built, the clatter of horses' hooves, and the cries of certain animals. The hard consonants *s, f, kh* [х], *ts* [ц], *ch* [ч], *sh* [ш], and liquid *r* are pronounced with resonance and speed; they can therefore help us to gain a clearer understanding of things and actions that are powerful, great, loud, terrible, and magnificent. The soft *zh* [ж], *z,* and liquid *v, l, m,* and *n* are pronounced gently and are therefore suitable for the depiction of gentle and soft things and actions; the same is true of the silent letter *ъ* through the reduction of consonants in the middle or end of a word. Joining hard,

> soft, and liquid consonants gives rise to *harmonies*, which are suitable for depicting powerful, magnificent, dull, terrible, gentle, and pleasant things and actions [3:241].

These ideas are based on the theory of correspondence between sounds and objects or emotions (*l'harmonie imitative*), and Lomonosov considers two main approaches: "sound imitation" and "mellifluence" (see Derzhavin's account of the difference between these two concepts in his "On the Ode").[21]

Lomonosov's contemporaries heard the "loudness" and "sound imitation" in his odes. It remains for modern scholarship to determine the influence of these qualities on the selection of templates for lexicon and imagery.

The question of the emotional connotations of poetic meters gave rise to a characteristic dispute between Lomonosov—who insisted that different meters (the trochee and iamb) had different functions—and Trediakovsky.

According to Lomonosov, the iamb "has an inherent sense of nobility in relation to that which [...] ascends from below." "All heroic verse, which is commonly used to sing of noble and lofty subject matter, should be composed using this meter." On the other hand, the trochee is "gentle and pleasantly sweet by nature," likewise "inherently," and "should [...] be used in composing elegiac poetry as well as other, similar genres."[22]

---

21 Derzhavin, *Works* 7:571—*YT.*

The problem of a motivated link between the phonic and semantic aspects of language has been addressed in various ways in twentieth-century Russian poetics. Some poets have made assertions that are close to Lomonosov's in principle. On the other hand, the Futurists'[T] "word as such," considered outside of meaning, embodied the view of poetic language as different from practical. [...] In *The Problem of Verse Language*, first published 1924, Tynianov developed his own conception of the interaction between the semantic and phonic factors of verse, which is also reflected in the present article; in this case he only gives the text from the *Rhetoric* and points to the functional connection between Lomonosov's corresponding premises and the oratorical orientation of his poetry. The same is true of Lomonosov's "metrical symbolism," which Tynianov addresses in the next section of the present article—*ET*. Also see "On the Composition of *Eugene Onegin*" (114–150), "On Khlebnikov" (217–229), and "Interlude" (173–216).

22 Trediakovsky sums up Lomonosov's views in the preface "For Informative Purposes" [Dlia izvestiia] in V. K Trediakovsky, *Three Odes Paraphrasing Psalm 143* ... [Tri ody parafrasticheskie psalma 143 ...] (St. Petersburg, 1744), which included versions by Lomonosov, Sumarokov (in iambs), and Trediakovsky (in trochees). Cf. on the iamb and the "depiction of the affects" in poems of other meters in Lomonosov's "Letter on the Rules of Russian Poetry" [Pis'mo o pravilakh rossiskogo stikhotvorstva] (*PSS*, vol. 8:15)—*ET*.

Meanwhile, Trediakovsky believed that meter did not have a simple semantic function, and that the semantic mode depended "solely on the images the poet uses in his compositions." In this respect, Lomonosov is characterized by a "systemic," functional relationship to each element of his art, as well as the desire to assign a specific formal element to each function. His approach to meter resembles that laid out in his theory of the three styles, where he associates specific lexical combinations with the functions of "high" and "low" genres.[23]

But there is another aspect of this debate which demonstrates yet again Lomonosov's orientation toward oratorical speech. Lomonosov's own position in the debate is that of a poet-orator, who evaluates each element of a poem with an eye to its oratorical function. He turned the poetic meter of a given word, which ordinarily acted as a constructive factor, into a factor with its own oratorical function, considering it a framework for sound.

When we study Lomonosov's lyric poetry, we should not neglect the declamatory, concrete meaning of each element of his style. Lomonosov's poems join the ranks of declamatory phenomena. We can and must think of every example he discusses as something meant to be spoken out loud. And Lomonosov left us a guide of sorts for reconstructing the basic features of his declamatory style. He left behind *gestural* illustrations of an oratorical nature, in application to his poems. These gestural directions in the tradition of Quintilian and Nicolas Caussin can, in this case, be used for a straightforward "declamatory reconstruction" of Lomonosov's odes.[24]

> While [pronouncing] an ordinary word, in which no passions are represented, skilled orators will stand up straight and refrain from virtually any movement. When, on the other hand, they try to prove something through forceful argument or express themselves with convincing or gentle figures of speech, they represent this conjointly with their hands, eyes, head, and

23 V. K. Trediakovsky, "On the Use of Church Books in the Russian Language" [O pol'ze knig tserkovnykh v rossiiskom iazyke] (1757), in V. K. Trediakovskii, *Izbrannye proizvedeniia* (Moscow/Leningrad: Sovetskii pisatel', 1963), Lomonosov proposed that all poetry should be written in one of three styles—high, middle, and low—each of which was distinguished by specific diction and form.

24 Quintilian and Caussin were among the sources Lomonosov worked with when composing his *Rhetoric*. See, in particular, M. I. Sukhomlinov's notes to vol. 3 of Lomonosov, *Sochineniia—ET.* Quintilian (35–100) was a Roman rhetorician whose work strongly influenced developments in medieval rhetoric. Caussin (1583–1681) was a French rhetorician and Jesuit known for his work *De Eloquentia sacra et humana* [On Holy and Human Eloquence].

> shoulders. By lifting up both arms, or just one, they offer a prayer to God, or make a vow, or swear an oath; when they hold out their hand with the palm facing away, they deliver a rebuke or drive someone away; by putting a hand to their lips, they indicate silence. With an outstretched hand, they point something out; by intensifying this with a gentle movement up and down, they show the importance of a thing; when they fling their arms open, they are in doubt or make a denial; they beat their own chests during a sorrowful speech; by wagging a finger, they threaten and admonish. They roll their eyes upward during prayer and exclamation; turn them away in denial or contempt, squeeze them shut with irony and ridicule, close them gently to indicate sorrow and weakness. By lifting up their head and face, they signify something magnificent, or their own pride; by lowering their head, they show sorrow and humiliation; by shaking it, they make a denial. By hunching their shoulders, they represent fear, doubt, and denial." (*Rhetoric*, 1744, section 138) [3:78–79].

Thus, oratorical intonation played a role as important as that of grammatical intonation. The word came to signify an impetus for gesture. For us, the "indication" in the following lines has been effaced:[25]

И се уже рукой багряной	And lo, with lovely crimson hand
Врата отверзла в мир заря,	Dawn flings open the world's gates,
От ризы сыплет свет румяный	Sprinkling rosy light from her robes
В поля, в леса, во град, в моря [8, 138]	Over fields and woods, cities and seas

—but for Lomonosov it was a specific gesture: "With an outstretched hand, they point something out; by intensifying this with a gentle movement up and down, they show the *importance* of a thing" (Lomonosov's example).

The latter gesture is particularly interesting. In addition to "illustrative" and "imitative" gestures, Lomonosov's system included "metaphorical" ones, which accentuated meaning indirectly, through the generally recognized (or fabricated) coloring of a word or gesture. An ode was to be constructed according to the principle of the "mixing of passions," along with other intonational and gestural elements.

25 The term "indication" [*ukazanie*] comes from the *Rhetoric*: "When we indicate a given object with a pronoun: lo, here." See section 101 of the 1744 *Rhetoric* or section 218 of the 1748 version, where Lomonosov refers to the above quotation from the ode to Elizaveta Petrovna's coronation (1746). See Lomonosov, *Complete Works*, 7:59.

The semantics of poetic language is also constructed around orientation. When the notion of oratorical impact, with its demand for variety, suddenness, and unexpectedness, is applied to poetry, it gives rise to a theory of imagery; for the word, the crucial thing is its "power of associative imagination," "the ability, when the mind is presented with one thing, to conjointly imagine other things which are, in one way or another, paired with the first." From an oratorical standpoint, the "conjoining of ideas" is more effective than "simple ideas" by themselves.[26] The word moves ever further away from its primary meaning: "Ornate discourse is somewhat unexpected or unnatural, but it is nevertheless appropriate to the proposed theme and, for this reason, is grand and pleasing" (section eleven) [3:27]. Ornate speeches are generated from "the transposition of things to an inappropriate setting" (section seventy-seven) [48]. The ode's oratorical organization breaks with the word's nearest associations, viewing them as the least effective; "*distant* ideas," "when paired [...] can form substantial compound ideas that are also appropriate to the theme" (*Rhetoric*, 1748, section twenty-seven) [3:111].

Thus, the linking or juxtaposition of "distant" words (in Lomonosov's terminology, "the conjoining of distant ideas," where an idea is a word in its constructive function, a word in the process of elaboration) creates an image; the ordinary semantic associations of the word are eliminated, leaving a semantic *fracture*.[27] This trope is understood as an "*aversion*" or "*perversion*," a term of Lomonosov's that superbly accentuates the fractured semantic line of the poetic word.[28] One of Lomonosov's favorite devices is using a conjunction to bring words together that belong to distant lexical and material series (zeugma):

---

26 "Ideas are either simple or compound. Simple ideas consist of one notion, while compound ones treat two or more, which are joined amongst themselves" (*Rhetoric* [1748], section four; *PSS*, 7:100)—*ET*.

27 Note the connection between Lomonosov's aesthetic principle and the general principles of the Baroque style, with its intentionally extravagant juxtaposition of strikingly different, if not dissonant, elements.

28 The term "aversion" [*otvrashchenie*] is found in section eighty-two of the 1744 *Rhetoric* (and in a different sense in section 100, where he writes about rhetorical figures); in section eight-three he uses the term "metaphor." In the 1748 *Rhetoric*, Lomonosov writes only about metaphor—*ET*. Note that the root of these words in Russian is "turn" [*vrat-*]—cf. *vertere* [Latin], also "trope" [from Greek, *tropos*]. See also "Tyutchev and Heine" (68) and "On the Composition of *Eugene Onegin*", note 9 (116).

С пшеницей, где покой насеян [8, 29]	Where peace, with wheat, is sown.
От Вас мои нагреты груди И Ваши все подданны люди [8, 35]	It was you who warmed my breasts, And all of your subjects.
Оставшей труп и стыд смердит [8, 49]	It reeks of a corpse and of shame.

Lomonosov often transposes his epithets onto a word from a neighboring lexical series, e.g., "fiery sound" in the line "The sign of triumph, the fiery sound" (note the repetition of the sounds *s-n-tr-f, fr-t-s-n*); also "the loyal thought," as in the line "Does wish this loyal thought of mine" (the syntactic inversion in this example is typical).[29]

Lomonosov chooses predicates that are striking, overdone, and that do not correspond to the basic feature of the grammatical subject. Every action is hyperbolic:

В пучине след его *горит* [8, 391].	Her trace *burns* in the [watery] abyss.
Что *бьет* за странный шум в мой слух? [8:21].	What noise so strange *beats* at my ear?[30]

Likewise, Lomonosov uses Biblical images that are similar in terms of their constructive principle:

Руками реки восплескали.[31]	The rivers clapped their hands together.

This is not about accidental "influence," but rather the selection of material that is close at hand. The image is meanwhile brought into being through the sustained development of one of the paired "ideas." The more powerful the verbal actualization, the deeper the semantic fracture, and the more obscured the clarity of the material-semantic series:

---

29 The examples in Russian are *paliashchii zvuk* [burning sound] and *pobedy znak* [the sign of victory], with the sound repetitions *pa-z-k*; and *podanna mysl'*.

30 Note how the sound-based metaphor is supported by the meter—*YT*.

31 Inexact quotation from the ode on the arrival of Elizaveta Petrovna to Petersburg from Moscow (Lomonosov, *PSS*, 8:93). The source of this metaphor, one of Lomonosov's favorites, is Psalm 97:8: "Let the floods clap their hands: let the hills be joyful together"—*ET* (it is Psalm ninety-eight in the King James Version).

Восторг внезапный ум *пленил*, *Ведет* на верьх горы высокой [8, 16]	A sudden rapture *seized* my mind And *leads* me up a lofty peak.
Там холмы и древа *взывают* И *громким гласом* возвышают До самых звезд Елисавет [8, 137–138]	The hills and trees are *calling* her, And in a *booming voice* they praise Elizaveta to the very stars.

The verbal actualization occurs in the last three lines (call—in a booming voice, praise—to the very stars); hence the semantic pallor of the grammatical subjects (the "terms of the ideas"), *hills and trees.*[32]

Given the vital role of sound in the ode, the "conjoining of ideas" had to be grounded in sound.[33]

The semanticization of individual word parts is typical of Lomonosov; see section 106 of his *Grammar*: "At the beginning (of a word—*YT*), one finds consonants followed by vowels, in the same order in which other words in the Russian language also begin; for example: *u—zha—snyi* [dread—ful], *chu—dnyi* [splen—did], *dria—khlyi* [flab—by], *to—pchu* [I—stamp], for the consonantal pairs *sn, dn, khl, pch* are at the beginnings of the words *sneg* [snow], *dno* [bottom, base], *khleb* [bread], *pchela* [bee]" [7:428].[34]

For Lomonosov, the word expands into a verbal group with parts that are not connected through direct semantic associations, but rather associations that emerge out of rhythmic (metrical and phonic) proximity. This is expressed through repetitions and the adjacency of words that are either identical or have similar roots.

Examples where the words are identical:

32 Here and subsequently, Tynianov uses the word "term" [*termin*] as it is used in Lomonosov's *Rhetoric*, where a "term" is a thematic element or motif.

33 Later, Jean François de La Harpe would write: "Quoique les pensees soient partout un merite essential, elles le sont dans une ode moins, que partout ailleurs, parce que l'harmonie peut plus aisement en tenir lieu" ["Although thought is everywhere an essential virtue, it is less so in an ode than anywhere else, since harmony can more easily take its place"]—*YT.* See J. P. La Harpe, *Lycee …*, vol. 6 (Paris, 1798), 96—*ET*.

34 Lomonosov draws his readers' attention to the consonantal pairs in the second part of the words that he breaks up; English words that might fit the second part of his proposition are "fulsome," "diddle," "bee," "amplify," but English morphology is such that they do not feature similar consonantal pairs.

Отца отечества отец! [8, 51]

O *father* to *fatherland's father!*

Отрада пойдет вслед *отраде*
<...........................>
И *плески плескам* весть дадут [8, 107]
Что *вихри в вихри* ударялись,
И *тучи с тучами* спирались,
И устремлялся *гром на гром* [8, 141]

Joy shall come on the heels of *joy*
[..............................]
And *splash* to *splash* will tidings tell
That *gust* with *gust* collided,
And *cloud* pressed upon *cloud,*
And *lightning* dashed at *lightning*

Герою молвил тут *Герой* [8, 23]

To *Hero* then the *Hero* said
etc.

Examples where the words are related by root:

Долы скрыты *далиной* [8, 10]

The dales by *distances* obscured.

К *хвале* Твоих доброт *прехвальных* [8, 41]
Твоей для *славы* лишь бы *слыло* [8, 51]
Превысить хочет *вышню* Власть [8, 38]
Успело твой *отпор попрать* [8, 49]

To the *praise* of your *praiseworthy* kindness
Only to *know* of your *renown*
Wants to *exceed* an *excellent* Power
Managed to *refuse* your *rebuff*

This can be seen further in the way Lomonosov surrounds words with a sonically related environment. The two factors that play a part here are, first, the distinct semanticization of individual words and groups, and second, the application of the rule that an "idea" can develop along purely sonic lines, as in an anagram (e.g., *mir—Rim* [cf. more—Rome]).[35]

За нами пушки, весь *припас,*
Прислал что сам Стокгольм про нас [8, 49]
Какую здесь достали *честь,*
Добычи *часть* друзьям дарите [8, 49]

Behind us, cannons, the whole *reserve,*
That Stockholm itself *remitted* to us
Whatever here you gained *importance,*
Give to friends *a portion* of the gain.

Во днях младых сильна *держава,*
Взмужав до звезд прославит ту? [8, 51]

In younger days the *state comes on* strong,
When it *comes of age,* will it praise her to the stars?

35 See sections eighteen and seventy-five of the 1744 *Rhetoric* and sections ten and 135 of the 1748 *Rhetoric—ET.* Note that in Russian *mir—Rim* means "the world—Rome," a more evocative combination.

Such sonically dense lines will often transition into sound-based metaphors:

Горят сердца их к бою жарко; *Гремит* Стокгольм трубами ярко [8, 46]	Their *hearts blaze* hot for battle; Stockholm *blares loud and clear* with trumpets
Стигийских вод шумят *брега,* *Гребут* по ним побитых души [8, 49]	The *flanks* of the Stygian waters rustle, Across them *ferry* the souls of the fallen.
Кумиров *мерсских мрак* прогнал [8, 39]	He chased away the *dire dark* of idols
Смущает *мрак и страх* дорогу [8, 25]	*Darkness and dread* confound the way
Полков лишь наших слышен *плеск* [8, 40] *За холмы,* где паляща *хлябь* [8, 19]	Only the *splashing* of our *squadrons* can be heard *Beyond the heights,* where flared the *hellpit*
Горы выше облаков *Гордыя* главы вздымают [8, 9]	Higher than the clouds *the mountains* Raise their *monumental* heads
Грозных туч не опасаюсь, *Гордость* что владык разят [8, 12] От *устья быстрых струй* Дунайских, До самых *уских* мест Ахайских [8, 40]	I do not fear the *prominent* clouds, *The pride* that eats away at chieftains From the *rapid* Danube's *torrent,* To the *tapered* Achaean stretches

This special predilection for the semanticization of sounds also provides a likely explanation for why Lomonosov's rhymes are based on sound similarity between final *words,* rather than between final syllables. The deciding factor is evidently the semantic vividness of certain sound groups, rather than the similarity of final syllables, e.g. *consternation—constitution, rapidity—rapacious, godly—golden.*[36]

In Lomonosov's poetry, the placement of these sound repetitions sometimes corresponds to rhythmic divisions, emphasizing the segmentation of rhythmic series into periods, and opposing these rhythmic periods to one another:

---

36 Tynianov gives the following examples in Russian: 1) *golubiami—golosami* [doves—voices], 2) *brega—beda* [riverbanks—woe], 3) *raby—rvy* [slaves—ditches], 4) *struiakh—stepiakh* [streams—steppes], 5) *vstupi—vsi* [enter (imperative, sing.)—all (plural)], 6) *rvy—kovry* [ditches—carpets], 7) *pora—tvortsa* [time—creator], 8) *zvezdami—nozrdriami* [stars—nostrils].

Победы *знак,* / **па**лящий *звук* [8, 43]	The *sign* of [**free**dom], / the **fier**y *sound*
Российский род / и **П**лод **П**етров [8, 108]	The **R**ussian race / and **P**eter's **P**rogeny
Тростник **под**слав, / **Тра**вой **по**крылся [8, 44]	The **re**eds be**hind** him / He **hides** in g**r**ass
Вас **т**ешил *мир,* / нас *Марс* **тр**удил, **С**олдат ваш **с**пал, / наш в **б**рани *был* [8, 50]	*Peace* **d**elighted you, / *Aries* **d**rove us down, Your **s**oldier **s**lept, / ours **b**attled *on*

These sound repetitions are completely in keeping with the orientation of Lomonosov's odes toward declamation and reading out loud. In this connection, Lomonosov made extensive use of seventeenth- and eighteenth-century theories on the emotional significance of sounds.

As a result, a Lomonosov ode can be seen as a grandiose verbal elaboration of a "term"; a verbal construction subordinated to the tasks of oratory.

Poetic speech is sharply delineated from ordinary speech, even in its phonetic make-up. Lomonosov strove to create an ideal phonetic standard for poetry: "high-style recitation" should tend toward the "precise articulation of letters," something not required in practical, conversational speech.[37] At the same time, the question of poetic language took on particular significance, as its effect now depended solely on its *lexical* make-up.

Existing outside its proper meaning, the words—in the context of the "conjoining of ideas"—were meant just to set a certain tone, to operate more through their lexical coloring than as words per se. The function of this lexical coloring was carried out by the words' lexical associations. *Lomonosov thought of linguistic phenomena as literary phenomena,* which resulted in his preference for Church Slavonic words ("On the Use of Church Books"). His innovation was not the division into three styles, which had become dominant before his time, but the actual selection of words according to their lexical associations, which he treated as lexical coloring: "Due to the importance of God's church as a sacred place, and its antiquity, we feel a special reverence for the Slavonic language, through which a versifier can elevate his magnificent thoughts still higher."[38] Here, the Church Slavonic word is important because it is colored by the lexical

---

37 *Russian Grammar* [Rossiiskaia grammatika], section 104 (*PSS,* 7:427, 623). Cf. the 1744 *Rhetoric,* section 137 (PSS, 7:78)—*ET.*

38 "On the Use of Church Books in the Russian Language," ibid., 591. For more on the significance of the lexical coloring of words and Church Slavonicisms, see Tynianov, *Problema stikhotvornogo iazyka,* 87–94—*ET.*

framework that surrounds it. From a literary standpoint, it is less important that a particular word be a true Church Slavonicism; what is important is how it is colored in the given context. No wonder, then, that Pushkin called Church Slavonicisms (or archaisms, as the case may be) *bibleisms.*[39] Church Slavonic lexical coloring is a tool for elevating poetic language and marking it off from colloquial speech, just as inversions do on the syntactic level, and as normative poetic sound orchestration does on the phonetic level.[40]

The aims of expressive speech do not align with the concept of "perfection": in place of euphony, it favors an impactful system of sounds; instead of the pleasure afforded by the aesthetic fact, it seeks the dynamism of that fact; in place of "perfect equilibrium," it prefers "beauty with blemishes."[41]

These "blemishes" play a special constructive role in the ode.[42] The ode's fundamental orientation justifies their inclusion as a source of variety, just as "cadences" are justified as a means of weakening, a pretext for relaxation.[43]

---

39 In margin notes to Konstantin Batyushkov,[N] *Polnoe sobranie sochinenii* (St. Petersburg: Tip. B. S. Balasheva, 1885–87)—*ET.*

40 It is curious that, years later, the Archaist[T] Shishkov[N] would assert the rights of "literary language." Shishkov defended the phonetic norm as an attribute of the high style: "The same manner of speaking is appropriate to elevated and eloquent language [...] In comedies, works which are close to colloquial language, it ("vulgar pronunciation"—*YT*) can still be tolerated, though not in every case, and depending on the simplicity or loftiness of the discourse ...]" (Aleksandr Shishkov, *Collected Works and Translations of Admiral Shishkov* [Sobranie sochinenii i perevodov admirala Shishkova], part 3 (St. Petersburg: V tip. Imperatorskoi rossiiskoi akademii, 1824), 31–33). Shishkov considered words and groups with *different meanings* to be doublets of a single word (or group), belonging to different lexical series. In copying out Lomonosov's line "Like an eagle ascending he soared up the mountain" (aiming to prove by this example that in the high style in Russian, *g* should be pronounced *h*), Shishkov remarks: "This example shows that lofty language differs from simple language not merely in the selection of words, but even in their stresses and pronunciation" (ibid, 40)—*YT.*

41 *On the Sublime. The Work of Dionysius Longinus* [O vysokom. Tvorenie Dionisiia Longina], Russian trans. I. Martynov (St. Petersburg, 1826), 143–161—*ET.*

42 See Boileau: "Dans un noble projet on tombe noblement" (Longinus) ["When the conception's grand, one falls with grandeur"]. See also the following chapters: "Si l'on doit preferer la mediocre parfait au sublime qui a quelques defauts" (chap. twenty-seven) ["Should one prefer mediocre perfection to the sublime that has a few defects"]; "Que les fautes dans le sublime se peuvent excuser" (chap. thirty) ["That defects in the sublime can be excused"]. "Traite du sublime on du merveilleux dans discours. Traduit du grec Longin" [Treatise on the sublime or on the marvelous in speech. Translated from the Greek of Longinus" (Paris: Denys Thierry, 1674), 3–102]—*YT.*

43 See Aleksei Merzlyakov[N] in his essay on Derzhavin (after Lomonosov's time): "Worth noting is a certain exhaustion on the part of the poet [...] Inspiration is and must be fleeting; such efforts surpass mankind's weak nature. The poet has achieved his insight and ought to

Incidentally, this constructive role of "blemishes" was, significantly later on, adopted with great enthusiasm by the Archaists[T] (Shishkov's[N] followers).

Lomonosov's odes can be called oratorical not because (or, not only because) they were conceived with a view to reading out loud, but primarily because the oratorical element became decisive for them; it became a constructive factor. The oratorical principles of maximum impact and verbal development subordinated and transfigured all the elements of the word. The potential for declamation is not just a given in Lomonosov's odes, it is how they were conceived in the first place.

3

The theory and practice of the lofty ode were formed through struggle. Sumarokov spoke out against "loudness" and the "conjoining of distant ideas." In his essay, "On Russian Liturgical Eloquence," Sumarokov makes an argument against the lofty oratorical element: "Many religious orators, lacking taste, keep both their hearts and all natural feeling out of their compositions; but philosophizing without foundation, imagining in an obscure fashion and trusting in the commoner's usual praise, offered up to everything beyond his understanding, they set out to climb Parnassus along crooked paths, and, bridling instead of Pegasus a wild stallion, and sometimes even a donkey, they drag themselves up some little foothill, along a crooked road."[44]

Against oratorical "fervor," Sumarokov offers "wit" [*ostroumie*]: "A sharp intelligence [*ostryi razum*] is defined by perspicacity, while fervent intelligence boasts mere speed. There are witty people who happen to be slow in the twists and turns of their intelligence, and there are likewise simpleminded people who, lacking perspicacity, sparkle by speed alone, blinding those who are as empty-headed as they are with their sham subtlety. [...] Only the general and the poet can do nothing without fervent intelligence. [...] But however beneficial fervor may be to a general or poet with wit, it proves no less harmful when wit is lacking."[45]

---

appear exhausted" ("Amphion" [July 1815], 114). Section five in the "Colloquy of Lovers of Literature" [Beseda liubitelei russkogo slova] in Moscow)—*YT.* See Archaism / Archaists in Terms.

44 A. P. Sumarokov, *Complete Works in Verse and Prose* [Polnoe sobranie vsekh sochinenii v stikhakh i proze] (Moscow: V univ. tip. N. Novikova, 1787), 6:279—*YT.*

45 "On the Difference Between Fervent and Sharp Intelligence" [O raznosti mezhdu pylkim i ostrym razumom]. Ibid, 298—*YT.*

The value of poetic language, according to Sumarokov, lies in its "stinginess," "brevity," and "precision": "Volubility is a sign of poverty of human intellect. All speech and writing in which there are more words than thoughts point to a dim-witted author. A quick-witted intelligence selects words to fit the measure of its thoughts, and is left with neither an overabundance nor a shortage of words. This applies to conversations as well as to written compositions."[46]

"[...] Begone, splendor that lacks clarity!"[47]

Naturally, the value of the constructive principle here is transferred to a different domain: "Happy are those," writes Sumarokov, ironically, " [...] who are little concerned with the beauty of their thoughts, and do not even entertain the vain hope of achieving it. They feel no compunction about sacrificing their thoughts at the altar of rhyme, caesura, and meter."[48]

Sumarokov fought against the metaphorical tendencies of the ode.

"'Blissful villages, fortified forts.' One cannot say 'fortified forts.' You can say 'fortified settlements,' but not 'fortified forts.' A fort is called a fort for the very reason that it is fortified."[49] For both Lomonosov and Sumarokov, verbal pairings such as "fortified forts" or "valley of the vale" constituted a specific device for the verbal elaboration of an image.

Sumarokov rejected Lomonosov's method for developing metaphor, which was based on the extended elaboration of a single metaphor and was inimical to the material concreteness that came, for Sumarokov, from joining words based on their closest associations. Sumarokov commented regarding the following lines by Lomonosov:

Сокровищ полны корабли	Piled with treasure, the ships
Дерзают в море за тобою [8:196]	Follow you boldly over the sea

where the pronominal substitute "you" allows for the development of a free-standing metaphorical series, and signals a break from the "main term" (which is "stillness"):[50] "I have grave doubts as to whether one can say that ships venture over the sea seeking stillness or that stillness precedes them. Stillness remains ashore, and the sea never asks whether a nation is at war or at peace.

46 "A Letter on the *mot juste*" [Pis'mo ob ostroumnom slove]. Ibid, 349—*YT*.

47 "To the Versifiers of Nonsense" [K nesmyslennym rifmotvortsam]. Ibid., 9:277—*YT*.

48 "To the Typesetters" [K tipografskim naborshchikam]. Ibid, 6:312—*YT*.

49 "Criticism of the Ode" [Kritika na odu]. Ibid., 10:77—*YT*.

50 Note that the word (the "main term") "stillness" [*tishina*] is mentioned earlier in the poem.

It grows restless whenever it likes [...]."[51] Here, Sumarokov also stresses his disagreement with the handling of the "main term"; he is opposed to its being used as allegory, and also opposes Lomonosov's symbolic use of words. Also cf. his commentary on Lomonosov's lines "Но краше в свете не находит, / .... и тебя [But none more beautiful on earth is found, / .... than you][52]—where "you" is also a disconnected pronominal substitute for the "main term" ("silence") in a freestanding metaphorical series: "It's true that the sun gazes upon filigree, gold, and porphyry; but for it to gaze upon silence, wisdom, and conscience is against our understanding."[53]

Opposing the "conjoining of distant ideas," Sumarokov advanced the need to conjoin close words, words that are connected in accordance with the material and lexical series closest at hand: "Upon pearls, gold and porphyry. Porphyry has little in common with pearls and gold. It would have been better to say: upon pearls, silver and gold; or, upon crown, scepter, and porphyry, in order that these words would be in greater harmony with one another."[54]

To Sumarokov, a deformed poetic mode of speech was unacceptable. This is why he waged his battle in the name of language itself. He singled out Lomonosov's "incorrect stresses" for their metrical deformation. Similarly, Sumarokov rejected the sound structure of Lomonosov's verse. He called for "eloquence" [*sladkorechie*] and euphony instead of "sound imitation" (for that historical period, we should understand this as encompassing both onomatopoeia in the standard sense and a broad range of sound-based metaphors): "Mr. Lomonosov is prone to lapses in eloquence, by which I mean poverty of rhymes, a cumbersome quality owing to the crowding of letters and pronunciation, impurity of scansion, obscurity of harmony, violations of grammar and spelling, and everything else offensive to the gentle ear and abominable to unsullied taste."[55] With reference to the requirements of eloquence, he objects to Lomonosov's system of inexact rhymes, as well as his cumbersome sound orchestration:

"И числа совесть рвет притворств гнилых завесу	"And unblemished conscience tears the veil from filthy affectation

51 Sumarokov, "Criticism of the Ode," *PSS*, 10:78—*YT*.

52 The ellipses in the second line of the quotation (see Lomonosov, *PSS*, 7:98) replace the word "Elizaveta" in Sumarokov's text: the empress's name could not be written in a critical context—*ET*.

53 Sumarokov, "Criticism of the Ode," *PSS*, 10:79—*YT*.

54 Ibid.—*YT*.

55 Sumarokov, "On the Use of Meter" [O stoposlozhenii], ibid, 51—*YT*.

The meter here is in good order, but there's no rhyme or reason.

> Стьрвет, Тпри, Рствгни
> [*st'rvet, tpri, rstvgni*]."[56]

But for the sake of semantic clarity [Sumarokov] was still willing to sacrifice euphony: "[...] harsh pronunciation is preferable to a bizarre arrangement of words."[57]

A curious admission by Sumarokov shows just how much these two tendencies saw themselves as fundamentally at odds with one another: "When Mr. Lomonosov recited his poems, he could hear the iambs sometimes deforming into dactyls, as well as the crude fusing of his consonants, but either he could not or would not take the trouble to render his language gentler. He knew, moreover, that many ignorant people held that this indolent style of composition, by very reason of its crudeness, was in fact the height of sublimity; and that many called my free-flowing style gentle, but considered this gentility to be nothing more than softhearted weakness; ascribing to him a certain loud quality, and to me one of gentility."[58]

Sumarokov's parodic "Nonsense Odes" speak to this as well.[59] There, the author emphasizes the key devices typically used by Lomonosov for linguistic elaboration: repetition, the syntactic grouping of words that have a single root, and so on. He also emphasizes the principle of unification around sound, the conjoining of distant ideas, and the sound principle of their combination and "non-euphony."

These parodies already contain formulas that have become clichés:

И столько хитро воспеваю,	And so ingenious is my singing
Что песни не пойму и сам.	I cannot grasp the song myself.

56 In the Russian, Tynianov gives Sumarokov's rendering of the unwieldy consonant clusters in the quoted line: "*st'rvet* [conscience rips], *tpri* [rips affectation], *rsvgni* [affectation [the] veil]."

57 Ibid., 74—*YT*. The quotation is from Lomonosov's "Letter on the Use of Glass" [Pis'mo o pol'ze stekla] (*PSS*, 7:510).

58 Ibid., 8:52—*YT*.

59 Tynianov included Sumarokov's "nonsense" odes in the *Apparent Poetry* [Mnimaia poeziia (Moscow: Academia, 1934)] collection he edited in 1931, which also includes other parodies of odic poetry—*ET*. For more on this topic, see "On Parody" (especially note 53, 314).

Остави прежний низкий стих!	Begone, o base verse of yore!
Он был *естествен, прост,* и *плавен,*	It was *easy, simple,* and *smooth,*
Но хладен, сух, бессилен, тих!	But cold, dry, powerless, quiet!
Гремите, Музы, сладко, красно,	Thunder, O muses, sweetly, beautifully,
Великолепно, велегласно![60]	Magnificently, with voices grand!

It's curious that in his parodies, Sumarokov tends to use the segmented stanzaic mode, which is so rare in his other works ("Nonsense Odes" 1, 3, 4).

Against the hyperbole, fluid imagery, intonational richness, and "loudness" of Lomonosov's odes, Sumarokov contrasts the semantic "clarity" of his own odes.

Sumarokov placed the following epigraph at the head of his "Solemn Odes" (1774):

Не громкость и не нежность	Neither loud nor gentle,
Прославят нашу песнь:	Our song will be praised otherwise:
Излишество всегда есть в стихотворстве плеснь;	Excess always leads, in verse-making, to mold;
Имей способности, искусство и прилежность![61]	Have ye skill and talent and be ye not too bold!

In this way, the high-style—"loud"—lofty ode was rejected in favor of the "middle"-style ode. Sumarokov's odes seemed deliberately antithetical to Lomonosov's in their number of stanzas (from four to twelve; averaging around ten—apparently the standard number),[62] and in the intonational mode of the stanzas, which is restrained and minimal. While Lomonosov saw the round, measured mode as a backdrop for intonational fluctuations, for Sumarokov it was the norm. His digressions are negligible, and they are understood precisely as *digressions.*

Toward the end of his literary career, Sumarokov summed up these arguments by juxtaposing "certain stanzas by two authors"—his own and Lomonosov's.[63] The stanzas chosen for juxtaposition were considered typical: they were juxtaposed according to their devices rather than their themes.

---

60 Quotations from "Nonsense Ode II" [Vzdornaia oda II] and "A Dithyramb for Pegasus" [Difiramb Pegasu]—*ET. Izbrannye proizvedeniia* (Lennigrad: Sovetskii pisatel', 1957), 289, 292.

61 See Sumarokov's 1774 *Solemn Odes* [Torzhestvennye ody], in *Poems* [Stikhotvoreniia] (Moscow: Sovetskii pisatel', 1935), 410.

62 These numbers are imprecise. Sumarokov's smallest ode has three stanzas, while his largest has twenty-seven—*ET.*

63 This was the title of Sumarokov's brochure (1774)—*ET.*

But the ode form actually used genre to justify the oratorical orientation of poetic language; any attempt to downplay this language within the ode could only be a compromise. The ode was recognized as the highest form of lyric poetry, a view supported by the theory of the three styles, with its definition of the value of different literary forms and their corresponding lexical frameworks. This way of thinking was so ingrained that the concept of *the ode* became practically a synonym for the concept of lyric poetry. The ode was important not only as a genre, but also as a distinct direction for poetry.

4

For literature, this *recognition of the value* of genre was decisive. The coexistence of other poetic forms alongside the main one during the entire period of the ode's development did not hinder this development, because these other forms were seen as *minor* ones. The senior genre, the ode, existed not as a finished, self-sufficient genre, but as a distinct constructive tendency.

This high-style genre could thus attract and absorb all kinds of new material, and be revitalized at the expense of other genres; ultimately, it could transform beyond all recognition as a genre, and nevertheless continue to be recognized as an ode, as long as its formal elements remained tied to its primary verbal function, its orientation.

This article does not seek to provide a history of the ode. I will only note that the subsequent phases of the ode were marked by a struggle between the approaches of Sumarokov and Lomonosov, and by occasional attempts to merge them in an eclectic fashion.[64]

Derzhavin's new approach involved eliminating the ode as a radically self-contained, canonical genre, *replacing* the "solemn ode" while at the same time preserving it as a tendency; that is, by preserving and developing the stylistic features that had been determined by its lofty oratorical element.[65]

---

64 The intonational layout of the stanza can indicate allegiance to one or another tendency. While the overall number of stanzas in the fluctuating and segmented modes (and their role within the poem) is very high for Lomonosov, Petrov, and Derzhavin, it occurs much less frequently in Sumarokov, [Vasily] Maikov, Kheraskov, and Kapnist. For the latter group, the round and measured mode is undoubtedly *the norm*, while for the former, it serves merely as a backdrop—*YT*.

65 In a well-known autobiographical statement, Derzhavin attested that he initially tried to imitate Lomonosov, but subsequently "chose [...] an entirely different approach"—ET. See "Zapiski Derzhavina," in *Works*, 6: 443.

In bringing about a revolution in the ode by introducing elements from the middle (and even low) styles into the lexicon of the high style, by reorienting the ode toward the prose of satirical journals in terms of both composition and style, and by building up his imagery to the very limits of the lyric fabula,[T] Derzhavin did not render the ode "lower." And it was characteristic that, although Derzhavin did not acknowledge "types" (genres) of lyric poetry and wished to focus on individual authors when writing about lyric poetry, he still titled his essay "A Treatise on Lyric Poetry, or the Ode" [Rassuzhdenie o liricheskoi poezii, ili ob ode].

The verbal elaboration of imagery ceased to be effective because the obscure space of incongruity between the verbal and material images could no longer be perceived. The semantic fracture caused by the "conjoining of distant ideas" stopped being a fracture; it became settled and stylistically commonplace.[66]

Under such conditions, importing radically different stylistic resources into the ode did not undermine the ode as a genre of the high style, but, on the

---

66 That said, it is impossible not to notice the enormous influence of Lomonosov's *principles* of verbal elaboration on Derzhavin's style:

Затихла тише тишина. [4:51]	Still quieter quieted the quiet.
Грохочет эхо по горам, Как гром гремящий по громам. [1:322]	The echo rumbles o'er the rocks Like thunder thunderously thundering.

The former example points us to Tyutchev, who took this device even further and changed it:

Утихло вкруг тебя молчанье И тень нахмурилась темней.	The silence hushed around you, The shade grew darker with a scowl.

The following lines are a striking example of Derzhavin's approach to verbal elaboration:

Твоей то правде нужно было, Чтоб *смертну бездну* преходило Мое *бессмертно* бытие; Чтоб дух мой в *смертность* облачился. И чтоб чрез *смерть* я возвратился, Отец!—в *бессмертие* твое. [1:132–133]	For your truth it was required That through the *mortal vale* should pass My being, *immortal* though it were; That my soul dress in *mortality*. And that, through *mortal wounds*, I should then, O Father! unto your *immortality* return.

Here it is as though we have a single word broken up into many parts (words). This device derives its special power from the fact that all of these words reiterate a single root, and yet differ from one another; this makes the word feel as though it were in *flow*, and charges it with dynamism; one could compare it to [Velimir] Khlebnikov's verbal constructions—*YT*. The quotes are from Derzhavin's poems "Sorrow of the Soul" [Toska dushi], "The Waterfall" [Vodopad;], and the ode "God" [Bog] (Derzhavin, *Works*, 3:51–53, 1:318–327, 1:130–133). F. I. Tyutchev, "Yesterday in enchanted dreams ..." [Vchera v mechtakh obvorozhennykh], in *Polnoe sobranie sochinenii*, 33–34.

contrary, reinforced its value.

Gogol[N] said of Derzhavin: "His language is *bigger* than that of any other of our poets. When it is dissected, we see that it is the result of an extraordinary *union of the loftiest terms with the lowest* and simplest ones, which no one but Derzhavin would venture."[67]

Earlier, this "proximity of unequally lofty words" in Derzhavin's poetry had bothered Merzlyakov.[68]

The picturesque quality of Derzhavin's imagery and its material concreteness are generally acknowledged. But Merzlyakov, who was closer to Derzhavin [chronologically and aesthetically], leveled the same accusations against him that Sumarokov had leveled against Lomonosov: "It seems to me [...] that such lines as '*it flings the towers beyond the clouds*' [*bashni rukoiu za oblak brosaet*] add nothing to Derzhavin's magnificent vision: it is too playful a thing to say of a violent wind. The same goes for the *city falling down* when *touched by the storm*: a city, in this context, can collapse, but not fall down."[69]

Merzlyakov's description of the function of Derzhavin's "material" images is spot on:

> Are we able to delight in the play of words; to look upon *hill and thicket*; to observe how sound [the "thunder of fame," as Derzhavin has it—*YT*] *rolls by*, and right away *passes on*, and right away *races past*, and right away *resounds from vale to vale, from hill to hill*; can we see anything in the light of that terrible sword, in the glow of the luminaries encircling the celestial globe, and of the stars tracing the heavens, girding them so magnificently with resplendent, fiery bands!—The mind cannot keep up with Derzhavin.[70]
>
> Such poetic imagery! But [...] [here—*YT*] there are two pictures that, being both skillfully wrought, cannot [...] follow on one another's heels [...] Every [image—*YT*] is very *fine* on its own, but taken together they

67 Nikolai Gogol, *Selected Passages from Correspondence with Friends* [Vybrannye mesta iz perepiski s druz'iami], trans. Jesse Zeldin (Vanderbilt University Press, 1969), 205–206 (translation slightly modified).

68 Tynianov refers to the "proximity of unequally lofty words" in his characterization of Vladimir Mayakovsky[N] in "Interlude" (185–90). See also "On Mayakovsky" (293).

69 "Amphion" (July 1815), 100—*YT*.

70 Ibid., 98–99—*YT*. The poem in question is most likely "On Satisfaction" [O udovol'stvii] (1808).

> hinder one another.[71]

This is perfectly in line with Derzhavin's own stance on poetics: "That which is lively is not also exalted; and that which is exalted is not also lively. And thus it follows that lyrical exaltation consists in the rapid soaring of thoughts, the uninterrupted representation of a multitude of brilliant pictures and feelings, expressed in language that is loud, grandiose, and florid; this fills one with rapture and amazement" [7:537].

The intonational structure of Derzhavin's odes is too complex a topic to cover here; there is no doubt, however, that Derzhavin built on and refined Lomonosov's intonational devices, and not just in the canonical ten-line stanza. By varying the odic stanza, he applied the stanzaic practices of the Lomonosovian canon to other stanzaic forms as well (for example, he applied the fluctuating mode to the eight-line stanza of the aAaA + bBbB type); because of the intonational foregrounding of the seventh and final lines of the canonical stanza, Derzhavin used them for aphorisms and maxims. At the same time, he varied the stanza in terms of intonation; for instance, he frequently used the stanza form aAaA + b, where a four-line stanza that is regular and metrically complete (though usually not syntactically complete) is followed by an unrhymed line:[72]

Седящ, увенчан осокою,	Seated, crowned with sedge,
В тени развесистых древес,	In shade of trees outspread,
На урну облегшись рукою,	My arm at rest on an urn's ledge,
Являющий лицо небес	Showing its face to heaven's stead
Прекрасный вижу я источник.	I behold a marvelous spring.
(«*Ключ*») [1:48]	("*The Fount*")

The intonational effect here is twofold: 1) stanzaic enjambment after the syntactically incomplete fourth line, and 2) the unusually forceful foregrounding of the final line.

Derzhavin worked out a theory (and practice) of "sound imitation" vis-

---

71 Ibid., 107—*YT*.

72 Derzhavin's foregrounding of the last line here undoubtedly shows the influence of classical stanzaic forms (which, in a number of instances, he transferred unchanged into his own work)—*YT*.

à-vis the sound organization of the line. For Derzhavin, the "onomatopoeic poem" was an ideal. And although Derzhavin understood sound imitation as something subordinate to the general requirement of "eloquence," he preferred Lomonosov's "magnificence and loud language."

Derzhavin was well aware of the difference between a line organized *intonationally,* and a *melodious* line. The ode, which is built around intonation, is a long way from the "song," which is built around melody.[73]

Curiously, Derzhavin vacillated when it came to delimiting the themes of these two genres. For him, the defining characteristics of the genres are, on the one hand, their contrasting frameworks of plot and semantics, and, on the other, their contrasting approaches to intonation and melody:

> The ode and the song have so much in common that each has the right to call itself by the other's name; however, it is still possible to point out certain differences between them, both in their internal and external organization. In terms of internal organization, the song always moves in a single unwavering direction, while the ode meanders in sinuous fashion through marginal and secondary ideas. The song explores only one passion, whatever it may be, while the ode flits to others as well [...] The song will sometimes sustain a single feeling for a long time, in order, through such prolongation, to impress it all the more firmly on the memory; whereas the ode uses variety to bring the mind into raptures and is quickly forgotten. As much as it can, the song eschews pictures and lofty oratory, while the ode eagerly adorns itself with them [...] The song has only one tune, or melody, with regard to the uniform organization of its couplets and the measure of the lines; it thus lends itself easily to being learned by heart, its voice revived in the memory. The ode, meanwhile, with its unequal stanzas and expression equally powerful in application to its various subjects, is obliged to use different harmonies and does not easily lend itself to being learned by heart. [7:609–10]

Derzhavin contrasts the ode's system of inexact rhymes to the exact rhymes of the "song"; the ode's "blemishes" to the "song's" immaculate style; the ode's "Slavonic language" to the "clarity and artificial simplicity of the song."

73 The "song" is a poetic genre of the late eighteenth to early nineteenth century, which often features a sentimental theme (intended to arouse emotion) and elements of musical form (such as a refrain or discernible melody).

He illustrates this song type with a "pastoral song" [7:610].

Derzhavin's illustration contradicts his own suggestions about the metrical nature of the "song": the new genre was only just making itself felt, but his example emphasized the melodic aspect of this form that was now vying with the ode. Meanwhile, his suggestions regarding the "sole passion," the single emotional tone that ought to run through the entire poem (unlike the ode's "mixing of passions"), and which proves here to be "in a minor key," as well as the theme of the example he provides—all these elements begin to point toward the thematic restrictedness of the *elegy*.

These elements, which left traces in the transitional genres of the "romance"[T] and the "song," would combine with the descendants of the monumental elegy to create a new "romance" form of the elegy.[74]

5

The turn to melodic forms, along with a decline in declamatory and oratorical ones (those organized around intonation) was a typical move. In contrast to the spoken word and the verbal image, there was now musicality, which subordinated all other features of the poem to itself; here, this sharp-edged language, more complex in its sound and meaning, had to be replaced by a smoother, simplified version ("artificial simplicity"). Accordingly, the intonational system that was manifest in and fundamental to the ode was completely subordinated to the melody of the verse ("reflected" melody, in Boris Eikhenbaum's formulation);[75] it ceased to exist as an organizing principle. Derzhavin responded to this by forbidding the use of enjambment in "songs," for packing too great an intonational punch and thereby weakening the melody: "Every line of a song should contain a complete thought and a conclusive period; while in the ode, a thought will often dart into both the neighboring lines and on into the following stanzas as well" [7:609].

The Lomonosovian impulse temporarily reached its limits in Derzhavin. Accordingly, small forms became a decisive factor; they became especially conspicuous once the grandiose ones had run their course. These "minutiae" sprang from extra-literary series—from epistolary forms (which were bound up with

74 See also note 87.

75 Eikhenbaum used the term "reflected" for a melody "mechanically generated by rhythm" while remaining firmly linked to certain meters (the context was a discussion of the "monotony" of ternary meters—see B[oris] Eikhenbaum, *On Poetry* [O poezii], 413 [...]—*ET*.

salon culture): letters were suddenly peppered with "quatrains." The cultivation of *bouts-rimés* and charades (even more bound up with salon culture) reflected a newfound interest in individual words, rather than large verbal masses. Words were "conjoined" through their closest material and lexical series. As a result, the associations that arose from words placed next to each other came to bear only secondary significance, and attention was focused instead on individual words. This can be seen in the detailed analysis of the lexical coloring of two words—"tweety-bird" [*pichuzhechka*] and "young fellow" [*paren'*]—which Karamzin[N] provided in a letter to Dmitriev.[76]

Karamzin liked to accentuate intonationally distinct words by inserting a conversational pause before the main parts of a sentence. He would mark the pause with an ellipsis, which was meant to suggest a kind of hesitation in choosing the right word, or temporarily forgetting it. He used the same device in his poetry; thus, conversational pauses foregrounding the words that followed them were brought into poetry.

The epistolary style of that period was marked by wordplay and the cultivation of puns, which also highlighted the importance of the individual word. At the same time, Zhukovsky[N]—first in his letters and then in his poems as well—used words that he set off from verbal masses by isolating them graphically, using italics. This turned them into personified allegorical symbols: *remembrance, yesterday, tomorrow, over there.* The elegy—with its songlike functions provided by the fading word and intonations subordinated to melody—would go through yet another phase of semantic purification: Zhukovsky's correspondence in verse with Batyushkov and Vyazemsky[N] (1814).[77] Alongside the elegy, the light *epistle* had risen in the ranks: this genre essentially existed to justify the introduction of *conversational* intonations into poetry. The ode fell so far out of favor that works which were thematically quite close to it were deliberately called either "songs" or "epistles." Karamzin wrote to Dmitriev about his

76 Letter of 22 June 1793.—N. M. Karamzin, *The Letters of N. M. Karamzin to I. I. Dmitriev* [*Pis'ma N. M. Karamzina k I.I. Dmitrievu*] (St. Petersburg: Tip. Imperatorskoi Akademii nauk, 1866), 39—*ET.*

77 Tynianov refers to Vasily Zhukovsky's "To Areopagus," in which he responds to criticisms of his epistle "To Emperor Alexander" made by Batyushkov in a letter to A. Turgenev in December 1814, as well as two epistles written by Zhukovsky to Vyazemsky and V. L. Pushkin (V. A Zhukovskii, *Sobranie sochinenii v chetyrekh tomakh* [Moscow/Leningrad: Gos. izd-vo khud. literatury, 1959–1960], 1:245–249). In one of them ("In this post all is in verse …"), Zhukovsky analyzes another one of his epistles written to the same addressees—"My friends, woe to the poet … ", which Tynianov considered to be a source for Lermontov's [famous poem] "Death of the Poet" […] (ibid., 1:221–224, 224–229)—*ET.*

"non-ode," which he called *a song*; Zhukovsky wrote an "epistle" to Emperor Alexander I (1814). The decline of the oratorical orientation caused the spoken aspect of poetry to go altogether dim. The romance, a popular form with both linguistic and musical elements,[78] quickly became a purely musical phenomenon; in poetry it persisted only as a narrow genre, or in the more songlike forms of the elegy. Declamation was meanwhile subordinated to other principles. One of the elder Karamzinists, M. N. Muravyov,[N] could already write the following:

> The Athenian people had such refined hearing that a single word pronounced incorrectly by a speaker would arouse general indignation against him. One can tell from how someone reads whether he understands what he is reading. There are numerous voices which nature itself makes available for the communication of our thoughts and states of mind. We affirm in one way, doubt in another. The question differs from the answer. All of our feelings—happiness, sorrow, hope, fear, desire, envy, love of mankind—have their own particular language. Discourses devoid of passion should be read simply, without excitement; but *the voice should always be coextensive with the meaning*. One should not read using only language, but thought and attention as well. The voice should be pleasant to hear, and should shift in accordance with the reason. [...] And those [words—*YT*] should not be separated that are united by a single meaning.[79]

One need only compare this injunction to accentuate semantic divisions to Aksakov's[N] "senseless" style of declamation (which had so thrilled Derzhavin), in order to fully appreciate the incompatibility of the two orientations.[80]

The movement that fostered the development of the elegy, the didactic and friendly epistle, and small forms such as the rondo, charade, etc., is generally known as "sentimentalism,"[T] and this term invariably covers both the movement's themes and its emotional coloring. But this fails to account for the fact that the evolution of themes was a subordinate rather than an independent

---

78 See Karamzin's 1791 letter to Dmitriev: "What's 'Sylphida' to you? If I'm not mistaken, in Petersburg we used to *sing* it like this:

Плавай, Сильфида, в весеннем эфире!	Cleave the vernal ether, Sylphida!

Karamzin, *Letters*, 24—*YT*.

79 M. N. Muravyov, "On Declamation" [O deklamatsi*i*], *Works* [Sochineniia], vol. 2 (Saint Petersburg: Tip. Imp. Akademii nauk, 1847), 262—*YT*.

80 S. T. Aksakov, "My Acquaintance with Derzhavin" [Znakomstvo s Derzhavinym], *Complete Works* [Polnoe sobranie sochinenii], vol. 3 (St. Petersburg: Kopeika, 1913), 503—*YT*.

factor.

The entire orientation of poetic language was changing, and the result was a particular thematic framework. Various themes proved to be either more or less functionally in line with this framework, and either became part of the overall orientation or fell away.

Derzhavin, who grasped perfectly well the differences and points of contention between the two opposing orientations, refused to make a clear distinction between them on the basis of their themes: "The specialists claim that it is difficult to draw a differentiating line between the song and the ode. But if this difference even exists, it can only be one that proceeds gradually. Parsing these various gradations among works of literature requires an altogether keen mind and highly refined sensibility, in order to specify precisely how they are different. The ode and the song have so much in common that each has the right to call itself by the other's name [...]" [7:609].

Much as the erotic themes in Batyushkov's poetry would later be based on his work on poetic language rather than his worldview (see his essay "On the Influence of Light Verse on Language"), the themes associated with "sentimentalism" simply proved to be the material best suited to this new orientation of the poetic word. They were suited to "personal" (conversational and songlike) intonations, which revived the poetic word as a living form of address, as well as the interrelations of this poetic word with ordinary speech series, and, further still, extra-literary series (the salon). This was, in fact, the task of literature at that time, given the obsolescence of the odic, oratorical orientation, which had been interrelated with solemn recitation and, further still, with the extra-literary series of official ceremonies. We tend to equate sentimentalism with "tearful effusiveness" on the basis of resultative and secondary phenomena. This is as unfair as equating "Symbolism" with "mysticism."

Cf. the following, strongly representative statement by Karamzin, from the preface to the second book of "The Aonides" (1797):

> I will make so bold as to point out only two of the chief defects of our youthful muses: excessive grandiloquence, thundering language when it isn't needed, and frequent *counterfeit tearfulness.* (Not to mention their careless rhymes, although irreproachable poetry demands that rhymes be exact.) Poetry is based not on overwrought descriptions of frightening scenes from nature, but on the vivacity of thoughts and feelings. If the poet does not write about what truly absorbs his soul; if he is not the slave, but the tyrant of his own imagination, forcing it to chase after

> unfamiliar and *remote* ideas that are alien to his nature; if he does not describe *objects that are close to him* and that take hold of his imagination spontaneously [...] then his works will always lack vitality, truthfulness, and that harmoniousness of parts which makes up a whole [...] The young pupil of the muses would do better to depict in his poems the first impressions of love, friendship, and the delicate charms of nature, rather than the destruction of the world, the conflagration of nature, and other things of this sort. [...] *Nor is it fitting* to talk incessantly *of tears*, finding various epithets for them, calling them gleaming or diamond-like; this is a very unreliable way *to stir the emotions*. It is better to find a striking way to describe the reasons behind them; to signify sorrow *not just by means of general features*, which are too ordinary to have a powerful effect on the reader's heart, but *by means of particular features*, those that *relate directly to the character and personal life of the poet*. It is these features, these *details* and this *personality*, so to speak, that convince us of the truth of the descriptions—and we are often deceived, but such deception is the triumph of art.[81]

It is this "personal quality" of the tone—the new orientation of literature in the age of Karamzin—that selected its own themes and even aggressively promoted them; but the "minor key" and "tearfulness" [of sentimentalism] were here the resultative, rather than the originary, attributes of the movement.

But the ode, at least as a tendency if not a genre, did not die out entirely. Relegated to a latent, underground existence, disgraced, it resurfaced in the revolt of the Archaists, first the elder ones (Shishkov), and then the younger ones (Katenin,[N] Griboedov,[N] Küchelbecker[N]).[82] The stated goal of the "Colloquy of Lovers of the Russian Word" was "to take pains over distinct pronunciation, clear articulation [...] over every alteration of the voice that can make a fine utterance even more agreeable and intelligible; which in turn is of great benefit to both language and poetry, or literature in general."[83] Shishkov presented a

81 Karamzin, "The Aonides, or A Collection of Diverse Poems" [Aonidy, ili sobranie raznykh stikhotvorenii (Moscow, 1797)], book 2, books 5–11—*ET*.

82 Tynianov closes the article with an outline of the conception he would develop fully in the long article "Pushkin and the Archaists", in *Pushkin and His Contemporaries* [Pushkin i ego sovremenniki] (Moscow: Nauka, 1968), 23–121. Cf. contemporary scholarship on literary tradition by Shklovsky and Eikhenbaum—*ET*.

83 "Reading in the Colloquy of Lovers of the Russian Word" [Chtenie v Besede liubitelei russkogo slova], Reading 1 (St. Petersburg, 1811), 3—*ET*.

theoretical argument for poetry as "sound imitation"; while the semantic investigations of the Arzamas Society typically dealt with the associations suggested by individual words, Shishkov's etymologies argued for the unexpected affinity of words sharing similar phonic elements.[84] A typical example of someone who straddled the two periods is Nikolai Gnedich, who united his poetic vocation with that of the public speaker; he was known as a skilled appraiser of poetry, and also for translating poems into the realm of declamation.

The middle of the 1820s was marked by this struggle over the ode; it was a turning point for the development of lyric poetry, with the epistle and elegy having run their course. This was the context for the experiments and theoretical essays of Griboedov and Küchelbecker.

The ode persisted in another side branch of lyric poetry as well: the poetry of Stepan Shevyryov and Fyodor Tyutchev,[N] where we see a complex synthesis of the oratorical principle with the melodic achievements of the elegy (cf. the convergence of Lomonosov and Italian influences in the poetry of Semyon Rayich[N]), as well as an extra-literary form, the dilettantish fragment (in Tyutchev).[85]

Thus, the struggle for genre was, in essence, a struggle for the future direction of the poetic word, for its orientation.[86] This struggle was complex; sometimes the greatest achievements resulted from using the methods of rival schools. But the struggle itself was, in essence, a struggle for the function of poetic language, for its orientation and its interrelations with literature and with various verbal and extra-literary series.

---

84 Though it must be said that Shishkov's etymologies were perfectly in line with the newer movement, with its keen interest in semantic units and the semantics of individual words, rather than large semantic groupings ("the conjoining of ideas")—*YT*. The Arzamas Society (1815–1818) was an exclusive group of poets that followed Karamzin's orientation toward clarity and neoclassical models, and was explicitly opposed to the Archaist group. Arzamas poets included Pushkin, Batyushkov, and Zhukovsky, among others.

85 For more on Tyutchev, see "Tyutchev and Heine" (64–76) and "On Parody" 294–328). For Rayich, see "Tyutchev and Heine" (75).

86 In our own time, this can be compared to an analogous battle between genres: Mayakovsky's new "satiric ode" and Esenin's[N] new (romance-type) "elegy." The battle between these two genres is, for all intents and purposes, the same old battle for the orientation of poetic language—*YT* (note appended to this article in 1928). For more on Mayakovsky, Esenin, and Tynianov's ideas in application to contemporary (1920s) poetry, see "Interlude".

On the Composition of *Eugene Onegin* (1921–22)[1]

1

All attempts to divide prose and poetry according to sound are thwarted by the facts, which contradict the usual notion that verse is organized around sound and prose is not.[2] On the one hand, we have the existence of *vers libre* and *freie Rhythmen* with their unlimited freedom of prosody, and on the other we have the rhythmically and phonically organized prose of writers like Gogol[N] and Andrei Bely,[N] or in Germany, Heine[N] and Nietzsche.[3] These phenomena reveal the concept of the sonic organization of poetry and prose to be extraordinarily tenuous; a clear dividing line between the two is absent. At the same time, these phenomena also point to the astonishing stability of, and clear boundary between, the categories of poetry and prose. No matter

1 First published in Dmitrii Likhachev, ed., *Pamiatniki kul'tury. Novye otkrytiia. Ezhegodnik. 1974* (Moscow, 1975; dated to 1921–1922 by Tynianov. Translation from Iurii Tynianov, "O kompozitsii 'Evgeniia Onegina'," *PILK*, 52–77. Selected notes to this publication by A. P. Chudakov [*AC*], 415–420. Additional notes by Yuri Tynianov [*YT*] and the translators [unmarked].

Chudakov notes that this article should by rights be read in tandem with Tynianov's 1924 monograph *Problems of Verse Language* [Problemy poeticheskogo iazyka, henceforth *PVL*]. The article can be read as an application of "general premises" to the analysis of a specific work. In *PVL*, Tynianov emphasized both the mobility of the border between verse and prose, and the stability—even indestructibility—of these two types of literary speech (as well as the corresponding opposition present in literary consciousness); although he was also interested in the possibility of introducing the elements of one series into another.

2 Tynianov tends to use the words *stikh* (verse line, line of poetry), *stikhi* (verse/verses or poem/poems) rather than the word "poetry" [*poeziia*] or "single poem" [*stikhotvorenie*]. The concepts of "verse" and "poetry" are, however, much closer in Russian than in English, where the former sounds both archaic and technical (used to talk specifically about versification), and the latter is perhaps less marked as a foreign (Latinate) borrowing. At the same time, Tynianov's preference for *stikh* reflects his aim of specificity and precision: sometimes he really does want "verse" to be a technical term. For this reason we have chosen to vary the terms in English, referring to "poetry" and "poems" when Tynianov speaks more generally, and giving "verse" in more technical constructions.

3 For more on these authors, see "Dostoyevsky and Gogol: Toward a Theory of Parody" (27–63) and "Tyutchev and Heine" (64–76).

how rhythmically and sonically organized prose might become, it is still not perceived as verse;[4] and for its part, no matter how much a poem may sound like prose, the claim that *vers libre* is equivalent to prose is nothing more than literary polemics.

At this point we should note the following: from the very beginning of modern Russian literature, the sonic features of literary prose have been organized with the same care that is accorded to verse. In Lomonosov's[N] work, prose developed under the influence of the theory of rhetoric, in line with the rules of oratorical rhythm and euphony; and Lomonosov's rhetoric, a crucial normative-theoretical factor in the development of literature, relates to prose as much as it does to poetry. But the sonic peculiarities of Lomonosov's and Karamzin's prose that stood out for their contemporaries become less conspicuous over time.[5] Take the endings of certain rhythmic sections in their prose (clausulas): we are more likely to treat these as syntactic-semantic than as sound phenomena, and we have a hard time reckoning with instances of euphony in their prose.[6]

Meanwhile, different elements of language in poetry become less conspicuous over time; customary groupings of words and the connections between individual words become less semantically conspicuous, while remaining associatively connected mostly through sound (the ossification of epithets).

We must not rush to the conclusion that prose and verse are distinguished by the fact that, in verse, the word as an external sign plays the vital role, while in prose that vital role is played by meaning.

This is confirmed by a phenomenon we can call the *semantic threshold*. The *exclusive* orientation toward immanent sound in poetry (*zaum*[T] language, *Zungenrede* [German: speaking in tongues])[7] brings about an extreme tension in the quest for meaning, and thus emphasizes the semantic element of

---

4 The very genres of *petites poèmes en prose* (Baudelaire) and "poems in prose" (Turgenev[N] and many others) are founded on the absolute dividing line between verse and prose; certain reactions to the verse form in this genre only emphasize its belonging to prose—*YT*.

5 For more on these authors, see "On Literary Fact" (157; 165–168) and "The Ode as an Oratorical Genre" (109–113).

6 This is evidently also typical of our relationship to Karamzin's adjectival inversions, which were initially explained by their sonic conspicuousness, but over time came to be felt exclusively in their syntactic-semantic sense. Here we can recall Shevyryov's curious opinion that the folk song, with its dactylic endings, had influenced Karamzin's prose, encouraging its dactylic clausulas (and deforming his syntax as a result). See *The Muscovite* [Moskvitianin] (1842), part 2, no. 3, 160–162—*YT*.

7 For more on *zaum*, see "Interlude" (191–196) and "On Khlebnikov" (217–229).

language. On the other hand, prose's utter disregard for sound can give rise to sound phenomena (special coincidences of sounds, etc.) that pull the center of gravity onto *themselves*.

And while there is no doubt about the sonic organization of prose, or the way it is influenced by poetry, there is also the fact that, for one of the Russian poetic traditions, the semantic principle of poetic language was not just occasionally present, but actually canonical. The theory of the ode for Lomonosov and Derzhavin[N] endowed poetic language with the emotionally persuasive function of oratorical speech; poetry is thus constructed according to the aural, pronunciation-based aspect of language. Words enter into an emotional, sonic relationship; tropes constitute the "conjoining of *distant* ideas," produced through a chain of emotional associations (based on oratory's aim to be unexpected and awe-inspiring), rather than a chain of logical associations based on the primary meaning of words.[8] But this theory of language was opposed by the hostile principles of a younger branch, which was in open conflict with the older odic school. This was the Russian *poesie fugitive* [French: light poetry—*YT*] of Bogdanovich, Karamzin,[N] M. N. Muravyov,[N] and Batyushkov,[N] in which the semantic side of the word began to play an important role. The theory of logically clear language directly opposed that of emotionally persuasive poetic language; the former favored great clarity in words, rather than the distortion of their semantic line. As a consequence, words would enter into relationships not because of their sound or emotional coloring, but rather according to their basic, usual (dictionary) points of meaning. This new theory of poetic language approaches a theory of prosaic language; poetry begins to learn from prose.

Regarding Karamzin's poems, Vyazemsky[N] wrote: "One might think that he was adhering to the well-known phrase: '*C'est beau comme de la prose* [French, "as beautiful as prose"—*YT*].' He demanded that everything be said economically and with literal precision. He allowed space for invention and feeling, but not expression."[9] And in 1817 Batyushkov[N] wrote in a similar vein:

---

8 Thus the semantic line of words proves to be a sort of zigzag, and Lomonosov translates the term *trope* as "aversion" [*otvrashchenie*]; cf. the Shishkov[N] group's use of the related term "perversion" [*izvrashchenie*]—*YT*. For more on these terms and concepts, see "The Ode as an Oratorical Genre" (91).

9 P. A. Vyazemsky, *Complete Works* [Polnoe sobranie sochinenii], vol. 7 (St. Petersburg: Izd. grafa S.D. Sheremet'eva, 1882), 149—*YT*.

> In order to write well in verse—of whatever variety—to write diversely, with a strong and pleasant turn of phrase, with original thoughts, with feeling, one should write a great deal in prose, but not for the public; simply write for oneself. I myself have often found that this method worked well for me; sooner or later, that which I had written in prose proved useful. Alfieri said that "[prose] provides the nourishment for poetry," if my memory serves me right.[10]

Pushkin[N] wrote prose plans and programs for his poems; in this case, prose plainly provided the nourishment for poetry. And, as if in answer to Batyushkov, the "lover of wisdom" Ivan Kireevsky—who was close to the older, Archaist[N] tradition of "high-style" (emotionally persuasive) poetry—wrote the following:

> Do you know why you still haven't written anything? Because you don't write verse. If you were to write verse, then you would love to express even aimless thoughts, and every well-spoken word would have for you the value of a well-formed thought, and this is necessary for a writer with soul. With poetry, one only writes when it cheers one to do so, but writing is never cheering for the person who does not see the unique beauty in elegant expression for its own sake, distinct from its object. Thus: if you want to be a good prose writer, then write poems.[11]

In this way, prose for Batyushkov and poetry for Kireevsky serve as sources of new meaning, the means to bring about some kind of semantic shift[T] [*sdvig*] within prose and poetry.[12] Evidently, what distinguishes prose from poetry is not any innate quality of sound, or the idea that verse is oriented toward sound and prose toward meaning. Instead, what distinguishes them is the way these elements influence one another: how sound in prose is deformed by semantics (the orientation toward semantics), and how the meaning of words is deformed by verse.[13]

---

10 K. N. Batiushkov, *Sochineniia* (St. Petersburg: Tip. B.S. Balasheva, 1885–87), 2:331–332—*YT*.

11 I. V. Kireevsky, *Complete Works* [Polnoe sobranie sochinenii], vol. 1. (Moscow: V tip. P. Bakhmeteva, 1861), 15 (letter to Koshelev, 1828)—*YT*. Ivan Kireyevsky (1806–1856) was a writer and Slavophile, member of the "Lovers of Wisdom" group (the name, *liubomudry*, is a Russian calque of the Greek word "philosophers").

12 For more on "shift," see "On Literary Evolution" (269–281).

13 An investigation of the semantic deformation of the word by verse is the subject of a separate study by the author, *PVL*. In what follows, partial *proof* of the above claims will be found

The deformation of sound through meaning is the constructive principle of prose; the deformation of meaning through sound is the constructive principle of poetry. Partial changes in the interrelation of these two elements are a driving force in both poetry and prose.

If sounds proper to poetry are inserted into a prose construction, these sounds will be deformed by their orientation toward meaning; if verbal masses combined according to their semantic principle are then placed in a poetic construction, then that principle will inevitably be deformed by the principle of sound.

This means that prose and poetry are closed semantic categories; meaning in prose is always distinct from meaning in poetry; this ties into the fact that the syntax, and even the lexicon, of poetry and prose are essentially different.

But when prose principles of construction are introduced into poetry (just as when poetic principles are introduced into prose), the relation between the deforming and deformed factors changes somewhat, although the closed semantic series of poetry and prose are not violated. This is how prose is enriched with new meaning through poetry, and poetry enriched with new meaning through prose (cf. Ivan Kireevsky's letter cited earlier).

In this way, the sound and meaning of language in prose and in poetry are not equal in value: studying only semantics or only sound in poetry and prose (something perhaps unavoidable when first separating out these materials, and pedagogically useful) essentially dismembers elements that are interdependent and at the same time complex in their significance. When we study sound in prose, we should bear in mind that it is deformed by semantics; when we talk about verse semantics, we must remember that we are dealing with deformed meaning. This comes across most clearly in the study of poetic styles that are rich in prose elements, and prose styles that have obviously incorporated poetic devices. Having entered a verse construction, prosaic ingredients become elements of meter, instrumentation, etc., and become subordinate to its principle—that of deformation of meaning through sound. When prose elements enter into sonic relationships with neighboring words, verse lines, etc., their sounds are refreshed to a surprising degree; as a result words and phrases that are entirely bland and indistinguishable in prose become highly

---

in *examples* from *Eugene Onegin*; cf. particularly: the metrification of words; rhyme and instrumentation as semantic factors; the origin and role of Gallicisms in prose and [their] deformation in verse—*YT* (emphasis *YT*). Also see Tynianov's note on his use of the term "deformation" (versus "transformation") in "Literary Fact" numbering at the end.

conspicuous semantic elements in poetry.[14] Similarly, the introduction of rhymes, etc. into prose—thanks to semantic anticipation—elevates the sonic conspicuousness of these elements; thus rhymes that sound hackneyed in poetry will not sound that way in prose. In this way, prose and poetry mutually enrich one another.[15]

But as soon as a prose element introduced into a poetic series is wholly absorbed by it, it begins to be deformed through sound *in the same way* as the elements of poetic speech. The refreshment of meaning disappears; the prose element moves entirely into the poetic series and becomes an element of poetic speech. At the other end of things, some verse sounds (certain rhythms) can merge with the sound composition of prose, becoming unremarkable in their sound and losing their sonic freshness. It follows that the historical presentation of the problem is particularly important.

Thus, it would be a mistake to treat the semantic elements of poetic speech in the same way that we treat the semantic elements of prosaic speech. The *meaning* of poetry is different from the *meaning* of prose. This mistake occurs most frequently when a form specific to prose (like the novel), which is fused with the constructive principle of prose, is introduced into verse. These semantic elements are then immediately subject to deformation by verse.

The main semantic unit of the prose novel is the *protagonist*—a set of heterogeneous dynamic elements united under a single external sign. But over the course of a *verse* novel these elements are deformed; the external sign acquires a different coloring in poetry that it would in prose. For this reason, the protagonist of a verse novel is not the protagonist of that same novel transposed into prose. When we characterize the protagonist as the main semantic unit, we should bear in mind the unique deformation which this unit underwent when it took root in verse. A leading example of this kind of verse novel is *Eugene Onegin*; and all of the novel's protagonists were subjected to this deformation.

---

14 This depends furthermore on the fact that a *prose element* in poetry is felt precisely *as a prose element,* that is, is associated simultaneously with two series—the prosaic and the poetic—*YT*.

15 Evidence of the lengths to which such enrichments can go without turning prose into poetry and poetry into prose (as long as the constructive principle is observed) can be found in phenomena like *vers libre,* at one end of the spectrum, and "poetry in prose," on the other (I have already mentioned the latter). Meanwhile, the division into verse lines is often merely an indicator of the verse-like nature of speech, its constructive principle, while the actual functions (related to physical movement) of this division are reduced to a minimum—*YT*.

2

Whenever there was talk of the literary forms in which verse was evidently meant to play a secondary, auxiliary role—for instance, in drama—Pushkin always emphasized the primacy of the verbal and poetic aspect. He wrote of Lobanov's translation of [Racine's] "Phèdre":

> Speaking of horrors—I read Lobanov's "Phèdre"—I wanted to write a critique of it, not for Lobanov's sake, but for the marquis Racine—I couldn't bring myself to write it. And where you are, everybody's talking about it, and your journalists are calling it the greatest-ever translation of Mr. Racine's famous tragedy! *Voulez-vous découvrir la trace de ses pas* [French: Would you like to discover his footprints—*YT*]—are you hoping to find
>
> "Theseus's hot footprint or dark pathways"—
>
> got the goddamn rhyme! and the whole thing's translated like that! But what else keeps Ivan Ivanovich Racine together but verses filled with meaning, precision, and harmony! The plan and characters of "Phèdre" are the height of stupidity and null in terms of invention—Theseus is nothing more than one of Molière's cuckolds; Hippolyte, *le superbe, le fier Hippolite—et même un peu farouche* [Even proud, arrogant Hippolyte is a little unhinged—*YT*], Hippolyte, the cruel Scythian [...] is nothing more than a well-mannered little boy, polite, and respectful
>
> "—*D'un mensonge si noir* ..." etc. ["Such a black lie"—*YT*]
>
> when you've read this much-vaunted tirade you'll be quite convinced that Racine had no idea how to create a tragic character. Compare this to the speech of the young lover in Byron's *Parisina* and you'll see the difference between minds. But Theramenes—the abbot and pimp—*Vous-même ou seriez vous* [Where would you yourselves be—*YT*], etc... .—now that's the depths of stupidity![16]

We have no reason to take this as a negative review; through Racine, Pushkin is upholding the law that Racine himself established, and which should condition judgment of his work—the *category* that Racine was writing in (not genre so much as the predominance of a certain aspect of form). For Racine, this predominating element was style, and more narrowly—verse. In just the same way,

---

16 Letter to L. S. Pushkin, January-February 1824—*YT*. Alexander Pushkin, *Collected Works* [Sobranie sochinenii v 10–i tomakh] (Moscow: GIKhL, 1959–1962), 9:89–90. Subsequent quotations from this collection will be given in the text in the format vol. no: page no(s).

Pushkin insists on the right to have a "feeble plan" and "lack of events" in his long poem:

> Byron was not particularly concerned with the plans of his works, or he may not have thought about them at all: a couple of loosely connected scenes was all he needed for this abyss of thoughts, feelings, and pictures. [...] What would we think of a writer who chose to take only the plan of "The Corsair"—worthy of an absurd Spanish tale—and on the basis of this childish plan composed a dramatic trilogy, replacing Byron's charming and profound poetry with pompous and hideous prose, worthy of our [Russian] imitators of dear departed Kotzebue? [17] [...] One has to ask: what impressed him so much in Byron's poem—could it really have been the plan? *O miratores*! [...][18] [6:280]

Thus "a couple of loosely connected scenes," "a plan worthy of *an absurd tale*" are more than sufficient for "charming and profound *poetry*." Even more decisive was Pushkin's review of Baratynsky's[N] "Eda": "Reread his "Eda" (which our critics found *insipid,* for they, like children, require a poem to have plenty of events) [...]" [6:370].[19]

And this is not merely a critic's judgment; it harks back to a practical struggle. Pushkin is eager to take on critics' reproaches regarding "characters" who had been rendered less than methodically, colorless "protagonists," and the unfinished quality of the plan.[20]

---

17 August von Kotzebue (1761–1819) was a Prussian playwright whose work was very popular in its time. He was particularly well known in Russia, having spent some years there, alternately in exile and as an imperial favorite, directing plays in St. Petersburg.

18 Pushkin, "On Olin's Tragedy 'The Corsair'" [O tragedii V. N. Olina "Korser"] (1827)—*YT*. The closing citation paraphrases an exhortation in Horace's *Epistles* (1:19), "Oh imitators [you servile herd]."

19 "Baratynsky" [Baratynskii] (1830)—*YT*. Note that "Eda" is the name of Baratynsky's heroine in this poem; despite the tie with Scandinavia, this should not be confused with the "Edda," the famous Icelandic saga.

20 Cf. Pushkin on "The Prisoner of the Caucasus": "The character of the Prisoner is unsuccessful" (letter to V. P. Gorchakov, October-November 1822) [9:55]; "The simplicity of the plan comes close to poverty of invention; the description of Circassian mores, which is the most tolerable episode in the whole poem, is not connected with any events and is nothing other than a geographical article or traveler's report" (letter to N. I. Gnedich, 29 April 1822) [9:39]. On "The Robber Brothers" [Razboiniki]: "Your criticism of my 'Robbers' is unfair; as far as the plot is concerned, *c'est un tour de force,* but this is no praise, quite the contrary; but as far as style is concerned, I've never written anything better" (letter to P. A. Vyazemsky,

Evidently, these poems' center of gravity lay elsewhere; evidently, for Pushkin the *verse* plan and *verse* protagonist were something not subject to the same demands that could be made of the plan and protagonist of a tale or novel.

In *Eugene Onegin*, the *unfinished quality* of the plan and "characters" stops being a feature justified by and inherent to the verse form, and itself becomes an element of the composition. We would be mistaken to assume that this "incompleteness" was something that Pushkin, too, was attempting to excuse or justify; that the indication of omitted lines and verses really was dictated by his desire not to interrupt the *coherence* of the novel; that Pushkin sensed that the plan was incomplete and sought to *finish* his novel. In the preface to *Onegin*'s first chapter (written when *three* chapters were already finished), Pushkin talks about the "deficiency of the plan" half-ironically: "Farsighted critics will note, of course, the deficiency of the plan. Everyone is free to judge the plan of the whole novel, having read its first chapter" [4:451]. The extent to which this careful remark about the "whole novel" was meant to be taken seriously becomes clear when we compare the preface with the final stanza of the first chapter:

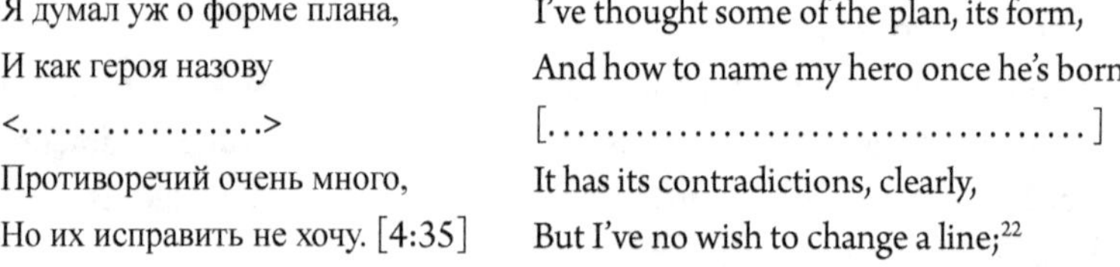

Я думал уж о форме плана,	I've thought some of the plan, its form,
И как героя назову	And how to name my hero once he's born
<................>	[......................................]
Противоречий очень много,	It has its contradictions, clearly,
Но их исправить не хочу. [4:35]	But I've no wish to change a line;[22]

This statement about the form of the plan is consistent with similar digressions that make the subject of the novel the novel itself (from this point of view, *Eugene Onegin* is not a novel, but a novel of a novel). The line containing the phrase "The hero's named," following multiple mentions of the protagonist's name, leads ironically to the line "It has its contradictions, clearly." The same game of contradictions can be seen in the last stanza of chapter seven:

---

14 October 1823) [9:73]. On "The Fountain of Bakhchisaray": "I'm glad my 'Fountain' is causing a fuss. The inadequacy of the plan isn't my fault. I faithfully transposed into verse the tale of a young woman" (letter to A. A. Bestuzhev, 8 February 1824) [9:91]—*YT*.

21 English translation from Alexander Pushkin, *Eugene Onegin: A Novel in Verse*, trans. James E. Falen (Oxford: Oxford University Press, 1990), 31 (translation modified). Subsequent references to this edition will give only the page number.

Но здесь с победою поздравим	But here let's honor with affection
Татьяну милую мою,	My Tanya's conquest taking wing,
И в сторону свой путь направим.	*And steer for now a new direction,*
Чтоб не забыть о ком пою ... [4:154]	*Lest I forget of whom I sing* ... (192) [emphasis *YT*]

Thus it is easy to *forget* about the protagonist, and returning to him is yet another digression in a novel of digressions ("And steer for now *a new direction*"). Also relevant is Pushkin's ironic note to the third chapter: "In the previous edition, the line *flying off toward home* was accidentally printed as *flying off in winter* (which didn't make any sense). Failing to figure out [the error], the critics discovered anachronisms in the following stanzas. I assure you that in my novel, time is measured according to the calendar" [4:180].

In his notes to the preface to the eighth and ninth chapters, Pushkin becomes openly ironic:[22] "Here are two more chapters of *Eugene Onegin*—the final ones, at least for print ... Anyone who plans to search for entertaining events in them can be sure that they have *even less action than all the previous ones*. I had wanted to destroy the eighth chapter entirely and substitute a single Roman numeral, but *I was afraid of the critics*. And in any event, many excerpts from it had already been printed" [6:358].

The question of omitting stanzas is of particular interest here. Consider the fact that *certain numbers* that are meant to indicate *omitted* stanzas hang, as it were, in midair—for these stanzas were never written in the first place. Pushkin himself explains his omissions in the following way: "The fact that there are stanzas in *Eugene Onegin* that I could or would not print is nothing to be surprised at. But, once omitted, *they break up the coherence of the story*, and this is why the place where they belong is indicated. It would have been better to substitute other stanzas, or transfer and combine others I'd saved. But I'm sorry, I'm too lazy for that. Let me humbly confess as well that there are two omitted stanzas in 'Don Juan' too" [6:348].

This note was written in 1830, and after his earlier statement about the plan and coherence of the novel, it sounds entirely ironic; but he emphasizes the

22 Prefaces and notes were yet another powerful way for Pushkin to emphasize or reveal the novel's dynamics, to create the *novel of the novel*, and furthermore justified the inclusion of *prosaic* introductions and digressions which, in this way, make the verse stand out. Pushkin gives only rare and meager prefaces and notes to his other works. The poem "Conversation between the Bookseller and the Poet" [Razgovor knigoprodavtsa s poetom] was placed as a gigantic introduction to the first chapter of *Eugene Onegin*—a curious example of the compositional implantation of a whole separate work—*YT*.

irony still further with a reference to laziness, and to a literary source in which omission also played a compositional role. If we recall that in the preface to the final chapter and to the "Fragments from Onegin's Journey" Pushkin talks about omitting *an entire chapter*, it becomes even clearer that the point here is not the *coherence* or elegance of the plan. This is what Pushkin writes in the preface:

> P. A. Katenin[N] (whom exquisite poetic talent does not prevent from being a subtle critic as well) has pointed out that this exclusion, *though perhaps to the readers' benefit*, is, however, detrimental to the *plan* of the whole work; because of it, the transition from Tatyana the provincial maiden to Tatyana the aristocratic lady becomes too sudden and unexplained. A criticism that exposes an experienced artist. The author himself sensed its fairness, but decided to skip that chapter *for reasons important to him, and not to the public*. [4:184]

Thus, omitting an entire chapter, which provoked Katenin's (indeed subtle) criticism[23] about the lack of motivation and suddenness of the heroine's dramatic change (reminiscent of a theatrical transformation), is declared to have been "*for the readers' benefit*" and is not motivated in any way. At this point, Pushkin's fastidiousness about the *interruption of the coherence of the story* begins to seem strange—he claims that this interruption gave rise to the empty numbers and omission of individual lines. An analysis of the omitted stanzas leaves us certain that, as far as the coherence and the plan are concerned, Pushkin did not need to indicate a single omitted line—for they all have to do either with digressions or small details of setting, and only a few contribute new features to the action itself, the *plan* (not to mention the empty numbers). Indeed, the mere fact that the empty numbers and *unwritten* stanzas exist eliminates the need to draw attention to explain the special role of the omitted lines, and likewise the fact that the deleted stanzas and lines were not deleted because they were incomplete, or for personal or censorship-related reasons.[24]

The situation becomes clearer, though no less complicated, if we understand this omission as a compositional device, one of unusual significance: and this significance lies entirely in the verbal dynamics of the work, rather than in the *plan, coherence* or *events of the story* (fabula)[T].[25]

---

23 Made regarding the *plan*—*YT.*

24 M. F. Gofman, "The Omitted Stanzas in *Eugene Onegin*" [Propushchennye strofy "Evgeniia Onegina""], in Iurii Tynianov, *Pushkin and His Contemporaries* [Pushkin i ego sovremenniki], issues 33–35 (Petersburg: Tip. Imperatorskoi Akademii nauk, 1922), 2—*YT*.

25 See "On Fabula and Plot in Film" (240–241).

The numbers give a kind of equivalent to stanzas and lines, which could contain anything; instead of verbal masses, there is a dynamic sign pointing toward them; instead of a specific semantic weight, there is an indeterminate, mysterious semantic hieroglyph. Given this hieroglyph, the following stanzas and lines are perceived as semantically complicated and pregnant with meaning. No matter what artistic merit the omitted stanza may have had, from the point of view of semantic complication and the increase in verbal dynamics, it would be weaker than these asterisks and periods. This is true, to the same or an even greater extent, of the omission of individual lines, since this emphasizes metrical phenomena.[26]

The end of *Eugene Onegin* shows a similar orientation toward the *verbal* plan, as do the ostensible attempts to continue the novel.

The true end of *Eugene Onegin* is actually not the fifty-first (51) stanza of the eighth chapter, but the "Fragments from Onegin's Journey" (1832) that follow it, and which are neither embedded in the novel nor chronologically consistent with any of its action. They conclude both the "Final Chapter of *Eugene Onegin*" (1832) as well as the publication of the whole novel during Pushkin's lifetime (1833). The inclusion of the "Fragments" was motivated by the preface, part of which was cited earlier:

> The author sincerely admits that he left an entire chapter out of his novel, which described Onegin's travels around Russia. It was up to him to indicate this omitted chapter with ellipses or a number; but in order to avoid temptation he decided to number the final chapter of *Eugene Onegin* as the eighth, rather than the ninth, and to sacrifice one of the final stanzas [...] [4:184].

(This is followed by a reference to Katenin's comment about the damage done to the plan by this exclusion, and about the resulting sudden and unmotivated nature of Tatyana's transition from provincial maiden to aristocratic lady.) The preface to the final chapter, which includes a detailed description of why the eighth chapter was not called the ninth ("to avoid temptation") and stresses the unmotivated change in the heroine, was even more ironic since it did nothing to justify placing the fragments after the eighth

26 These ideas are strengthened rather than weakened by the fact that omitting chapters (and rearranging them) is a frequent device of compositional play (Sterne, Byron, Cl. Brentano, Pueckler-Muskau, Hoffmann, etc.)—*YT.*

chapter.[27] Once again, Pushkin was drawing attention to the verbal dynamics of his novel, and the end of *Eugene Onegin* is undoubtedly in the "Fragments from Onegin's Journey"—this is the only way to explain its placement.[28] The digressions in these fragments are maximally condensed and concentrated within the space of a single sentence, a single phrase; they basically stretch from the sixty-third verse to the end (verse 203):

63. Я жил тогда в Одессе пыльной ... [4:188]	63. I lived then in dusty Odessa ...
91. А где, бишь, мой рассказ несвязный? В Одессе пыльной, я сказал. Я б мог сказать: в Одессе грязной [4:189]	91. But where, pray, was my rambling tale? "In dusty Odessa," I had said. I might have said "in muddy Odessa"
109. Однако в сей Одессе влажной Еще есть недостаток важный. [4:190]	109. However, in this moist Odessa There is another grave deficiency. (222)

And finally, the concluding line of all of *Eugene Onegin* (for this line *concludes* the novel), is the 203rd line of the "Fragments":

> Итак, я жил тогда в Одессе ... [4:193][29] [And so, I lived then in Odessa ...]

The above line is the culminating point of the whole novel; it was only [in the "Fragments"] that Pushkin fully realized what he had been working toward in the fifty-first [LI] (final) stanza of the eighth chapter:

---

27 In this preface, Pushkin explains that the "journey" actually precedes the events of chapter eight, which should by rights be called "chapter nine." The preface appears, however, at the beginning the "Fragments from Onegin's Journey," which was published *after* the full publication of *Eugene Onegin*.

28 This becomes particularly clear if we consider the fact that Pushkin not only failed to include any of the unfinished fragments in the first full edition of *Eugene Onegin*, but *excluded* from the first and second edition the preface to the first chapter, the "Conversation between the Bookseller and the Poet," several notes, and four stanzas that had previously been printed (the thirty-sixth stanza of the first chapter, the thirty-seventh and thirty-eighth stanzas of the fifth chapter). He also moved the forty-seventh stanza of the sixth chapter to the notes, while *leaving* the "Fragments from Onegin's Journey" at the end—*YT*.

29 Meanwhile, it is interesting that Pushkin had a whole stanza ready (see Gofman, "Omitted Stanzas," 254–255), beginning with this verse, but he preferred to conclude *Onegin* with a fragment, the first line—*YT*.

И *вдруг* умел расстаться с ним,
Как я с Онегиным моим, — [4:178]
[But *all at once* for good withdrew, / As I from my Onegin do. (222)

In the "Fragments," the compositional substance of the digressions is condensed into a linguistic, syntactic game, and the purely verbal dynamics of *Onegin* become exceptionally visible. As far as Pushkin's attempts at a "continuation" are concerned—it would seem that we must be extremely careful when talking about a real *continuation* of *Eugene Onegin*. To begin with, a preliminary note: out of the seven fragments identified by P. O. Morozov in connection with this idea (really, eight: the second fragment quite naturally falls into two parts, for its second half was written in a different meter and repeats the theme of the first fragment), three (written in 1833) are usually attributed to the beginning of the unknown "epistle to Pletnyov and to my friends" and only the remaining ones (written in 1835) to the "continuation" itself.[30] The distinction between them is based on the differences in the meters and the stanzaic forms. The first two fragments (evidently representing a single whole) are written in iambic pentameter; while the stanzaic form of the first is *ottava rima*, the second is, characteristically, not sustained.[31] The latter starts off in pentameter as well, but subsequently Pushkin hesitates and slips back into his Onegin tetrameter:

Ты говоришь: «Пока Онегин жив,	You say: "As long as Onegin lives,
Дотоль роман не кончен; нет причины	The novel will not end; there is no reason
Его кончать <...>	To end it [...]
и т.д.	etc.
Со славы, вняв ее призванью,	From glory, heeding its calling,
Сбирай оброк хвалой и бранью	Collect your tithe through praise and abuse
и т.д. [2:628]	etc.

The third fragment is written in alexandrines.[32] A simple comparison of the first fragments with the others adequately demonstrates that they are all

30 Tynianov refers to this work as "unknown" since there is no known complete text of the epistle, just a few different versions of the opening.

31 *Ottava rima* is a kind of rhyming stanza of eight iambic lines, usually iambic pentameter, with the rhyme scheme *abababcc*. It dates back to Boccaccio and has been used in the European (including Russian) poetic tradition for long narrative poems on heroic or mock-heroic themes (Byron's "Don Juan" and Pushkin's "Little House in Kolomna" are prime examples).

32 Alexandrines in Russian verse are rhymed couplets of iambic hexameter lines with an obligatory caesura after the sixth syllable; the number of syllables ranges depending on whether the rhyme is masculine (twelve) or feminine (thirteen).

variations on the same theme—and if the first fragments have been acknowledged (on entirely reasonable grounds) as the beginning of the "continuation," the same beginning of the "continuation" can be found in the others as well.

1

Ты мне советуешь, Плетнев любезный,
Оставленный роман мой продолжать
<.................................>
Ты думаешь, что с целию полезной
Тревогу славы можно сочетать.
А для того советуешь собрату
<........................>
Брать с публики умеренную плату.
Оброк пустой для нынешних людей.
Неужто жаль кому пяти рублей?
<..............................>

1

You advise me, dear Pletnyov,
To continue my abandoned novel
[.............................]
You think that a useful aim
With fame's unease can be joined.
And toward this you advise your confrere
[.................................]
To ask his public for a modest fee.
A trifling tithe for modern folk today.
Five rubles—who would refuse to pay?
[.................................]

2

Ты говоришь: «Пока Онегин жив,
Дотоль роман не кончен; нет причины
Его кончать; к тому же план счастлив
<...> кончины
<............................> [2:628]

2

You say: "As long as Onegin lives
The novel will not end; there's no reason
To end it; and plus the plan is fine
[...] death
[..............................]

3

Вы за Онегина *советуете, други,*
Опять приняться *мне в осенние досуги;*
Вы говорите мне: «*Он жив и не женат* —
Итак, еще *роман не кончен:* это клад!
В его свободную, вместительную раму
Ты вставишь ряд картин, откроешь диораму.
Прихлынет публика, платя тебе за вход,
Что даст тебе и *славу и доход*». [2:629]

3

You advise, friends, that Onegin mine
Should be taken up again *in my free time;*
You tell me: "He's not *married off* and still *alive*—
And so the *novel's not finished*: it's a goldmine!
Into this open, spacious frame you'll fit
A series of pictures, a splendid diorama.
The audiences will flood in, paying entrance fees,
This will bring you *money and prestige.*

4
В мои осенние досуги
<………………..>
Вы мне советуете други
Рассказ забытый продолжать.
<…………………………>
Что должно своего героя
Как бы то ни было *женить,*
По крайней мере — *уморить.*
<…………………………>

4
in the autumn, in my free time
[……………………..]
You advise, o friends of mine
I continue this forgotten story.
[…………………………]
That my hero must
At all costs be *married off,*
Or at very least—*killed off.*
[……………………..]

5
Вы говорите: «Слава богу!
Покамест твой Онегин *жив,*
Роман не кончен.
<…………….>
Со славы, вняв ее призванью.
Сбирай оброк
<………….>
И с нашей публики меж тем
Бери умеренную плату». <…> [2:630]

5
You tell me: "Thank God!
As long as your Onegin *lives,*
The novel's not finished.
[……………………]
From glory, heeding its calling,
Collect your tithe
[………………]
And meanwhile ask your public
For a modest fee. […]"

We are thus not dealing with the *ottava rima* and alexandrines of an epistle, but rather the *ottava rima* and alexandrines of "Onegin's continuation." This alone provides ample proof for the idea that, with its "established hero" and "excellent plan," the continuation should have been a perfectly independent variant; the emotional tone of the beginning is also completely different:

> И, потчуя стихами, век железный
> Рассказами пустыми угощать.[33]
> [And, regaling it with verses, to treat / this iron age to empty stories.]

The novel's "series of pictures" in "an open, spacious frame" was meant to be different and to come together only by means of the familiar synthetic sign of the protagonist (an "*established* hero"); meanwhile, the "continuation" (actually a new, independent work) was perhaps meant to stand out in [implicit] parodic contrast to *Eugene Onegin*:

33 Variation on the above-quoted poem "To Pletnyov" [Pletnevu].

< … > должно своего героя
Как бы то ни было женить.
По крайней мере — уморить. [2:630]

[…] his hero must
At all costs be married off.
Or if nothing else—killed off.

Thus the "continuation" was not prompted by the novel's (parodic) unfinished state so much as by the use of its "frame" for new purposes.

Pushkin did everything he could to underscore the *verbal* plan of *Eugene Onegin*. Moreover, his practice of publishing the novel one chapter at a time, at several-year-long intervals, also blatantly undermined any orientation toward a plan of *action, plot* and *fabula*[T]; instead of a dynamics of semantic emblems, this is the dynamics of *language* in its poetic sense. Instead of the development of action, we have the development of the *verbal* plan.

3

For Pushkin, the decisive factor in *Onegin*'s *verbal* plan was the fact that it was a *novel in verse*. At the very beginning of his work on *Onegin*, Pushkin wrote to Prince Vyazemsky: "As far as my activities are concerned, I'm not writing a novel, I'm writing a novel in verse—a devilish difference! Along the lines of 'Don Juan'—no reason to even think about publishing it; I'm really letting things slide" [9:77].[34]

Pushkin was faced with the task of incorporating an entire prosaic category into verse, and he wavered. For him, *Eugene Onegin* was a novel one moment and a long poem [*poema*] the next; the novel's chapters turned into the cantos [*pesni*] of an epic poem; a novel that parodies the conventional plot models of novels through compositional play vacillates and becomes intertwined with parodic epic.

On 16 November 1823, Pushkin wrote: "Now I'm writing a new *poema* […]"; on 1 December 1823: "[…] writing a new *poema* […] Two *cantos* are already ready"; 8 February 1824: "No reason to think at all about my *poema* […]"; 13 June 1824: "I'm trying to hustle my way to the censor's gates with the first *chapter* or *canto* from *Onegin*"; 24 March 1825: "You compare the first *chapter* with 'Don Juan' […]"; in the same letter: "Wait to read more of the *cantos* … […] The first *canto* is just a quick introduction […]"; in early April 1825: "[…] I'm ready to add a whole couplet in his honor to the first *canto* of *Onegin* […]"; 23 April 1825: "Tolstoy makes a dashing appearance

34 From a letter to P. A. Vyazemsky, 4 November 1823—*AC*.

in the fourth *canto* of *Onegin* [...]"; late April 1825: "[...] I'm sending you the second *chapter* of *Onegin* [...]"; 8 June 1825: "Let me know what he thinks of the second *chapter* of *Onegin* [...]"; 14 September 1825: "[...] I have four of the Onegin *cantos* ready [...] I'm so glad you liked the first *canto* [...]"; 27 May 1826: "In the fourth *canto* of *Onegin* I depict my own life"; 1 December 1826: "In Pskov, instead of writing the seventh *chapter* of *Onegin,* I'm losing the fourth at faro"; December 1827: "[...] could you send me the second *chapter* [...] thanks to you all the bookshops have stopped selling the first and third *chapters*"; late March 1828: "[...] include the hostile stanzas in *Onegin*'s eighth *ch.*?"; late February 1829: "Let me send you the three final *cantos* of *Onegin*"; early 1829: "Who is the wise man from *Athenaeum* who discussed the fourth and fifth *chapters* so beautifully?"; 9 December 1830: "The last two *chapters* of *Onegin*"; in October and November 1830: "The first hostile articles, as I recall, began appearing after I printed the fourth or fifth *canto* of *Eugene Onegin.* The discussion of these *chapters* that was printed in *Athenaeum,*" etc.; from the same time: "In the journal he'd begun publishing, Mr. B. Fyodorov discussed the fourth and fifth *chapters* quite favorably [...]"; "They didn't discuss the sixth *canto* [...]";[35] "I quickly read through the criticism of the VII *canto* in *The Northern Bee* while I was out visiting [...]";[36] from the same time: "When the seventh *canto* of *Onegin* appeared, the journals' overall response was highly unfavorable. I'd be glad to believe them if it weren't for the fact that their judgment strongly contradicts what they said about the previous *chapters* of my novel. After the unrestrained and undeserved praise heaped on the six *parts* of one and the same work [...]"; "It was said in one of our journals that the seventh *chapter* could never have any success [...]"; "Here are two more *chapters* of *Eugene Onegin* [...] I had wanted to do away entirely with the eighth *chapter* [...]."[37] In Pushkin's manuscript, *Eugene Onegin* is split into three parts of three *cantos* each [emphasis *YT*].[38]

35 For all quotations from correspondence, see Pushkin, *Collected Works,* vol. 9.

36 From the "Rebuttal to my Critics" (Pushkin, *Sobranie sochinenii,* 6:349).—*AC.* The *Athenaeum* [Atenei] and *The Northern Bee* [Severnaia pchela] were literary journals of Pushkin's time.

37 From the preface to the planned separate edition of the eighth and ninth chapters of *Eugene Onegin* (ibid., 6:358)—*AC.*

38 Tynianov refers to a sheet with a plan for the full publication of *Eugene Onegin* (1830), found by P. V. Annenkov in Pushkin's papers—*AC.*

4

The verse form [in *Eugene Onegin*] made itself felt in the vacillations between long poem and novel, canto and chapter. But this is precisely why, in a verse text, Pushkin put such emphasis on the *novel*,[39] which, by being superimposed onto the verse (and thus shifting), became especially conspicuous:

Впервые именем таким
Страницы нежные романа
Мы своевольно освятим (2:24). [4:46]

And now we press our willful claim
To be the first who thus shall honor
A tender novel with that name. (56)

С героем моего романа
<........................>
Позвольте познакомить вас (1:2) [4:12]

May I present, as we set sail,
The hero of my current novel: (15)

Покаместь моего романа
Я кончил первую главу (1:60) [4:35]

And meantime I've just now completed
My present novel's Chapter One. (41)

В начале моего романа
(Смотрите первую тетрадь) (5:40)
[4:109]

At the beginning of my novel
(In Chapter One, if you recall),
(137; translation modified)

This *novel* is wholly literary: against a backdrop of old novels, the hero and heroine appear effectively as parodic shadows. *Onegin* is a sort of imaginary novel; Onegin imagines himself as [Childe] Harold, Tatyana imagines herself as a whole gallery of literary heroines, as does her mother. Besides these, there are stereotypes (Olga), which are also markedly literary.[40]

Onegin:

Как Child-Harold, угрюмый, томный
В гостиных появлялся он (1:38) [4:26]

Like Byron's Harold, lost in trances,
Through drawing rooms he'd pass and
stare; (32)

Онегин жил анахоретом
<........................>
Певцу Гюльнары подражая,

Onegin lived in his own heaven:
[........................]
Gulnare's proud singer his example,

---

39 This is the subtitle in all published editions: *A Novel in Verse* [roman v stikhakh]—*AC.*

40 Eugene Onegin is the hero of Pushkin's eponymous novel; Tatyana Larina is the female protagonist and primary romantic interest; Olga is her sister and a more minor figure. For more on Tynianov's views on parody, see "Dostoevsky and Gogol" (27–63) and "On Parody" (294–328).

Сей Геллеспонт переплывал,
Потом свой кофе выпивал (4:36, 37)
[4:88]

He'd swim across this Hellespont;
Then afterwards, as was his wont,
He'd drink his coffee […] (110)

Olga:

Всегда скромна, всегда послушна,
Всегда как утро весела,
Как жизнь поэта простодушна,
Как поцалуй любви мила,
Глаза как небо голубые,
Улыбка, локоны льняные,
Движенья, голос, легкий стан,
Все в Ольге … но любой роман
Возьмите и найдете верно
Ее портрет: он очень мил,
Я прежде сам его любил,
Но надоел он мне безмерно (2:23)
[4:46]

Forever modest, meek in bearing,
As gay as morning's rosy dress,
Like any poet—open, caring,
As sweet as love's own soft caress;
Her sky-blue eyes, devoid of guile,
Her flaxen curls, her lovely smile,
Her voice, her form, her graceful stance,
Oh, Olga's every trait … But glance
In any novel—you'll discover
Her portrait there; it's charming, true;
I liked it once no less than you,
But round it boredom seems to hover;
(56)

Tatyana:

Ей рано нравились романы;
Они ей заменяли все. (2:29)

From early youth she read romances,
And novels set her heart aglow; (87)

Воображаясь героиней
Своих возлюбленных творцов,
Клариссой, Юлией, Дельфиной (3:10).

Perceives herself as *heroïne*—
Some favorite author's fond creation:
Clarissa, Julia or Delphine. (100)

The Mother:

Она любила Ричардсона
<……………………>
Сей Грандисон был славный франт
(2:30) [4:49]

For Richardson [she] was simply mad.
[……………………………]
This Grandison was fashion's pet, (59)

(We should also note the similarities between the initial sketch of Tatyana, who was also infatuated with Richardson, and the sketch of her mother.) All of the novel's clichés are markedly parodic:

Господский дом уединенный,
Горой от ветров огражденный,
Стоял над речкою. <…>
Огромный, запущенный сад,
Приют задумчивых дриад (2:1)

The manor house, in proud seclusion,
Screened by a hill from wind's intrusion,
Stood by a river. […]
A vast neglected garden made
A nook where pensive dryads played. (45)

Почтенный *замок* был построен,
Как замки строиться должны (2:2) [4:36]

The ancient *manse* had been erected
For placid comfort—and to last; (stanza 2:45)

And right away, in the next stanza, there is a parodic opposition:

Он в том покое поселился,
Где деревенский старожил
Лет сорок с ключницей бранился,
В окно смотрел и мух давил. (2:3)

He settled where the former squire
For forty years had heaved his sighs,
Had cursed the cook in useless ire,
Stared out the window, and squashed flies. (46)

Один среди своих владений
<…………………………>
В своей глуши мудрец пустынный
<………………………………>
И раб судьбу благословил. (2:4) [4:37]

Alone amid his new possessions,
[……………………………]
A backwoods genius, he commuted
[………………………………]
His peasants thanked their lucky fate (stanza 4, 46)

Везде, везде перед тобой
Твой искуситель роковой. (3:15) [4: 60]

While everywhere before your eyes
Your fateful tempter's figure lies. (74)

Блистая взорами, Евгений
Стоит подобно грозной тени,
И как огнем обожжена
Остановилася она. (3:41) [4:74–75]

His eyes ablaze, Eugene stood waiting—
Like some grim shade of night's creating;
And she, as if by fire seared,
Drew back and stopped when he
Appeared … (91)

Быть может, чувствий пыл старинный
Им на минуту овладел. (4:11) [4:78]

Perhaps an ancient glow of passion
Possessed him for a moment's sway … (97)

И пилигримке молодой
Пора, давно пора домой, <…>

And now it's time, indeed long past,
That our young pilgrim leave at last. […]

Но прежде просит позволенья Пустынный замок навещать. (7:20) [4:139]	But, taking leave, requests permission To see the vacant house alone. (175)
В возок боярский их впрягают. (7:32) [4:144]	They're harnessed to the coach and steadied; (181)
Стремится к жизни полевой, В деревню, к бедным поселянам. (7:53) [4:153]	Calls up the life she left behind, The countryside, poor village neighbors; (191)
Она его не будет видеть; Она должна в нем ненавидеть Убийцу брата своего. (7:14) [4:136]	She'll never see him … and be grateful, She finds her brother's slayer hateful And loathes the awful thing he's done. (172)

(The last two examples follow the heroine's motivations; we see them through her prism.)

This plan for a *grand* novel is joined with a plan for a novel of everyday life [*byt*], made up of conversations and narrative devices. The problem of a prose substratum in the epic—a prose plan underlying the development of a long poem—came up repeatedly for Pushkin. He wrote the following about "The Prisoner of the Caucasus": "The description of Circassian mores, which is the most tolerable episode in the whole long poem, is not connected with any events and is nothing other than a geographical *article or traveler's report*. The personality of the main character (more like, sole character), and of the other characters (there are only two) is *more appropriate for a novel than a long poem* […]" [9:383]. Regarding "The Fountain of Bakhchisaray," he also wrote: "I faithfully transposed the story of a young woman into verse.

> Aux douces loix des vers je pliais les accents
> De sa bouche aimable et naïve" [9:91][41]

41 From a draft of a letter to N. I. Gnedich, 29 April 1822, and a letter to A. A. Bestuzhev, 8 February, 1824—*YT*. French: "Into sweet regular verse I plied/the accents of her charming and naive mouth."

If we recall his prose plans and programs for these poems, it becomes clear that the interrelation between prose and poetry was a familiar one for Pushkin; the existence of Pushkin's programs and plans proves that the overall compositional framework of his works can be traced back to a plan, a prose outline.[42] In this way, the digressions in *Eugene Onegin* are without a doubt part of the fundamental compositional conception, rather than a secondary phenomenon prompted by the verse (one critic aptly dubbed them "outgrowths of Sterne").[43] Yet this interrelation never became an independent, conspicuous part of the work, instead always remaining a *substratum*.

5

The conjoining of prose and poetry, which is the compositional premise of *Eugene Onegin,* itself became conspicuous and, over the course of the work, proved to have important consequences. Here are a few examples of this dynamic usage. The novel opens with Onegin's speech:

«Но, боже мой, какая скука	But God, what deadly boredom, brothers,
С больным сидеть и день и ночь,	To tend a sick man night and day,
Не отходя ни шагу прочь!	Not daring once to steal away!
Какое низкое коварство	And, oh, how base to pamper grossly
Полуживого забавлять,	And entertain the nearly dead,
Ему подушки поправлять,	To fluff the pillows for his head,
Печально подносить лекарство,	And pass him medicines morosely—
Вздыхать и думать про себя:	While thinking under every sigh:
Когда же черт возьмет тебя?» [4:10]	The devil take you, Uncle. Die! (15)

That this direct speech serves as the opening of a novel is interesting, but it is even more interesting as the opening of a *novel in verse.* The pacing of conversational intonation barges into verse: that which in prose only stands out for its meaning, in poetry is felt as a consequence of the unusual combination of conversational intonation with *verse.* Pushkin's intonational devices become ever more striking once the intonation has made itself felt:

---

42 The prose programs were a *primary* phenomenon for Pushkin, in contrast to the verse; this concurs with the Karamzinian (writing) tradition. Meanwhile, in this connection we have to ask whether Pushkin's prose can be traced back to verse plans and programs. (A different solution can be found in B. M. Eikhenbaum[N])—*YT.*

43 In direct contradiction to Gofman's opinion that the digressions in *Eugene Onegin* are not an overall compositional premise, but are rather generated *by the verse,* the "form of the *lyric* novel"—*YT.*

«Представь меня». — «Ты шутишь.—
«Нету». (3:2) [4:55]

"Present me, do."—"You must be joking!"
"I'm not." (67)

(three intonations in the space of a single verse line).

«Но куча будет там народу
И всякого такого сброду ... »
— И, никого, уверен я! (4:49); [4:92–93]
— И, полно, Таня! В эти лета
Мы не слыхали про любовь (3:18) [4:61]

"But there's be lots of noise and babble
And all that crowd of local rabble."
—Why not at all! (115);
"Oh come! Our world was quite another!
We'd never heard of love, you see" (75)

(a striking conversational intonation introduced by the intonational word *and* [in English, *Why* and *Oh come!—trans.*]).

— Дитя мое, ты нездорова;
Господь помилуй и спаси!
Чего ты хочешь, попроси ...
Дай окроплю святой водою,
Ты вся горишь ... — «Я не больна:
Я ... знаешь, няня ... влюблена»
(3:19) [4:62]

"My goodness, girl, you must be ailing;
Dear Lord have mercy. God, I plead!
Just tell me, dearest, what you need.
I'll sprinkle you with holy water,
You're burning up ... —"Oh, do be still,
I'm ... you know, nurse ... in love, not ill."
(76)

(fragmentary dialogue intonation; repetitions).

— Итак, пошли тихонько внука
С запиской этой к О ... к тому ...
К соседу ... да велеть ему —
Чтоб он не говорил ни слова,
Чтоб он не называл меня ... (3:34)
[4:71]

"Then send your grandson, little Thomas,
To take this note of mine to O—,
Our neighbor, nurse, the one ... you
know!
And tell him that he's not to mention,
My name, or breathe a single word ..."
(87)

(even more fragmentary intonation, word left unspoken).

Князь на Онегина глядит.
— Ага! давно ж ты не был в свете (7:17)
[4:162]

The prince looked Onegin up and down.
"You *have* been out of circulation." (203)

(intonational gesture [in English, through the emphasis on *have*]).

«А я так на руки брала!
А я так за уши драла!
А я так пряником кормила!» (7:44)
[4:149]

"And since I dried your baby tears!
And since I pulled you by the ears!
And since my gingerbread surprised
you!" (187)

(monotonous, rising intonation).

These conversational intonations arise naturally out of dialogue and become particularly significant in *verse*. Pushkin also uses them for other ends; in narration, for example, where the intonational coloring makes the narration itself into a sort of indirect speech on the part of the protagonists:

Ее находят что-то странной,	They find her stranger than expected,
Провинциальной и жеманной,	A bit provincial and affected,
И что-то бледной и худой,	And somewhat pale, too thin and small,
А впрочем очень недурной. (7:46) [4:150]	But on the whole, not bad at all (188).

Та, от которой он хранит	The girl whose letter he still kept—
Письмо, где сердце говорит	In which a maiden heart had wept;
Где все наруже, все на воле,	Where all was shown ... all unprotected?
Та девочка … иль это сон? …	Was this that girl ... or did he dream?
Та девочка, которой он	That little girl whose warm esteem
Пренебрегал в смиренной доле,	And humble lot he'd once rejected?
Ужели с ним сейчас была	And could she now have been so bold,
Так равнодушна, так смела? (8:20) [4:163]	So unconcerned with him ... so cold? (204)

А он не едет; он заране	But he refused to go. He's ready
Писать ко прадедам готов	to join his forbears any day;
О скорой встрече; а Татьяне	Tatyana, though, stayed calm and steady
И дела нет (их пол таков);	(Their sex, alas, is hard to sway).
А он упрям, отстать не хочет,	And yet he's stubborn. ... still resistant,
Еще надеется, хлопочет. (8:32) [4:168]	Still hopeful and indeed persistent. (210)

У! как теперь окружена	My god! How stern that haughty brow,
Крещенским холодом она! (8:33) [4:170]	What wintry frost surrounds her now! (213)

Ей-ей! не то, чтоб содрогнулась,	It's true! The lady didn't shiver,
Иль стала вдруг бледна, красна …	Or blush, or suddenly turn white ...
У ней и бровь не шевельнулась;	Or even let an eyebrow quiver,
Не сжала даже губ она. (8:19) [4:163]	Or press her lips together tight. (204)

The final example straddles the border between intonations conveyed through the prism of the protagonists and entirely unmotivated intonations, introduced as authorial speech. The authorial remarks and addresses, etc., were a device specific to prose; the author was sometimes promoted to the status of an active character, sometimes remained inactive (but a character),[44] and sometimes played a distinctive narrating role. Because of the primacy of the semantic principle in prose, this device remained barely noticeable (consider Dostoevsky 's "I"); but in verse it was strongly foregrounded by the fact that all of these authorial remarks—presented intonationally as fragmentary asides—violated the ordinary intonational framework of verse and became a kind of play with intonations:

Латынь из моды вышла ныне:
Так, *если правду вам сказать,*
Он знал довольно по латыне. (1:6) [4:13]

The Latin vogue today is waning,
And yet *I'll say on his behalf,*
He had sufficient Latin training (17)

Замечу кстати: все поэты —
Любви мечтательной друзья. (1:57) [4:33]

All poets, *I need hardly mention,*
Have drawn from love abundant themes (40)

И запищит она *(бог мой!)*:
Приди в чертог ко мне златой! ... (2:12). [4:42]

And then, *good God,* she starts to bawl:
"Come to my golden chamberhall!" (50)

Враги его, друзья его
(Что, может быть, одно и то же)
Его честили так и сяк. <...>
Уж эти мне друзья, друзья! (4:18) [4:81]

Good friends no less than ardent foes
(*But aren't they one, if they offend us?*)
Abused him roundly, used the knife. [...]
Ah, friends, those friends! ... (100)

Так он писал темно и вяло
(Что романтизмом мы зовем,
Хоть романтизма тут ни мало
Не вижу я; да что нам в том?)
И наконец перед зарею <...> (6:23) [4:120]

He wrote thus—*limply and obscurely.*
(We say "romantically"—although,
That's not romanticism, surely:
And if it is, who wants to know?)
But then at last, as it was dawning, [...] (153)

(the size of the free-standing interjection).

---

44 There are hints of this in *Eugene Onegin* too ("Onegin, my good friend"); and the sketch "Pushkin with Onegin"; "Wandering in the same direction, Onegin thought of me" ("Onegin's Journey")—*YT. Collected Works,* 4:188.

А что? Да так. Я усыпляю
Пустые черные мечты. (4:19) [4:81]

What's that? Just that. Mere conversation
To lull black empty thoughts awhile; (101)

Еще есть недостаток важный;
Чего б вы думали? — воды. [4:190]
(*Отрывки из* «Путешествия Онегина»).

There is one important drawback;
What did you think?—no water.
(*Excerpts from* Onegin's Journey).

Того, что модой самовластной
В высоком лондонском кругу
Зовется *vulgar*. (Не могу … (8:15)
[4:161]

Of what, with fashion's sense of duty,
The London social sets decry
As *vulgar*. (I won't even try
(8:15, 202)

Люблю я очень это слово,
Но не могу перевести. (8:16) [4:161]

To find an adequate translation
For this delicious epithet; (8:16, 202)

The last example is especially interesting because the break occurs at the border of two lines, which creates something like a gesture at the end of the first line.

Pushkin goes even further, and introduces intonational particles or interjections into the authorial addresses:

Кого твой стих боготворил?
И, други, никого, ей-богу! (1:58)
[4:34]

"Whose form, in pensive adoration,
Do you now clothe in sacred dress?"
Why, no one, friends, as God's my witness
(40)

Тьфу! прозаические бредни <…>
А где, бишь, мой рассказ несвязный?
[4:188]

Bah! Just prosaic ravings […]
But where'd my wandering tale leave off?[46]

Гм! Гм! Читатель благородный,
Здорова ль ваша вся родня? (4:20) [4:81]

Hm, hm, dear reader, feeling mellow?
And are your kinfolk well today? (101)

The last example is especially interesting since it renders the intonational interjections particularly conspicuous by making them, from the poetic or metrical point of view, equivalent to real words.

45 Excerpts from "Onegin's Journey" [Puteshestvie Onegina]—*YT.*

We see the same thing in conversational elisions:

> Да щей горшок, да сам большой [4:188]
> (*Отрывки из* «Путешествия Онегина»).
> ["A bowl of soup, and big 'nough for my britches." (*from* Onegin's Journey)]

Intonation even affects the metrical features of the work:

> Визг, хохот, свист и хлоп,
> Людская молвь и конский топ! (5:17)
> [Guffawing, barking, whistles, claps, / And human speech and hoofbeat taps! (127)

(the lines are from an 1828 edition; caving to the critics, Pushkin changed this line, which was metrically too bold:[46]

> Лай, хохот, пенье, свист и хлоп! [4:101]
> [Barking, laughing, singing, whistling and bang!]).

This device becomes condensed to the point of mere verbal gesture:

> Татьяна *ах!* а он реветь (5:12). [4:99]
> [Tatyana *oh!* He growled and reared (124; translation slightly modified)]

In verse, something which in a prose novel would have purely semantic significance, and be taken as a mere plot point, becomes a conspicuous and concrete image of physical movement:

Вдруг топот!.. кровь ее застыла	Then sudden hoofbeats! ... Now she's quaking ...
Вот ближе! Скачут ... и на двор	They're closer ... coming here ... it's he!
Евгений! «Ах!» — и легче тени	Onegin! "Oh!"—And light as air,
Татьяна прыг в другие сени,	Tatyana—hop—and down the stair
С крыльца на двор, и прямо в сад,	From porch to yard, to garden straight;
Летит, летит; взглянуть назад	She runs, she flies; she dare not wait
Не смеет; мигом обежала	To glance behind her; on she pushes—
Куртины, мостики, лужок,	

46 The first line cited (*Vizg, khokhot ...*) is "metrically too bold" because it is iambic trimeter, unlike the iambic tetrameter used universally in the rest of the work (as in the *Lai, khokhot* replacement line).

Аллею к озеру, лесок,	Past garden plots, small bridges, lawn,
Кусты сирен переломала,	The lakeway path, the wood; and on
По цветникам летя к ручью,	She flies and breaks through lilac bushes,
И, задыхаясь, на скамью (3:38) [4:73]	Past seedbeds to the brook—so fast
	That, panting, on a bench at last (3:38)
	(89, translation slightly modified)
Упала ... (3:39)	She falls ... (3:39) (89)

In this excerpt, the dynamic force of the verse line is clearly felt; here, enjambment takes on its primitive sense, of a representation of physical movement: *coming here...* (a rise and pause, with the latter more conspicuous precisely because it shouldn't be there, because the previous line is connected to the following one) *Onegin* (a drop and pause again); and the lines meanwhile acquire remarkable dynamic force from the enjambment:[47]

взглянуть назад	she dare not wait
Не смеет; мигом обежала	To glance behind her; on she pushes

down to:

Упала ...	She falls ...

These lines are not read with an eye to meaning at all—they are a sort of impediment to the image of physical movement—and this is why "*she falls*" achieves the concreteness of a verbal gesture,[48] a concreteness achieved exclusively through the dynamics of the verse.[49]

---

47 Note that this is an interstanzaic enjambment, which comes at a moment of great fear and surprise; this is very rare even in *Eugene Onegin*.

48 Compare this to the term "sound gesture"—*YT.*

49 Internal rhymes play a major role here: in combination with enjambment, they go even further in violating the borders of rhythmic series:

1) coming here ...
Onegin! "Oh!"—and light as *air*
She's out ... down the *stair*

2) on she pushes
lawn
[the wood], and on
breaks through
[to the brook] so fast
[to the bench] at last
She falls.
—*YT.*

1) Similarly, the simplest phenomena of a prose novel are deformed by verse in a way that is so conspicuous that it becomes comic (this is the direct consequence of what happens when a prose phenomenon, for which semantics is the organizing principle, is transformed into a verse phenomenon, for which phonic elements fulfill that role).

Pushkin achieves this effect as early as stanza thirty-four of chapter three, where the conversational intonations, as it were, break down individual words. But the broken elements, which in prose cannot play the role of independent words (only their equivalent), in verse finds themselves on equal footing with other metrical elements; they are verse words:

С запиской этой к О … к тому К соседу … [4:71]	To take this note of mine to O— Our neighbor … (87)

And in stanza 37 of the same chapter:

Задумавшись, моя душа, Прелестным пальчиком писала На отуманенном стекле Заветный вензель О да *Е*. [4:72]	All lost in thought, the gentle lass Begins to trace with lovely fingers Across the misted planes a row Of hallowed letters: *E* and *O*. (88)

Here, the device is concentrated; the concreteness of the image retreats before the purely phonic phenomenon whereby letters are assimilated (through verse) into full-fledged words (and rhyming ones, at that).

We see this take the form of a pun in a draft version, in stanza thirty-two of the same chapter: [50]

И думала: что скажут люди И подписала: Т. Л.	And she thought: what will people think And signed it: T. L.[51]

We can see the same thing to varying degrees elsewhere:

И подпись: t. à. v. Annete. (5:28) [4:85]	And neath it: *t. à v. Annette*: (105) [French: *toute à vous*]
О ком твердили целый век: N. N. прекрасный человек. (8:10) [4:159]	Of whom lifelong the verdict ran: "Old X is quite a splendid man." (199)

50 Note that each letter of the Russian alphabet used to correspond to a specific word, thus *T*—*tverdo* [firmly] and *L*—*liudi* [people]. If the line is read with these words substituted for the letters, it scans properly.

Письмо: князь N. покорно просит. (7:21) [4:164]

Prince N. had send an invitation. (205)

Шестого был у В. на бале,
Довольно пусто было в зале —
R. C. как ангел хороша [4:478]
(*«Альбом Онегина»*, 5).

Was at V's ball on the sixth,
The hall was pretty empty—
R. C. is lovely as an angel
(from "Onegin's Album").

Вчера у В., оставя пир,
R. C. летела как зефир
(*«Альбом»*, 9). [4:480]

At V's yesterday, leaving the feast,
R. C. flew off like an easterly breeze
("Album").

Вечор сказала мне R. C.:
Давно желала я вас видеть.
Зачем?—мне говорили все,
Что я вас буду ненавидеть.
(*«Альбом»*, 6). [4:478]

Yesterday R. C. said to me:
So long I've wished to meet you.
Why?—everyone kept saying,
That I would simply hate you.
("Album").

And finally, the consolidation of the device:

Боитесь вы графини -овой —
Сказала им Элиза К.
Да, возразил N. N. суровый,
Боимся мы графини -овой,
Как вы боитесь паука.
(*«Альбом»*, 2). [4:478]

You steer clear of Countess -ova—
Said Eliza K. to them.
Yes, objected stern N.N.,
We're afraid of Countess -ova
Just like you're afraid of spiders.
("Album").

The conventional prose device of abbreviating last names by their first letter or ending (Eliza K., the Countess -ova) acquired an entirely unconventional meaning here as a result of having been embedded in verse;[51] because these bits and pieces of words are both playing the role of independent words and, by rhyming with full words (*-ovoi* rhymes with *surovyi* [stern], Eliza *K.* rhymes with *pauka* [spider]), they even acquire a hint of meaning. It is highly typical that Pushkin hesitates in the first line; in the draft version it reads:

51 The entire fragment is built on this device, which is presented as a sort of experiment—*YT.*

Боитесь вы княжны-овой,
[You're afraid of Princess -ova,]

But the line, which is metrically unstable, would force one to think about the *omission* and would be an undeniable prose element (in prose, such patterns have a purely visual character and sound awkward when read out loud). Rejecting this version, Pushkin followed his principle: that this would be not a novel, but a novel in verse.[52]

Finally, a draft fragment from "Onegin's Album" openly plays with this device:[53]

Вчера был день довольно скучный;	Yesterday was rather dull;
Чего же так хотелось ей?	What was it she wanted?
Сказать ли первые три буквы?	Should I say the first three letters?
К-Л-Ю-Клю … возможно ль, клюквы! [4:480]	C-R-A … maybe cranberries!

2) Similarly, words of secondary significance or a secondary grammatical category of relations (particles, etc.) are presented as *verse*; their metrical role in the verse is on a level with fully legitimate words. This partly determines the difference between the language of poetry and prose; poetic language has a hard time reconciling itself with function words (*for*, *which*, etc.).

Чему-нибудь и как-нибудь. (1:5) [4:13]	In something somehow, have we not? (17)
То есть умел судить о том,	Which is to say that he could tell
Как государство богатеет,	The ways in which a state progresses—
И чем живет, и почему	The actual things that make it thrive,
Не нужно золота ему (1:7) [4:14]	And why for gold it need not strive. (18)
Что? Приглашенья? В самом деле,	What? Invitations? Yes, three houses
Три дома на вечер зовут. (1:15) [4:16]	Had asked him to a grand soiree. (20)
Вдруг получил он в самом деле	And sure enough a note came flying;
От управителя доклад. (1:52) [4:31]	The bailiff wrote as if on cue: (37)

52 Using the Russian word "countess" [*grafinia*] means that the line is in perfect iambs, while the word "princess" [*kniazhna*] in the draft version leaves a missed syllable before "-ova," forcing the reader to register that information is missing.

53 "Onegin's Album" appears as a section in an early draft of the novel in verse.

Но так как с заднего крыльца
Обыкновенно подавали
Ему донского жеребца. (2:5) [4:38]

But when they learned that in the rear
Onegin kept his stallion ready
So he could quickly disappear (47)

Но вот
Неполный, слабый перевод. (3:31) [4:67]

But nonetheless
Here's a feeble part-translation. (82; translation slightly modified)

3) This role of verse comes through particularly vividly in the phonic deformation of proper nouns and foreign words.

4) Likewise, the combination of words (the device of enumeration, which can play various roles in prose) can, depending on the nature of the verse, acquire a completely different meaning.

Слова: бор, буря, ведьма, ель
Еж, мрак, мосток, медведь, метель
И прочая <...> (5:24) [4:104]

There's bear and blizzard, bridge, and crow,
Fir, forest, hedgehog, night, and snow,
And many more. [...] (130)

Мелькают мимо будки, бабы,
Мальчишки, лавки, фонари,
Дворцы, сады, монастыри,
Бухарцы, сани, огороды,
Купцы, лачужки, мужики,
Бульвары, башни, казаки,
Аптеки, магазины моды,
Балконы, львы на воротах
И стаи галок на крестах. (7:38) [4:147]

By sentry booths and peasant lasses;
By gardens, mansions, fashion shops;
Past urchins, streetlamps, strolling fops,
Bokharins, sleighs, apothecaries,
Muzhiks and merchants, Cossack guards;
Past towers, hovels, boulevards,
Great balconies and monasteries;
Past gateway lions' lifted paws,
And crosses dense with flocks of daws. (184)

The distinctively comic quality of the enumeration here is due not only to the intonational equivalence of the *different* objects being counted (which exists in prose as well), but also to their metrical equivalence, the monotony of the verse.[54]

---

54 Cf. 1:35, where the depiction of morning "While Petersburg, already rousing" (30) is comic because of the *resolution* of the stanza:

И хлебник, немец аккуратный,
В бумажном колпаке, не раз
Уж отворял свой васисдас. [4:25]

The German baker's up and baking,
And more than once, in cap of cotton,
He has thrown his Fenster offen. (30)

—*YT.*

5) Quotations; comic syntax; mosaic composition.

6) In this way, the word is brought outside of its ordinary limits and becomes a sort of word-gesture.

6

The deformation of the novel by verse could be seen in the deformation both of small units and of large groups of text, until the whole novel was deformed as a result. The fusion of these two essences, their struggle and interpenetration, gave rise to a new form.

The deforming element in *Eugene Onegin* was verse; the word as a signifying element retreated before the verse word, was overshadowed by it. This affected the small groups within the novel in verse: because of the power of verse and the metrical role played in it by function words, these little words, expressing the relations between grammatical categories, became equivalent to full-fledged words. The same thing happened with the shorthand designations (abbreviated words, initial letters) that in prose always signal a convergence with reality. Because they were part of the meter, and sometimes even appeared in rhyming position (i.e. were verse words generally), these words were deformed in their *meaning* as well; they acquired a certain semantic (comic) coloring from neighboring words; when brought into the verse mechanism, intonational particles became concrete to the point of being sound gestures.

In novels, fragments are usually structured according to various prose principles, and give the impression of being motivated by actual reality. Such fragments may not be involved in the development of the fabula, but thanks to the great affinity of literary prose for prosaic speech, the separation of the essential from the less important is inevitable (at least in the conventional sense of the word "important"). But verse fragments are perceived as *verse*; their uniformity is sanctified by verse—the essential is brought to the same level as the inessential. Sterne's dynamics in *Tristram Shandy* seemed like a digression, while in *Eugene Onegin*, where verse makes digressions equivalent to "the action," this does not occur.[55] Emotional shifts in a prose novel are always noticeable; in verse fragments, they are created by the verse itself.

55 See Shklovsky, "Sterne's *Tristram Shandy* and the Theory of the Novel" [*Tristam Shendi* Sterna i teoriia romana (Petrograd: Izd. OPOIAZ, 1921)].

The deforming element in *Eugene Onegin* was verse: its metrical forms, its sound (in the narrow sense), and finally its stanzaic structure.[56]

> a It is characteristic of the whole organization of the stanza that only one rhythmic
> A period is structured according to the principle of alternating rhymes; in addition
> a to this one period, there are three periods with paired rhymes and one with
> A enclosed rhyme. The positioning of the periods is meanwhile important: the
> b period with alternating rhymes is followed immediately by two periods with paired
> b rhyme, then one with belted rhyme, and the stanza closes with yet another paired
> B period. Meanwhile, the stanza features a preponderance of masculine paired rhymes
> B over feminine: there are six paired masculine rhymed lines and only two feminine.
> c In the theory and practice of poetic speech, rhyme is the earliest element to
> D demonstrate the deforming role of sound in relation to meaning. While for most
> D nineteenth-century critics, rhyme was just a phonic element,[57] Schlegel
> c emphasized the role of rhyme in determining meaning—the alexandrine,
> E the semantic role of rhyme in the sonnet.
> E

Rhyme was a semantic phenomenon for these writers. Two words that sounded alike had mutually intersecting meanings, and the degree and direction of this intersection was determined by multiple factors: 1) the *proximity* of

---

56 The following paragraph demonstrates the rhyme scheme of the "Onegin stanza," invented by Pushkin for his novel in verse. As noted earlier, Tynianov employs an unconventional notation for rhymes: his masculine rhymes are indicated with uppercase letters and feminine with lowercase.

57 The extent to which this question is improperly posed can be seen in phenomena like Mayakovsky's[N] rhymes, where the phonic element takes a back seat to the semantic—*YT*.

rhyming words in lines of poetry (the deformation of meaning in poems with ABAB rhyme will be weaker than in poems with ABBA or AABB rhymes); 2) the kinship or grammatical similarity of rhyming words (the deformation of meaning in related or grammatically similar words will be different than in conjoined words from dissimilar grammatical categories); 3) the phonic similarity of rhyming words (we know that sonically dissimilar words can also engage in rhyme—through assonance, etc.; the quality of the rhyme—masculine, feminine, dactylic, etc.—and how commonly it is used can be a significant factor here).[58]

Pushkin was very conscious of the semantic role of rhyme. For him, the transition to blank verse was a transition to a new semantics of verse. In his "Thoughts on the Road" he writes:

> I think that with time we will turn to blank verse. There are too few rhymes in the Russian language. One immediately evokes the next. *Flame* inevitably drags behind it *fame*. *Healing* is always peeking out from behind *feeling*. Find me a person who isn't sick of *love* and *dove*, *hard* and *starred*, *true* and *blue*, etc?[59]
>
> Much has been said about Russian folk verse. A. Vostokov defined it with great scholarship and *savoir-faire*.[60] Probably some future epic poet of ours will embrace it and make it popular [6:401].[61]

An ordinary rhyme, however, can be used precisely because of its strong associative connections: because *flame* drags *fame* behind it, *flame* also

---

58 We take the same point of view on the so-called instrumentation of the verse (*ochei ocharovan'e* [eyes' exaltation], "The Talisman," etc.)—*YT*.

59 The Russian pairs are: *plamen'* / *kamen'* [flame / stone], *chuvstvo* / *iskusstvo* [feeling / art], *liubov'* / *krov'* [love / blood], *trudnoi* / *chudnoi* [difficult / wondrous], *vernoi* / *litsemernoi* [faithful / hypocritical].

60 Alexander Vostokov (1781–1864) was a poet and philologist, one of the first serious scholars of Russian verse and versification.

61 Prince Vyazemsky writes about the same thing in an epistle to Zhukovsky (1821):

> The mind says one thing, the scandalmonger something else.
> Would I try to say which Russians Phoebus favored,
> Derzhavin bursts into verse, but it comes out Kheraskov.
> [See "Ostaf'evo archive," vol. 2 (1899–1913), 173]

Cf. Pushkin's comment—*YT*. P. A. Viazemskii, *Poems* [Stikhotvoreniia] (Leningrad, 1958), 125. What Tynianov calls "Thoughts on the Road" is given in the *Collected Works* as "Journey from Moscow to Petersburg."

experiences a semantic shift. The significance of an unexpected rhyme is similar to that of a banal one: it, too, shifts the word semantically. But a banal rhyme tends primarily to shift the *first* word (*flame,* which already seems to contain the shadow of *fame*), and the second word—already anticipated—then plays an auxiliary role. Meanwhile, with an unexpected rhyme, the *second* word experiences this kind of shift in meaning: only afterwards will it be associatively connected with and able to shift the meaning of the first word.[62]

62 This is why a rich rhyme is not favored as more valuable than a banal one—it all depends on what kind of deformation of meaning it brings about. (Cf. the polemics between Panaev[N] and Pavlova[N] around rich rhymes—given Nekrasov's poor rhymes.)—*YT.*

Part Two

THEORY THROUGH HISTORY—NOW

Literary Fact (1924)[1]

FOR VIKTOR SHKLOVSKY

What is literature?

What is a genre?

Every self-respecting literary theory textbook necessarily starts out with these definitions. The theory of literature stubbornly vies with mathematics in its extraordinarily dense and confident static definitions, forgetting that, while mathematics is built on definitions, definitions in literary theory are, far from forming the foundation, a constantly shape-shifting[T] consequence of the ever evolving literary fact.[2] And it's becoming more and more difficult to define things. Ordinary speech uses the terms "literature," "verbal art" [*slovesnost'*], and "poetry," and the need arises to affix them and render them serviceable for science, which is so fond of definitions.

We end up with three levels: the lowest is verbal art, the highest is poetry and the middle is literature. It is quite difficult to figure out what distinguishes them individually.

And it's even worse when people hold to the old-fashioned belief that verbal art refers to absolutely everything that has ever been written, while poetry is thinking in images. Because it's clear, to begin with, that poetry is not just thinking, and that thinking in images is furthermore not poetry.

We might just as well not bother looking for exact definitions for all the terms that are in use, or trying to advance them to the rank of scientific definitions. All the more since things are not going so well with the definitions themselves. For instance, let's try to define the concept of the long poem [*poema*[T]] as a genre. All attempts at a single static definition fail. Just look at Russian literature. The whole revolutionary essence of Pushkin's[N] long poem "Ruslan and Ludmila" lay in the fact that it was a "non-*poema*" (likewise his

1 First published in *LEF* no. 2 (1924), 101–116. Translation from "Literaturnyi fakt," *PILK*, 255–270. Selected notes by A. P. Chudakov, M. O. Chudakova, and E. A. Toddes [*CCT*], 507–518. Additional notes by Yuri Tynianov [*YT*] and the translators [unmarked].

2 For more on "shift," see "On Literary Evolution" (269–281).

"Prisoner of the Caucasus").[3] A frivolous eighteenth-century "fairy tale" was contending for the spot of the heroic long poem, without making apologies for its frivolity; the critics felt that this was a kind of anomaly in the system. In fact, it was a *shifting* of the system. The same thing happened with the individual elements of the long poem: Pushkin intentionally created the "hero"—the protagonist in "Prisoner of the Caucasus"—"for the critics," while the plot was a *tour de force* [a curiosity (Fr.)—*YT*].[4] *And once again, the critics perceived this as an anomaly in the system, a mistake; and once again it was a shifting of the system.* Pushkin had changed the meaning of the protagonist, but the protagonist went on being contrasted with the epic hero and seen as "lowered." Pushkin wrote:

> One lady noted of "The Gypsies" that there is only one honest person in the whole long poem, and it's the bear. Dear departed Ryleev was indignant that Aleko dragged a bear around and even took money from the gaggling crowds. Vyazemsky[N] had the same criticism. (Ryleev asked me to at least make Aleko into a blacksmith, which would be far more noble.) Really the best thing would be to make him a collegiate assessor or a landowner instead of a Gypsy. In that case, though, the whole poema wouldn't exist: *ma tanto meglio* [Italian: so much the better—*trans.*].[5]

Not gradual evolution, but a leap; not development, but shift. The genre is unrecognizable, and yet there remains enough of something to make this "non-*poema* " a *poema*. And this "enough" does not mean enough "fundamental" or "major" distinctive features of the genre, but rather the secondary features, the ones that are taken for granted and that do not seem to characterize the genre at all. In this case, the distinctive feature needed to preserve the genre was *size*.

At the outset, the concept of "size" is an energy-based concept: we tend to say "large form" about one whose construction requires a greater amount

---

3 For more on Pushkin, see "On the Composition of *Eugene Onegin*" (114–150). "Prisoner of the Caucasus" [Kavkazskii plennik] (1820–21) is one of Pushkin's long narrative poems written in a Byronic vein; "The Gypsies" [Tsygane] (1824) is another.

4 From a letter Pushkin wrote to Vyazemsky regarding the "Robber Brothers" plot on 15 October, 1823—*CCT*. Alexander Pushkin, *Sobranie sochinenii v 10–i tomakh* [Collected Works; henceforth *PSS*] (Moscow, 1959–1962), 9:73. Subsequent references to this edition will give the volume and page numbers in brackets.

5 "Rebuttal to My Critics" (1830)—*CCT*. See PSS, 6:344. Kondratii Ryleev (1795–1826) was a poet of Pushkin's circle and a political activist, sentenced to death following his participation in the Decembrist revolt in St. Petersburg in 1825.

of energy. But a "large form," such as a long poem, can be written using a small quantity of lines (cf. Pushkin's "Prisoner"). A form that is large in terms of expended energy can also happen to be large in spatial terms. But in certain historical periods this form also determines the laws of construction. The novel is distinguished from the novella by being a *large form*. The long poem is distinct from just a "poem" in the same way. The expectations for large forms are not the same as those for small ones: depending on the size of the construction, every detail and every stylistic device has a different function, possesses different power, and carries different weight.

Where this principle of construction has been preserved, the sense of genre is also preserved; but in preserving this principle, the construction can then shift to any number of new positions. A lofty long poem can be switched out for a frivolous fairytale, and a noble hero (like Pushkin's parodic "senator" or "litterateur")[6] can be replaced by a prosaic protagonist; the fabula can be downshifted in importance, etc.

But then it becomes clear that it is impossible to give a *static* definition of a genre that would cover all the associated phenomena: the genre *shifts*. We are looking at an irregular zigzag instead of a direct line of evolution. Moreover, that evolution is able to take place precisely due to the "fundamental" features of the genre: the epic as narrative, the lyric as emotional art, etc. The sufficient and necessary condition for the unity of a genre from one historical period to the next lies in "secondary" features like the size of the construction.

But the actual *genre* is not a constant, immobile system. It's interesting to see how the concept of genre vacillates when we are faced with an excerpt or fragment. An excerpt from a long poem can be experienced as an excerpt *from a long poem*, but it can also be experienced as an *excerpt*; that is, we can be aware of the fragment as its own genre. This sense of genre does not depend on the perceiver's arbitrary reaction; rather, it depends on the prevalence or even just the presence of a genre. In the eighteenth century, the excerpt was only a *fragment* [of a larger form], but in Pushkin's time it was *a long poem* in its own right. Interestingly, the functions of all of a work's stylistic methods and devices depend upon the definition of the genre: they will function differently in a long poem than in a fragment.

In this way, the genre as system can vacillate. It arises (from anomalies and embryonic ideas in other systems) and declines, turning into the rudiments of other systems. The genre function of a device is not fixed.

It is impossible to conceive of a genre as a static system because the very awareness of a genre emerges as the result of its clash with a traditional genre

6 "Ode to his Grace Count Dm. Iv. Khvostov" (1825) [2:72]—*CCT*.

(i.e. the sense of a shift—at least partial—from the traditional genre to a "new" one taking its place). The whole point here is that the new phenomenon *supplants* the old one, takes its place and, without being a "development" of the old one, nevertheless acts as its substitute. When this "substitution" does not occur, the genre as such disappears, falls apart.

The same is true for "literature." The fact of evolution sweeps away all firm and static definitions.

The definitions of literature that proceed from its "fundamental" features run up against living *literary fact.* Even as it becomes more and more difficult to give a firm *definition of literature*, any contemporary can tell you exactly what makes a *literary fact.* He will say that X has nothing to do with literature and is a fact of everyday life [*byt*][T] or of the poet's personal life, whereas Y is definitely a literary fact.[7] An older contemporary, who has lived through one or two—if not more—literary revolutions, will point out that in his day, this or that phenomenon was not a literary fact, but has now become one; and vice versa. Literary journals and almanacs are nothing new, but only in our day have they come to be perceived as "literary works" and "literary facts" in their own right. *Zaum*[T] has always existed, in the language of children, sectarians, etc., but only in our day has it become a literary fact.[8] Conversely, something that is a literary fact today may tomorrow become an ordinary fact of life and disappear from literature. For us, charades and logogriphs are games for children, but in the age of Karamzin,[N] with its emphasis on verbal minutiae and play with literary devices, they were a literary genre.[9] As it turns out, it's not just the *borders* of literature—its periphery and frontiers—that are fluid: the center itself is fluid as well. Instead of one primordial, regular stream of succession flowing and evolving at the center of literature, with new phenomena congregating around its edges, it is these new phenomena that come to occupy the center, while what was previously in the center is in turn relegated to the periphery.

When a genre is in the process of disintegrating, it migrates from the center to the periphery, and a new phenomenon moves in from the minutiae of literature, its backwoods and lowlands, and takes the previous genre's place at the center (this

---

7 For *byt*, see also "On Literary Evolution" (especially 277–279).

8 The reference to sectarians concerns the role of glossolalia, or speaking in tongues, in a state of religious ecstasy—something observed in many religions but particularly in the Old Believers sect widespread in Russia.

9 For more on Karamzin, see both "On Literary Fact" (165–168) and "The Ode as an Oratorical Genre" (109–113).

is the same phenomenon as the "canonization of minor genres" described by Viktor Shklovsky).[N] This is how the adventure novel became cheap, "dime-store" fiction, and why the psychological narrative is now becoming cheapened as well.

The same is true of shifts in literary tendencies: In the 1830s and 1840s, "Pushkinian verse" (i.e., not verse by Pushkin, but its most popular elements) was taken up by his imitators in literary journals, where it became drastically impoverished and vulgarized (Baron [Egor] Rozen, V. Shchastnyi, A. A. Krylov, et al.).[10] It became literally the "dime-store" verse of its time, while phenomena from other historical traditions and strata ended up in the center.

By setting up a "firm" "ontological" definition of literature as a "quintessence," historians of literature were boxed into viewing manifestations of historical shifts as part of a serene continuity, as the serene and gradual elaboration of this "quintessence." This produced a harmonious picture: Lomonosov[N] begat Derzhavin[N], Derzhavin begat Zhukovsky,[N] Zhukovsky begat Pushkin, Pushkin begat Lermontov.[11]

Pushkin's unvarnished remarks about his supposed predecessors (Derzhavin was an "illiterate crank" [9:161]; Lomonosov "had a pernicious influence on literature" [6:385])[12] were overlooked. Also, the fact that Derzhavin only succeeded Lomonosov by bringing about a *shift in his ode*; that Pushkin inherited the large form of the eighteenth century only *by turning the Karamzinists' minutiae into a large form*; that all of them only managed to succeed their predecessors insofar as they *supplanted* their style and genres—all of this was overlooked. The fact that every new phenomenon *supplanted* an old one, and that every substitution of this sort was extremely complex in its makeup, also escaped notice; as did the fact that *continuity need only be discussed in reference to literary schools and imitations, not to phenomena of literary evolution, which is driven by struggle and shift.* The historians also completely overlooked exceptionally dynamic phenomena which, though of enormous significance for literary evolution, do not have dealings with the usual, customary literary material, and therefore do not leave behind sufficiently compelling, static "tracks"; their construction stands apart from preceding literary phenomena so starkly that they are left out of the textbooks. (This is the case with both *zaum* and the *enor-*

---

10 Tynianov offers a short list of minor poets of the 1830s. Krylov actually died before Pushkin, and Tynianov includes him here by mistake—*CCT*.

11 For Lomonosov, see also "The Ode as an Oratorical Genre" (77–113).

12 Imprecise quotations from a letter to Delvig[N] (no later than 8 June, 1825) and "Journey from Moscow to St. Petersburg" (1833–35)—*CCT.*

mous body of nineteenth-century epistolary literature. All these phenomena dealt with unusual material; they are enormously significant for literary evolution, but are omitted from static definitions of literary fact.) And here we see the faultiness of a static approach.

You can't judge a bullet by its color, taste or smell: a bullet must be judged by its dynamics. It is rash to talk about the overall aesthetic qualities of a work of literature. (By the way, the phrases "overall aesthetic merits," "overall beauty" keep popping up in the most unexpected quarters).

When scholars deal with a work of literature in isolation, ostensibly outside of historical considerations, they fail entirely; they just end up approaching it with the poor-quality, imperfect historical apparatus of a person from a different time.

Individual literary periods, or the literary present, do not represent an immobile system opposed to the mobile, evolving historical series.

Today we are witness to the same historical struggle between various strata and formations that can be found in the historical series of different periods. Like all contemporaries, we equate the "new" and the "good." But there are periods when all poets write "well," such that the "bad" poet will be the genius. The "impossible," unacceptable forms of Nikolai Nekrasov,[N] his "bad" poems, were good because they got automatized verse moving—they were *new.*[13] Outside of this evolutionary moment the work falls out of literature, and even though its devices can be studied, we risk studying them outside of their functions, for *the whole point of a new construction can lie in its new use of old devices, in their new constructive significance*, and that is what drops out of sight with the "static" approach.

(This does not mean that works cannot exist "for the ages." Things that are automatized can still be used. Every historical period puts forward bygone phenomena that seem kindred to it in spirit, while letting others be forgotten. Of course, these are secondary phenomena; new work made from ready-made material. The historical Pushkin differs from the Symbolists'[T] Pushkin, but the Symbolists' Pushkin cannot be compared to the evolutionary significance of Pushkin in Russian literature; each period always seeks out the materials it needs, but the way these materials are used characterizes only the period itself.)

By isolating a work of literature or a writer, we do not break through to the author's originality. Authorial individuality is not a static system; the literary personality is as dynamic as the literary period with which, and within which,

13 For more on the idea of "bad" poetry being good, see "Interlude" (173–216).

it moves. It is not like a closed space containing certain things; it is more like a zigzag line that is being continuously broken and redirected by the literary period.

(By the way, it's now become very fashionable to switch out the question of "the writer's individuality" for the question of "literary individuality." The question of evolution and the substitution of literary phenomena is replaced by the question of the psychological genesis of each phenomenon, and instead of literature we are encouraged to study the "personality of the creator." It's clear that the genesis of each phenomenon is one question, and its evolutionary significance, its place in the evolutionary series, is a different one. To talk about the individual psychology of the author and to ascribe to him the uniqueness of the phenomenon and its evolutionary literary significance is like claiming, when explaining the origins and significance of the Russian revolution, that it was brought about by the personal peculiarities of the leaders of the two opposing sides.)

Here's a curious testimony to the need to be extremely careful when dealing with the "psychology of creativity," even with questions of "theme" or "thematics," which are enthusiastically linked to authorial psychology. Vyazemsky wrote the following to Alexander Turgenev,[N] who had detected personal feelings in the former's poems:

> If I were in love, as you think I am, if I believed in the immortality of the soul, perhaps I would not have written for your pleasure:
>
> Душа, не умирая,
> Вне жизни будет жить бессмертием любви.
> [The soul, not dying, / Beyond life will live through love's immortality.]
>
> For instance, I have often noted that when my heart is raging, my tongue always misfires; an innocent passerby gets in its way and all of a sudden, it goes off. Diderot says, "Why seek the writer in his characters? What do Racine and Athalie have in common, [or] Molière and Tartuffe?"[14] What he said about writers of drama can be said about all writers. The main thing to note is not the selection of objects but the device: how, from what angle you look at a thing, what you see in it and what you can root out

14 Jean Racine and Molière were prominent seventeenth-century French playwrights; Vyazemsky refers to their plays, respectively, "Athalie" (1691) and "Le Tartuffe" (1664). Denis Diderot was an eighteenth-century French philosopher. All three are major figures of the French Enlightenment.

> that others will not notice. One cannot judge the singer's character by the words he sings [...] As if Batyushkov[N] could really be like the characters in his poems. He himself is not the source of this sensuality.[15]

Static isolation doesn't reveal any paths to the writer's literary personality; it only palms off the concept of psychological genesis for the concepts of literary evolution and literary genesis.

We have an example of this kind of static isolation right in front of us—in studies of Pushkin. Pushkin is removed from his historical moment and evolutionary line and studied outside of it (while the entire literary era is often studied under his aegis). And for this reason (and this reason alone), many literary historians continue to claim that the final stage of Pushkin's lyric is the highest point of its development, not noticing the actual decline in Pushkin's lyric production during this time, or the fact that he was withdrawing into series adjacent to literature: journals and history.

When you switch out the evolutionary viewpoint for a static one, many important and valuable literary phenomena will suffer. The unimaginative literary critic who scoffs at the phenomena of early Futurism has won an easy victory: judging a dynamic fact from a static viewpoint is no different than judging the qualities of a cannon ball without bringing up the question of flight. A "cannon ball" may look nice but not be able to fly, i.e., not actually be a cannon ball; or it may be "unwieldy" and "misshapen" but fly just fine, i.e., actually be a cannon ball.

It is only in evolution that we can successfully analyze the "definition" of literature. We will then discover that the properties of *literature* that seemed *fundamental* and primary are in constant flux and do not characterize literature as such—for instance, notions of the "aesthetic" in the sense of "the beautiful."

What remains is something that is often taken for granted: literature is a verbal construction that is felt precisely as a construction; i.e., literature is a *dynamic verbal construction.*

The demand for uninterrupted dynamics is the driving force behind evolution, for every dynamic system necessarily becomes automatized, and the opposing constructive principle takes shape dialectically.[16]

---

15 Ostaf'evo archive, vol. 1 (St. Petersburg: Tip. M.M. Stasiulevicha, 1899), 382; letter dated 1819—*YT*.

16 Defining literature as a dynamic verbal construction does not of itself necessitate a laying bare of the device. In some historical periods, the "bared" device becomes automatized like any other, which naturally gives rise to the need for a dialectically opposed "polished" device.

The uniqueness of a work of literature lies in its application of the constructive factor to the material, its "formatting" (essentially "deformation") of the material.[17] Every literary work is eccentric, in the technical sense: the constructive factor does not dissolve in the material or "correspond" to it, but is connected to it eccentrically, taking form on its surface.

And it goes without saying that "material" is by no means the antithesis of "form"; "material" is also "formal," for there is no such thing as material outside of the constructive principle. Any attempt to transcend construction will lead to results like those of Potebnya's[N] theorem: say one image aspires toward an idea (point X), but it converges there with many different images; this renders the most specific and varied constructions indistinguishable from one another.[18] The material is the element of form that is subordinated to the foregrounded constructive elements.

In verse, this crucial constructive factor is *rhythm*, while the material, in a general sense, is made up of *semantic groups*; in prose, the constructive factor is a *semantic grouping* (plot), and the material—again, in a general sense—is made up of the rhythmic elements of the word.

Every principle of construction determines both the specific connections within these constructive series and the relationship between the constructive factor and subordinated factors. (The principle of construction can also involve a particular *orientation*[T] [*ustanovka*] toward a role or use for the construction; to give a straightforward example, the constructive principle of oratorical speech, or even of oratorical poetry, involves an orientation toward language *spoken aloud*.)[19]

Thus, while "constructive factor" and "material" are constants for some constructions, the "constructive principle" is an ever-changing, complex and evolving concept. The whole point of a "new form" is its new principle of con-

---

Under these conditions, a "polished" device will be more dynamic than one that is bared, as it will shift, and thereby accentuate, the habituated relationship between the constructive principle and its material. The "minus sign" in front of a "polished" device comes into force in cases where the "plus sign" of a bared device has been automatized—*YT*.

17 In his subsequent work, Tynianov came to have doubts about his use of the term "deformation"; in a 1924 letter to G. Vinokur, he wrote "The term 'deformation' is inapt, I should have said "transformation"—then everything would make sense" (TsGALI, fond 2164, op. 1, item 334)—*CCT.*

18 Tynianov refers obliquely to some of [Oleksandr] Potebnya's positions at the beginning of this article, when he refutes the notion that poetry is "thinking in images."

19 For more on orientation [*ustanovka*], see "On Literary Evolution" (especially 273–280) and "The Ode as an Oratorical Genre" (284–285).

struction, its novel handling of the relationship between the constructive factor and subordinated factors (material).

To be dynamic, the reciprocal relationship between the constructive factor and the material must constantly vacillate, diversify, and change shape.

It is easy to approach a literary work of another era with one's own apperceptive baggage and to see, instead of an original constructive principle, nothing but withered and irrelevant connections tinted by our apperceptive lenses. But a *contemporary* can always appreciate these relationships and interactions in all their dynamism. Without separating "meter" from "diction," he always recognizes the novelty of their relationship. And this novelty is in fact an awareness of evolution.

One law of the dynamism of form is the widest possible vacillation, the greatest variation in the interrelations between the constructive principle and the material.

For example, in poems with a certain kind of stanza, Pushkin uses *blank spaces.* (These are not merely "gaps," since in this case lines are omitted for constructive reasons, and sometimes the blank spaces have no text at all—this is how it works in *Eugene Onegin*).[20]

We see something similar in [Innokenty] Annensky and Mayakovsky[N] ("About That").[21]

These are not pauses; they are verse lines extrinsic to the speech material; their meaning is any meaning, "some meaning"; as a result, the constructive factor—meter—is laid bare and its role emphasized.

The construction is elaborated using zero verbal material. The borders of the material of verbal art are so broad that they allow for the most profound rifts and ruptures, since the constructive factor welds them back together. Leapfrogging over material or using zero material only further emphasizes the durability of the constructive factor.

And so, when analyzing literary evolution, we encounter the following stages: 1) in response to an automatized principle of construction, an opposing constructive principle takes shape dialectically; 2) the new constructive principle begins to be applied—seeking out the easiest possible application; 3) the constructive principle spreads to the greatest mass of phenomena; 4) it gets automatized and gives rise to opposing principles of construction.

---

20 Tynianov discusses this and other features of Pushkin's novel in verse in greater detail in "On the Composition of *Eugene Onegin*" (114–150).

21 For more on Mayakovsky, see "On Mayakovsky" (293) and "Interlude" (173–216).

The new constructive principle makes its appearance dialectically when the predominant central trends are disintegrating. As large forms become automatized, they emphasize the significance of small forms (and vice versa); an image that presents a purely verbal arabesque or a semantic fracture, when automatized, clarifies the significance of the image motivated by an object (and vice versa).

But it would be strange to think that the new trend, the successor, makes its debut instantly, like Minerva springing from the head of Jupiter.

No, this important fact of evolutionary shift is preceded by a complex process.

The first thing is the emergence of the opposing constructive principle. It takes shape from *"incidental" results and "incidental" anomalies, mistakes.* Thus, for instance, when small forms are dominant (the sonnet and quatrain, etc., in lyric poetry), this kind of "incidental" result can come from banding together the sonnets, quatrains, etc., into a *collection.*

But when small forms become automatized, this *incidental result gets consolidated*—the collection comes to be understood as a construction, i.e. a large form comes into being.

Thus August Schlegel called Petrarch's sonnets a fragmentary lyric novel; thus Heine[N]—a poet of small forms—considered one of the main constructive features of his *Buch der Lieder* [Book of Songs] and other cycles of "little poems" to be the element of their *unification* in the collection, the element of connection, and he created collections that were lyric novels in which each small poem served as a chapter.[22]

On the other hand, one of the "incidental" results of a large form can be the recognition of incompleteness and fragmentariness as a device, as a method of construction—one which leads directly to small forms. But this "incomplete," "fragmentary" quality will obviously be perceived as a mistake, an anomaly in the system, and only when the system itself is automatized will it provide the necessary background for that mistake to take shape as a new constructive principle.

Actually, every deformity, every "mistake," every "irregularity" in normative poetics is—potentially—a new constructive principle (this is exactly what happened with the Futurists' use of careless and "incorrect" language as a means of semantic shift [*sdvig*]).[23]

22 For Heine, also see "Tyutchev and Heine" (64–76).

23 This is why every "purism" is a specific purism based on a given system, rather than "purism in general." The same is true of linguistic purism. The long lists of Pushkin's "mistakes" and

As it develops, the constructive principle seeks opportunities for application. For a constructive principle to apply itself in practice, special conditions—the most favorable ones—are needed.

This is how it is in our day with the Russian adventure novel. The principle of the plot-centered novel arose in dialectical opposition to the principle of the plotless vignette, or tale. However, the constructive principle has yet to find the appropriate application; it is still working with foreign material. For it to fuse with Russian material, it needs special conditions. This union is not so easy to bring about: the interaction between plot and style can be established only under particular conditions. This is the crux of the matter. If these conditions are not in place, the phenomenon will stall as a mere attempt.

The more "subtle" and unusual the phenomenon, the more clearly the new constructive principle comes into view.

Art locates these phenomena in the realm of everyday life [*byt*]. *Byt* teems with the rudiments of different intellectual activities. In terms of its makeup, everyday life is a rudimentary science, rudimentary art and technology. It differs from fully developed science, art, and technology in the way it interacts with them. For this reason, "artistic *byt*" is different from art—art plays a functional role in it—but in the form of their respective phenomena, the two do come into contact. Different ways of interacting with the same phenomena are conducive to different selections of these phenomena, which is why the forms of the artistic everyday are themselves distinct from art. But while a foundational, central principle of construction in art is developing, the new constructive principle is seeking "new," fresh, and "unfamiliar" phenomena. These cannot be old, habitual phenomena linked to the decomposing constructive principle.

And so the new constructive principle alights on phenomena from the realm of everyday life, ones that are fresh and easily accessible.

An example:

In the first half of the eighteenth century, written correspondence meant more or less the same thing that, until lately, it meant to us: a phenomenon

---

"irregularities" take up whole pages in the Archaists'[N] journal *Galatea* (1829 and 1830). Contemporary Russian prose "acts the prude" on two fronts: it's afraid of simple sentences and avoids carelessness even when it is fully motivated by language. Pisemsky[N] wasn't afraid of this when he mixed the genitive and instrumental cases in the following passage: "The smell of cheap tobacco [genitive] and some rancid cabbage soup [instrumental] coming from over there made life in this place nearly unbearable" (A. F. Pisemskii,[N] *Complete Works* [Polnoe sobranie sochinenii], vol. 4 [St. Petersburg: A.F. Marks, 1910], 46–47)—*YT*.

belonging exclusively to everyday life. Letters did not meddle with literature. They borrowed a good deal from the style of literary prose, but were themselves a long way from literature—instead these were notes, receipts, petitions, news from friends, etc.

Poetry was the predominant genre in literature, and within poetry the more high-style genres predominated. There was no outlet, no gap for the letter to slip through and become a literary fact. But this state of affairs ran its course, and the interest in prose and minor genres began to crowd out the solemn ode.

As the predominant genre, the ode began its decline into "overcoat odes"[T]—i.e., poems of praise offered for money—in other words, into everyday life. The constructive principle of any new movement finds its way forward dialectically.[24]

The main principle of the "grandificence" of the eighteenth century was the oratorical, emotionally dazzling function of poetic language. Lomonosov's imagery was built on the principle of transferring things into "inappropriate," unseemly contexts. This principle of "conjoining distant ideas" legitimized the union of words that were semantically distant from one another. An image would function more as a semantic "fracture" than a "picture" (meanwhile, the principle of conjoining words according to sound was also foregrounded).

"Grandiose" emotion would alternately build and subside ("rests," "weaker parts," and duller passages were included by design).

This accounts for the allegorical and anti-psychological tendency of eighteenth-century "high-style" literature.

The oratorical ode evolved into the ode as practiced by Derzhavin, whose grandiosity lay in the combination of words from high and low registers, of the ode with the comic elements of poetic satire.[25]

The collapse of grandiose poetry occurred in the age of Karamzin. In opposition to oratorical language, "romances"[T]—songs—took on special significance. The image-as-semantic-fracture became automatized and sparked an affinity for images oriented toward the associations closest at hand.

Minor forms and intimate emotions appeared, and the psychological replaced the allegorical. This is how constructive principles dialectically build on their predecessors.

---

24 For more on "overcoat odes," see "On Literary Evolution" (278) and "Interlude" (186).

25 For more about the ode and its evolutionary path in Russian literature, see "The Ode as an Oratorical Genre" (77–113).

But the application of these principles requires the most transparent and amenable phenomena, and these are found in everyday life.

Salons, the conversations of "fair ladies," and albums cultivated trivial, minor poetic forms: "songs," bagatelles, quatrains, rondos, acrostics, charades, *bouts-rimés,* and games were transformed into important literary phenomena.

And finally, *the letter.*

Letters provided the most amenable, effortless and necessary phenomena for advancing the new principles of construction in a singularly forceful way: the minor, "domestic" form of the letter, with its emphasis on things left unsaid, on fragmentariness and hints, prompted the induction of minutiae and stylistic devices antithetical to the "grandiose" devices of the eighteenth century. This much-needed material had been part of everyday life, outside of literature. And thus, from its status as a commonplace document, the letter ascended to the very center of literature. Karamzin's letters to [Alexander] Petrov surpassed his own experiments in the old oratorical canonical prose and led to the *Letters of a Russian Traveler,* where the travel letter became a *genre.* These letters became an apologia for a genre, a way for the genre to hold together new devices. In his foreword, Karamzin writes:

> Variegation and irregularity in language is a consequence of various objects acting on the soul ... of the traveler: he ... described his impressions not at his leisure, in the quiet of his study, but wherever and however he could: on the road, on foolscap, in pencil. Certainly there is much here that is unimportant, trivial ... but why not forgive the traveler a few idle details? A man in his travel clothes, staff in hand, knapsack slung over his shoulder, is not expected to speak with the careful scrupulousness of a courtier surrounded by similar courtiers, or of a professor in a Spanish periwig seated in big learned chairs.[26]

But the everyday letter continued to exist alongside the literary version. Instead of exclusively print genres, the center of literature also contained the everyday letter: peppered with lines of poetry, jokes, and stories, it was no longer merely a "notification" or "receipt."

Having once been a document, the letter became a literary fact.

The work of younger Karamzinists like A. Turgenev and P. Vyazemsky shows the constant evolution of the everyday letter. Letters were read, and not

---

26 N. M. Karamzin, *Selected Works* [Izbrannye proizvedeniia], vol. 1 (Moscow/Leningrad: Khudozh. literatura, 1964), 79—*CCT.*

only to their addressees; letters were appreciated and analyzed as works of literature in the very letters written in response. The model of a Karamzin letter—a mosaic of embedded poems, unexpected transitions and with a well-rounded closing aphorism—held for a long time. (See Pushkin's first letters to Vyazemsky and V. Pushkin.) But the style of the letter evolved. From the very beginning, elements like intimate jokes between friends, humorous circumlocutions, parodies, teasing, and hints at erotica played a role in these letters; these elements emphasized the intimate and non-literary nature of the genre. This is the line of development (of evolution) followed by the letters of A. Turgenev, Vyazemsky, and particularly Pushkin—but already toward a different end.

The mannered quality and circumlocutions began to disappear and fell into disfavor; things evolved in the direction of coarse simplicity (in Pushkin's case there was some influence from the Archaists with their struggle for "primeval simplicity" against Karamzinist aestheticism). This was not the neutral simplicity of the document, report, or receipt—it was [a] literary simplicity discovered anew. The extra-literary and intimate nature of the genre continued to be emphasized, but it was emphasized through overt coarseness, intimate ribaldry, and crude eroticism.

At the same time, writers recognized this genre as profoundly literary; letters were read out loud and shared. Vyazemsky planned to write a Russian *manuel du style epistolaire.*[27] Pushkin wrote drafts even for inconsequential private letters. He was scrupulous about his epistolary style, guarding its simplicity from any reversions to the mannered Karamzinist style. ("[…] *Adieu,* Prince Flibber and Princess Chatterbox. You see that I don't even have enough of my own simplicity to keep up correspondence" [Letter to Vyazemsky, 1 December 1826 (9:248)].

The language of everyday conversation was chiefly French, but Pushkin gave his brother a hard time for mixing French with Russian in his letters, like some Moscow *mademoiselle.*[28]

Thus the letter, while remaining a private and non-literary fact, was simultaneously and for this very reason a literary fact of tremendous significance. This literary fact is what defined the canonized genre of "literary correspondence," but even in its pure form it remained a literary fact.

And it's not hard to find periods of time when the letter, having exhausted its literary role, falls back into everyday use, ceases to have any

---

27 French: guide to epistolary style—*YT*. It was Alexander Turgenev, not Vyazemsky, who expressed this ambition. Ostaf'evo archive, vol. 3 (Saint Petersburg, 1899), 115—*CCT*.

28 Letter from 24 January, 1822 [9:37]—*CCT*.

further impact on literature, becomes a fact of everyday life—a document or receipt. But in the right circumstances, this everyday fact can once again become a literary fact.

It is curious to observe how the historians and theoreticians of literature who worked to build a firm definition of literature managed to miss a literary fact of tremendous significance, one that rose up to the surface of everyday life, then dove back down into it. To date, Pushkin's letters have only been used for fact-checking, or occasionally as a source for inquiries into his love life. And no one has yet studied the letters of Vyazemsky, A. Turgenev and Batyushkov as literary facts.[29]

In the case of Karamzin, the letter form justified the particular devices of the construction: as an everyday object, something fresh and "not ready-made," it suited the new constructive principle better than any "ready-made" literary objects could.

But there are other ways of making an everyday object literary, other ways of transforming facts of everyday life into facts of literature.

When the constructive principle is applied in one area, it strives to further expand and extend itself over the broadest possible areas.

We can call this the "imperialism" of the constructive principle. We can observe this imperialism, this quest to seize the greatest possible territory, in virtually any area. For instance, the generalization of poetic epithets described by Veselovsky: if poets today are using "golden sun," "golden hair," then tomorrow we will see "golden sky," "golden earth," and "golden blood."[30] Another example is the fact of orientation toward the domineering framework or genre—periods of rhythmic prose coincide with the predominance of poetry over prose. The development of *vers libre* proves that the constructive significance of rhythm was recognized to an extent sufficient for it to cover the broadest possible series of phenomena.

The constructive principle strives to reach beyond its habitual limits, since when it stays within the limits of habitual phenomena, it quickly becomes automatized. This explains why poets change their themes.

An example: Heine's art is based on fracture and dissonance. In the last lines of his poems, he breaks the continuity of the entire poem (its *pointe*), and his images are constructed through contrasts. The love theme in his work is also

29 Written in 1924. There are now articles on the topic by N. Stepanov and others—*YT*.

30 See Alexander Veselovsky, *Historical Poetics* [Istoricheskaia poetika] (Moscow: Khud. literatury, 1940), 21—*CCT*.

developed under these conditions. As Gotschall writes: "Heine took the contrast between sacred and profane love to its limit, until it threatened to break free of poetry altogether. In time, his variations on this theme no longer 'rang true,' and his interminable self-ridicule brought to mind a circus clown. His humor had to seek out new territory, step outside the narrow circle of 'love' and take on the themes of nation, literature, art, and the objective world."[31]

As it extends to cover ever-broader areas, the constructive principle strives to break through the boundary of the specifically literary and "secondhand," and alights, at long last, upon everyday life [*byt*]. For example, the constructive factor of prose—the plot dynamics—becomes its main principle of construction and strives for the highest degree of development. Works with *minimal fabulas*, with plots that develop outside of the fabula, come to be perceived as plot-centered. (See V. Shklovsky, "Tristram Shandy.")[32] This can be compared to the phenomenon of free verse, which, though distanced from the usual verse system, emphasizes the verse line).

In our day this constructive principle has alighted upon everyday life. Newspapers and journals have been around for many years, but only as a fact of everyday life. Today, however, there is a heightened interest in newspapers, journals, and literary almanacs as literary works in their own right—as constructions.

What is revitalizing in a fact of everyday life is its constructive side. The layout of a newspaper or journal is of interest to us. A journal can be good as far as content goes, but we might nevertheless find its construction or layout disappointing, and for that reason denounce it as a journal. If we trace the evolution of the journal, and its replacement by the almanac, etc., it becomes obvious that this evolution does not proceed in a straight line. At times, the journal is an ordinary fact of everyday life; its layout is irrelevant; at other times, it develops into a literary fact. During periods of increased intensification and expansion of facts such as "montage-type" composition in the story or novel (where plot is

---

31 R. Gotschall, *Die deutsche National-Literatur des 19. Jahrhunderts*, Bd. 2 (Beslau, 1872), 92. To suggest that these thematic shifts were determined by extra-literary causes (e.g., personal experiences) would be to conflate genesis and evolution into a single concept. The psychological genesis of a phenomenon does not correspond to that phenomenon's evolutionary significance—*YT*.

32 In "Sterne's *Tristam Shandy* and the Theory of the Novel" [*Tristam Shendi* Sterna i teorii romana, in *Sborniki po teorii poeticheskogo iazyka*, vol. 4, no. 2 (Petrograd: Opoiaz, 1921)], Shklovsky used Lawrence Sterne's 1767 novel to demonstrate his hypothesis of the prevalence of narrative style over plot.

constructed out of deliberately disconnected segments), this principle of construction quite naturally crosses over to neighboring phenomena, and later to those further afield.

Let me mention one more typical phenomenon that also helps in discerning how a constructive principle that is cramped by purely literary material can cross over into real-life phenomena. I have in mind the "literary personality."

There are certain phenomena of style that point to the *person* of the author. We can observe this in embryonic form in an ordinary short story: the peculiarities of lexicon and syntax, and, most importantly, the phrasal and intonational pattern, all hint at certain elusive and yet concrete features of the narrator. If the narrative foregrounds the narrator and his point of view, then these elusive features become palpably concrete and take on a form—a persona. (This is, of course, a special kind of concreteness, which has little to do with how something is visualized in an illustration. If we were asked what this narrator *looked like*, our answer would be of necessity subjective.) The outer limit of literary concreteness for this stylistic character is the *name*.

Naming a character instantly introduces a great deal of minor features, which reach far beyond the names themselves. When a nineteenth-century author signed his articles "A Resident of New Village" instead of giving his name,[33] he naturally had no intention of informing readers that he lived in New Village, since there was no reason why they should need to know that.

But precisely because of its "pointlessness," the name took on other features. The reader selected only concepts that were *true-to-character*, that somehow hinted at the author's features, and overlaid these features onto the ones that emerged for him out of the style, the idiosyncrasies of *skaz*,[T] or the assortment of other already existing, similar names. Thus for the reader, New Village meant "outskirts" and the author of the article had to be a "hermit."

Proper names and last names are even more expressive. In everyday life, the name or last name is the same thing as the person who carries it. When we hear an unfamiliar last name, we say: "That name doesn't tell me anything." In a work of literature there are no nonspeaking names. All the names tell you something. Every name mentioned in a work of literature is already a designation, one that plays with all the meanings at its disposal. It does everything it can to develop the nuances that we would simply ignore in everyday life. For a literary protagonist, the name "Ivan Petrovich Ivanov"

33 The mysterious Resident is Nikolai Gnedich (1784–1833), a poet and translator—*CCT*.

is not colorless at all, because colorlessness is only a negative characteristic in everyday life—within the construction, it instantly becomes a positive characteristic.[34]

Thus, signatures like "A Resident of the Village of *Tentelevo*" or "An Elder from *Luzhniki*" which appear to be just indications of place (or age), are actually very specific, very concrete appellations not only because of the features inherent in the words "elder" or "village resident," but also because of the great expressiveness of place-names like "Tentelevo" and "Luzhniki."

Meanwhile, the institution of the *pseudonym* also plays a role in literary-artistic everyday life (and will continue to do so). When considered in these everyday terms, the pseudonym is a phenomenon of the same order as the anonymous author. The everyday and historical conditions and the reasons behind this phenomenon are complex and do not concern us here. But during periods of literature when the "author's personality" comes to the fore, this everyday phenomenon finds a use within literature.

In the 1820s pseudonyms like the ones mentioned became "concentrated," more concrete in proportion to the growth of the stylistic phenomena linked to *skaz*. In the 1830s, this led to the creation of the literary personality of Baron Brambeus.

Later on, the "personality" of Kozma Prutkov was created in the same way.[35] Under special conditions of literary evolution, a legal fact connected mostly with the question of copyright and responsibility—a note in one's file at the Writers' Union—becomes a *literary fact.*

Literary phenomena belong to various strata; in this sense, no one literary trend can completely supplant another. But this shift does happen in a different sense—the *prevailing* trends, prevailing genres, are supplanted by others.

However broad and numerous the branches of literature may be, whatever multitude of individual features might be present in these individual branches, history leads them along certain channels: a trend of seemingly infinite diversity at some point inevitably grows shallow, and phenomena that were initially insignificant and barely noticeable arise to take its place.

The "merging of the constructive principle with the material" that I mentioned before is infinitely diverse, and takes place through many different forms;

34 "Ivan Petrovich Ivanov" is approximately "John Peter Johnson,"—that is, an unmarked and common-sounding name here in the Anglo-American context.

35 For other literary personalities, including Kozma Prutkov, see also "On Parody" (318–319; 326–327).

but every literary trend ultimately faces its hour of historical generalization, its reduction to the simple and uncomplicated.

Consider, for instance, the manifestations of unoriginal, derivative writing that can speed up this kind of shift in the prevailing trend, a shift that can entail revolutions of varying scale and varying depth.[36] There are domestic ("political") revolutions; there are revolutions that are *sui generis* "social." And these revolutions usually break through the realm of "literature" proper and seize upon the realm of everyday life.

This variable make-up of the literary fact should be taken into account every time we talk about "*literature.*"

The literary fact is variable in its composition, and in this sense literature is a ceaselessly evolving series.

Every term in literary theory must be the concrete consequence of concrete facts. One must not proceed from the extra- and super-literary heights of metaphysical aesthetics and forcibly "cherry-pick" "suitable" phenomena for a given term. The term is concrete, while the definition evolves, as does the literary fact itself.

---

36 We give "unoriginal, derivative writing" where Tynianov uses the word *epigonstvo,* which derives from "epigone" [*epigon*], meaning an unimpressive, imitative follower of a great artist. The word is part of common usage in Russian, not felt as a specialized Greek word as in English—*CCT.*

Interlude (1924)[1]

FOR BORIS PASTERNAK

Здесь жили поэты.
[Poets once lived here.][2]
Blok

1

These days writing about poems is almost as hard as writing them.[3] And writing poems is almost as hard as reading them. Such is the vicious circle of our time. There are fewer and fewer poems being written, and what is really front and center right now is not poems, but poets. And this is not nearly as inconsequential as it may seem.

Three years ago prose ordered poetry to leave the premises once and for all. The poets cleared out in a sort of panic, and prose writers moved in and occupied all the empty seats. Along with this development, the number of poets fell dramatically, while that of prose writers grew. Many of these writers did not actually exist yet, but nevertheless were considered wholly existent and, subsequently, really did come to exist. There was a rush; these were premature, hurried births—the Serapion Brothers, for example, were translated into Spanish long before they wrote anything in Russian.[4] We could all see that

1 First published (in part) in *The Russian Contemporary* [Russkii sovremennik], no. 4 (1924), 209–221; subsequently and in full, in *Archaists and Innovators* [Arkhaisty i novatory] (1929). Translation from "Promezhutok," *PILK*, 168–195. Selected notes by Marietta Chudakova [*MC*], 471–482. Additional notes by Yuri Tynianov [*YT*] and the translators [unmarked].

2 Inexact quotation from "Poets" [Poety], a poem by Alexander Blok[N]—*MC*. The line is actually "Poets lived there" [Tam zhili poety]. See Alexander Blok, *Complete Works in Two Volumes* [Polnoe sobranie stikhotvorenii v dvukh tomakh], vol. 1 (Leningrad: Sovetskii pisatel', 1946), 432–433.

3 Tynianov tends to use the words *stikh* (verse line, line of poetry) and *stikhi* (verses or poems), rather than *poeziia* (poetry) or *stikhotvorenie* (a single poem). See Verse / Poetry in Terms.

4 The Serapion Brothers, who borrowed their name from the German Romantic writer E. T. A. Hoffmann, was a group of early 1920s prose writers, including, among others, Evgenii Zamiatin, Mikhail Zoshchenko, Tynianov's brother-in-law Veniamin Kaverin, fellow

prose was victorious, poetry was in retreat, and for some reason we were all happy about it (those poets' evenings had really gotten old). But what the point of it all was, what this victory might mean, and where poetry's retreat would ultimately take it—we somehow didn't think about any of that. Now poetry has fully "retreated," and the situation has turned out to be rather complicated.

The fact remains: prose won. In the past, when a reader would pick up a journal or an almanac, he would immediately rush to the poems and, only after he'd cooled down a bit, skim through the prose. The reader of a more recent vintage carefully avoids the poems as if they were comrades long past their prime, and rushes headlong for the prose. Instead of poetesses there are now prosettes. (The very newest readers have started to avoid both the poems and the prose. These readers are still timid, still won't admit to it; and yet, in a way, they are the most peculiar of all—they go straight to the current events, the reviews, the editorials—to the journalistic back alleys that are beginning to point toward a new type of journal.)

So, "our prose is blossoming." This situation is now established, so to speak, and I have no intention of challenging it. According to critics these days, writing a short story no worse than Tolstoy is not so difficult. And prose production really is growing, while poetic production is falling. The watches of prose writers and of poets tick differently. The time of a poem is no longer determined by the day it appears; the time of prose is determined by cash advances. And meanwhile, the relationship between the victors and the defeated is, I repeat, rather complex.

These days, prose exists through tremendous inertia.[5] This inertia can only be overcome with a huge effort, bit by bit, and making the effort has become ever more difficult and, evidently, ever more pointless. Sometimes it seems

---

Formalist theorist Viktor Shklovsky,[N] and the poet Nikolai Tikhonov. For more on the latter, see section eleven of this article.

5 Tynianov uses the word *inertsiia*, a calque from the Latin that means, as in English, "inertia"—the continuation of matter in its state of rest or uniform motion. Unlike English, however, *inertsiia* in Russian also has the colloquial meaning of something happening automatically: "I started boiling water to do laundry but *by inertia* [*po inertsii*] made myself a cup of tea." The latter meaning is important for Tynianov, in light of the central importance of "automation" / "automatization" in Formalist thought (note, however, that Tynianov does not use the word "automatization" per se). For consistency's sake, we have used "inertia" throughout, but readers should be aware that the idea of uniform motion in a straight line is more important here than that of "inertness" or lack of movement; for this reason, in some contexts the English word "momentum" ("Prose is being carried along by its own momentum") might better approximate the meaning.

that inertia itself, rather than any particular writer, has written a short story and inevitably ended it with the death of the protagonist, or at least of Europe.[6] For poetry, the period of inertia has ended. Belonging to a school or holding a poetic passport won't save the poet any longer. The schools have disappeared, the movements have quite predictably ceased to be, as if on command. They gained prominence in geometric progression, became differentiated, and fell apart; subsequently, the self-determination of minor poetic nationalities began to take place within the confines of individual apartments and, finally, each poet was left to his own devices.

Now all of this belongs to the distant past, but just a couple of years ago even the Emotionalists, who had declared love the best thing in the world, along with some other more or less joyful feelings—I think even they were considered, if not a school, then at least a movement.[7]

This phenomenon of schools being replaced by solitary individuals is characteristic of literature overall, but the rapid pace of succession, the brutality of the struggle, and the swiftness of the fall—this is the tempo of our age. The nineteenth century was slower. There are no poets now who would not outlive their movements—Blok's death was *all too* predictable.[8]

Poetic inertia has ended; the groupings have mixed together; the scale has grown immeasurably broader. Poets who have absolutely nothing in common are joining forces; names remote from one another are standing side by side. The ones surviving are the solitaries.

And right now, the stakes for poetry are high. Poetry is speech transformed; it is human speech that has outgrown itself. Language in poetry has thousands of unexpected shades of meaning; poetry gives language a new dimension. New poetry is new vision. And the growth of these new phenomena happens only in the interludes when inertia loses its grip. The action of inertia is, essentially, all we know—in skewed historical perspective, an interlude without inertia seems like a dead end. (Every innovator is ultimately working for inertia; every revolution is produced for the canon.) But there are no dead ends in history. There are only interludes.

---

6 Tynianov refers obliquely to Ilya Ehrenburg's novels *The Life and Ruin of Nikolai Kurbov* [Zhizn' i gibel' Nikolaia Kurbova] and *D. E. Trust: A History of the Death of Europe* [Trest D. E. Istoriia gibeli Evropy]—*MC*. Ilya Ehrenburg (1891–1967) was a major prose writer of the early to mid-Soviet period.

7 See the "Declaration of Emotionalism" [Deklaratsiia emotsionalizma] signed by Mikhail Kuzmin, A. Radlova, S. Radlov, and Yuri Yurkun, published in *Abraxas* no. 3 (1923)—*MC*.

8 The death of Alexander Blok in 1921 was seen by many as marking the passing of an era.

One of these solitary poets told me that "every hour changes the situation." Poetry itself has become a favorite topic for poets. The better half of Pasternak's poems are about poetry. Mandelstam[N] writes about his "dear sound sequence," Mayakovsky[N] about his "poetic blinders."[9] It's hard to say anything about works, fully formed poems, let alone about whole books during an interlude. The poets passing through the interlude make for an easier subject.

2

Прокатилась дурная слава
[*An ill fame rolled through*][10]

During an interlude, there is no need to observe poetic hierarchies. Esenin comes first. He is one of the most characteristic poets of the interlude. When one stops to take a breath at battle's end, the landscape inevitably comes into view. When inertia ends, the first and most pressing need is to test one's own voice. Esenin is testing his for public response, for echo. This line of approach is typical.

When literature is having a hard time, people start talking about readers. When a voice needs to be retuned, they talk about resonance. This approach is sometimes successful—when *readers* are brought into literature, they prove to be a literary engine, the only thing still needed to nudge language out of its standstill. Thinking of readers is a sort of "motivation" for getting out of a dead end. In poetry the way out sometimes manifests as a change in intonation—the angle of "addressing the reader" can change the entire intonational framework. In prose, *skaz*[T] has the reader in mind, forcing him to "perform" all the speech. And this kind of "internalized" consideration of the reader helps during periods of crisis (Nekrasov).[N]

But there is another way of addressing the reader—the verse can be made commonplace, the language more familiar. Doing so is a slide into poverty.

Esenin is inexorably retreating.

Esenin's early lyric poetry was, of course, deeply traditional; it had roots in Fet,[N] and in an abstract kind of poetic "populism," and in Blok crudely understood via Klyuev.[11] In fact, Esenin was never strong in novelty or radicalism or

9 For more on Mayakovsky, see "On Mayakovsky" (293).

10 Epigraph from Sergei Esenin,[N] "I only have one amusement left …" [Mne ostalas' odna zabava …]. See Sergei Esenin, *V stikhakh i zhizni*, vol. 1 (Moscow: Respublika, 1997), 223.

11 For more on Afanasy Fet, see Tynianov's comments on Pasternak in section nine of this article. Nikolai Klyuev (1884–1937) was a "peasant" poet affiliated with the Symbolists

self-sufficiency. The least convincing of all his supposed affiliations is with the Imaginists, who were likewise neither new nor a distinct group, and actually, who knows whether they ever even existed?[12] Esenin's strength was the emotional tone of his lyric poetry. Naïve, archetypal and therefore unusually vital poetic emotion makes up the backbone of Esenin. His entire poetic project is a ceaseless search for decorations for this naked emotion. First it was Church Slavonicisms, a painstakingly rustic veneer, and an equally traditional "peasant's Christ"; later, obscene vocabulary from the Imaginists, which was essentially just as much a decoration for Esenin's emotions as the lofty church language had been.

Art that leans so heavily on powerful, archetypal emotion is always closely tied to the personality. Behind the words, the reader sees a person; something "personal" can be conjectured behind the verse intonation. It is for this reason that Blok's literary personality (which was not the living, "biographical" Blok, but an entirely distinct, "verse Blok" that existed on an entirely different level) loomed so extraordinarily large in his poems.[13] Esenin's "Pugachov" is remarkable because, in it, this emotion appeared in a new light and took up a far-off theme, rendering it extraordinarily vital and close at hand:

— Дорогие мои, хорошие![14]
["My dear friends, my darlings!"]

Esenin's literary (poetic) personality has been inflated to the outer reaches of illusion. Readers treat his poems like documents, like letters received in the mail from Esenin. This is of course powerful and necessary. But it is also dangerous. A breakdown or dissociation could occur—the literary personality could fall out of the poems and begin living alongside them, and the abandoned poems could turn out to be poor. Esenin's literary personality—from the "shining novice" in Klyuev's skullcap to the "foulmouthed scandal-monger" of *Bawdy Moscow*—is profoundly literary. This personality is nearly a literary borrowing—sometimes

---

whose work drew heavily on Russian religious motifs and folklore. He was an early mentor to, and perhaps a lover of, Esenin.

12 Imaginism did exist (from 1918–1925, with a manifesto published in 1919); its adherents, who also included Vadim Shershenevich and Anatoly Mariengof, had much in common with the Futurists,[N] despite attempts to distinguish themselves through an emphasis on "vivid images."

13 Tynianov treats the problem of the "literary personality" more extensively in"Literary Fact" (especially 170–172) and "On Parody" (especially 318–328).

14 Esenin's "Pugachov," which refers to the famous leader (Emelyan Pugachov) of an eighteenth-century rebellion of Cossacks and peasants, was published in 1922. See Esenin, *V stikhakh*, 2:39.

it seems like an unusually schematized, degraded Blok or a parodied Pushkin;[N] even the little dog by the village gate barks at Esenin in a Byronic manner.[15] And still, this personality, tied to emotion, was sufficiently convincing to overshadow the poems, to grow into its own kind of extra-verbal literary fact. In Esenin's most recent poems, the "personality" has played out its final act. He is neither a "novice in a skullcap" nor a poet "gulping down pure alcohol."[16] The "scandal-monger" has repented from his scandals; the dramatic tension has weakened. The personality no longer overshadows the poems. But, in the meantime, if you draw the viewer away from the actor, a form like *Lesedrama* becomes suspect; remove the title from the painting and it turns out to be an oleograph.[17] The poet who was once so dear to worshippers of the "visceral," to those who grumbled about literature having become a "craft" (that is, an art, as if it hadn't always been one), discovers that the "visceral" is much more literary than any "craft." Esenin used this primitive emotional force, the almost intrusive immediacy of his literary personality, to downplay the literariness of his verse. These days he can sometimes seem like an anthology ("from Pushkin to the present day"):

Я посетил родимые места	I visited my childhood haunts
-------	-------
Да! теперь решено. Без возврата	Yes! it's decided. No looking back
Я покинул родные поля.	I left the fields of home for good.
-------	-------
Ах! какая смешная потеря!	Ah! What a ridiculous loss!
<.........................>	[......................]
Золотые, далекие дали!	The golden, distant expanses![18]

But maybe these banalities are not so bad? Maybe we need them? The emotional poet has the right to be banal. Hackneyed words can act with remarkable force, precisely because they have been overused, because they

---

15 Tynianov has in mind Esenin's 1924 poem "Returning Home" [Vozvrashchenie na rodinu]—*MC*. See ibid., 1:236. For Pushkin, see also "On the Composition of *Eugene Onegin*" (114–150).

16 Tynianov refers to the poems "I will go as a meek novice in a skullcap ..." [Poidu v skuf'e smirennym inokom] (1914) and "Yes! it's decided. No looking back ..." [Da! Teper' resheno. Bez vozvrata ...] (1922–1923)—*MC*. See ibid., 1:66, 1:217.

17 *Lesedrama* (literally "reading-drama") is the German term for what in English is called "closet drama": plays written to be read by a solitary reader or to a small group, rather than performed onstage.

18 Lines from Esenin's "Returning Home," "Yes! it's decided. No looking back ..." and "I have only one trick left ... " *MC*. See ibid., 1:236, 1:217. By referring to an "anthology," Tynianov emphasizes the generically "poetic" meter, diction, and themes of the cited extracts; likewise, the frequent and obvious motifs and quotations from Pushkin.

occur every other second. They are the source of the magnetic pull of the Gypsy theme; and also the source of the banality of Polonsky, Annensky, and Sluchevsky, as well as Blok's Apukhtin-esque[N] howling.[19] But that is the whole point: in Esenin's desire to bring lyric down to the level of simple, archetypal emotion, he is actually translating it into traditions that are annoying and not at all simple. There are annoying traditions—worn-out ones. (For us these days Blok—as a tradition—is worn-out in this way.) There are commonplaces that simply cannot come across as poetry, and there is poetry that has become a kind of "stock verse" and has ceased to be poetry as such. Rosenheim was (and is) annoying (though at one point people mistook his poetry for Lermontov[N]).[20] The Rosenheim tradition—the one-dimensionality of his poetry—is likewise annoying.[21] What Esenin is moving toward is stock verse:

> И полилась печальная беседа
> Слезами теплыми на пыльные листы.[22]
> [And our sorrowful conversing / Flowed in warm tears onto the dusty leaves]

This banality is too epic, too comprehensive to be on par with Esenin's previous banalities. The intonation here is false; there is no "address" to anybody. Instead there is an ossified, stock-verse intonation, which seems like a withdrawal to the one-dimensionality of stock verse (but, actually, to the flattened-out poetry of the late nineteenth century). The public's response has played Esenin false. His poems are poems for light reading, but to a large extent they are no longer poems at all.

3

Au dessus de la mêlée [23]

Another retreat.

One can try to stand on the sidelines. This is a more or less dignified and tempting position.

---

19 Yakov Polonsky (1819–1898), Innokenty Annensky (1855–1909), and Konstantin Sluchevsky (1837–1904) are all nineteenth-century poets (of rather different profiles).

20 For more on Lermontov, see also "Interlude" (179; 201–202); "Literary Evolution" (269–272); "On Parody" (299–302)

21 Mikhail Rosenheim (1820–1887) was a poet and journalist remembered for his banal progressivism and, subsequently, patriotism.

22 Ibid., 1:236—*MC*.

23 French: "above the fray."

Just as Esenin makes his retreat into the ranks of his readers, so Khodasevich's role lies in retreating to the ranks of literary culture.[24]

But this retreat is also unexpectedly a retreat to readers' notion of poetic culture.

We have a rich culture of poetry (immeasurably richer than our prose culture).

We remember the nineteenth century more profoundly than nineteenth-century people remembered the eighteenth century. In 1834 Belinsky[N] boldly wrote a bunch of nonsense about the eighteenth century in his *Literary Daydreams*; he declared his ignorance with pride, even enthusiasm—and all just to say what he needed to say (even if it was completely untrue then, as it is now): "We have no literature." Our thirties haven't yet begun, but there probably won't be another discovery of this negative America, even in the thirties. We have been denied that option. We have one of the greatest poetic cultures of all time; it brought real movement, but skewed historical perspective means that we perceive this culture first and foremost through its products (its poems). In Pushkin's era, poetic language was the center of the same kind of struggle that is going on today; and the poetry of that era was a powerful factor in that struggle. This poetry hits us like a clot, a ready-made object, and it takes archaeological investigation of this clot to reveal the movement that once was.

Так ярый ток, оледенев,	Thus raging torrents turn to ice,
Над бездною висит,	suspended above the deep,
Утратив прежний грозный рев,	and sound no more their awesome voice,
Храня движенья вид.[25]	yet motion's semblance keep.[26]

The simplest approach is to deal with the poem itself. It is a closed circle and can serve as an excellent frame (if we cut out the middle).

---

24 Vladislav Khodasevich (1886–1939) was something of an anachronism among Modernist poets, since he felt that Pushkin's poetry should serve as the model for all contemporary poets. He was an influential literary critic in Russia and, from the mid-1920s, in the Russian émigré community of Berlin and Paris.

25 Tynianov used this poem as an epigraph to his 1928 novel *The Death of the Vazir-Mukhtar*—*MC*. See Evgenii Baratynskii,[N] "Inscription" [Nadpis'], in *Polnoe sobranie sochinenii* (St. Petersburg: Akademproekt, 2000), 113.

26 English translation from Yevgeny Baratynsky, *A Science Not for the Earth*, trans. Rawley Grau (Brooklyn, NY: Ugly Duckling Presse, 2015), 65.

Poetry that "has been bequeathed to us by the ages" cannot easily accommodate contemporary meanings.[27] If Pushkin and Baratynsky[N] had lived in our time, they might have maintained their constructive principles, but probably would have rejected their verse formulas, their clots. "The Smolensk Market," written in Pushkin's and Baratynsky's iambic dimeter and in their manner is, of course, recognizably a poem, a poem of our time, but as a work of verse, it does not belong to us.[28]

This doesn't mean that Khodasevich hasn't written any "good" or even "beautiful" poems. He has, and it's possible that twenty years from now some critic will say that we underestimated Khodasevich. The "underestimations" of contemporaries are always an issue. Their "blindness" is entirely conscious. (This can even apply to the way Tyutchev[N] was underestimated in the nineteenth century.)[29] We consciously underestimate Khodasevich because we want to read verse that belongs to us; we have a right to this. (I'm not talking about new meter per se. Meter can be new while the verse stays old. I'm talking about newness in the interaction between all aspects of the verse line, which generates new verse meanings.)

Meanwhile, Khodasevich has poems that suggest he might not be listening to them very carefully. Such is his "Ballad" ("I sit, illuminated from above ..." [Sizhu, osveshchaemyi sverkhu ...]), with its grim angularity, the intentional awkwardness of its verse. Such is the scribbled note-in-verse: "Stride over, jump over ..." [Pereshagni, pereskochi ...], with its muttering domestic rhymes and unexpected brevity, is nearly a scrap of Rozanov[N]—as if some casual scribbled notes had abruptly burst into the classroom of High Lyric. Both of these are out of step with Khodasevich's canon.[30] Indeed, for us Khodasevich's usual voice, his full voice, is inauthentic. His poetry is neutralized by the poetic culture of the nineteenth century. The reader, who can only see clots in this culture, demands that the poet see better than he can.

---

27 Tynianov refers to Vladislav Khodasevich's poem "Ne mater'iu, no tul'skoi krest'iankoi ..." ("No mother, but a Tula peasant woman..."). See Vladislav Khodasevich, *Collected Works in 4 vols.* [Sobranie sochinenii v 4–kh tomakh], vol. 1 (Moscow: Soglasie, 1996), 195–196.

28 Tynianov refers here to Khodasevich's poem "The Smolensk Market" (1916). Ibid., 156.

29 For more on Tyutchev, see "Tyutchev and Heine" (1922) (64–76) and "On Parody".

30 Both of these poems were published in Vladislav Khodasevich, *The Heavy Lyre* [Tiazhelaia lira] (1922)—*MC*. Tynianov refers to Vasily Rozanov.

4

И быстрые ноги к земле приросли.[31]
[*And feet once quick took root in the ground.*]

There is another danger: seeing one's own poems as clots; becoming a captive of one's own poetic culture.

The primary question here is that of theme. Entire movements can be held hostage by their own themes—this is a lesson of history. How surprised our schoolchildren would be to learn that the themes of "sentimentalism"[T]—its "love," "friendship," "weepiness"—are not at all characteristic of the movement itself (which means that "sentimentalism" is not sentimentalism at all). Yes, love, friendship, and regret over lost youth—all these themes emerged through the working process as a means of joining together specific principles of construction, as a justification for the intimate style of Karamzin[N] and his followers,[32] and as a kind of domestic, intimate resistance to the lofty and grandiose themes of their elders. It was only later that the theme was legitimized, became itself a driving force: Karamzin capitulated to Shalikov.[33]

But we can find a more familiar example in Symbolism,[T] which only toward the end decided that its *themes* were its foremost asset, its driving force—and set off after those themes, and left the realm of living poetry.

The same thing occurred with individual poets. Our era talks so much and so eagerly about Pushkin but has actually learned little from him. And yet Pushkin made his mark by retreating from old themes and seizing on new ones. There is a tremendously long evolutionary line between "Ruslan and Ludmila" and "Boris Godunov," but a mere five-year interlude separates the two.[34] For Pushkin, this transition was always a revolutionary act. Thus, toward the end, he was retreating into history, prose, journalism—and again finding new themes. The boldness of his transitions is hard for us to grasp. We prefer to cling to our themes. Our era prefers to learn from Gogol[N]—from the Gogol of part two of

---

31 From Anna Akhmatova's poem "Lot's Wife" [Lotova zhena] (1922–1924). Tynianov refers to this same poem later in the section—*MC*. See Anna Akhmatova, *Poems and Long Poems* [Stikhotvoreniia i poemy] (Leningrad: Sovetskii pisatel, 1977), 160.

32 For more on Karamzin, also see "On Literary Evolution" (267–282) and "The Ode as an Oratorical Genre" (77–113).

33 For more on Shalikov, see "On Parody" (319; 324–325).

34 Tynianov refers to Alexander Pushkin's heroic-comic epic poem "Ruslan and Ludmila" (1820), and to his historical drama "Boris Godunov" (1825, published 1831).

Dead Souls, who was led by his theme; bowing their heads, our poets shamble into their own thematic captivity.[35]

Nor do they remember the funny example of Heine, who struggled to free himself from the canon of his own themes, from the "Heine manner," as he himself called it. And such themes! Love, which became canonical for the entire nineteenth century. Like Pushkin, Heine was unashamed of infidelities. In poetry, fidelity to one's themes is not rewarded.

Today, Akhmatova[N] is captive to her own themes. The theme is leading her along, dictating her images, quietly blanketing the whole verse line. But it is worth noting that when Akhmatova was just starting out, her novelty and significance did not derive from her themes, but *in spite of* them. Almost all of her themes were "prohibited" among the Acmeists.[36] And the theme was not interesting in itself; it was alive by virtue of its intonational angle, as it were, the new angle of verse from which it was presented. It was made indispensable by her nearly whispering syntax and the abruptness of her ordinary lexicon. Akhmatova's intimate style and her rough-edged, domestic diction were a new phenomenon, and the verse itself paced along the corners of the room. There's a reason Akhmatova's diction is organically linked to a specific culture of the metrically foregrounded word (which got stuck with the inaccurate, hideous label *pauznik*).[T] Her style naturally gravitated toward a narrowed range of themes and to "minor emotions": these elements constituted a sort of new perspective and led Akhmatova to the poetic genre of "stories" and "conversations," which had not solidified or been canonized prior to her arrival. And these "stories" were linked up into collections, or into novels (B. Eikhenbaum[N]).[37]

The theme was not alive outside of the poem: it was a verse theme, which was the source of its unexpected nuances. Verse ages as people do—old age consists of a loss of nuance, of complexity; the verse smooths out and, instead of posing a problem, immediately provides the solution. In this sense, the wonderful "When in suicidal sorrow ... " [Kogda v toske samoubiistva ...] was already typical. And it's likewise typical that Akhmatova's verse has gradually retreated from meter, which at first was organically linked to her diction.

35 See also "Dostoyevsky and Gogol" (27–63).

36 Nikolai Gumilyov (1886–1921) founded the Poets' Guild, also known as the Acmeists, an early twentieth-century group of poets founded by Nikolai Gumilyov (1886–1921); Akhmatova was an early member and Gumilyov's wife at the time.

37 Tynianov refers to Boris Eikhenbaum's article on Akhmatova, "Lyric-Novel" [Lirika-roman], first published in *Literary Herald* [Vestnik literatury] 5–6 (1921)—*MC*.

The lines have straightened out, their edges have softened; the verse line has become "more beautiful" and comprehensive; the intonations are weaker, the language loftier; the Bible, which used to lie on the table as a part of the décor, is now a source of images:

Взглянула — и, скованы смертною болью,	She glanced over—and, by mortal pain all bound,
Глаза ее больше смотреть не могли;	Her eyes could see no longer;
И сделалось тело прозрачною солью,	And her body turned to translucent salt,
И быстрые ноги к земле приросли.[38]	And feet once quick took root in the ground.

Akhmatova's primary theme is attempting to vary and renew itself at the expense of Akhmatova herself.

5

Без эпиграфа
[*No epigraph*]

Being held captive by a poet is no good for the theme, either. It remains no more than a theme, loses its urgency, and eventually begins to decompose.

Vyazemsky,[N] who was never one for sitting still, once criticized this tendency in Zhukovsky[N]:

> Zhukovsky has to be especially wary of monotony: he's awfully quick to settle down into a habit. Once he hit upon the idea of death, all of his poems ended with his burial. The premonition of death *is striking when it bursts forth*; but if we see that a person awaits death every day, but nevertheless enjoys full health, then his premonitions will eventually make us laugh. [...] Evdokim Davydov used to relate how the crippled Evgraf Davydov would tell him he was thinking constantly of death: "[...] well, so you think you're going to die that very evening; well, brother, so you ask them to bring you some tea; well, brother, you drink that tea and think you're about to die; well, you're not dying yet, brother; you ask them to serve you dinner, brother; well, you eat dinner and think you're about to die; well, you finish dinner, brother, and you're not dying yet; you go to

38 Akhmatova, *Stikhotvoreniia i poemy*, 160.

> bed; well, brother, you go to sleep and think you're going to die, brother; you wake up in the morning, brother; well, I'm not dead yet; well, brother, once again you ask them to serve you tea, brother."[39]

Even the theme of death, which would seem immune to parody, is capable, as we see here, of engendering a funny parody, as well as being handled in a manner diametrically opposed to the usual one. All themes, whether domestic or global, have identical dimensions. They are necessary until they fall out of step with the work and begin to stand out in an obvious way, triggering a shift in interpretation.

6

Эта тема придет, прикажет[40]
[This theme will come and demand]

The theme is suffocating Mayakovsky too, sticking right out of him. Russian Futurism[T] broke loose from the middling poetic culture of the nineteenth century. In its brutal struggles and its conquests, it was much like the eighteenth century. [Futurism] reached over the nineteenth century's head to shake hands with the eighteenth. Khlebnikov[N] is akin to Lomonosov[N]. Mayakovsky is akin to Derzhavin.[N] The geological shifts of the eighteenth century are closer to us today than the calm evolution of the nineteenth. Nevertheless, we are not of the eighteenth century, and so we have to talk first about our Derzhavin and only later about our Lomonosov.[41]

Mayakovsky revitalized the grandiose image that was lost to us after the age of Derzhavin. Like Derzhavin, he knew that the secret of the grandiose image is less in its "loftiness" than in the extreme contrast of linked levels—the high style and the low style—in what the eighteenth century called "the proximity of unequally lofty words" (as well as in the "conjoining of distant ideas").

39 (Prince) Pyotr Vyazemsky, Ostaf'evo archive, vol. 1, 305–306 (letter to A. I. Turgenev, September 5, 1819)—*MC*.

40 Vladimir Mayakovsky, "About That" [Pro eto] (1923)—*MC*. See V. V. Maiakovskii, *Polnoe sobranie sochinenii v 13–i tomakh*, vol. 4 (Moscow: Gos. izd. khud. literatury, 1957), 138.

41 For the major eighteenth-century poets (including Lomonosov) and Gavrila Derzhavin, and on eighteenth-century poetics in general, also see "The Ode as an Oratorical Genre" (77–113); for more on Velimir Khlebnikov; see section eight of this article; "On Khlebnikov" (217–229)

Mayakovsky's demonstration-ready, bellowing poems, calculated to elicit the response of big crowds (just as Derzhavin's poems were constructed with a view to the resonance of palace halls), was nothing like the poetry of the nineteenth century. His poetry ushered in a distinct system of verse meaning. A word could take up a whole line, stand on its own, and so a phrase (which could also take up a whole line) became equivalent to a single word, shrank and contracted. The semantic weight was redistributed—in this, Mayakovsky is close to comic poetry (the fable being another genre that works by redistributing semantic weight). Mayakovsky's verse line is always on the razor's edge between the comic and the tragic. The vulgar genre, or "burlesque," has always been both a supplement to, and a stylistic tool of, "high-style poetry," and both streams (the high and the low) have been equally inimical to the nature of "the middle style."[42]

The intimate, whispering style is in danger of becoming a middle, common voice, but the vulgar style threatens to break into a falsetto.

This threat is present in Mayakovsky's latest poems. He has always had his poetic sights set on linking the two levels—high and low—but the levels keep breaking down; the low devolves into satire ("Mayakovsky Gallery") and the high into the ode ("To the Workers of Kursk"). Naked satire and the naked ode alike begin to lose their sharpness, and Mayakovsky's verse ceases to operate on two levels. Satire opens a path to poor Demian Bedny—a poor path, in any case, for Mayakovsky.[43] The naked ode, meanwhile, has shown that it can degenerate very quickly into "overcoat poems." Only the Chamber Theater runs plays where people shout from start from finish.[44]

And it is a theme that pushes Mayakovsky toward this fork in the road, a theme that now looms over his poems rather than being contained within them—an obnoxious, naked theme that drives Mayakovsky to repeat himself:

Эта тема придет,	This theme will come
прикажет:	and demand:
—Истина! —	"Truth!"
Эта тема придет,	This theme will come
велит:	and order:
—Красота! —	"Beauty!"

---

42 Tynianov refers to the theory of the "three styles" (high, middle, and low) governing lexicon and literature which was popularized in eighteenth-century Russia by Mikhail Lomonosov.

43 Demian Bednyi (1883–1945) was an early Soviet poet who was quite popular in the early 1920s. Tynianov puns on his last name / pseudonym ("Bednyi"), which means "poor" in Russian.

44 The Kamerny (Chamber) Theater was directed in Moscow between 1914 and 1950 by Alexander Tairov. It was known for its Constructivist, avant-garde-leaning aesthetics.

The theme holds sway over the verse. And the heartbeat of Mayakovsky's verse is experiencing arrhythmia. Imperceptibly, bit by bit, Mayakovsky has moved away from his previous verse line (short, written in columns, with variable meter)—with its conspicuous, shouting, and weighty words—toward traditional meter. It's true that he openly parodies this kind of poetry, but secretly he has been drawing closer to it:

В этой теме,	Inside this theme,
и личной	so personal
и мелкой,	so petty,
перепетой не раз	sung over and over
и не пять,	again,
я кружил поэтической белкой	I spun around like a squirrel of poetry
и хочу кружиться опять.[45]	and want to go spinning again.

And elsewhere, no longer parodically:[46]

Бежало от немцев,	It fled from the Germans,
боялось французов,	fearing the French,
глаза	squinting
косивших	their eyes
на лакомый кус,	at a tempting piece,
пока доплелось,	until it came limping,
задыхаясь от груза,	breathless and wrenched,
запряталось	and hid deep
в сердце России	in Russia's heart
под Курск.[47]	by Kursk.

This kind of short verse line has lately become Mayakovsky's means of fusing together different meters. Mayakovsky is seeking a way out of his poetics through *parodic hyper-awareness of his verse.* (Mayakovsky set out on this path with the success of his unexpected Koltsov-like lines in "150 000 000.")[47]

45 From "About That" [Pro eto]—*MC*. Ibid., 4:137. This poem's meter is mixed but leans amphibrachic, while the following citation (from "To the Workers of Kursk") is written in regular amphibrachs.

46 "To the Workers of Kursk, First Miners, a Temporary Memorial Built by Vladimir Mayakovsky" [Rabochim Kurska, dobyvshim pervuiu rudu, vremennyi pamiatnik raboty Vladimira Maiakovskogo] (1923)—*MC*. Ibid., 5:156. The "it" in question is iron.

47 Aleksei Koltsov (1809–1842) was a Romantic poet of unusually humble (peasant-merchant) origins for the time, known for his celebrations of peasant life and his use of stylized folk-song meters and diction.

In "About That," he tried on, got a feel for, every possible verse system, all the existing established genres, as if he were seeking a way out of his own self. This poem has echoes of Mayakovsky's early poems, like "The Backbone Flute" [Fleita-pozvonochnik]; it is a kind of summary of his entire work. In it, he is trying to push aside the literariness of everyday life [*byt*][T] so that he can get the object back into the word's crosshairs; but it is hard to get back down from the high falsetto notes. And the deeper the rut dug into poetry, the harder it is to keep the wheel from spinning in place. In his early lyric poems, Mayakovsky introduced the *personality* of a poet who was still fresh: an "I" that wasn't vague or nebulous, that didn't belong to the traditional "novice" or "scandal-monger," but rather to a poet with a known home address. That address keeps spreading to cover ever more territory; his biography, verifiable details from everyday life, and memoirs are taking root in his poems ("About That"). Mayakovsky's most hyperbolic image, which connects the sublime—tensed to the point of hysteria—with the street, is Mayakovsky himself.

Any more, and this hyperbolic image will protrude headfirst out of the poem, tear it open, and stand up in its place. In "About That," Mayakovsky once again emphasizes that the nature of his language is inimical to the plot-centered epic, and that his large form is distinctive in being a "great ode," not an epic.

Mayakovsky's position is unique. He cannot rest on his canon, which has already become the darling of various eclectics and imitators. He has a good feeling for the seismic shocks of history, because he himself was once just such a shock. And it is for this reason that he—a poet very little theorized—is so self-aware during this interlude. He is consciously returning to a theme "so personal, so petty, sung over and over again" (and immediately making it as grandiose as it once was); but he is consciously crippling his verse in order to free it once and for all from "poetic blinders":

Хотя б без размеров
Хотя б без рифм.[48]
[Even without meter / Even without rhyme.]

At last, feeling helpless, he heads back to the trusty old street, so indissolubly linked to early Futurism. His ads for Mosselprom, disguised as his contribution

48 From Mayakovsky's poem "May 1st" ("Poets ...")—*MC*. Ibid., 5:43.

to the production effort, are a retreat—for reinforcements.[49] When the canon begins to weigh on a poet, the poet takes his craft and escapes into everyday life—the way Pushkin wrote poems that were half epigram, half madrigal, in ladies' albums. (Thus, it seems incorrect to bemoan poets "wasting" their talents in such a manner; instead of "wasting," they are actually expanding their scope.) In everyday life, poetry is given such tasks that it must come down from its comfortable perch whether it wants to or not—and that is the whole point.[50]

These days, compliments are not handed out for free; the madrigal of our time is the advertisement. Mayakovsky's madrigals for Mosselprom are an occasionally much needed "poetic philandering." But

> И стих,
> И дни не те.
> [Both the verse, / and the times are not what they were.][51]

Neither is the street. Futurism has moved away from the street (and, to tell the truth, Futurism itself is essentially over); meanwhile, the street doesn't have time for either Futurism or poetry.

Жестоких опытов сбирая поздний плод,	Gathering the late fruits of savage experiments,
Они торопятся с расходом свесть приход.	They rush to make credits and debits come even.
Им некогда шутить <…>	They have no time to joke [...]
Иль спорить о стихах.[52]	Or argue over poems.

And if anyone does argue about poems, they do it in a businesslike manner, mentioning projects and estimates with everything calculated in advance, to

49 Mosselprom—the Moscow Association of Enterprises Processing Agro-Industrial Products—was a state-owned entity that produced and sold small consumer items such as food, drinks, and cigarettes. Mayakovsky and several other avant-garde artists worked for the association in the 1920s, designing advertisements that combined images and text in Constructivist fashion.

50 For more of Tynianov's views on the relationship between literature and "everyday life" [*byt*], see "Literary Fact" (especially 169–172) and "On Literary Evolution" (especially 271; 277–280).

51 Tynianov mimics Mayakovsky's visually dramatic layout by giving the first of these two lines from "About That" (I stikh/I dni ne te) as an indented quotation. Ibid., 4:167.

52 Pushkin, "To a Grandee" [K vel'mozhe] (1830)—*MC*. Alexander Pushkin, *Sobranie sochinenii v 10–i tomakh* (Moscow: GIKhL, 1959–1962), 2:289–292.

the last cent. Can cold-blooded Mosselprom stimulate Mayakovsky to produce, as the hot-blooded posters of ROSTA once stimulated him?[53]

7

А у меня, понимаешь ты,
шанец жить! [54]
[But hey, dontcha know, I got a
chance to live!]

There's something else curious about this exodus into the street. Every *new* phenomenon in poetry is felt primarily through the *newness of its intonation.* Akhmatova had new intonations, and, though different, Mayakovsky's intonations were also new. When intonations age and cease to be noticeable, the poems themselves stand out less boldly. By going out into the street, Mayakovsky is attempting to change his intonation.

There were glimpses of a new intonation in a poet who debuted recently—Selvinsky.[55] He brings a thief's intonation into his verse, the intonation of a Gypsy romance song. Selvinsky's "thieves' lyric" is a kind of Babel in verse:[56]

И я себе прошел как какой-нибудь
 ферть,
Скинул джонку и подмигнул глазом:
«Вам сегодня не везло, дорогая мадам
 Смерть,
Адью до следующего раза».

And I passed on by like some kinda
 popinjay,
Slipped off my cappy and winked my eye
fine:
"Today's just not your day, my dear
 Madame Death,
Adieu until next time."

53 In the last years of the Civil War (1919–21), Mayakovsky had worked for the Russian Telegraph Agency (ROSTA), making stenciled propaganda posters usually displayed in windows.

54 From Ilya Selvinsky's poem "The Thief" [Vor], part of the collection *Swap Everybody, Constructivist-Poets* [Mena vsekh. Konstruktivisty-poety] (1924). The following quotation is from the same poem—*MC*. See Ilya Sel'vinskii, *Sobranie sochinenii v 6–i tomakh*: vol. 1 (Moscow: Khudozhestvennaia literatura, 1971), 102.

55 Ilya Selvinsky (1899–1968) was an experimental poet affiliated in the later 1920s with the Constructivist movement.

56 Tynianov refers to Isaac Babel (1894–1940), a prose writer of the early 1920s, known particularly for his rich evocations of nonstandard speech (of Cossacks, Odessa Jews, and petty thieves, for example.).

Of course, here in "The Thief," the introduction of thieves' jargon into the poem isn't so important—with a little help from Trachtenberg's dictionary we can translate the poem fairly easily into ordinary Russian (just as the *Introduction to Linguistics* makes it easy to decode the poems of the rest of the poets in *Swap Everybody*). The curious thing here is the new intonation, fresh off the street.

The Gypsy intonation has already managed to "turn literary"—there is such a thing as *high* Gypsy lyric. Selvinsky offers a new Gypsy intonation, one that hasn't had time to settle:

Погляжу, холоднылигорячи**и**ль	Lemme see, are they coldorhot these
П**а**ды ножом ваши ласки женские.	Feminine caresses o'yours, under the knife.
Вы грызитесь, подкидывая пыль.	You're at each other's throats, kicking up the dust.
Вы. Жеребцы. Мои. Оболенские.[57]	You. Studs. All mine. Obolensky stallions.

The poem almost becomes an open-air stage. Selvinsky is fortunate to be working with an unusually bad tradition. Traditions that are bad sometimes produce vital phenomena, provided that the tradition doesn't turn out to be an ordinary bad *literary* tradition, as in his long poems "in crowns of sonnets," which are just bad, ordinary, and traditional.

Selvinsky's "Gypsy Waltz for Guitar" really is a Gypsy waltz; it must be sung and not read, from an open-air stage. Poetry doesn't gain anything from being performed, but it doesn't lose anything, either. Will Selvinsky be able to avoid bad literature and the actual open-air stage, and develop into a living phenomenon? This is a question for the future.

8

Огромный, неуклюжий,
Скрипучий поворот руля.[58]
[A groaning wide, ungainly / sweep of the rudder]

In these "retreats," the twentieth century instinctively clings to the poetic culture of the nineteenth century, instinctively tries to be its heir; the poems are

57 Ibid., 103.

58 From Mandel'shtam, "The Twilight of Freedom" [Sumerki svobody] (1918)—*MC*. See O. E. Mandel'shtam, *Poems* [Stikhotvoreniia] (Leningrad: Khudozhestvennaia literatura, 1973), 109. Translation from Mandel'shtam, *The Selected Poems. Osip Mandelstam*, trans. Clarence Brown and W. S. Merwin (New York: New York Review of Books, 2004), 22.

atoning for the guilt they feel toward their predecessors. We are still apologizing to the nineteenth century. But the leap has already been made, and we more closely resemble our grandfathers than the fathers who struggled against them. We carry the nineteenth century deep in our memory, but in essence we have already moved far away from it:

> Чтоб вы сказали, сей соблазн увидя?
> Наш век обидел вас, ваш стих обидя!
> [What would you say upon seeing this lure? / Our epoch spurned you when it spurned your verse!][59]

The silent struggle between Khlebnikov and Gumilyov recalls the struggle between Lomonosov and Sumarokov.[N] And it's likely that both struggles contained at least a grain of love.

At the crossroads of two elemental forces of poetry lies the work of Khlebnikov. Velimir Khlebnikov has died, but he is a living phenomenon. Just two years ago, before he died, it was still possible to call him a half-mad versifier. No one would say this now; Khlebnikov's name is on the tip of every poet's tongue. Now Khlebnikov faces a different kind of threat—his own biography. His is an unusually canonical biography, the biography of a madman and a seeker who died of starvation. But a biography—and death, above all—can sweep away whatever a person has done. The name is remembered and for some reason respected, but what the person actually did is forgotten with astonishing speed. There is a whole pantheon of "great men remembered only by their portraits."

And if the study of Pushkin has been replaced for so long by the study of his duel, who knows to what extent this is due to all the speeches and poems that have been recited, are being recited, and will be recited on his many anniversaries?[60]

Without naming Khlebnikov and sometimes without even having heard of him, poets are using him; he is present as a framework, a tendency. Moreover, his theories get conflated with "*zaum*,"[T] and he is known as a poet "not

---

59 From Alexander Pushkin's "skipped" stanza of "The Little House in Kolomna" [Domik v Kolomne]—*MC*. Pushkin, *Sobranie sochinenii*, 3:456. The stanza addresses great French poets of the past, including Boileau, Racine, and Voltaire, imagining their dismay over the new poetic boldness of Pushkin's own era. Tynianov quotes the same line in "The Foundations of Film" (258).

60 Pushkin died at age thirty-seven from wounds received in a duel. For more on the problem of literary biography, see "Literary Fact" (170–172).

for reading." (There have been other poets of this variety. From the very beginning, Lomonosov "had no need for the petty honors of a fashionable writer," as Pushkin diplomatically put it.)[61]

Khlebnikov's language theory was hurriedly declared *zaum*, and everyone settled happily for the notion that he had invented a kind of meaningless sound-speech.

But the point of Khlebnikov's theory lay elsewhere. He shifted poetry's center of gravity from questions of sound to the question of meaning.[62] Taking the meaning of a word, he revived its long-forgotten kinship with other similar words, or *brought* the word into kinship with unrelated words. He achieved this through his recognition of the verse line as a *framework*. If unrelated but similar-sounding words are placed in a *series*, a framework, they become relatives. And here is the source of Khlebnikov's "word declensions," of the new "etymology" that met the same derision in our time as Shishkov's[N] "etymology" had in his day.[63] And yet Khlebnikov did not (as Shishkov had done) present his theory as scientific truth; rather, Khlebnikov thought of it as a structural principle. He did not think of himself as a scholar—he was a "railwayman of artistic language":

"[...] Language has no railwaymen on permanent duty," wrote Khlebnikov. "Who wants to travel from Moscow to Kiev via New York? And yet what phrase from contemporary literary language is free from such detours?"[64]

"This is because whatever single ordinary meaning a word may possess will hide all its other meanings, as daylight effaces the luminous bodies of the

61 Pushkin, "On Mr. Lémontey's Preface to Krylov's Fable Translations" (1825)—*MC*. See Pushkin, *Sobranie sochinenii*, 6:13.

62 Tynianov's line of thinking here is highly characteristic: *zaum* is seen as accentuating the semantic aspect of literary speech (compare his essay "On the Composition of *Eugene Onegin*"). For Tynianov, Khlebnikov's work represents the "purest" possible realization of his own ideas about poetic language in general and verse semantics first and foremost, about verse as a "dynamic speech construction." At the same time, Khlebnikov stood out as a unique embodiment of Tynianov's conception of the historical movement of Russian poetry, beginning with Lomonosov, which he expressed in the formula "archaists are innovators" [...]—*MC*.

63 Tynianov gives the example *bog-beg*, which sees the word "god" "decline" into "running" through a vowel shift. Khlebnikov conducted similar experiments in his search for an immanent etymology of Russian and Slavic roots.

64 Quotations from Khlebnikov, "Our Fundamentals" [Nasha osnova] (first published 1920)—*MC*. See Velimir Khlebnikov, *Collected Works of Velimir Khlebnikov*, 3 vols., trans. Paul Schmidt (Cambridge, MA: Harvard University Press, 1997), 1:367. Translation slightly modified. Subsequent citations from these volumes given in brackets.

starry night. But for an astronomer the sun is simply another speck of dust, like any other star." For Khlebnikov, ordinary language is "the dim visions we see at night"—"the night of everyday reality [*byt*]." Literary language that follows ordinary language is thus, for Khlebnikov, a wheel spinning in place. He preaches an "explosion of verbal silence, the deaf and dumb layers of language":[65] a controlled explosion, a revolution that is simultaneously a framework. (He also used the long poem to illustrate and prove his theory—this method is the source of his word series and outlandish juxtapositions of words and numbers, as well as of his long "number" poems.)

Khlebnikov's final long poems, which were printed in *LEF*—"Ladomir" and "Razin's Adze" [Ustrug Razina]—are a summation of his poetry. These poems could have been written today.

In an Onegin stanza, phrases that border on nonsense sound almost comprehensible; in a variable verse system, where the iamb slips into a trochee and the trochee into an iamb, an almost comprehensible phrase will be colored in a new way. In high-style language, an ordinary object is no longer ordinary; it becomes monstrously complex.

Here is an image whose novelty lies precisely in its everyday familiarity—the Kschessinska Palace:[66]

Море вспомнит и расскажет	The sea will remember, will always recount
Грозовым своим глаголом —	in its awful threatening language,
Замок кружев девой нажит	How a castle of lace was the prize of a maiden
Пляской девы пред престолом.	Who won it by dancing in front of a throne.
Море вспомнит и расскажет	The sea will remember, will always recount
Громовым своим раскатом,	in its thundering racket and roar
Что дворец был пляской нажит	that the palace was once a prize for a dance
Перед ста народов катом.	danced for the assassin of a hundred nations.[67]

65 Ibid., 1:377. Translation slightly modified.

66 The palace, which is situated in the Petrogradskaya neighborhood in St. Petersburg, was built for and belonged to Matilda Kshessinska, an illustrious ballerina who had been the lover of the future Tsar Nicholas II back in the 1890s (hence Khlebnikov's Salome imagery). In 1917, Kshessinska fled the country and the palace was temporarily seized to become Bolshevik headquarters.

67 From "Ladomir." The following quotation is from the same long poem—*MC*. See Velimir Khlebnikov, *Tvoreniia* (Moscow: Soglasie, 1986), 284. For the English translation, see Khlebnikov, *Collected Works*, 3:171. Translations modified.

Archaic language thrown into the present doesn't transport us back in time; by bringing antiquity closer to us, such language merely colors the present in a particular way. The themes of our current reality sound almost Lomonosovian—but, strange though it may seem, this [quality] makes them newer:

Лети, созвездье человечье,
Все дальше, далее в простор
И перелей земли наречья
В единый смертных разговор.
[283]
<...>

Soar, you great constellation, star-clustered humanity,
Fly farther and deeper into space,
And melt all forms of human speech
Into one unified conversation of mortals! [170]
[...]

Сметя с лица земли торговлю
И замки торгов бросив ниц,
Из звездных глыб построишь кровлю —
Стеклянный колокол столиц.
[290]

Sweep from the face of earth the filth of commerce
and level the castles and fortresses of trade,
You'll use the stars to build a shelter
A glass bell of capital cities. [179]

But Khlebnikov's importance does not lie in his "revitalizing" themes. He is above all a poet-theorist. The foremost element in his poems is their bared construction. He is a poet of his principles.

There is no one true theory of construction for poetry, just as there are no false ones. There are only historically necessary and unnecessary theories, useful and useless ones; just as in literary struggles, there are no guilty parties, but there are losers.

Khlebnikov counters nineteenth-century verse culture with principles of construction that are, to a large extent, close to those of Lomonosov. This is not a regression to old forms; it is a struggle with the fathers, in which the grandson has come to resemble his grandfather. Sumarokov took a rationalist's stance in his struggle with Lomonosov—he kept exposing the falsity of the latter's construction, and this was his undoing. It was only later that Pushkin could turn up and declare that "the Lomonosov tendency is pernicious."[68] Pushkin was victorious through the simple fact of his existence. We face a long streak of Khlebnikov's influence, a lengthy process of his merging with the nineteenth century, of his seeping into its traditions, and we are a long way off from a Pushkin of

68 Inexact quotation from Pushkin's "Journey from Moscow to St. Petersburg"—*MC*. Pushkin, *Sobranie sochinenii*, 6:385.

the twentieth century. (And we should meanwhile not forget that Pushkin was never a Pushkin scholar.)

9

Вещи рвут с себя личину.[69]
[Objects tear off their masks.]

The revolt led by Khlebnikov and Mayakovsky got literary language moving and revealed the possibility for new shades of meaning within it.

At the same time, this revolt pushed language—the word—extremely far away. Khlebnikov's poems make their mark primarily through the principle they represent. In them, the rebellious word tore free, separated from its object. (Here, Khlebnikov's "self-sufficient word" [*samovitoe slovo*] meets Mayakovsky's "hyperbolic word.") The word became a little too free; it lost its bite. This is why the key figures of Futurism were so drawn to the object, the naked object of everyday reality, and also why the "rejection of poetry" was seen as a logical way out. (A little too logical: the more infallible our logical approach is to things that move and change, as literature does, the more straightforward and correct that logic, the less right it always turns out to be.)

This excessive freedom also gives rise to another desire—to target the object with language, to try to somehow arrange words and objects so that words do not hang in midair and objects are not naked; to reconcile them, mix them up in a friendly way. This also marks a natural pulling away from hyperbole, as well as the yearning of those positioned at a new phase of poetic culture to use the nineteenth century as material: neither treating it as a norm or starting point, nor being ashamed to acknowledge kinship with the fathers.

Here is where Pasternak's mission lies.

Pasternak has been writing for a long time, but he did not make it into the first ranks right away—only over the past two years.[70] He was sorely needed. Pasternak gives us a new literary object. This is why his themes are so inevitable.

---

69 Epigraph to his section from Boris Pasternak, "Those crooked pictures pouring down ..." [Kosykh kartin, letiashchikh livmia ...], from the collection *Themes and Variations* [Temy i variatsii]—*MC*. See Boris Pasternak, *Poems and Long Poems* [Stikhotvoreniia i poemy] (Leningrad: Khudozhestvennaia literatura, 1990), 184. Pasternak (1890–1960) began as an experimental Futurist and ended as one of Russia's foremost late Modernists.

70 That is, following the collection *My Sister Life* [Sestra moia zhizn'] (first published 1922). Tynianov draws primarily on the material of this book and the following one (Pasternak's fourth), *Themes and Variations* (1923)—*MC*.

His theme does not obtrude in the slightest; it is so robustly motivated that no one even mentions it.

What are the themes that make poetry and objects collide?

First of all, the process of wandering itself, the actual birth of poetry among objects:[71]

Отростки ливня грязнут в гроздьях	The downpour's offshoots sink into clusters
И долго, долго до зари	And endlessly before the dawn
Кропают с кровель свой акростих,	Drip their acrostic in drops from rooftops,
Пуская в рифму пузыри.[72]	Blowing bubbles in regular rhyme.

Language merges with the pouring rain (the downpour is Pasternak's favorite image and landscape); the verse is incorporated into the surrounding landscape and intertwined with the images that have themselves merged together through their sounds. The result is nearly "nonsensical sound-speech," and yet it is relentlessly logical; we are looking at a somehow transparent imitation of syntax, but the syntax here is impeccable.

And as a result of this poetic alchemy, the downpour begins to live as verse: "both the March night and the author" are walking side by side, shifted one square to the right "by a three-tiered hexameter"[73]—and the end result is an object coming to life:

Косых картин, летящих ливмя С шоссе, задувшего свечу, С крюков и стен срываться к рифме И падать в такт не отучу.	These crooked pictures pouring down From the high-road that's snuffed the candle, Tearing off their hooks and walls toward the rhyme And falling into rhythm—I can't make them stop.
Что в том, что на вселенной — маска? Что в том, что нет таких широт, Которым на зиму замазкой Зажать не вызвались бы рот?	So what if the universe is wearing a mask? So what if there are no such latitudes That would not opt to plaster white Their mouths tight before the winter?
Но вещи рвут с себя личину, Теряют власть, роняют честь, Когда у них есть петь причина, Когда для ливня повод есть.	But objects tear off their masks, Lose authority, defile their honor, When they have a reason to sing, When there is cause for a downpour.

71 "Poetry" [Poeziia] (from *Themes and Variations*)—*MC*. See ibid., 196.

72 "Meeting" [*Vstrecha*] (from *Themes and Variations*)—*MC*. See ibid., 162.

This poem has not only torn off its mask, it has "defiled its honor."

This is how Pasternak's "Pushkinian Variations" came to be. The faded postcard image of the "swarthy youth" was replaced by a descendant of the "thick-lipped Hamite,"[73] wandering among sounds:

> Но шорох гроздий перебив,
> Какой-то рокот мёр и мучил.[74]
> [But interrupting the rustle of the grapevines, / Some distant clatter gripped and tortured]

Pasternak's Pushkin, like all of his verse objects, is like an attic that "starts declaiming"—tears off its mask and begins to ramble through sounds.[75]

What sorts of themes make the best springboard for throwing oneself at an object in order to revive it? Illness, childhood, basically all of the *incidental* and therefore intimate points of view that are ordinarily lacquered over and forgotten:

Так начинают. Года в два
От мамки рвутся в тьму мелодий,
Щебечут, свищут, — а слова
Являются о третьем годе.
<…>

Так открываются, паря
Поверх плетней, где быть домам бы,

So they begin. Around age two
Tearing from nurse into darkness of
 melodies,
They twitter and whistle, and then the words
Appear around year three.
[…]
So they come to light, soaring

73 Tynianov refers to Pasternak's poem "Theme" [Tema] (ibid., 166), which addresses Pushkin, and particularly his African lineage. On his mother's side, Pushkin was descended from Abram Petrovich Gannibal, of unclear but perhaps Abyssinian origin, who was adopted as a child by Peter the Great. Tynianov contrasts Pasternak's more realistic rendering of this heritage with the previously popular romanticized images of "swarthy young Pushkin":

Скала и Пушкин. Тот, кто и сейчас,
Закрыв глаза, стоит и видит в сфинксе
Не нашу дичь, не домыслы втупик
Поставленного грека, не загадку,
Но - предка: плоскогубого хамита. <…>

A cliff and Pushkin. The one who even now,
Eyes closed, stands before the Sphinx and
 sees
Not our wild game, not the the wild guesses
Of a bewildered Greek, not a riddle but—
An ancestor: the thick-lipped Hamite. […]

74 "Reaching for Gypsy colors …" [Tsyganskikh krasok dostigal …]—*MC*. See ibid., 170.

75 Indirect quotation from "About this Poem" [Pro eti stikhi] (from *My Sister Life*)—*MC*. See ibid., 119.

Внезапные, как вздох, моря,
Так будут начинаться ямбы.
<…>
Так начинают жить стихом.[76]

Above wicker fences, where there might be houses,
Sudden as a breath—these seas,
So the iambs will start to be.
[…]
So they begin to live through verse.

We begin to understand one of the strangest definitions of poetry ever offered:

Поэзия, я буду клясться
Тобой, и кончу, прохрипев:
Ты не осанка сладкогласца,
Ты — лето с местом в третьем классе,
Ты — пригород, а не припев.[77]

Poetry, I will swear an oath
By you, and wheeze out at the end:
You're not the poise of the honey-tongued,
You're summer with a third-class seat,
The city's fringes, not refrain.

A definition such as this could be expected from no one but Verlaine, a poet with an obscure longing for the object.[78]

Childhood—not canonical "childhood" but childhood as a different way of seeing—mixes up the object and verse; and the object comes to stand right next to us, while the verse can be prodded with one's fingers. Childhood justifies, and makes inevitable, images that tie together the most diverse, incommensurate things:

> Галчонком глянет Рождество.[79]
> [Christmas peeks with jackdaw-eyes.]

What makes Pasternak's language unique is its unbelievable precision; its difficulty notwithstanding, it is an intimate conversation, a conversation in the nursery. (Pasternak needs the nursery in his poetry for the same reason that Tolstoy needed it in prose.) There's a good reason why *My Sister Life* is essentially a diary, with its conscientious noting of location ("Balashov") and much-needed (at first for the author, but later for the reader as well) notes at the end of each

76 "This is how they start. Around age two" [Tak nachinaiut. Goda v dva] (from *Themes and Variations*)—*MC*. See ibid., 182.

77 "Poetry"—*MC*. See ibid., 196.

78 Tynianov refers here to Paul Verlaine[N] (1844–1896), the poet who coined the term *poète maudit* [accursed poet] to describe the French Symbolists and Decadents.

79 "About this Poem"—*MC*.

section: "These amusements ceased when, leaving for good, she passed her mission on to her replacement" or "To get there that summer, one had to leave from [Moscow's] Paveletsky Station."

This is why Pasternak has a prosaic quality, a domestic efficiency to his language. Its origin is the nursery:

> Небо в бездне поводов,
> Чтоб набедокурить.[80]
> [The sky has a sea of reasons / To make a pile of mischief.]

Pasternak's exaggerated language also comes from children's language:

> Гроза моментальная навек.
> [A storm instantaneous forever.][81]

(In Pasternak's early poems this intimate transparency was different; it recalled Igor Severyanin.[82] An example from Pasternak: [83]

Любимая, безотлагательно,	Darling mine, without delay,
Не дав заре с пути рассесться,	Before the dawn has a chance to settle,
Ответь чем свет с его подателем	Get word to me quick, at first sight of light
О ходе твоего процесса.)[84]	Regarding the course of your proceedings.)

This intimate mode is also the source of the strange visual perspective typical of someone who is ill: the attention to nearby objects, beyond which lies endless space:

---

80 "Summer Stars" [Zvezdy letom] (from *My Sister Life*)—*MC*. See ibid., 132.

81 Pasternak, "A storm instantaneous forever" [Groza momental'naia navek] (from my *My Sister Life*)—*MC*. Ibid., 154. English translation from Boris Pasternak, *My Sister Life and the Zhivago Poems* trans. James Falen (Evanston, IL: Northwestern University press, 2012), 92. Subsequent citations from this edition will be given in parentheses; all other translations are our own.

82 Igor' Severianin (1887–1941) was briefly the leader of the pre-revolutionary Ego-Futurists and cultivated a poetic stance combining bourgeois decadence with *épatage*.

83 Pasternak, "Two Letters" [Dva pis'ma] (from *Themes and Variations*), dated 1921, such that Tynianov's reference to "early work" is not entirely correct—*MC*. See Pasternak, *Stikhotvoreniia*, 197.

От окна на аршин,
Пробирая шерстинки бурнуса,
Клялся льдами вершин:
Спи, подруга, лавиной вернуся.[85]

At a yard from the window,
As he picked at the threads of his burnous,
By the icy peaks he swore:
"Sleep, my love, I'll return as an avalanche." (7, modified)

We see the same strange perspective in the illness that projects "love" through "the eyes of medicine vials."[86] The same goes for any incidental angle of vision:

В трюмо испаряется чашка какао,
Качается тюль, и прямой
Дорожкою в сад, в бурелом и хаос
К качелям бежит трюмо.

A cocoa cup steams the mirror with mist,
The curtains of lace are asway,
And straight into chaos—to garden and swing—
The mirror runs off to play. (16, modified)

This is why Pasternak's stock of images is unusual, selected at random; the objects there are very loosely connected, they are merely neighbors, close only through contiguity (the second object in any given image is very humdrum and abstract). And this incidental quality makes for a more powerful connection than the tightest imaginable logical connection:

Топтался дождик у дверей
И пахло винной пробкой.

The drizzle tiptoed at the door
And smelled like cork from wine.

Так пахла пыль. Так пах бурьян.
И если разобраться,
Так пахли прописи дворян
О равснстве и братстве.[88]

So smelled the dust. So smelled the weeds.
And if we chanced to read them,
So smelled as well the gentry's screeds
On brotherhood and freedom. (90, modified)

(For Pasternak, these half-abstract "screeds" that form part of his simile are part of a whole lexicon of such abstractions: "pretext," "right," "excerpt"—curiously, this makes him close to Fet, who also uses "pretext" and "right" and "honor" in astonishing combinations with extremely concrete objects.)

---

84 Pasternak, "In Demon's Memory" [Pamiati Demona] (from *My Sister Life*)—*MC*. See ibid., 118. Note that this poem refers extensively to the world of "Demon," a long poem by Mikhail Lermontov.

85 Pasternak, "In the twilight you seem so like a boarder ..." [Mne v sumerki ty vse—pansionerkoiu ...] (from *Themes and Variations*)—*MC*. See ibid., 176.

86 From Pasternak's poems "The Mirror" [Zerkalo] and "Summer" [Leto] (from *My Sister Life*)—*MC*. See ibid., 121, 153.

There is such a thing as déjà vu. You're having a conversation and it seems to you that all this has already happened, that you were once sitting in this very place and the other person was saying the exact same thing, and you already know what he's going to say next. And indeed this other person says exactly what he's supposed to. (Of course, the situation is actually quite the opposite: the other person is talking and *at that time* it seems to you that he said the exact same words once before.)

Something similar is at play in Pasternak's images. The connection between objects that he proffers is unknown to you—it is incidental—but once he has laid it out, you seem to recall it, as though it had already happened. And the image becomes inevitable.

The image and the theme are also inevitable because they are not obtrusive, because they are a consequence of the verse rather than the reason behind it. The theme is inextricable; it exists in the spongy tissue, the coarse texture of the verse. (This coarse, spongy quality is a marker of young tissue; old age is as smooth as a billiard ball.)

The theme does not hang in midair. The language has a key, which lies in the "incidental" vocabulary, the "monstrous" syntax:

Осторожных капель	Of cautious droplets
Юность в счастье плавала, как	Youth was rocked in bliss,
В тихом детском храпе	The way in children's snoring
Наспанная наволока.	A sleepy pillow drifts. (87–88)[87]

Likewise, rather than hanging in midair, this "free" word moves the object around. For this to occur, the word and object must come into contact: and this happens through emotion. Not Esenin's naked, everyday emotion, assigned as a theme and supplied from the outset of the poem. This emotion is indistinct, resolving toward the end, a musical emotion that glimmers in all of the words, all the objects; an emotion closely related to that of Fet.

This is why Pasternak's traditions—the references that he himself points out—are emotional poets. *My Sister Life* is dedicated to Lermontov, its epigraphs are from Lenau and Verlaine; hence in Pasternak's variations we catch glimpses of themes like the Demon, Ophelia, Gretchen, Desdemona.[88] He even has an Apukhtin-esque romance:

---

87 Pasternak, "To Elena" [Elene] (*My Sister Life*)—*MC*. See ibid., 151. Translation slightly modified.

88 Tynianov refers here to Nikolaus Lenau (1802–1850), an Austrian Romantic poet.

> Век мой безумный, когда образумлю
> Темп потемнелый былого бездонного?[89]
> [O my mad age, when will I bring to reason / The darkened pace of the fathomless past?]

But, more than anything else, we hear echoes of Fet:

Лодка колотится в сонной груди,	Rockaway boat in a somnolent breast,
Ивы нависли, целуют в ключицы,	Willows sweep down kissing collarbones
В локти, в уключины — о, погоди,	Elbows and oarlocks ... but, oh, wait now,
Это ведь может со всяким случиться!	This here could happen to anyone! (36)[90]

It's best to avoid pinning historical labels onto living people. Mayakovsky gets compared to Nekrasov. (Worse still, I myself have compared him to Derzhavin, and Khlebnikov to Lomonosov.)

I know I shouldn't, but this bad habit comes from how hard it is to make predictions and how important it is to keep careful watch. I refer to Pasternak himself (and to Hegel in the same breath):

Однажды Гегель ненароком	Once upon a time old Hegel
И, вероятно, наугад	At random and probably by chance
Назвал историка пророком,	Called a historian a prophet,
Предсказывающим назад.[91]	Predicting things by backward glance.

I will refrain from making predictions about Pasternak. Ours is a high-stakes time, and I don't know where he's headed (which is a good thing—it's bad when a critic knows where a poet is headed). Pasternak is wandering, and in this wandering touches other poets—there's a reason no other poet turns up so frequently in other poets' work. He's not just a wanderer; he's the source of all this fermentation.[92]

---

89 Pasternak, "Drink and write, a ceaseless patrol [Pei i pishi, nepreryvnym patrulem ...] (from *Themes and Variations*)—*MC*. See ibid., 196.

90 Pasternak, "Slozha vesla" ("Folding the Oars," from *My Sister Life*)—*MC*. See ibid., 130. Translation slightly modified.

91 Pasternak, "A Lofty Ailment" [Vysokaia bolezn'], journal version (published in *LEF*, no. 1 [1924]: 16).

92 Tynianov puns here on *brodit'*, to wander or roam, and *brodilo*, ferment (as in wine- or bread making).

10

Я слово позабыл, что я хотел сказать.
[I have forgotten the word I wanted to say.][93]

Coming from a different place entirely—seemingly close to Pasternak but actually foreign to him—we have Mandelstam.

Mandelstam is an astonishingly stingy poet—two slender books, a few poems a year. And yet he is a weighty poet; his books have great vitality.

There have already been a few poets of this sort—their poems are few and spare; this trait has cropped up at various times. The model for this kind of writing is, of course, Tyutchev—"weightier still than many volumes."[94] Still, Tyutchev as a poet is far from stingy; his poetry is compact because it is fragmentary, not miserly. And this fragmentariness is a function of literary dilettantism. There is another kind of stinginess—that of Batyushkov, who was working to develop verse language at the beginning of a new era in poetic culture. This example is closer to Mandelstam.

Mandelstam is solving one of the most difficult problems of verse language. The old theorists were already working with the difficult concept of "harmony": "harmony requires a fullness of sounds, in accordance with the breadth of the thought." Although they, as if anticipating our time, requested that "harmony" and "melody" not be lumped together.[95]

Leo Tolstoy, who understood Pushkin well, wrote that Pushkin's harmony resulted from a distinct "*hierarchy of objects*."[96] Every work of art places objects of the same kind into a hierarchical series, and levels objects that are different into a single, uniform series; every construction rearranges the world. This is particularly clear in poetry. The semantic weight carried by words gets redistributed through the verbal exigency of verse, the equivalence (or non-equivalence) of one verse line to another, the way some words stand out in a line or do not stand out. This—the distinct hierarchy of *objects*—is why Pasternak is so significant. He rearranges objects, brings about shifts in material perspective.

---

93 Osip Mandelstam, "The Sparrow" [Lastochka] (from the collection *Tristia*)—*MC*. See Mandelstam, *Stikhotvoreniia*, 117.

94 Tynianov refers here to an 1885 poem by Afanasy Fet, "On a Book of Tyutchev's Poems" [Na knizhke stikhotvorenii Tyutcheva (*Lirika*. Moscow: Khudozhestvennaia literatura, 1966), 133].

95 P. A. Pletnev, *Writings and Correspondence of P. A. Pletnyov* [Sochineniia i perepiska P. A. Pletneva], vol. 1 (St. Petersburg: Tip. Imperatorskoi Akademii nauk, 1885), 24–25—*MC*.

96 [Tolstoy], letter to E. G. Golokhvastov (April, 1873)—*MC*. See L. N. Tolstoi, *Sobranie sochinenii v 22 tomakh*, vol. 18 (Moscow: Gos. izd-vo khud. literatury, 1984), 731.

But the verse line as a framework does not merely rearrange things; a framework can add color, has *its own* power, generates *its own, verse-specific* shadings of meaning.

The time when meter or rhyme could be a novelty, or "musicality" a kind of decoration, is behind us. But by the same token, we have become attuned to the music of meanings in verse (and this is the basis for a new poetic culture—which is why Khlebnikov is so important) and to the order, the framework in which words are transformed in poetry. And this—in the specific *shadings* of words, their distinctive semantic music—is where Mandelstam comes in. Mandelstam borrowed his musical verse from the nineteenth century—the melody of his verse is almost Batyushkovian:

Я в хоровод теней, топтавших нежный луг,	A ring of shades danced on the springing meadow.
С певучим именем вмешался,	I threw among them a name like a song.
Но все растаяло, и только слабый звук	Everything melted. Only a weak sound
В туманной памяти остался.	Remained in my dim memory.[97]

But Mandelstam needs this melody (just as Batyushkov needed it) for a specific purpose; it helps him knit together shadings of meaning, to construct them in a particular way.

Rendered equivalent by this single, familiar melody, the words become colored by a single emotion, and their strange order, their hierarchy, becomes inevitable.

Every restructuring of melody in Mandelstam is primarily a switch in the semantic framework:

И подумал: зачем будить	And I thought, why stir up the swarm
Удлиненных звучаний рой,	of long drawn-out lines of sound?
В этой вечной склоке ловить	Why run after the miraculous Aeolian harmony
Эолийский чудесный строй?[98]	In this ceaseless squabble? (42, modified)

Mandelstam's semantic framework is such that *one* image, one verbal series, takes on a decisive role for the whole poem and quietly colors all of the others—it becomes the key to the whole hierarchy of images:

97 *Stikhotvoreniia*, 124. See also *Selected Poems*, 34. Translation slightly modified. Subsequent citations from this edition will be given in parentheses.

98 From "I climbed the ladder ..." [Ia po lesenke pristavnoi ...]—*MC*. See *Stikhotvoreniia*, 129.

Как я ненавижу *пахучие,* древние *срубы*	How I loathe the *odorous,* aging *stockades*
<…>	[…]
Зубчатыми *пилами* в стены *врезаются* крепко	*Hacking out* the sides with their dented *saws*
<…>	[…]
Еще в *древесину* горячий топор не *врезался.*	Nor the *hot axe hacked into* wood.
Прозрачной слезой на *стенах* проступила *смола,*	*Resin* has seeped from the *stockade* like transparent tears
И чувствует город свои *деревянные ребра*	And the town is conscious of its own *wooden ribs*
<…>	[…]
И падают стрелы сухим *деревянным дождем,*	While arrows rattle like dry *wooden rain*
И стрелы другие растут на земле, *как орешник.*[99]	and grow from the ground *like shoots from a hazel.* (32, modified)

Mandelstam's key also restructures the image of blood:

Никак не уляжется *крови сухая возня*	Nothing quiets the *blood's dry fussing*
<…>	[…]
Но хлынула к *лестницам кровь* и на приступ пошла.	But *blood* has rushed to the *stairs* and started climbing. (32, translation modified)

Mandelstam's key is still more noticeable in places where he trades his "elongated" melody for a shorter mode:

Я не знаю, с каких пор	No way of knowing
Эта *песенка* началась—	when this *song* began.
Но по ней ли *шуршит вор,*	Does the *thief rustle* to its tune? … .
Комариный звенит князь?	Does the *prince of mosquitoes hum it*?
<…>	[…]

99 "Because I could not hold onto your hands …" [Za to, chto ia ruki tvoi ne sumel uderzhat']—*MC*. See ibid., 121.

Прошуршать спичкой, плечом	*rustle* up like a struck *match,*
Растолкать ночь—разбудить.	*nudge* night awake with my shoulder,
Приподнять, как душный стог,	*Heave up like a smothering haystack,*
Воздух, что шапкой томит,	the muffling hat of *air,*
Перетряхнуть мешок	*shake* out the stitches
<…>	[…]
Чтобы розовой крови связь,	then the pink link of blood,
Этих *сухоньких трав звон,*	the *hushing of these dry grasses*
Уворованная нашлась	*stolen away,* would be found after
Через век, *сеновал, сон.*	a century, a *hayloft,* a *dream.*[100]

The rustling of the verse has brought the century, the hayloft, and the dream very close together; they have taken on distinct shadings. But we find the key only in the next poem:

Я по лесенке приставной	I climbed the ladder leaning against the hay,
Лез на *всклоченный сеновал,* —	Into the uncombed *loft,*—
Я дышал *звезд* млечной *трухой,*	I breathed the *haydust* of milky *stars,*
Колтуном пространства дышал.	I breathed *the elf-lock of the void.*
	(42, modified)

But we don't even need the key: the "stolen link" can always be found in Mandelstam. It is made *line by line*; the shadings and coloring of a given word in each line are not lost, and they become still more concentrated in the following line. In his latest poem ("1 January 1924"), there is an almost insane association—"Underwood typewriter" and "pike bone."[101] It is as though it were created for fans of talking about "senselessness" (these fans are known for trying to use their own keys to open doors into spaces that belong to others, even when they are not locked).

But these strange meanings are actually justified by the movement of the whole poem, the passage from shading to shading that ultimately leads to *new meaning*. In this sense, the main point of Mandelstam's work is the creation of distinctive meanings. His definitions are only apparent; they are oblique definitions of the sort that can emerge only in verse, and that become inevitable through verse alone. Instead of words he has the shadows of words.

---

100 See ibid., 129. See *Selected Poems*, 42. Translation modified.

101 Writing in 1924, Tynianov refers to Mandelstam's "last poem": Mandelstam effectively stopped writing poetry during the second half of the 1920s, resuming again in 1930.

With Pasternak, the word becomes a nearly tangible verse object; with Mandelstam, the object becomes a verse abstraction.

This is why he has a knack for the abstract philosophical ode in which, as in Schiller, "sober concepts whirl in a Bacchic dance" (Heine).

This is also why the theme of the "forgotten word" recurs in Mandelstam:

Я слово позабыл, что я хотел сказать.
<…>
О, если бы вернуть и зрячих пальцев стыд,
И выпуклую радость узнаванья.
Я так боюсь рыданья Аонид:
Тумана, звона и зиянья.
<…>
Все не о том прозрачная твердит.

I have forgotten the word I wanted to say.
[…]
Oh to bring back also the shyness of clairvoyant
fingers, the swelling joy of recognition.
I shrink from the wild grieving of the Muses,
from the mists, the ringing, the opening void.
[…]
The Spectral One still speaks, but not of this. (28, translation modified)

And for this very reason, Mandelstam understands the power of verbal coloring better than any other contemporary poet. He is fond of proper nouns, because they are not words but word shadings. Shadings are what make language significant for him:

Слаще пенья итальянской речи
Для меня родной язык,
Ибо в нем таинственно лепечет
Чужеземных арф родник.

Sweeter to me
than the singing speech of Italy
is the language to which I was born.
Notes of foreign harps well up in it mysteriously.[102]

Here is one "foreign harp" built *almost entirely* without foreign words:

Я изучил науку расставанья
В простоволосых жалобах ночных.
Жуют волы, и длится ожиданье,
Последний час *вигилий* городских.[103]

I learned the art of parting ways,
In night laments, with hair undone.
The oxen chew, the waiting lasts.
The final hour of *vigils* in the town.[104]

102 "Slightly shimmers the transparent stage …" [Chut' mertsaet prizrachnaia stsena …]—*MC*. See *Stikhotvoreniia*, 118; See *Selected Poems*, 29. Translation slightly modified.

103 "Tristia"—*MC*. *Stikhotvoreniia*, 110.

104 Ibid. Translation by Daria Khitrova.

Here is another:

Идем туда, где разные науки,	Let's go where they've a collection of sciences,
И ремесло — *шашлык и чебуреки,*	and the art of making *shashlyk* and *chebureki,*
Где вывеска, изображая брюки,	where the sign shows a pair of pants
Дает понятье нам о человеке.[105]	to tell us what a man is. (26)

In this highly receptive verse culture, the smallest foreign grafting is enough for ordinary Russian words like *parting ways* [rasstavaniie], *hair undone* [prostovolosaia], and *waiting* [*ozhidanie*] to become as Latinate as *vigils,* and for *sciences* [nauki] and *pants* [briuki] to become *chebureki.*[106]

Mandelstam's admission about himself is also characteristic:

И с известью в крови для племени чужого	and with lime slaking in the veins, to hunt
Ночные травы собирать.[107]	for night herbs for a tribe of strangers! (52)

His work on the literary language is that of a near foreigner. This is why Mandelstam is a pure lyricist, a poet of small forms. His chemistry experiments are possible only on a small scale. He is unconcerned with the question of moving beyond the lyric (consider his love for the ode). His shadings would be unthinkable in the space of the epic.

Mandelstam doesn't have any hard-currency words. He has shadings, promissory notes that are passed from line to line. For now, this is where his strength lies. For now—because during an interlude, hard currency usually turns out to be counterfeit. We saw this when discussing Esenin.

---

105 "Theodosia" [Feodosia]—*MC.* Ibid., 115.

106 *Shashlyk* (grilled meat kebabs) and *chebureki* (fried meat pastries) are common foods of Transcaucasia that had become ubiquitous in Russia by the early twentieth century.

107 Mandelstam, "1 January 1924"—*MC.* Ibid, 138.

11

Баллада, скорость голая.
[A ballad, naked speed.]

И в эпос выслали пикет.[108]
[And scouts have been sent to the epic.]

"The ballad's manner's not so young": one might even say that it has aged out for the second time already.[109] The ballad as a genre was all played out in under two years. Why?

We still treat genres as if they were ready-made objects. The poet gets up, opens up some kind of cabinet, and takes out the genre he needs. Any poet can open this cabinet. And there are plenty of genres, from the ode all the way to the long poem. There should be more than enough to go around.

But the interlude teaches us a different lesson. That is what an interlude is for: there are no ready-made genres; they are in the process of being created, slowly and anarchically, and not for general use.

A poetic genre is created when verse language, gathering momentum and bringing itself to fruition, has all the qualities it needs to present a completed form. A genre is the realization, the concentration, of all of the wandering, glimmering energies of the word. This is why a new and convincing genre arises only sporadically. The poet is only occasionally aware of the quality of his language, and this recognition leads him to the genre. (This ability was Pushkin's great strength. In *Eugene Onegin*, you can see how the distinctive properties of existing poetic language are *projected* into a genre, how *that distinctiveness itself* essentially creates it.)[110] Needless to say, this quality of poetic language (which, as it becomes more concentrated and self-aware, leads to the genre) does not have to do with meter or rhyme; it comes from the semantic distinctiveness of the language, whereby it comes to live in verse. This is why the eighteenth century was only capable of creating a

---

108 The first epigraph is from Nikolai Tikhonov's long poem "Face to Face" [Litsom k litsu] (Moscow/Leningrad, 1927); the second is from Pasternak, "A Lofty Ailment" [Vysokaia bolezn'], *LEF* 1 (1924): 16.

109 Inexact quotation from Mayakovsky's long poem "About That"—*MC*. The line actually reads "The ballad's manner's not young at all" [Nemolod ochen' lad ballad]. Mayakovksii, *Polnoe sobranie*, 4:140.

110 For more on Pushkin's novel in verse, see "On the Composition of *Eugene Onegin*" (114–150).

burlesque verse tale, and why the nineteenth century could only produce a *parodic* epic.[111]

Right now, poets are in search of a genre. This means that they are trying to fully realize their poetic language.

The ballad of our time was started by Tikhonov:[112]

Шеренги мертвых — быль бывалую,	Ranks of the dead—seen-it-all true story,
Пакеты с доставкою на дом,	Home-delivery packages,
Коней и гвозди брал я	Steeds and nails—I drew
На твой прицел, баллада.	Your bead on them, ballad.
Баллада, скорость голая,	O ballad, naked speed,
Романтики откос,	Sheltering slope of romance,
Я дал тебе поступь и рост,	I gave you a gait and growth,
Памятью имя выжег.	Used memory to brand on your name.
Ступай к другим, веселая,	Now move on, smiling girl,
Служи, как мне служила,	Serve others as you served me,
Живи прямой и рыжей.	Live on, straight-backed and red-haired.

This farewell is portentous, and the definition provided works: the ballad is "naked speed,"

> Озеро — в озеро, в карьер луга.[113]
> [Lake into lake, meadows into the quarry.]

The ballad was able to form on the basis of precise, almost prosaically honest language; there is a reason Tikhonov belongs to a circle of prose writers. The language of his ballads has lost almost all of its verse coloring, in order to become a support for the plot—a plot point. The drum of the plot beats out a rat-a-tat of words as precise as arithmetic:

---

111 For more on Tynianov's understanding of parody, see "Dostoyevsky and Gogol" (27–63) and "On Parody" (294–328).

112 Nikolai Tikhonov (1896–1979) was an experimental Modernist poet known particularly for his ballads of the 1920s. Though a poet, he was affiliated with the Serapion Brothers, a group of prose writers.

113 Quotations from Tikhonov's long poems "Face to Face" [Litsom k litsu] and "Ballad of the Blue Package" [Ballada o sinem pakete]—*MC*. See Nikolai Tikhonov, *Collected Works* [*Sobranie sochinenii*], vol. 1 (Moscow: Gos. izd-vo khud. literatury, 1958), 103–105.

114 Tikhonov, "The Deserter" [Dezertir] (from *The Horde* [Orda], 1922)—*MC*. See ibid., 66–67.

Хлеб, два куска	Bread, two chunks
Сахарного леденца,	Of sugar candy, and,
А вечером сверх пайка	Come evening, on top of rations
Шесть золотников свинца.[114]	A single ounce of lead.

And the plot, with no delay, without being transformed through the verse—with "naked speed"—goes flying through three-four-five stanzas down to the "sheltering slope of romance."

Tikhonov's ballads made a big impression. No one before him had put the question of genre so bluntly, no one had perceived poetic language as a plot point. In the ballad, Tikhonov pushed to the limit what we might call the *Gumilyov* tendency of poetic language; he discovered the genre that this tendency had been moving toward.

Do you remember what happened next? Well-meaning but naïve imitators, who thought that genres could be plucked ready-made out of the cabinet, rushed to rewrite Tikhonov's ballads, occasionally making changes to the proper nouns, the heroes' ranks, and the punctuation.

Tikhonov himself didn't stop with the ballad, and that is perhaps the source of his stamina. The language of the ballad is a fast sprinter, but it can't handle long distances. It gets carried home, along with the blue package in the seventh stanza.[115]

Now Tikhonov has fallen for the epic. He has sidestepped the temptation of Zhukovsky: to group several ballads together, which in its day led to "The Twelve Sleeping Maidens," but never turned into a long poem.[116]

For us, the most obvious form that the epic can take is the verse tale. We forget that "Ruslan and Ludmila" was for a long time *not a genre*; people who had been raised on epics refused to consider it a *genre*. And *Eugene Onegin* was yet another *non-genre*, one that was difficult to reconcile with after "Ruslan and Ludmila." The verse tale was a younger version of the epic; all its distinctiveness lay in the poetic language built around a prose skeleton, a plot.

---

115 The reference is to Tikhonov's "Ballad of the Blue Package" [Ballada o sinem pakete]. See ibid., 103–105.

116 Zhukovsky's popular verse tale "The Twelve Sleeping Maidens" [Dvenadtsat' spiashchikh dev] was published in 1811. Also see "On Parody" (294–328, especially 301–303).

But the descriptive long poem, an older genre, never had a prose skeleton, and language unfolded in it according to the principle of the image.

In their large-scale works, the Symbolists had been hypnotized by the verse tale of the nineteenth century. There was a reason why Vyacheslav Ivanov, when it came time for him to write a long poem, seized upon something ready-made—the Onegin stanza.[117] (No one remembered that it had not always been ready-made.) Khlebnikov brought about a rupture with his poetic language that unfolded according to other laws, that changed from stanza to stanza (or really, from paragraph to paragraph, sometimes from line to line—in his work the concept of the stanza as a unit loses significance), and from image to image. In "Chess," Tikhonov has arrived at a descriptive long poem. In much the same way that the nineteenth-century verse tale resisted the purely descriptive long poem, his purely descriptive long poem has come to resist the verse tale.

But while the ballad is "naked speed" and dashes too quickly to the end (and is thus inimical to the epic), the descriptive long poem is static and has no end at all.

In Tikhonov's long poem "Face to Face" [Litsom k litsu], we already find a hero wandering through the large masses of the descriptive long poem, and the large masses themselves are beginning to move. In this way, the long poem marks a new phase for Tikhonov: description here is plot-oriented; description and plot are aligned. Disconnected from the ballad in accordance with the basic principle of construction, the descriptive masses are nevertheless built using *ballad material.* Looking ahead, this large-form tendency of Tikhonov's will most likely go still deeper.

We can see another interesting genre turn in another poet—a turn in the opposite direction. Nikolai Aseev is a poet who slowly discovered the importance of the foregrounded word.[118] As early as his "Rusty Lyre," it's as if a dense clot of words is broken up into stanzas and sentences:

117 In Ivanov's poem "Infancy" [Mladenchestvo] (1918)—*MC*. Vyacheslav Ivanov (1866–1949) was a Russian Symbolist poet known for extremely complicated form.

118 Nikolai Aseev (1889–1963) was a poet who got his start with the Russian Futurists and by the mid-1920s was associated with the politically engaged LEF group.

119 The cycle "The Rusty Lyre" [Zarzhavlennaia lira] (Tynianov cites an eponymous poem from the cycle) is dated 1916–1918 in Aseev's *Select* [Izbran'] (1923)—*MC*. See Nikolai Aseev, *Stikhotvoreniia i poemy* (Leningrad: Sovetskii pisatel', 1967), 113–115.

И вот —	And here—
Завод	A factory
Стальных гибчайших песен,	Of songs, flexible steel and rapid,
И вот —	And here—
Зевот	Autumnal
Осенних мир так пресен,	Yawns make the world vapid,
И вот —	And here—
Ревет	Wailing
Ветров крепчайших рев …	The howl of strongest winds …
И вот	And here
Гавот	A gavotte
На струнах всех дерев.[119]	Strummed by all the trees.

(This device evidently came out of the one-word song chorus, of which Aseev was very fond.)

From here it is but one step to "The Northern Lights" and "The Coming Ones":

Скрути струн	Twirl the screws'	Screw tea true
Винтики.	Strings.	Win teak.
Сквозь ночь лун	Through the moons' night	Squaws no chill one
Синь теки,	Flow the blue,	Seen the key,
Сквозь день дунь	Through the day blow	Squaws zen dune
Даль дым,	The distances smoke,	Dal dim,
По льду	Along the ice	Pole dew
Скальды!	The skalds!	Scolds![120]

Every word here is a rhythmic stride. (The poem itself is subtitled "Running.")

At the same time, Aseev is always aiming for distinct genres, albeit not of his own invention. His collection *Select* [Izbran'] opens with "songs," and contains a *naigrysh,* a distinctive folk melody. Aseev often introduces a chapter-based structure for his poems, which suggests a love of plot and dissatisfaction with formlessness. Aseev is making the transition to the ballad. His ballad, unlike Tikhonov's—which is built around precise language and a prosaic, fast-moving plot—is built on the *foregrounded* word (which actually does kind of stand out in the poem). For him, this kind of language has preserved its kinship with the song from which it emerged

120 Aseev, "The Northern Lights" [Severnoe siian'e] (*Select*)—*MC*. See ibid., 122–124. The two English versions (from left to right, respectively) offer a more or less literal and a phonetic translation. This poem depends heavily on sound-play for its effect.

(at first as a chorus); this is why, in Aseev's ballads, the *stanza* with its melodic pacing is so strong (with Tikhonov, it is the *line*). Aseev's ballads are songlike:

Белые бивни	White tusks
бьют	batter
ют.	tar.
В шумную пену	Into gurgling foam
бушприт	the bowsprit
врыт.	bit.
Кто говорит,	Who would say
шторм —	a storm is
вздор,	silly,
если утес — в упор.[121]	when the cliffs are clamoring.

(Previously, Polezhayev was known to work with that kind of language, which is both foregrounded and, at the same time, melodic.)[122]

Each of the ballads' little chapters has a different melodic pacing—the melody illustrates the plot in the same way that music illustrates the film in the cinema. This melody makes it possible once again to assimilate unexpectedly strange choices. For instance, the assimilation of Koltsov's verse:

Той стране стоять,	That country will stand,
Той земле цвести,	That land will bloom,
Где могила есть	Where lies the tomb
Двадцати шести.[123]	Of twenty-six men.

This is why Aseev's ballads are longer than Tikhonov's, and why they do not show any straightforward plot development (cf. "The Black Prince"). Tikhonov's and Aseev's ballads constitute different genres, because different verse elements have been condensed into each.

But this difference is also what proves to us that genre is not a "ready-made object," but a crucial connection—when it comes about as a result, when it is not just provided, but recognized as the direction that language is taking.

Meanwhile, Pasternak has sent his scouts out toward the epic.

His "A Lofty Ailment" offers an epic beyond the reaches of plot, like a slow stirring, a slow crescendo of the theme—and, in the end, a recognition of the

121 Nikolai Aseev, *Long Poems* [*Poemy* (Leningrad/Moscow: Gosizdat, 1925), 49]—*MC*.

122 Alexander Polezhaev (1804–1838) was a Romantic poet and contemporary of Pushkin.

123 Inexact quotation from Aseev, "Twenty-six"—*MC*. See ibid., 438.

theme. It is clear that, in this endeavor, Pasternak has come up against Pushkin's poetic language and is trying to renew *the principles of the Pushkinian image* (which provided the support for Pushkin's epic):

В те дни на всех припала страсть	Those days all were seized by a passion
К рассказам, и зима ночами	For stories, and the winter by nights
Не уставала вшами прясть,	Never tired of spinning its lice,
Как лошади прядут ушами.	Like horses flicking their ears.
То шевелились тихой тьмы	Then the quiet darkness went dashing
Засыпанные снегом уши,	Its ears dusted heavily with snow,
И сказками метались мы	And fairy-tales had us thrashing
На мятных пряниках подушек.[124]	On pillows' minty gingerbreads.

It is characteristic that this vitality cannot be sustained in the poem. By the end, it is supplanted by the "naked word"; here and there, it is obscured by associative detritus, and the iambic tetrameter is periodically interrupted.

No one has yet really pulled off the epic; that doesn't mean that it *has* to be pulled off. The idea that a perfect epic is due in our time is all too logical, and history has played us false plenty of times before. Instead of delivering something expected and simple, or something unexpected but still simple, history offers us yet another, a third, option, something utterly unheralded and, moreover, complicated—and a fourth option, and a fifth.

These experiments by Tikhonov and Pasternak teach us one more lesson. During an interlude, "successes" and "ready-made objects" are the last things we need. We don't know what to do with good poems, just as children don't know what to do with toys that are too fancy. What we need is a way out. Poems can be "unsuccessful"—what matters is that the failures bring closer the possibility of "successes."

---

124 Pasternak, "A Lofty Ailment," *LEF* 1 (1924): 10–11.

On Khlebnikov (1928)[1]

1

When talking about Khlebnikov,[N] you do not actually have to mention Symbolism[T] or Futurism,[T] or even talk about *zaum*[T]. Up until now, people who have done so were not talking about Khlebnikov, but about "Khlebnikov and" instead: "Futurism and Khlebnikov," "Khlebnikov and *zaum*." A less frequent pairing is: "Khlebnikov and Mayakovsky"[N] (but it has happened) and a very frequent one: "Khlebnikov and Kruchenykh."[2]

This has proved to be wrong. First of all, neither Futurism nor *zaum* is a known entity. They are more like conventional designations covering various phenomena, a lexical unity bringing together various words; something like a last name, which is shared by various relatives and even just people with the same name.

After all, there was a reason why Khlebnikov called himself a Futurian (not a Futurist), and a reason why this word did not catch on.[3]

Secondly, and most importantly, generalizations happen at various times and for various reasons. There is no such thing as a stock individual, a generic person: in school, he gets assigned to groups by age, in the army—by height. Military, medical, and class-based statistics take one and the same person and enter him into different columns. Time keeps moving and adjusts these generalizations. Finally, there comes a time that demands an individual persona. Pushkin[N] was pegged as the poet of Romanticism, while Tyutchev[N] was a poet "of the German school."[4] It was just easier for reviewers that way, and more convenient for textbooks. Trends are broken down into schools; schools narrow into circles. In 1928, Russian poetry and literature wants to see Khlebnikov.

---

1 "O Khlebnikove," first published as a preface to Khlebnikov's 1928 selected Works. See Velimir Khlebnikov, *Collected Works* [Sobranie proizvedenii, vol. 1 (Leningrad, 1928), 19–30]. Also published in the 1965 volume of Tynianov's *Problema stikhotvornogo iazyka.* Notes by the translators.

2 For more on Mayakovsky, *zaum*, and related fenomena see "On Mayakovsky" (293) and "Interlude" (173–216).

3 Khlebnikov coined the word "Futurian" [*budetlianin*], which takes as its root the future tense of the Russian verb "to be" [*budet*] (as opposed to the Latinate "futur-").

4 For more on these authors, see "On the Composition of *Eugene Onegin*" (114–150) and "Tyutchev and Heine" (64–76).

Why? Because a substantially bigger "and" has suddenly come into view—"contemporary poetry and Khlebnikov"—and another "and" is on the horizon: "contemporary literature and Khlebnikov."

2

When Khlebnikov died, one overly cautious critic (perhaps, in fact, because of this cautiousness) called Khlebnikov's entire enterprise "a harebrained attempt to renew speech and verse," and on behalf "not only of literary conservatives" declared his "non-poetic poetry" unnecessary. Everything depends, of course, on what the critic meant by the word literature. If literature is understood as the periphery of literary and journalistic production, the ease of cautious thinking, then he's right. But there is literature that runs deeper; there is a fierce struggle for a new way of seeing, with empty victories and necessary, deliberate "mistakes"; there are decisive uprisings, with negotiations, battles, and deaths. And the deaths in this enterprise can be literal, not metaphorical. The deaths of people and of generations.

3

It is a common notion that the teacher paves the way for how his students will be received. But, in fact, the opposite happens: the way for Tyutchev's reception and acceptance was paved by Fet[N] and the Symbolists. Tyutchev did things that in Pushkin's time were considered bold, but unnecessary; Then, to Turgenev[N], these things seemed like illiterate blunders. Turgenev corrected Tyutchev; the poetic periphery smoothed out the center.[5] Only with the Symbolists was the true significance of Tyutchev's metrical "illiteracies" restored. Musicians tell us that Mussorgsky's "illiteracies" and "harebrained moments" were "corrected" in just the same way—he remains only half-published to this day. All of these illiteracies are as illiterate as a phonetic transcription seems when compared to Grot's orthography.[6] It takes a fermentation element many years of hidden, underground work before it can rise to the surface as a "phenomenon," no longer just an "element."

Khlebnikov's voice has already had its effect on contemporary poetry: it has already fermented the poetry of some and lent individual devices to others.

---

5 For Gogol, see also "Dostoevskii and Gogol" (27–63).

6 Yakov Grot (1812–1893) was a scholar of Russian and other literatures, remembered for his pioneering work on Russian orthography. Modest Mussorgsky (1839–1881) was a composer in the Russian Romantic tradition.

The students have paved the way for the appearance of their teacher. The influence of his poetry is an established fact. The influence of his lucid prose lies in the future.

4

Within poetry, Verlaine[N] distinguished "poetry" from "literature." Perhaps there are such things as "poetic poetry" and "literary poetry." In this sense, Khlebnikov's poetry, despite the fact that it is quietly nourishing the poetry of today, is perhaps closer to contemporary painting than poetry. (I am obviously not talking about all of the poetry currently being written: I am talking about the strong current of poetry, published in mainstream journals, which just recently emerged out of nowhere). In any event, today's poetry has paved the way for Khlebnikov's appearance in literature.

How does poetic poetry "go literary"; how does it get incorporated into literary poetry? Baratynsky[N] wrote:

Сначала мысль, воплощена
В поэму сжатую поэта,
Как дева юная, темна
Для невнимательного света;
Потом, осмелившись, она
Уже увертлива, речиста,
Со всех сторон своих видна,
Как искушенная жена,
В свободной прозе романиста;
Болтунья старая, затем
Она, подъемля крик нахальный,
Плодит в полемике журнальной
Давно уж ведомое всем.[7]

At first the thought, when it's made flesh
in the concise poem of the poet,
is like a young girl, still obscure
to the eyes of a heedless world.
Then, grown bolder, she becomes
more artful and more smooth of tongue,
displays herself on every side,
like a woman of experience,
in the free prose of the novelist.
Finally, an old chatterbox,
she instigates a shameless clamor
and brings forth in opinion columns
what everyone knew long ago.[8]

If we set aside the aristocratic poet's reproachful and biting tone, there remains a formula, one of the laws of literature. The "young girl" has preserved her youth despite the novelist's prose and the opinion columns. But she is no longer obscure to the eyes of a heedless world.

---

7 Evgenii Baratynskii, *Complete Poems* [Polnoe sobranie stikhotvorenii] (St. Petersburg: Akademproekt, 2000), 260.

8 "At first the thought, when it's made flesh … " (1838). Yevgeny Baratynsky, *A Science not for the Earth*, trans. Rawley Grau (Brooklyn, NY: Ugly Duckling Presse, 2015), 201.

5

We are living in a great time; it's unlikely that anyone could really doubt it. But many still adhere to yesterday's standards, while others cling to the familiar. Greatness has always been difficult to grasp. This goes for literature as well. Dostoyevsky wrote to Strakhov regarding the latter's book on Tolstoy, saying that he agreed with everything in the book, except for one thing: that Tolstoy had said something new in literature. This was when *War and Peace* was coming out. In Dostoyevsky's opinion, neither Tolstoy, nor he, Dostoyevsky, had said anything new, and Turgenev and Pisemsky[N] hadn't either. Something new had been said by Pushkin and Gogol[N]. Dostoyevsky was not just being modest. He had high standards, and, most importantly—it is hard for a contemporary to recognize the greatness of contemporaneity, and even harder to discern the "new language" that it brings.[9] The problem of greatness has been solved in different ways for centuries. Contemporaries always have a sense of failure, the sense that literature is failing, and new language in literature always looks like a particular failure. Speaking of the brilliant writer Lomonosov,[N] Sumarokov[N]—a talented man of letters—noted "the poverty of [his] rhymes, a cumbersome quality owing to the crowding of letters and pronunciation, impurity of scansion, obscurity of harmony, violations of grammar and spelling, and everything else offensive to the gentle ear and abominable to unsullied taste."[10]

Sumarokov took the following lines as his motto:

> Излишество всегда есть в стихотворстве плеснь:
> Имей способности, искусство и прилежность.[11]
> [Excess always leads, in verse-making, to mold: / Have ye skill and talent and be ye not too bold.]

Lomonosov's poems were and remain incomprehensible, "senseless" in their "excess." This was a failure.

9 In this paragraph, Tynianov uses the metaphor of Tolstoy, Dostoyevsky, et al. bringing a "new word" to literature. For his conception of the "word" as language, see *slovo*.[T]

10 Sumarokov, "On the Use of Meter" [O stoposlozhenii], *PSS*, part 10, 51—*YT*. See A. P. Sumarokov, *Polnoe sobranie vsekh sochinenii v stikhakh i proze* (Moscow: V univ. tip. N. Novikova, 1787). For more on Lomonosov and Sumarokov, see "The Ode as an Oratorical Genre" (77–113).

11 Sumarokov, *Solemn Odes* [Torzhestvennye ody], 410.

Lomonosov's sap fed directly into the literature of the eighteenth-century, into Derzhavin.[N] His struggle with Sumarokov constituted the upbringing and education of Russian poetry, including Pushkin. In the 1820s Pushkin was diplomatically relieving him of the "honors of the fashionable writer," while also making a careful study of him. And Lermontov[N] would go on to use stanzas from Lomonosov. There are flashes of Lomonosov here and there throughout the poetic environment of the nineteenth century.

Lomonosov had chemistry on his side, the greatness of science. If it hadn't been for science, he would probably have fallen into disfavor as a poet. One shouldn't fear one's own vision: Khlebnikov's great failure brought new language into poetry. For now, it's impossible to predict the extent of his fermenting influence.

6

Khlebnikov was aware of his own fate. Laughter never frightened him. In "Zangezi," his Romantic drama (in Novalis's sense of this word), where mathematical computations became a new kind of material for poetry, where numbers and letters were linked to the destruction of cities and empires, and the life of a new poet to birdsong, where laughter and woe are a prerequisite for earnest irony, Khlebnikov presents the voices of his critics as the voices of passersby:

„Дурак. Проповедь лесного дурака" …	"A fool! The sermons of a forest fool … "
„Он миловиден. Женствен. Но долго не продержится".	"He's kind of cute. Almost feminine. But he won't last long." [2:335]
„Бабочкой захотелось быть, вот чего хитрец захотел".	"He wants to be a butterfly, he thinks he's so smart" [2:338]
„Сырье, настоящее сырье его проповедь. Сырая колода".	"It's all just raw material, his sermon. Just a lot of unworked stuff." [2:342]
„Он божественно врет. Он врет, как соловей ночью".	"He's a divine liar. He lies like a night full of nightingales." [2:344]
„Что-нибудь земное! Довольно неба! Грянь камаринскую! Мыслитель, скажи что-нибудь	"We want something more down to earth! We've had enough of this sky stuff! Play us a tune we can dance to! You're

веселенькое. Толпа хочет веселого. Что поделаешь — время послеобеденное".	supposed to be a thinker, think us up something fun. We all want fun. That's how it is. That's the way things are—we just had a good dinner and we want to relax!" [2:352–353]
А мыслитель отвечает: „Я таковичˮ.[12]	"I am the only son of who I am." [2:354][13]

7

In the same work, Khlebnikov says:

Мне, бабочке, залетевшей В комнату человеческой жизни, Оставить почерк моей пыли По суровым окнам подписью узника.[14]	I have come like a butterfly Into the hall of human life, And must spatter my dusty coat As signature across its bleak windows [2:338]

Khlebnikov's handwriting really did resemble the pollen caught on the wings of a butterfly. In his poetry, the child's viewpoint and infantilism of poetic language come across not through "psychology" but in its very elements, in the tiniest phrasal and verbal segments. The child and the savage were a new face for poetry, one that brought the firm "norms" of word and meter into collision. The childlike syntax, the infantile repetitions of "here now" [*vot*], the pinning down of fleeting and non-obligatory successions of verbal series—all these devices struggled with the uttermost naked honesty against that dishonest literary phrase that had grown distant from people and the present moment.

The word "seeking," which many consider significant, is applied to Khlebnikov in vain. He didn't "seek," he "found."

This is why his individual lines seem to be simple "finds," just as simple and indispensable as individual lines from *Eugene Onegin* were in their time:

---

12 From the "supersaga" [sverkhpovest'] "Zangezi," in Velimir Khlebnikov, *Tvoreniia* (Moscow, 1987), 475–495.

13 Quotations from "Zangezi," in Velmir Khlebinkov, *Collected Works of Velimir Khlebnikov*, trans. Paul Schmidt (Cambridge, MA, 1997). Volume and page numbers given in brackets.

14 Khlebnikov, *Tvoreniia*, 477.

Как часто после мы жалеем
О том, что раньше бросим[15]
[How often later we regret / The things we earlier abandon]

8

Khlebnikov was a new way of seeing—new vision. This vision alights on different objects at the same time. This is not only "learning to live through verse," as Pasternak so wonderfully put it, but learning to live through epic. And Khlebnikov is our only twentieth-century epic poet. His small-form lyric poems make up that butterfly signature: they are sudden, "infinite" notations that stretch out into the distance; observations that—either themselves, or their relatives—will become part of the epic.

At its most crucial moments, the epic has arisen from the fairy-tale. This was the origin of "Ruslan and Ludmila," a work that determined the path of Pushkin's epic and of the nineteenth-century verse tale more generally; this was also the origin of the democratic version of "Ruslan"—Nekrasov's[N] "Who is Happy in Russia?"[16]

The pagan fairy-tale is Khlebnikov's first epic. He has also provided us with a new "light" long poem in the pre-Pushkinian sense of the term, nearly Anacreontic ("The Tale of the Stone Age" [Povest' kamennogo veka]), and a new bucolic idyll ("The Shaman and Venus" [Shaman i Venera], "Three Sisters" [Tri sestry], "Sylvan Sorrow" [Lesnaia toska]). Of course, readers of "Ladomir," "Razin's Adze" [Ustrug Razina], "The Night before the Soviets" [Noch' pered Sovetami] and "Zangezi" will consider these poems to be immature, works of the poet's youth. But this does not diminish their significance. This pagan world, so near to us, swarming close at hand, imperceptibly merging with our cities and villages, could only have been built by an artist whose verbal vision was new, childlike and pagan:

Голубые цветы,
В петлицу продетые Ладою.[17]
[the blue-petaled flowers / he wears in his buttonhole, Lada's devotion.]
[3:153]

15 "Venus and the Shaman" [Shaman i Venera] (1912), in ibid., 236.

16 Nekrosov's epic poem "Who is Happy in Russia?" [Komu na Rusi zhit' khorosho?] (1869–1877) explores the circumstances of Russians from various walks of life to demonstrate that the existing social system was no good for anyone.

17 From the long poem "The Poet" [Poet] (1919–21), in ibid., 263–271.

9

Khlebnikov is not a collector of themes assigned to him from outside. It's highly unlikely that this concept—an assigned theme, an assignment—even exists for him. The artists' method, his character, and vision themselves develop into themes. Infantilism, a pagan relationship to the word, the ignorance of the new man—all naturally lead to the theme of paganism. Khlebnikov himself "anticipates" his themes. The strength and completeness of this relationship must be taken into account in order to understand how Khlebnikov, a revolutionary of the word, "predicted" the revolution in his numbers poem.[18]

10

The brutal verbal battles of Futurism, which overturned the notion of the word's prosperity, its slow, predictable evolution, were clearly not just incidental. Khlebnikov's new vision, which combined the minor and the major in pagan and childlike fashion, would not accept the fact that the most crucial and most intimate things could not get past the dense and cramped language of literature; that these crucial things of the present moment were sidelined by the "packaging" of literary language and declared to be "incidental." And this is how the *incidental* became the main element of art for Khlebnikov.

This happens in science as well. Minor errors and "flukes," explained away by senior scientists as discrepancies caused by "defects in the experiment," are shown to be the workings of unknown laws.

Khlebnikov the theorist became a Lobachevsky of language: rather than bring to light minor deficiencies in old systems, he discovered a new framework based on incidental combinations.[19]

This new, very intimate, nearly infantile vision ("butterfly") turned out to be a new framework for words and objects.

There was a rush to simplify his language theory (it helped that it was called *zaum*); eventually, everyone calmed down and decided that Khlebnikov had created "senseless sound-speech." This is wrong. The whole point of his

---

18 Tynianov refers to "The Teacher and the Student" [Uchitel' i uchenik], a 1912 essay in dialogue between the two title characters, equipped with multiple charts and tables illustrating the mathematical laws of history. At one point the Student asks, "shouldn't we expect the fall of the state in 1917?" See ibid., 589.

19 Tynianov refers to Nikolai Lobachevsky (1792–1856), a groundbreaking Russian mathematician and one of the founders of non-Euclidian geometry.

theory lies in his having shifted poetry's center of gravity from questions of sound to the question of meaning. Sounds uncolored by meaning do not exist for him, just as the questions of "meter" and of "theme" do not exist in isolation. In Khlebnikov's hands, the "orchestration" which had previously served to imitate sound became a tool that could change meaning, that revitalized the long-forgotten kinship between familiar words and brought to light new kinships between domestic and unfamiliar words.

11

The "Dreamer" did not separate everyday life from dreams, life from poetry. His vision became a new framework, while he himself became an "railwayman of artistic language." "Language has no railwaymen on permanent duty," he wrote. "Who wants to travel from Moscow to Kiev via New York? And yet what phrase from contemporary literary language is free from such detours?" [1:367] He preached an "explosion of verbal silence, the deaf-and-dumb layers of language" [1:377].[20] Those who think of his speech as "senseless" do not see how a revolution can simultaneously be a new framework. Those who talk about Khlebnikov's "senselessness" need to reexamine this question. It's not nonsense—it's a new semantic system.

Lomonosov was not the only one who was "senseless" (this "nonsense" spurred Sumarokov to write parodies);[21] there are also parodies of Zhukovsky[N] (quite a few of them) where this poet is mocked for being senseless, although today he is used to teach children how to read. To Dobrolyubov, Fet was pure nonsense.[22] Any poet who made the slightest change to his semantic system was declared to be senseless, and only later became comprehensible—not in and of himself, but because readers worked their way up to his semantic system. Blok's[N] early poems did not become more comprehensible on their own; but who doesn't "understand" them today?

Nevertheless, those who want the central question about Khlebnikov to be that of poetic nonsense should just read his prose: "Nikolai," "Usa-Gali the Hunter," "Ka," and go forth. His prose, which is semantically as clear as

20 Quotations from Khlebnikov, "Our Fundamentals" [Nasha osnova] (first published 1920)—*MC*. Translation slightly modified. See full quotation in "Interlude" (193).

21 For a discussion of Sumarokov's "nonsense odes" parodying Lomonosov, see "The Ode as an Oratorical Genre" (101–102).

22 The critic Nikolai Dobrolyubov (1836–1861) was a major figure in the mid-nineteenth-century "radical" movement in literary criticism, which advocated a realist, materialist approach against aesthetic or spiritual concerns.

Pushkin's, will convince them that the point of this question is not "nonsense": it's the new semantic framework and the fact that this framework produces different results depending on the material—from Khlebnikov's *zaum* (which is semantic rather than senseless) to the "logic" of his prose.

After all, if you write a phrase truly lacking all "meaning" in immaculate iambs, it will be nearly "comprehensible." And so many of Pushkin's terrible "senseless passages," which were obvious to his contemporaries, no longer stand out because of the familiarity of his meter. For instance:

Две тени милые, два данные судьбой	Two lovely shades, two fate-appointed
Мне ангела во дни былые …	Angels to me in days long past …
Но оба с крыльями и с пламенным мечом	But both with wings and flaming sword
И стерегут и мстят мне оба.[23]	Do guard and take revenge on me both.

How many people have stopped to think that these wings are, entirely incongruously, a terrible attribute of angels, which is in contrast with their lovely meaning—wings that in and of themselves are not terrible at all? And to what an extent did this "nonsense" deepen and broaden the progression of associations? A meticulous and unedited transcription of human conversation with no authorial commentary will meanwhile look senseless; and a variable system of verse (here an iamb, there a trochee, here a masculine and there a feminine ending) will impart even to traditional verse speech a variable semantics, variable meaning.

Khlebnikov's verse speech is not a constructive binding agent—it is the intimate speech of a contemporary person, as if overheard by a bystander, with all of its immediacy and its combination of the high style with domestic details, with the disjointed precision our language inherited from the science of the nineteenth and twentieth centuries, with the infantilism of the city dweller. This book[24] includes commentary (to the poem "The Gul-Mullah's Trumpet" [*Gul'-Mulla*]) by someone who knew Khlebnikov during his wanderings around Persia, and every fleeting image turns out to be precise, only not "retold" in literary fashion, but rather created anew.

---

23 These lines are part of an alternative ending to Pushkin's 1828 poem "Recollection" [Vospominanie]. See Alexander Pushkin, *Sobranie sochinenii v 10–i tomakh* (Moscow: GIKhL, 1959–1962), 2:206.

24 Tynianov refers to the 1928 collection of Khlebnikov's work which this article prefaced.

12

Standing before the judgment of Khlebnikov's new framework, literary traditions find themselves flung wide open. The result is an enormous shift[T] in traditions. "The Igor Tale" is suddenly more modern than Briusov.[25] Pushkin enters the new order no longer tied to the ossified and undigested clots that are the pride and joy of stylizers; he is transformed:

Видно, так хотело небо	It seems that heaven so desired
Року тайному служить,	To serve its secret fate,
Чтобы клич любви и хлеба	To imbue the cry of love and bread
Всем бывающим вложить.[26]	To all those being on the earth.

Lomonosov's and Pushkin's odes, "The Igor Tale" and the "Sobakevna" character (who recalls Nekrasov) from "Night Before the Soviets" are all indistinguishable as individual "traditions": they are fully incorporated into the new system.

The new framework wields a compelling power and strives for expansion. There can be a variety of opinions regarding Khlebnikov's numerical explorations. Perhaps they seem groundless to experts, and a mere curiosity to readers. But in order for new phenomena to emerge in literature, this relentless labor of thinking is necessary, as is faith in that labor, labor that is scientific in terms of its material—even if science does not recognize it. The gulf between the methods of science and art is not so wide after all. Only that which has an independent value in science can be a reservoir of energy for art.

This is why Khlebnikov could bring about a revolution in literature: because his framework was not exclusively literary, because he used it to make sense of both the language of verse and the language of numbers, incidental street conversations, and world-historical events; because the methods of literary revolution and historical revolutions are similar. His long numerical historical poem may not be truly scientific, and perhaps his angle of vision is only a poetic one; but "Lightland," "Razin's Adze," "Night Before the Soviets," part XVI of "Zangezi" and "Night Raid" [Nochnoi obysk] may be among the most significant poetic works written in Russian about the revolution.

25 "The Lay of the Host of Igor" [Slovo o polku Igoreve], known more colloquially as the Igor Tale, is a twelfth-century epic poem. Valery Briusov (1873–1924) was a major Symbolist poet and literary figure in pre-revolutionary Russian literature.

26 "I and E. A Tale of the Stone Age" [I i E. Povest' kamennogo veka] (1911–1912). See Khlebnikov, *Tvoreniia*, 196.

Если в пальцах запрятался нож,	If a knife is concealed in a fist
А зрачки открывала настежью месть,	and revenge stares hard from the eyes,
Это время завыло: даешь,	then it's Time who howls: "I want!"—
А судьба отвечала послушная: есть.[27]	and "Yessir," obedient Fate replies. [2:363]

13

In its methods, poetry is close to science—this is what Khlebnikov teaches us. Like science, it should be opened up to encounters with phenomena. The poet who treats words, poetry, like an object whose use is long since familiar to him (and has even become a bit boring) will also relate to an everyday object as hopelessly outdated, no matter how new it is.

The poet's stance usually requires either looking at things from above (satire) or from below (the ode), or with eyes closed (the song). There are poets who look to the side, and poets who don't look anywhere. Khlebnikov looks at objects as phenomena, with the gaze of a scientist, gradually gaining an understanding of the process and its progress. This is why "low" things do not exist for him. His village poems certainly do not present the countryside from the viewpoint of weekend visitors (cf. our "village lyric"); "The Gul-Mullah's Trumpet" does not present the East from the viewpoint of a European dilettante: there is no trace of condescension or excessive deference. Up close and on equal terms.

This was the case with his poetic diction.

He is not a collector of words, not a property owner, and not a scandal-mongering wheeler-dealer. Like a scientist, he re-evaluates linguistic dimensions: dialects. The Kharkov "pilferer," considered appropriate only for the humor column, is invited into the ode as an equal: "you pilferers, madmen and screaming marauders."[28]

Ancient European artefacts are folded into contemporary speech, expanding it geographically and historically.

Khlebnikov has no "poetic household," he has a "poetic observatory."[29]

---

27 From "Zangezi," Plane 18. See ibid., 495.

28 From the long poem "Ladomir"(ibid., 284); Khlebnikov uses the dialectal words *raklo* [pilferer, petty thief], used primarily in Eastern Ukraine, and *galakh* [screamer/yeller, association with shaved heads]: *Rakly, bezumtsy, galakhi.*

29 The term "poetic household" [*poeticheskoe khoziastvo*] comes from the title of a 1924 book by Khodasevich about Pushkin. See Vladislav Khodasevich, *Poeticheskoe khoziastvo Pushkina* (Berlin: Mysl', 1924).

14

This is how Khlebnikov's poetic persona changed: the wise man Zangezi, the woodland pagan, the child-poet, Gul-Mullah (priest of flowers), the Russian dervish [*ursu-dervish*], as he was known in Persia—was, at the same time, an engineer of artistic language.

Khlebnikov's biography—the biography of a poet who stood outside of the literature of books and journals, who in his own way was happy and also in his own way unhappy, complicated, ironic, "antisocial" and friendly—had a terrible ending. This biography is linked to his poetic persona. No matter how strange and striking the life of this wanderer and poet, no matter how dreadful his death, this biography should not be allowed to stifle his poetry. The biography should not be used to dispose of the person. Russian literature has many such cases. Venevitinov, a complicated and curious poet, died at twenty-two, and to this day only one thing is remembered about him: that he died at twenty-two.[30]

15

Khlebnikov should not be assigned to any schools or movements. His poetry is just as inimitable as that of any other poet. And we can learn from him merely by tracing the path of his development, his starting points, and by making a careful study of his methods. Because these methods contain the ethos of a new poet. This is an ethos of attention and fearlessness: attention to the "incidental" (which, when it comes down to it, is representative and real), which is usually suppressed by rhetoric and blind habit; and fearless use of honest poetic language that gets onto paper without any literary "packaging," fearlessness before words that are necessary and cannot be replaced by any others, words "not borrowed from the neighbors," as Vyazemsky[N] used to say.

And so what if that language is childlike, if sometimes the most banal language is also the most honest? This is Khlebnikov's boldness—his freedom. Without exception, all of the literary schools of our time live by prohibitions: this isn't allowed, that isn't allowed, this is banal, that is ridiculous. But Khlebnikov existed through poetic freedom, which in each case was indispensable.

30 Tynianov has in mind Dmitri Venevitinov (1805–1827), a philosophically minded Romantic poet and member of the "Lovers of Wisdom" group.

Film—Word—Music (1924)[1]

1

Film and theater are not competing with one another. Film and theater are refining one another, showing each other the way forward as they mark out their own boundaries. This younger art has preserved the easy freedom of youth ("maybe we should go to the movies?"), but has also acquired a forbidding power. In terms of the *power* of its impressions, film has overtaken theater. In terms of complexity it will never overtake it. They are on different paths.

First and foremost: *space*. No matter how much you deepen stage perspective, there's no escaping the facts: the boxes like matchboxes and the stage under a bell-jar. The actor is bound by this bell-jar. He keeps running into the walls. (It's so dreadful that in operas they even have people riding in on horseback! The horse stamps its feet and shakes its mane. Everyone is so relieved when they finally lead the unhappy animal out again. Otherwise it might have leapt off of the stage and fallen into the orchestra pit.) The theater gives you a close-up, a bas-relief. If the actor turns his back to you, all that exists for you is his back.

Then we have the *actor's body*. From the upper balcony of the Bolshoi Theater, even an actor playing Wotan looks like a little doll.[2] (This is the connection between theater and marionette theater.) From the upper balcony Hamlet looks like a fly. The Itinerants, meanwhile, put the actor right up in your face.[3] Also unpleasant.

---

1 First published (under the pseudonym Yu. Van-Vezen) in the journal *Life of Art* [Zhizn' iskusstva] no. 1 (1924), 26–27. Translation from "Kino-slovo-muzyka," *PILK*, 1977), 320–322. Selected notes to this publication by Marietta Chudakova [*MC*], 548–549. Additional notes by Yuri Tynianov [*YT*] and the translators [unmarked].

2 Wotan is another name for the Norse god Odin. Tynianov refers to a performance of Wagner's opera cycle *Der Ring des Nibelungen*. The Bolshoi Theater is a major ballet and opera theater in downtown Moscow, built in 1825.

3 Tynianov refers to the Itinerant Theater [Peredvizhnoi teatr], a democratically minded experimental theater (its first iteration was the "Public" or "Generally Accessible Theater") that operated in St. Petersburg / Petrograd / Leningrad between 1905–1928. The name of the theater refers to, but should not be confused with, the Itinerant movement in nineteenth-century painting.

The actor is bound by his body.

The actor's speech is bound to his body, to his voice and to space.

Film is an abstract art.

Experiments with space—unprecedented heights, leaps from Mars to Earth—are achieved using the most elementary, insultingly simple methods.

The space of film is, in and of itself, abstract—two-dimensional. The actor turns away from the viewer—but look, here's his face: he's whispering and smiling. The viewer sees more than any participant in a play would see.

In the theater, time is broken up into pieces, but it moves in a straight line—not backwards or to the side. This is why there can be no *Vorgeschichte* [backstory—*trans.*] in a drama (it can only be provided through language). (In fact, this is what gave rise to the specificity of drama as a literary genre.) In film, time is fluid; it has been untethered from a specific place. This fluid time fills the screen with an unheard-of variety of things and objects. It allows for forays both backwards and to the side. This is a path for a new literary genre: the broad "epic" time of film suggests a cine-novel.

The *actor's body* in film is abstract. Watch him shrink down to a dot—and now watch his enormous hands shuffling cards, grown to fill the entire screen. Watch him grow and change. The film protagonist will never be a fly. This is why film has such intense interest in the *actor*. The names of film actors mean something completely different from the names of theater actors. There is new interest every time: how will Conrad Veidt transform this time, what will Werner Krauss's "abstraction" be like today?[4] The actor's body is light, it can be stretched and compressed. (And in theater? Remember all those ponderous theatrical "deaths": when the actor falls, you can't help worrying that he has hurt himself.) All of the *props* of film are abstract: close the door in front of the fakir and he will walk through the wall.

Finally, language ...[5]

But this is the most important part.

---

4 Conrad Veidt (1893–1943) was a German actor known for his work in films including *The Cabinet of Dr. Caligari* (Robert Weine, dir.; 1919; UFA GmbH) and *The Indian Tomb* (Joe May, dir.; 1921; May-Film). Werner Krauss (1889–1959) was a German actor known for *The Cabinet of Dr. Caligari, Othello* (Dmitri Buchowetzki, dir.; 1922; Wörner-Filmgesellschaft), and *Waxworks* (Leo Birinsky and Paul Leni, dirs..; 1924; Neptune-Film AG)—*MC*. Veidt and Krauss were known as the faces of German Expressionist cinema.

5 Note that "language" here is the "word" [*slovo*[T]] of the article's title.

2

They used to call film the Great Silent. It would make more sense to call the gramophone the "great strangled."

Film is not silent. Pantomime is silent, but film has nothing in common with pantomime.

Film uses speech, but it is abstracted speech, broken down into its component parts.

You are looking at the face of a speaking actor—his lips are moving, his facial expressions are dramatically strained. You cannot make out the words (and this is good—you are not meant to be able to make them out), but you have been given a certain *element* of speech.

Then an intertitle is trotted out—you know what the actor said, but you know it *after* (or *before*) he said it. The meaning of the words is abstracted, divorced from their pronunciation. They are separated out in time.

But where is the sound? The sound comes from the music.

The music in film is *internalized*—you barely hear it and don't pay much attention to it. (And rightly so—music that is interesting on its own distracts you from the action; it barges into film like an outside force.)

The music is internalized, but not for nothing: it gives actors' speech the final element they were missing—sound.

In this abstract art, speech is broken down into component parts. Rather than in its unsullied, real-life coherence, speech appears as a new combination of its elements. And each element can therefore be developed to the ultimate limit of expressiveness: the actor is not obligated to say what is expected of him, he can say whatever words provide the greatest abundance of facial expressions.

The intertitle is free to choose words with the most appropriate meaning.

Music provides an abundance and subtlety of sound unknown to human speech. It makes it possible to reduce the characters' speech to a tense, trenchant minimum. Music allows film to do away with all of its lubricants, all of the extra "packaging" of speech.

Film is the art of abstract language.

3

In film, as soon as the music stops, a tense silence ensues. It buzzes (even if the projector is not buzzing) and hampers the viewing. This is not because we are simply *used* to music in the cinema. If you remove the music from film, it will empty out and become a defective, inadequate art form. When there is no music, the pits of the gaping, speaking mouths are excruciating.

Look closely at the movement onscreen: how heavily the horses are leaping in that emptiness! You can't keep watching them running. Movements lose their lightness and the escalation of the action weighs on you like a stone.

When you take music out of film, you make film truly mute; deprived of one of its elements, the characters' speech becomes a hindrance, an abomination. You lay waste to the action. This is an important second point: music in film gives rhythm to the action.

4

Theater is built around a cohesive, unified language (encompassing meaning, facial expression, sound). Film is built around the broken-down abstraction of language. Film is not capable of "competing" with theater. But theater should likewise not compete with film. Physical stunts in theater run into the walls, just as dialogue in film runs into the screen.

5

When inventing a poison, it is customary to invent the antidote as well.

The antidote that is capable of killing film is the Kinetophone.[6]

The Kinetophone is an unhappy invention.

The characters will speak "like in a real theater." But film's whole power lies in the fact that the characters do not "speak"—"speech" is provided. Provided in the minimal and abstracted way that makes film art.

The Kinetophone is a misbegotten child of film and the theater, a pathetic compromise. It takes the abstraction of film and carefully and awkwardly gathers the parts back together.

---

6 The Kinetophone was an early (1894), largely unsuccessful, attempt by Thomas Edison and William Dickson to create a soundtrack synchronized with film. The Kinetophone was first demonstrated in Moscow in 1913, but by the time of Tynianov's article other, more successful sound-film technologies had been introduced. By 1930, Soviet film had begun its shift toward sound, though a majority of feature films were silent until 1935.

6

Film pulled apart speech. Stretched out time. Shifted space. And this is why it is maximalist. It works with very large numbers. "200,000 meters" [of film strip] recalls the abstract exchange rate of our ruble.

We are abstract people. Every day sees us split among ten different areas of activity. This is why we go to the movies.

Part Three

EVOLUTION IN LITERATURE AND FILM

On the Screenplay (1926)[1]

1

A certain monumental director took umbrage at a screenwriter for the literariness of his narrative: "What do I need style for, why do I need these trifling details? Just write: he came in, he sat down, he shot the pistol. Everything else is my problem."

Another director, less monumental but also respected, would say: "A fabula?[T] Why do I need a fabula? I can give you thirty fabulas without even getting up from my chair. No, what I need from you is details. Everything else is my problem."[2]

It would appear they were both right.

2

It's too bad I don't know the names of the two anonymous screenwriters who are perhaps the most remarkable out of all the screenwriters alive today. Plus, they probably have no idea of their own tremendous significance. One of them sent in, as a libretto, a complete edition of [Beethoven's] Ninth Symphony (unbound); the other sent in the *ABCs of Communism* (bound).

And it would appear that they too were right.

3

The only ones who are wrong are those who say we still don't have any screenplays. By and large everyone is writing screenplays, especially the people who

1 First published in the newspaper *Cinema* [Kino], no. 9 (2 March 1926), 1. "O stsenarii," in Iurii Tynianov, *Poetika. Istoriia literatury. Kino* (Moscow, 1977), 323–324. Selected notes to this publication by Marietta Chudakova [*MC*], 550–552. Additional notes by Yuri Tynianov [*YT*] and the translators [unmarked].

2 For more on fabula, or "storyline," see "On Plot and Fabula in Film" (240–241).

only rarely go to the movies. It's hard to find a self-respecting person who has never even once written a screenplay. There are lots of screenwriters and lots of screenplays. The only thing we are short of is decent screenplays.

4

There are many reasons for this, but the two examples given above help to clarify the main one: it is not known what a screenplay is, and it is therefore difficult to talk about what it should be. Naturally, you can take any old book off the shelf—even an index of bibliographical sources—and break it up into frames. It's even easier to think of a film that has already run and apply it to contemporary circumstances. (The latter approach is taken all the time in mass-market "comic" screenplays: they take Charlie Chaplin—but actually just a distant idea of what Chaplin is, or even just Glupyshkin—and paste him onto a Soviet background.)[3] The important question here, however, relates not just to slush-pile screenplays, but screenplays overall.

5

Film was slow to liberate itself from the neighboring arts—from painting and theater. Now it has to liberate itself from literature. For the time being film is still three-quarters literary, just like the Itinerants' painting was.[4]

Nautically themed films are finally starting to lose the obligatory blue *virage*.[5] There are fewer and fewer postcard shots onscreen.

The theatrical structure of conversations is also changing. Businesslike mouths wide open in honest conversation are gaping from the screen ever less frequently.

The same thing must happen with the literary fabula[T]. The very approach to it has to change, because the film plot has its own path of development and its own rules. Some of the features of a literary fabula become a part of cinema, but not all of them.

Even the "screen versions" of "classics" should not be illustrative—literary devices and styles can only be stimulants and ferments for the devices and styles

3 Glupyshkin [Foolshead] was the Russian name for Boireau, a personage of the French silent film actor André Deed.

4 The Itinerants [*Peredvizhniki*] were a group of mid-late nineteenth-century painters whose paintings depicted socially topical and literary themes.

5 In Russian, *virage* [French—film toning] meant film tinting.

of film (of course, not just any literary devices; and naturally, not every "classic" can provide material for film). Film can give an *analogue* of literary style in its structure.

6

We still do not have anything like a clear division of film genres, though it is film genres that should be dictating the very principles of screenplay structure. Any old fabula cannot just become a part of any old genre; rather, the genre of a given film either justifies the fabula, or makes it implausible. The director who took umbrage at the excessively "literary narrative" was wrong. As long as the question of genres is unresolved for everyone (including directors), screenwriters should be both developing the fabula and suggesting (at least by analogy) a possible genre.[6]

7

The concepts of theme and material have not been delimited in the popular consciousness. Ideology is part of the concrete material and style of a film, not an abstract theme. Meanwhile, there are countless screenplays that proceed from material rather than theme.[7] The two anonymous screenwriters mentioned above are a symbol rather than an exception.

8

The relationship of film to literature needs to be readdressed; until this happens, even the best kind of screenplay will be stuck in the middle ground between the debased novel and the half-baked drama. And even the best type of screenwriter will be stuck between the roles of unsuccessful playwright and writer of *belles lettres* who has grown sick of *belles lettres*.

---

6 For more on the problem of film genres, see "The Foundations of Film" (242–266).

7 Note the understanding of the word "theme" specific to literary scholarship of Tynianov's time (see Boris Tomashevsky, *The Theory of Literature. Poetics* [Teoriia literatury. Poetika] (Moscow/Leningrad: Gos. izd-vo, 1931), 131–132—*MC*. Also see "Interlude" (173–216) and "The Ode as an Oratorical Genre," particularly page 82 and 91.

On Plot and Fabula in Film (1926)[1]

Mechnikov's favorite author was Dumas. Mechnikov insisted to anyone who would listen that Dumas was a most tranquil writer: "Five people get killed on every page and it's not frightening at all."[2]

Films with an "adventure plot" have, essentially, a devilishly tiny range: there is the obligatory chase, the more or less successful follow-up and almost always—the happy ending.

The question of plot in film is just as fraught as in literature: the works considered plot-rich are those that feature a complicated story structure. But a fabula[T] is not, after all, a plot. The fabula outline of Gogol's[N] "The Nose" strongly resembles the ravings of a madman: Major Kovalyov's nose goes missing, then wakes up on Nevsky Prospekt, then, when it gets into a carriage to go to Riga, is seized and brought back to the major in a handkerchief by a police inspector.[3] It is obvious that specific conditions of style and language, and the splicing and movement of the material, were needed for this delirium to become an element of a work of art.

When schoolchildren are forced to recount the fabula of Pushkin's[N] "The Fountain of Bakhchisaray," they forget that Pushkin made the poem's resolution intentionally vague, giving it only through hints and innuendo.[4] To degrade this innuendo into a straightforward statement of "fact" is to subject the material to naïve violence. "Fabula" is usually understood to mean the story's *outline*. It is more correct to take "fabula" to mean the entire fabula blueprint of the

---

1 First published in the newspaper *Cinema* [Kino], 30 March 1926. Translation from "O siuzhete i fabule v kino," Iurii Tynianov, *Poetika. Istoriia literatury. Kino* (Moscow, 1977), 324–325. Selected notes to this publication by Marietta Chudakova [*MC*], 552. Additional notes by Yuri Tynianov [*YT*] and the translators [unmarked].

2 Tynianov probably refers to Ilya Mechnikov, a famous microbiologist whom he would have known through his brother-in-law Lev Zilber. Another possibility is Lev (Léon) Mechnikov (1838–1888), a Russian-born Swiss revolutionary and geographer who met the famous French author of adventure novels Alexandre Dumas (1802–1870) while fighting for Italian independence.

3 For Gogol, also see "Dostoevsky and Gogol" (27–63).

4 For Pushkin, see "On the Composition of *Eugene Onegin*."

work. The plot, meanwhile, is the overall dynamics of the work, formed from the *interaction* between the movement of the fabula and the movement through the buildup and setbacks of the elements of style. The fabula may only be hinted at, rather than given; the viewer may only be able to guess at it from the evolving plot—and this riddle will be an even greater plot mover than the fabula that unfolds straightforwardly right in front of the viewer.

The fabula and plot are eccentric in relation to one another.

In *The Bay of Death*, an episode that has absolutely no significance to the fabula—when the sailor pulls a bottle out of his pocket instead of the expected revolver—is given in a style that undermines the main foundation of the fabula and shoves it to the sidelines. And this is a good thing—it is just a result that compels the viewer to think twice about the relationship between the fabula and the plot. In *The Devil's Wheel*, the slowly developing fabula is given at a frenzied plot tempo.[5] The fact that the tempo is equally frenzied throughout the film is illegitimate (there is no buildup, the frenzy is static), but the device per se is legitimate and can serve as a point of departure for further developments.

Chases, captures, the punishment of vice and the triumph of good deeds in the cinema are starting to get old, and we will just as quickly become indifferent to bloodletting in film. (Though this blood is still not real, it's cinematic blood—but the law of habituation holds in art.) The moment will soon come when the viewer will be bored during the most brutal chase scene of airplane after automobile and automobile after horse and carriage. But when you get used to an artistic device, you start catching glimpses of the hand behind the device that is making it happen—the hand of the director or screenwriter pulling the strings.

When the character facing imminent death leaps onto an automobile, the viewer will say: "They were leaping around in that movie we saw just yesterday. That guy made it, and this one's going to make it too." When five people are being murdered at once right in front of the viewer, he will say: "That's not that many; remember, in that movie we saw yesterday …" The viewer will discern the author's act of violence behind the combinations of the fabula, and this will lead to a different interpretation of the plot—and to a nearly static fabula, as simple as two plus two, provided as part of an escalating, genuinely "adventurous" plot. Even without any chases or obligatory bloodletting.

5 Both films released by the FEX group in 1926. For more on FEX and *The Devil's Wheel* [Chortovo koleso (Grigorii Kozintsev and Leonid Trauberg, dirs.; 1926; Leningradkino)], see "On FEX" (289–292).

The Foundations of Film (1927)[1]

1

The invention of the cinematograph was greeted with the same delight as the invention of the gramophone. This delight had in it something of what primitive man must have felt when he first drew a leopard head on his rough blade, and simultaneously figured out how to pierce his nose with a stick. The hoopla in the press resembled a chorus of savages singing hymns of praise to these early inventions.

It probably did not take long for primitive man to decide that a stick through the nose was nothing to write home about; though in any case it took him longer than it took Europeans to despair of the gramophone. The point, it would seem, lies less in the fact that the cinematograph is a technology than that cinema is an art.

I remember hearing complaints about cinema being flat and colorless. I have no doubt that the primitive inventor who etched a leopard head onto his weapon was very quickly approached by a critic who pointed out the poor likeness of his depiction; and after the critic there doubtless came a second inventor who advised the first one to glue some real leopard fur onto his picture and stick in a real-looking eye. But the fur probably wouldn't stick to the stone very well, and meanwhile the carelessly drawn leopard head gave rise to writing, because instead of hindering, this carelessness and imprecision actually *helped* turn the drawing into a sign. Second-wave inventors don't usually have much luck, and we feel little enthusiasm over the future of the Kinetophone, stereoscopic cinema, or color cinema.[2] Because you'll never end up with a real leopard, and also because art has nothing to do with real leopards. Art—like language—

1 First published in B. Eikhenbaum, ed., *Poetika kino* (Moscow/Leningrad: Academia, 1927), 55–85. Translation from "Ob osnovakh kino," *PILK*, 326–345. Selected notes to this publication by Marietta Chudakova [*MC*], 552–556. Additional notes by Yuri Tynianov [*YT*] and the translators [unmarked].

2 For more on Tynianov's attitude toward sound and color in film, including the Kinetophone and other transitional cinematic inventions, see "Film—Word—Music" (230–234) and "On the Screenplay" (237–239).

endeavors to render its resources ever more abstract. And this is why not just any old resources are up to the task.

When this man drew an animal head on his blade, he wasn't just *drawing* it; it was also providing him with magical courage. His totem was with him, on his weapon; his totem pierced the chest of his enemy. In other words, his drawing had two functions: a material, reproductive function, and a magical function. An unintended result of this was that, once the leopard head appeared on all the weapons of the entire tribe, it became a sign distinguishing their weapons from the enemy's: a mnemonic sign that later became an ideogram and ultimately, a letter. How did this happen? One of several initial results was consolidated, and its functions switched over.

This is how technical resources become the resources of art. Naturalistic photography, whose main function was to resemble the natural world it sought to depict, passed into the art of cinema. With this transition, the function of all its resources was switched; instead of being resources in and of themselves, they became resources for art. Thus the "poverty" of cinema, its flatness and colorlessness, were revealed to be *positive* and genuine artistic resources, just as the imperfect and primitive qualities of ancient totemic depictions turned out to be positive tools in the development of written language.

2

As inventions, the Kinetophone and stereoscopic cinema belong to the early stages of cinema; their implied function is material and reproductive, "photography as such." Rather than proceeding from the frame sequence [*kadr-kusok*], which carries a semantic sign contingent on the frames' dynamic unity, they treat the shot (frame) as an undifferentiated whole.[3]

Viewers of stereoscopic cinema would doubtless be impressed by the close resemblance to reality of the bulging, three-dimensional walls of houses and bulging human faces. But bulging forms succeeded by other bulging forms in a montage, or bulging faces dissolving into other bulging faces, would seem like an unrealistic chaos made up of individual bits of verisimilitude.

No doubt nature and people would look just like the real thing if they were tinted with naturalistic color, but a gigantic face in close-up, naturalistically

3 In Russian, the direct relationship between the "shot" [*kadr*, also "frame"] and the "frame sequence" [*kadr-kusok*, literally: frame/shot-fragment or piece] is more evident in the terms themselves.

colored, would be monstrous, far-fetched and completely unnecessary, akin to a colorfully painted statue with swiveling eyes. Not to mention that the addition of color marginalizes one of film's most important stylistic resources: various shifts in the *lighting* of monochrome material.

Even the most unimaginably ideal Kinetophone would have to use such fiendishly meticulous montage that the actors would make the sounds they need (and that cinema does not need) completely independently of the laws for the development of cinematic material. Not only would this result in a cacophony of pointless speech and noise; it would also make even legitimate sequences of shots seem far-fetched.

We have only to think of a device like the dissolve, when a speaker recalls an earlier conversation, to feel unimpressed by this much-vaunted invention. The "poverty" of cinema is, in fact, its constructive principle. It's high time we stopped repeating that feeble compliment, "The Great Silent." After all, we don't complain that poems don't come with photographs of the rhapsodized heroines; no one calls poetry The Great Blind.[4] Every art form uses some element of the sensory world as a crucial, constructive element, while the other elements only exist in potential, under its sign. Thus visual and pictorial representations are not banished from the realm of poetry, but they take on a specific quality and specific application: in the descriptive long poem [*poema*[T]] of the eighteenth century, for instance, objects of nature aren't named, but are "described" metaphorically through connections and associations from other series.[T] To say "tea pouring from a kettle," a poem like this would say "the boiling, fragrant jet, streaming from glittering bronze." We are not given a pictorial, visual representation, and this serves to motivate connections between many verbal series; their dynamics depends on the riddle being posed. Needless to say, instead of true-to-life, visual representations, what we get here are verbal representations whose importance lies in the semantic coloring of words and the play of this coloring, rather than in the objects themselves. If we were to replace verbal series with series of actual objects, we would end up with an incredible chaos of objects and nothing more.

In the same way, cinema only uses words to motivate the linking together of different shots, or as an element whose role, either contrastive or illustrative,

4 For Tynianov's attitude toward silent film, see "Film—Word—Music" (230–234).

is entirely defined by its relation to the shot. If the cinema were stuffed full of words, we would end up with nothing but a cacophony of words.[5]

For cinema as an art, there are no further innovations per se, only the technical resources for refining its given elements; these are in turn selected for how well they correspond to its principal devices. This results in a mode of interaction between technology and art that is the opposite of what was happening initially. Now, art itself is *spurring on* technical devices; as art moves incrementally along, it selects the devices it needs, changes their application and their function, and, ultimately, casts them aside. No longer is technology spurring on art.

The art of the cinema already has its material. This material can become more varied and refined, but nothing more.

3

The "poverty" of cinema, its flatness and colorlessness, are, in fact, its constructive essence. This essence does not inspire the creation of new, supplemental devices; rather, it itself generates new devices—they grow out of its foundation. Cinema's flatness (which does not rob it of perspective), a technical "deficiency," manifests in the art of cinema as a positive constructive principle, that of the *simultaneity* of several series of visual representations, which in turn inspire entirely new interpretations of gesture and movement.

Consider the dissolve, a device well known to everyone. We see a piece of paper with typed text in sharp relief, held in someone's fingers; the letters start to fade, the outline of the paper grows indistinct, and through it, a new shot takes shape—the outlines of moving figures, gradually gaining solidity and, finally, completely superseding the shot of the paper with the text. Obviously, this linking of shots can only take place if they are flat: if the shots were three-dimensional, in relief, then their interpenetration, their simultaneity, would be unconvincing. Only through the use of this simultaneity is such a composition possible: a composition that both reproduces movement and is itself constructed through the principles of this movement. A shot can convey dancing

5 See the "Statement on Sound" made by Sergei Eisenstein, Vsevolod Pudovkin, and Grigori Alexandrov in *Zhizn' iskusstva*, 5 August 1928—*MC*. English version in *The Film Factory: Russian and Soviet Cinema in Documents*, ed. and trans. Richard Taylor and Ian Christie (Cambridge, MA, 1988), 234–235.

not just by showing "dancing," but also through the use of a "dancing shot," by "moving the camera" or "moving the shot": everything in this shot would sway, one row of people would be dancing on top of another. What we have here is a particular spatial simultaneity. The law of the impenetrability of bodies is overthrown by cinema's two dimensions: its flatness and abstraction.

Moreover, this simultaneity of time and space is not important in and of itself, but only insofar as it constitutes the semantic sign of a shot. As one shot follows another, it retains the semantic sign of that previous shot and is semantically colored by it for its entire duration. A shot that is *constructed* according to the principles of movement has little to do with the material reproduction of movement; it conveys a semantic representation of movement. (This is how Andrei Bely[N] sometimes constructs his phrases: the literal meaning of the phrase is less important than its phrasal patterning.)

Cinema's lack of color allows it to convey a *semantic*, rather than material, juxtaposition of sizes, a prodigious discrepancy in perspectives. There is a Chekhov story where a child draws a big person next to a small house.[6] This is perhaps the quintessential device of art: size is disassociated from its material and reproductive basis and turned into a semantic sign of art; a shot filmed with all the objects enlarged is followed by a shot with a diminished perspective. A shot of a small person filmed from above is followed by a shot of another person filmed from below (cf. the shot of Akaky Akakievich and the "important personage" in the "scolding" scene of *The Overcoat*).[7] Natural coloration here would cancel out the principal orientation—the semantic relation to size. The close-up, which isolates a single object from the spatial and temporal interrelation[T] of all the objects, would lose its *meaning* if there were natural coloration.

Finally, the wordlessness of cinema, or rather the constructive impossibility of filling shots with words and noises, exposes the nature of its construction: cinema has its own "protagonist" (its own specific element) and its own means of joining things together.

4

There has been a difference of opinion regarding this "protagonist" that is characteristic of the nature of cinema itself. In its material, cinema is close to the

6 Anton Chekhov, "At Home," in *Anton Chekov's Short Stories*, trans. Ralph E. Matlaw (New York, 1979), 52–59.

7 Tynianov wrote the screenplay for the Kozintsev/Trauberg film version of Nikolai Gogol's[N] *The Overcoat* (Grigorii Kozintsev and Leonid Trauberg, dirs.; 1926; Sevzapkino). For more on this film, see "On FEX" (290).

visual and spatial arts, to painting; meanwhile, the way it works with this material is closer to the temporal (verbal and musical) arts.

This is the source of such lush, metaphorical definitions as "film is painting in motion" (Louis Delluc),[8] or "film is the music of light" (Abel Gance).[9] But these definitions are scarcely different from "The Great Silent." Finding names for cinema through its relation to neighboring art forms is just as fruitless as defining those other art forms through their relation to cinema: calling painting "motionless cinema," or music "the cinema of sounds," or literature "the cinema of language." New art forms are particularly vulnerable to this. It smacks of reactionary deference to the past: naming a new phenomenon in relation to old ones.

But art doesn't need definitions; it needs studying. And it is completely understandable that the reproductive and material object of cinema—the "visible man" and "visible object" (Béla Balázs)—was initially proclaimed its "protagonist."[10] But the arts differ from each other not only, or even primarily, in their objects, but rather more in their relation to these objects. Otherwise, the art of the word would be ordinary conversation, speech. After all, the "protagonist" of speech is the same as that of poetry—language[T]. But that's just it: there is no stock "language." Language plays a completely different role in poetry than in conversation, and language in prose—across all its genres—plays a different role than in poetry.

The choice of "visible man" and "visible object" as the "protagonist" of the art of cinema is mistaken not because an objectless cinema is a real possibility, but because this choice fails to highlight the specific way the material is used (and this use alone is what turns a material element into an element of art); because this choice fails to highlight the specific function of this element in art.

Cinema does not convey the visible world per se, but in terms of its semantic interrelations; otherwise, cinema would be just a living (and lifeless) photograph. The visible man and visible object only become elements of cinematic art when they are given, and function, as a semantic sign.

This first premise gives rise to the concept of film style; the second to the concept of film construction. The semantic interrelations of the visible world are conveyed through its stylistic transformation. Meanwhile, the relations between people in a shot, between people and things, and between the part and

8 Louis Delluc (1890–1924) was a French film director, screenwriter and film theorist—*MC.*

9 Abel Gance (1889–1981) was a French film director and the inventor of Polyvision—*MC.* Gance's formal experiments (with montage, unusual angles, etc.) made his work extremely influential for early Soviet filmmakers.

10 Béla Balázs (Herbert Bauer, 1884–1949) was a Hungarian writer and film theorist—*MC.* Balázs authored a 1924 essay entitled "Visible Man." See *Early Film Theory*, ed. Erica Carter (New York/Oxford: Berghahn, 2010), 9–17.

the whole (what is usually called "the composition of a shot"), the camera angle and perspective from which they are filmed, and the lighting—all these take on tremendous significance. At this point, because of its technical flatness and monochrome palette, cinema transcends its own flatness. Compared to the prodigious freedom of cinema in its use of perspective and point of view, theater, which has at its disposal technical three-dimensionality and bulging forms, is condemned (due to this special quality) to a single point of view and to flatness as an element of its art.

The camera angle stylistically transfigures the visible world. A *horizontal*, slightly tilted factory smokestack, the crossing of a bridge filmed from below—this transformation of objects in the art of cinema is tantamount to a whole array of stylistic resources for making things new in verbal art.

Of course, not all camera angles or kinds of lighting are equally forceful as stylistic resources, and the most powerful stylistic resources are not always suitable for application; but here lies the persistent artistic difference between cinema and theater.

5

Unity of place is not a problem for cinema; the only serious problem is that of the unity of camera angle and lighting. A single film set involves hundreds of different camera angles and types of lighting, which in turn means hundreds of different interrelations between people and things, and of things among themselves; hundreds of different "locations." Five different stage sets in a theater are really just five "locations" from a single angle. This is why elaborate theatrical film sets with complicated perspectival calculations look phony on film. It is also why pursuit of the photogenic is fruitless. Objects are not photogenic in and of themselves; they are made so by camera angle and lighting. Thus, the very concept of "the photogenic" should yield to the concept of "*the cinegenic.*"

The same goes for all stylistic devices in film. The detail of moving legs, instead of people walking, focuses the attention on an associative detail just as synecdoche does in poetry. In both cases it's important that, in place of the object nominally drawing our attention, we are shown a *different object*, associatively linked to it (in cinema, an associative relation would typically be a movement or a pose). This substitution of a detail for an object makes our attention switch over: different objects (a whole and a detail) are provided under a single orienting sign, and this switch dismembers, as it were, the visible object, turning it into a series of objects that share a single semantic sign: the *semantic object* of cinema.

It goes without saying that with this stylistic (and therefore semantic) transformation, the "protagonist" of cinema is not the "visible man" or "visible object," but the "new" person and "new" object; people and objects transformed on the level of art; hence, the cinematic "person" and "object." The visible interrelations between visible people are interrupted and swapped out for interrelations between cinematic "people"; this occurs continually, unconsciously, almost naively—so deeply is it embedded in the very foundations of this art. When Mary Pickford plays a young girl, she surrounds herself exclusively with tall actors and "pulls the wool over our eyes," probably without even thinking about how in the theater she wouldn't be able to pull off a trick like that. (This is not a stylistic transformation, of course, just a technical application of one of the laws of this art.)

6

But what are the grounds for the emergence of these phenomena, this *new* person and *new* object? Why are they transformed by film style?

Because every stylistic resource is simultaneously a semantic factor. Under one condition: that the style be organized, that the camera angle and lighting are not incidental, but constitute a system.

There are works of literature where the simplest events and relationships are conveyed through such stylistic resources that they grow into an enigma; the reader experiences a shift[T] in his awareness of the relation between big and small, between ordinary and strange. He follows the author hesitantly, his "perspective" on objects and their "lighting" is shifted (we see this, for instance, in Joseph Conrad's story "The Shadow Line," where a straightforward event—a young naval officer is given command of a ship—grows into something grandiose and "off-kilter"). The point here lies in the particular semantic organization of objects, and the particular way in which the reader is brought into the action.

Film style offers essentially the same possibilities, and the situation there is essentially the same: the shifting of the viewer's perspective is simultaneously a shifting of the *interrelations* between objects and people, a semantic reconfiguring of the world in general. Changes in different kinds of lighting (or the persistence of a single lighting style) reconfigure the *environment* in the exact same way that a camera angle reconfigures the relationships among people and objects.

The "visible object" is once again replaced by the object of art.

The same goes for the significance of metaphor in film: one and the same action is conveyed by different vehicles; we don't see people kissing, but "lovebirds," doves. Here as well, the visible object is dismembered, and different vehicles, different objects, are conveyed under a single semantic sign; at the same time, the action itself is dismembered, and its specific semantic coloring is conveyed by the second parallel (the doves).

Even these simple examples are enough to show that cinema transforms both natural and "visible" *movement*—this visible movement can be dismembered and conveyed through a different object. Movement in cinema exists either to motivate *a camera angle* via association with the point of view of a moving person, or as a person's defining characteristic (a gesture), or as a *change in the interrelation* between people and objects, e.g. particular people and objects moving closer to and away from a person (or object); that is, movement in cinema exists not in and of itself, but as a kind of semantic sign. This is why movement within a shot is entirely non-obligatory outside of its semantic function. Montage can fulfil this semantic function; moreover, the shots can even be static. (Movement within a shot is greatly overstated as an element of cinema anyway; lots of running around for no apparent reason is exhausting.)

And if what we have in cinema is not "visible movement," it stands to reason that film operates on its "own time" as well. To establish the *duration* of a given situation, cinema uses the *recurrence* of a shot: a shot is broken up some minimum number of times, either through alterations or in its unchanged form, and this constitutes its duration, which is undoubtedly a far cry from the usual, "visible" concept of duration—this duration is completely relational. If the recurring shot is interrupted by a large number of other shots, then this "duration" will be substantial, even though the "visible duration" of the recurring shot is negligible. The same goes for the provisional significance of the *iris-in / iris-out* and *fade-out* as signs of major spatial and temporal demarcation.

The specificity of cinematic time is made evident through devices like the close-up. Close-ups take objects, or details, or faces, and abstract them, both from their spatial interrelations and from their temporal framework. There's a scene in *The Devil's Wheel* where bandits come out of a ransacked house.[11] The directors needed to show the bandits. They did this through a wide shot of the whole group. This resulted in a strange disparity: why were the bandits moving

11 *The Devil's Wheel* [Chortovo koleso (Grigorii Kozintsev and Leonid Trauberg, dirs.; 1926; Leningradkino)] was a FEX film made in 1924. For this film and the FEX crew, also see "On FEX" (289–292).

so slowly? If they had been shown in close-up, they could have taken all the time they wanted, because the close-up would have abstracted them, detached them from their temporal framework.

The duration of a shot is thus created by its recurrence; that is, by the interrelations of shots among themselves. On the other hand, temporal abstraction results from the absence of interrelations among objects (or groups of objects) with each other, within a shot.

Both of these things underscore the fact that "film time" is not real duration, but duration as a matter of convention, based on the interdependence of shots or of visual elements within a shot.

7

The specific nature of an art form is always reflected in the evolution of its devices. The evolution of cinematic devices can teach us a great deal.

At first, the motivation for a given camera angle was the viewer's point of view, or the point of view of a character. In the same way, close-ups of a detail were motivated by what a character was perceiving.

An unusual camera angle, which was once motivated by a character's point of view, shed this motivation and was presented in its own right; it thereby became the viewer's point of view, and by the same token, a stylistic device of cinema.

Initially the gaze of a character in a shot would alight on some object or detail, and this object would be shown in close-up. When this motivation was eliminated, the close-up became an independent device for isolating and accentuating objects as semantic signs, irrespective of temporal and spatial relations. Usually, a close-up plays the part of an "epithet" or "verb" (e.g., a face whose expression is emphasized through close-up); but other applications are also possible: the extra-temporal and extra-spatial nature of the close-up is itself treated as a stylistic resource, for figures such as simile, metaphor, etc.

Now, if a close-up of someone in a meadow is followed by a close-up of a pig strolling through the same meadow, the law of *the semantic interrelation* of shots and the law of *the extra-temporal, extra-spatial meaning of the close-up* would trounce the ostensibly firm and naturalistic motivation of the person's and pig's stroll taking place in the same space and time. The result of this sequence of shots is not a temporal or spatial progression from person to pig, but a semantic figure, a simile: the person is like a pig.

In this way, the independent semantic laws of cinema as an art form take shape and become established.

The significance of the evolution of cinematic devices lies in this formation of its independent semantic laws, and in their being stripped of the need for naturalistic "motivation."

This evolution has affected devices with an ostensibly strong motivation, such as the "dissolve." This device has been strongly and, at the same time, unambiguously motivated as "a recollection," "a vision," or "telling a story." But the device of "superimposition"—when the face of the person remembering is still visible through the shot of the "recollection"—nullifies the now external, literary motivation of "recollection" as a moment alternating with ordinary time; it shifts the center of gravity onto the *concurrence,* the *simultaneity* of the shots. There is no "recollection" or "storytelling" in the literary sense; there is a "recollection" in which the face of the person remembering persists. In a purely cinematographic sense, this device comes close to that of the dissolve of a face onto a disproportionately sized landscape or scene. In terms of its outside literary motivation, this latter device is very far from "recollection" or "story-telling," but cinematographically, the meaning of the two devices is very similar.

Such is the evolutionary path of cinematic devices: they become detached from outside motivations, and acquire "their own" meaning. In other words, they become detached from a *single,* external meaning, and acquire *many* of "their own," internal meanings. This multiplicity and multivalence of meanings is what allows a particular device to take root, and what allows that device to become its own distinctive artistic element, in this case: the "language" of cinema.

With some astonishment, we observe that language and literature have no word adequate to the dissolve. We can *describe* it using words in each given case, each application; but it is impossible to find a word or concept adequate to it in language.

The same can be said of the multivalence of the close-up, which alternates between showing a detail from a character's, or the viewer's, point of view, and using the result of this isolation of a detail—extra-temporality and extra-spatiality—as an independent semantic sign.

8

Cinema came out of photography.

The umbilical cord joining them was cut the moment cinema acknowledged itself as an art form. But photography has qualities of which it is unaware;

illegitimate aesthetic qualities, as it were. Photography is oriented toward resemblance. Resemblance is offensive; we are offended when a photograph looks too much like its subject. That is why photography surreptitiously deforms its material. But this deformation is allowed under one condition: that the basic orientation (toward resemblance) holds. No matter how a photographer deforms our face with poses, lighting, etc., it is all done with the tacit agreement that the portrait will resemble us. From the point of view of photography's basic orientation toward resemblance, any deformation is a "deficiency"; its aesthetic function is, in a sense, illegitimate.

Cinema has a different orientation, and what in photography would be a "deficiency" becomes its advantage, an aesthetic quality. Herein lies the radical difference between photography and cinema.

And photography has other "deficiencies" that turn into "positive qualities" in cinema.

Essentially, every photograph deforms its material. Just look at "landscapes": this could just be a subjective claim, but I only see the resemblance in landscapes when there are some orienting (or rather, differentiating) details present: a particular tree, bench, or shop sign. This is not because it "doesn't look like that," but because the landscape *stands out.* Something that in nature exists only in connection with other things, which is not delimited, stands out in a photograph as an independent whole. A bridge, pier, tree, a group of trees, etc., don't exist in our consciousness as independent units; they are always connected to their surroundings; they can be captured only in a momentary and fleeting way. But if their capture is lasting, it magnifies the individual features of the landscape a million times over, and for this very reason creates the effect of "non-resemblance."

The same is true of wide shots: the choice of camera angle, no matter how artless, and the focus on a given place, no matter how vast, lead to the same results.

In a photograph, the focus on material leads to the *unity* of every photograph, the unique *density of interrelations*[T] among all the objects, or all elements of a single object, within the picture.[12] As a result of this internal unity, the interrelations between objects, or among the elements within an object, are redistributed. The objects are deformed.

---

12 Note that from this point onward Tynianov applies to film his concept of "the unity and density of the verse line," which is fully developed in his *Problems of Verse Language*—*MC.* For a partial discussion of interrelation, see "On the Composition of *Eugene Onegin*" (especially 118 and 136).

But this "deficiency" of photography, these unconscious, "uncanonical" qualities—as Viktor Shklovsky[N] put it—are canonized in cinema; they become its foundational qualities, its points of reference.

Photography conveys a *single* situation; in cinema, this becomes a *unit*, a yardstick.

A shot is just as much a unity as a photograph or a self-contained line of verse.[13] According to this law, in a line of verse all the words that make up the line exist in a particular set of interrelations, in a denser state of interaction. This is why the meaning of a word in a poem is different, both in comparison to all the forms of practical speech and in comparison to prose. And all the purely functional little words, all the inconspicuous, auxiliary words of our speech, become highly conspicuous and meaningful in poetry.

It's the same with a shot: its unity reconfigures the semantic significance of everything in it, and each object becomes interrelated with all the other objects, and with the shot as a whole.

With this in mind, we ought to consider another situation as well: under what conditions do all the "protagonists" or characters in a shot (people and objects) become interrelated? Or, rather, are there conditions that might hinder this state of mutual interrelation? Indeed, there are.

The "characters" in a shot, like words (and sounds) in poetry, must be differentiated; they must be *diverse*. Only then can they be interrelated with one another; only then do they interact and imbue one another with shades of meaning. This explains the *selection* of people and objects, why the camera angle can function as a stylistic tool for demarcation, distinction, *differentiation*.

This "selection" came out of naturalistic resemblance, a correspondence between the person and object of cinema and the person and object of everyday life; what is called "typecasting" in the industry.[14] But in cinema, as in any art, something introduced for one set of reasons begins to play a part that no longer matches up with those reasons. "Selection" serves first and foremost to *differentiate the actors* within the film; this selection thus takes place within the film as well as outside it.

---

13 Here and elsewhere I use the standard term "shot" to mean a sequence of frames unified by the same camera angle and lighting. An actual single frame will have the same relation to this frame-sequence [*kadr-kusok*] as a poetic foot has to a line. The idea of a foot in poetry is more academic than anything else, and, in any case, applies only to a few metrical systems; current theories of poetry treat the line as a metrical series, rather than the foot as a fixed unit. In film theory, the technical concept of the single frame is essentially immaterial, and is wholly superseded by that of the length of the frame sequence—*YT*.

14 For the everyday [*byt*[T]], see also "Literary Fact" (especially 156, 164 and 169) and "On Literary Evolution" (especially 271, 277 and 279).

This need to differentiate the "protagonists of the shot" also led to the significance of *movement* within a shot. Smoke from a steamship and slow-moving clouds are necessary, not just in and of themselves; the same is true of a random person walking down a deserted street, or a person's facial expressions and gestures in relation to some other person or object. These things are needed in their capacity as differentiating signs.

9

This seemingly simple fact determines the whole system of *facial expression and gesture* in cinema, and marks it off decisively from the system of expressions and gestures connected with speech. In speech, facial expressions and gestures make speech intonations happen, "embody" them in a physical, visual sense. In this regard, they can be seen as supplementing the words.[15]

Such is the role of gestures and facial expressions in spoken theater. The role of facial expression in pantomime is to "substitute for" the omitted words. Pantomime is an art based on omission, a kind of giveaway game, where the whole point is to compensate for the missing element with other elements. But even in art that foregrounds language we can already find cases where "supplemental" facial expressions and gestures present an obstacle. Heinrich Heine[N] maintained that expressions and gestures sabotage verbal *wit*: "The facial muscles move in a way that is too intense, too excited, such that the observer can see the speaker's thoughts before they are expressed. This stymies unexpected jokes."[16]

This means that the embodiment of speech intonation in facial expression and gesture stymies (in this case) the verbal construction, violates its internal relationships. Heine makes an unexpected joke at the end of a poem and is loath to have sprightly facial expressions, or even the beginning of a gesture, signal this joke before it is made. Thus, a speech-gesture doesn't just accompany a word, it also signals or anticipates it.

---

15 In this connection, the debate among linguists regarding impersonal constructions is extremely intriguing. According to Wundt's proposition (refuted by Paul), in the impersonal sentence "[It's] burning!" the role of the subject is played by the *gesture* indicating the burning object (a house, or metaphorically speaking, one's breast, etc.). Shakhmatov suggests that the role of the subject is fulfilled in such cases by the speech *intonation*. From this example, the connection between speech gestures and facial expressions, on the one hand, and speech intonations, on the other, is readily apparent—*YT*.

16 For more on Heine, see "Tyutchev and Heine" (64–76).

This is why theatrical facial expressions are so incompatible with cinema: they cannot accompany language, since it is absent from cinema, but they signal language, *prompt* the words. These gesture-prompted words turn cinema into a kind of half-baked Kinetophone.

The facial expressions and gestures in a shot constitute, first and foremost, a *system of relations among its "characters."*

10

But the facial expressions in a shot can also function in a non-relational way, and the clouds don't have to move slowly. Relativity and differentiation can be shifted to another domain, from the *shot* to the succession of shots, to *montage*. Likewise, still frames, when they succeed one another in a particular way, allow for the movement within shots to be minimized.

Montage is not the linking together of shots, it is their differentiated *succession* [*smena*]—this is exactly why any shots that are interrelated in at least some way can displace one another.[17] These can be interrelations both at the level of plot,[T] and—much more so—at the level of style.[18] In current cinematic practice, we only have plot-centered montage; meanwhile, the camera angles and lighting are typically reshuffled into a chaotic jumble. This is a mistake.

We have agreed that style is a semantic fact. It follows that a lack of stylistic organization and a haphazard sequence of camera angles and lighting arrangements is roughly the same thing as mixing up the intonations in a single line of verse. At the same time, lighting and camera angles, by virtue of their semantic nature, are, of course, contrastive and differentiated. This is why shifts in lighting and/or camera angles effectively "edit" shots into a montage (make them interrelated and differentiated) in the same way as shifts or turns [*smena*] in plot do in a story.

Shots in cinema do not "unfold" in a sequential order, a gradual sequence—they *displace one another*. This is the basis of montage. They displace one another in the same way a single line of verse, one metrical unit, is succeeded by another: at a precise boundary. Cinema *jumps* from shot to shot, just as a poem jumps from line to line. Oddly enough, if we draw an analogy between cinema and the verbal arts, then the only legitimate analogy would be that of cinema and poetry—not cinema and prose.[19]

---

17 In discussing the displacement of shots, Tynianov uses the same concept of "shift" or "succession" (smena) that he uses in talking about literary evolution or the organization of verse lines.

18 For more on plot, see "On Plot and Fabula in Film" (240–241).

19 For more on the formal similarities of cinema and poetry, see "On FEX" (especially 292).

One of the main consequences of film's "jumpy" nature is the differentiated character of shots, their existence as a unity. *Shots, considered as unities, are equivalent.* A long take can be succeeded by a very brief one. The brevity of the shot does not mean that it ceases to be a free-standing entity, interrelated with other shots.

Essentially, the shot is important as a "*representative*": when a recollection is given via "dissolve," we don't see all of the shots of the scene remembered by the character—we see a detail, a single shot. In this way, a shot doesn't exhaust a given plot point, it merely acts as its "representative" in the way the shots are interrelated. In practice, this allows for the reduction of shots to a minimum during re-editing, or the use of a shot from an entirely different point in the plot as a "representative."[20]

One difference between the "old" and "new" cinema is in their interpretation of montage. While in the old cinema, montage was a means of bonding or pasting things together and explaining plot points, a tool that, in itself, was inconspicuous and concealed, in the new cinema it has become a crucial and conspicuous element, a tangible rhythm.

Something similar happened in poetry: a kind of satisfying monotony and inconspicuous, ossified metrical systems were succeeded by the jarring sensation of rhythm in "free verse" (*vers libre*). In Mayakovsky's[N] early poetry, a line consisting of a single word would follow a long line;[21] the same amount of energy carried by the long line would be spent on the short one as well (considered as rhythmic series, lines of verse are equivalent). As a result, this energy would proceed in bursts. Similarly, in tangible montage, the same energy carried by a lengthy frame-sequence will then be spent on a short one. A short sequence consisting of a "representative" shot is equivalent to a long one, and, like a line in a poem consisting of just a couple of words, a brief shot such as this stands out in terms of its significance and value.

In this way, the progression of montage helps to make the culminating points of a film stand out. While with tangible montage, the greatest amount of time would be spent on the culminating point, in montage that has become the tangible rhythm of a film, *the culminating point stands out precisely because of its brevity.*

This would not be the case if the frame sequence as a unity were not an interrelational *yardstick*, a measure of the film. We measure film involuntarily, pushing away from one unity as we proceed to the next one. This is why the

20 Re-editing [*peremontazh*] refers to the practice of reediting foreign films to make them more acceptable to Soviet audiences.

21 For Mayakovsky, see also "On Mayakovsky" (293) and "Interlude" (185–190).

works of eclectic directors are so viscerally irritating: one part follows the old principle of montage—montage-as-gluing-together, where the only measure is the extent to which a "scene" (plot point) exhausts all of its possibilities—while another part may follow the new principle of montage, where montage has become a conspicuous element of the construction. Our energy is assigned a certain task, a certain progression, and suddenly this task changes. The initial impulse is lost, and since we already accepted it in the first part of the film, we are unable to pick up on a new one. Such is the power of measure in film; its role resembles that of measure—of meter—in poetry.

If we look at the problem this way, then what is meant by the *rhythm* of film, a term that is often used, and just as often misused?

Rhythm is the interaction of stylistic and metrical elements in the unfolding of a film, in its dynamics. Camera angles and changes in lighting are significant not just as markers of change in the succession of frame sequences, but also in making certain sequences stand out as culminating points. This should be taken into account in cases where unusual camera angles or unusual lighting are used. These should not be arbitrary, or "good," or "beautiful" per se; instead they should be good for this particular case, in terms of their interaction with the metrical unfolding of the film and with the measure of the montage. Camera angles and lighting that make a metrically prominent sequence stand out will play an entirely different role from camera angles and lighting that make a metrically unobtrusive sequence stand out.

The analogy between film and poetry isn't really necessary. It goes without saying that film, like poetry, is its own specific art form. But the generation of the 1880s wouldn't have understood our cinema, just as they wouldn't have understood our contemporary poetry:

> Наш век обидел вас, ваш стих обидя
> [Our epoch spurned you when it spurned your verse].[22]

The "jumpy" nature of cinema, the role played in it by the unity of the shot, the semantic transformation of ordinary objects (the word in poetry, the object in cinema)—these are what cinema and poetry have in common.

---

22 Tynianov quotes a line from Alexander Pushkin's[N] narrative poem "A Little House in Kolomna" [Domik v Kolomne] (Alexander Pushkin, *Sobranie sochinenii v 10–i tomakh* [Moscow: GIKhL, 1959–1962], 3:456); the stanza addresses great French poets of the past like Boileau, Racine, and Voltaire, imagining their dismay over the new poetic boldness of Pushkin's own age.

11

For this reason, the cine-novel is just as distinctive a genre as the novel in verse. As Pushkin said: "[...] I am writing not a novel, but a novel in verse—a devilish difference."[23]

So what is the "devilish difference" between the cine-novel and the novel as a literary genre?

It's not just the material, but also the fact that in cinema, the style and laws of construction transform all the elements that would otherwise seem to be universal, equally applicable to all the arts and to all their genres.

The situation with fabula and plot in cinema is much the same.[24] When dealing with this problem, we must always keep in mind the specific material and style of the art.

In his new theory of plot, Viktor Shklovsky has advanced two basic premises: 1) plot as an unfolding, and 2) the connection between plot devices and style. The first premise has taken the study of plot away from examining static motifs (and their various historical manifestations) to address how these motifs pop up in the construction of the whole; this premise has already proved fruitful and has been widely accepted. The second premise has not yet been accepted and appears to have been forgotten.

It is this latter premise that I wish to discuss here.

Since the question of fabula and plot in cinema has been so little studied, and since this would require major preliminary research which has yet to be undertaken, I will allow myself to elucidate the question through literary material that has been more thoroughly studied: my aim here is just to *pose* the question of fabula and plot in cinema. I think this will not be amiss.

Let us first define our terms: fabula and plot.

Fabula is usually what one calls a static outline of relations, such as: "She was fair, and he loved her. However, he was not fair, and she did not love him" (one of Heine's epigraphs). In "The Fountain of Bakhchisaray" the *outline of relations* ("fabula") would be roughly the following: "Girey loves Maria, Maria does not love him. Zarema loves Girey, he does not love her." It's obvious that this outline does not elucidate anything in either "The Fountain of Bakhchisaray" or Heine's epigraph, and that it would apply just as well to thousands of different works, from the single phrase of an epigraph to a lengthy narrative poem.[25] Let's try another

---

23 See also "On the Composition of *Eugene Onegin*" (114–150, especially 130–131).

24 See also "On Plot and Fabula in Film" (240–241).

25 Tynianov refers to Pushkin's narrative poem "The Fountain of Bakhchisaray" [Bakhchisaraiskii fontan] (1821–1823).

common definition of fabula: an *outline of action.* In this case the fabula, at its minimum, would be roughly the following: "Girey fell out of love with Zarema because of Maria. Zarema kills Maria." But what do we do when this dénouement *does not actually appear* in Pushkin's poem? Pushkin merely lets us *guess at* this dénouement, which is deliberately veiled. To say that Pushkin deviated from our fabula-based outline would be bold indeed, since he disregarded it completely. This would be like tapping out the poetic feet (the outline of iambs) in his lines:

> "Мой дядя самых честных правил, / Когда не в шутку занемог,
> ["My uncle, man of firm convictions… / By falling gravely ill, he's won"][26]

and saying that Pushkin deviated from iambic meter because of the skipped stress in the second line's final word.[27] Wouldn't it be better to toss out the outline, rather than consider a work of art a "deviation" from it? And indeed, it would be closer to the mark to think of a poem's meter not in terms of its "foot" (an outline), but in terms of its entire accentual (stressed) blueprint. In that case, the "rhythm" would be constituted by the entire dynamics of the poem, comprising the interaction of meter (the pattern of stresses) with speech connections (syntax) and with sound connections (repetitions).

The same goes for the question of fabula and plot. Either we risk creating outlines that don't fit a given work of art, or we are compelled to define fabula as the *entire* semantic blueprint of the action. In this case, the plot of a work would be defined as its dynamics, comprising the interaction between all the linkages of the material (including the fabula as a linkage of actions): stylistic linkage, story-driven linkage, etc. Lyric poems have plots as well, but the fabula in a poem is something else entirely, and plays a completely different role in the development of the plot. The concept of plot goes beyond the concept of fabula. Plot can be eccentric in relation to fabula.[28] Several types are possible in this relationship between plot and fabula:

---

26 These very famous lines open Pushkin's novel in verse, *Eugene Onegin*. Pushkin, *Sobranie sochinenii*, 4:10; Alexander Pushkin, *Eugene Onegin: A Novel in Verse*, trans. James Falen (Oxford: Oxford University Press, 1995), 5. For more on this work, see "On the Composition of *Eugene Onegin*".

27 Falen's English translation actually provides perfect iambs all the way through, but in the original Russian the second line ends with *zanemOg*: while observing the obligatory end-stress "MOG," the first syllable of the word (*za*) is unstressed.

28 This was first demonstrated by Viktor Shklovsky in his works on [Laurence] Sterne and [Vasily] Rozanov[N]—*YT.*

1. The plot is, for the most part, dependent on the fabula, on the semantics of the action.

Here, the arrangement of fabulas becomes particularly important; one line slows another down, but this is what moves the plot forward. A curious example of the type where the plot develops along a false storyline is Ambrose Bierce's "An Occurrence at Owl Creek Bridge": a man is hanged, he breaks loose and falls into a creek—the plot continues to unfold along a false storyline—he swims out and runs away, flees to a house, and only there does he die. In the last lines we find out that the whole escape was a hallucination experienced in the instant before his death. Leo Perutz's "Between Nine and Nine" uses a similar device.

Interestingly, in one of the most fabula-driven novels ever written—Victor Hugo's *Les Misérables*—this "slowing" is accomplished through both an abundance of secondary storylines, and the *incorporation of historical, scientific, and descriptive materials as such.* This device is more typically used in the development of plot, not of fabula. As a large form, the novel requires this type of plot development outside of the fabula. Plot development that is exactly proportionate to the development of fabula is typical of adventure novels. (Incidentally, "large forms" in literature are not determined by the page count, just as in cinema they are not determined by the amount of footage. The concept of "large forms" is energetic; it must account for the effort expended by the reader (or viewer) in grasping the structure. Pushkin created a large poetic form based on digressions. "The Prisoner of the Caucasus" is no longer than some of Zhukovsky's[N] epistles, but it is a large form because the "digressions," which are based on material far removed from the fabula, drastically expand the "space" of the poem. This forces the reader to devote completely different amounts of work to get through the same number of lines in Zhukovsky's epistle "To Voyeikov" and Pushkin's "Prisoner of the Caucasus."[29] I chose this particular example because Pushkin used material from Zhukovsky's epistles in his "Prisoner," but made it a *digression* from the fabula.) This element of "slowing" through the use of distantly related material is indeed characteristic of large forms.

The same goes for cinema: "large genres" differ from intimate, "small-scale" ones in both the number of storylines and the amount of "slowing" material overall.

29 Vasily Zhukovsky's epistle "To Voyeikov" [*Voeikovu*] was published in 1814; Pushkin's "The Prisoner of the Caucasus" [Kavkazskii plennik] was another long narrative poem from the early 1820s (1820–1821).

2. The plot develops independently of the fabula.

The fabula is meanwhile hinted at, but this riddle and its solution are only there to motivate plot development; the solution may not even be given. The plot meanwhile shifts over to the segmentation and bonding of pieces of speech material that exist outside of the fabula. No fabula is given; in its place, the "search for a fabula" is what keeps things elastic and moving forward, as the fabula's equivalent, its proxy. We can see this in many works by Pilnyak, Leonhard Frank, et al.[30] In "searching for a fabula," the reader links together and breaks apart various individual segments that are connected only stylistically (or through the broadest possible motivation, such as unity of place or time).

It is perfectly clear that in the latter type of work the main engine of plot is *style*, meaning the stylistic interrelations among the interconnected units.

12

The link between plotting devices and style can also be found in works where the plot is not eccentric to the fabula.

Take Gogol's "Nose," for instance.

The fabula blueprint of this work and the semantics of its action inevitably make one think of a madhouse. All one has to do is to trace the outline of one of its storylines, that of the "nose": the severed nose of Major Kovalyov strolls down Nevsky Prospekt in its capacity as a Nose. The Nose wants to run off to Riga in a stagecoach, but is seized by a police inspector and returned to its erstwhile owner wrapped in a rag.

How could such a storyline be borne out by the plot? How did a simple absurdity become an artistic "absurdity"? As it turns out, the entire semantic system of the work was involved. The system of naming things in "The Nose" is what it makes its fabula possible.

Here we have the first appearance of the severed nose:

> "[...] saw *something there that looked white.* [...] '*It's solid,*' he said to himself. '*What in the world is it?*'
>
> "[...] it actually was a nose [...] it looked to him *somehow familiar.*
>
> "'I'll wrap *it* up in a rag and put it in a corner. Let it stay there for a while; I'll return *it* later on.'

30 Boris Pilnyak (1894–1938) was a contemporary prose writer, a typically experimental "fellow traveler" of the Soviet 1920s. Leonhard Frank (1882–1961) was a German expressionist writer known for his politically socialist, socially critical works.

> "'As though I would *allow* a stray *nose* to lay about in my room? [...] Away with *it*, away with *it*! Don't let me *set eyes on it* again!'
>
> " [...] 'bread is a thing that is baked, while a nose is something quite different.'"[31]

A thorough stylistic analysis of the reader's first encounter with the severed nose would lead us too far astray, but even the few lines quoted here make it clear that the semantic system of phrases turns the severed nose into something ambiguous: "*something*," "*solid*" (neuter gender), "*it, its*" (an extremely common pronoun that always diminishes substantive, material attributes), "allow *the nose*" (animate), etc. This semantic atmosphere, which is present in every line, constructs the storyline of the "severed nose" stylistically such that the reader—who has already been primed, already drawn into this semantic atmosphere—is later unfazed by such bizarre phrases as: "The *nose* looked at the major and his *eyebrows* slightly furrowed."[32]

This is how a discrete fabula becomes a plot component: through style, which conveys the semantic atmosphere of the work.

One possible objection to this is that "The Nose" is a one-of-a-kind work. But only lack of space prevents me from demonstrating that the very same thing is true of Andrei Bely's *Petersburg* and *The Moscow Eccentric* (we should also note the "hackneyed" nature of the fabula in these nevertheless extraordinary novels), and many others.

It would be wrong to think that style doesn't play a role in these works, or in works by authors whose style is "restrained" or "anemic." Every literary work is always a semantic system, and no matter how "restrained" the style, it functions as a resource for constructing a semantic system; moreover, there is a direct link between this system and the plot, whether this plot unfolds in step with or outside of the fabula.

Of course, different works have different systems. But in the verbal arts there are instances where the profound connection between the semantic system and plot is particularly striking. Such is the semantic system we see in poetry.

In poetry, whether in an eighteenth-century heroic long poem or a Pushkin epic, this connection is clear-cut. The debates over metrical systems in poetry always turn out to be debates over *semantic systems*, and ultimately these debates

31 See Nikolai Gogol, *The Complete Tales of Nikolai Gogol,* trans. Constance Garnett, ed. Leonard J. Kent (Chicago: University of Chicago Press, 1985), 2:217. For further discussion of Gogol's story, see "Dostoyevsky and Gogol" (especially 28–35).

32 Ibid., 2:223, translation slightly modified.

determine how plot is understood in poetry, as well as the relationship between plot and fabula.

Because this question (about the relationship between plot and fabula) is tied to the question of genre.

This relationship is not only different in different novels, novellas, long poems, and lyric poems; it also differs between the novel and the novella, between the long poem and the lyric poem.

13

In this article, I seek merely to *pose* the questions: 1) of the relationship between plot and style in cinema, and 2) of how cinematic genres are determined by the relationship of plot to fabula.

Posing these questions was the reason behind my "buildup" articulating the problem in terms of literature. Making the "leap" to cinema requires extensive research. In the literary context, we saw that one may not talk about fabula and plot in general terms; that plot is closely bound up with a given semantic system, which, in turn, is determined by style.

In *Battleship Potemkin,* the role of stylistic and semantic resources in determining plot is obvious, but has not been studied. Further research will uncover this phenomenon in less obvious examples as well. Noting the stylistic "restraint" or "naturalism" of certain films or directors does not deny the role of style. These are just different styles, and they play different roles in relation to plot development.

Further study of cinematic plot depends on the study of its style and of the distinctive qualities of its material.

Our naïveté in this regard is proven by the widely accepted way critics routinely talk about a film: first comes a discussion of the screenplay (on the basis of the finished film), then of the director, etc. But there is no need to talk about the screenplay of a finished film. The screenplay almost always gives us the "fabula in general," only reflecting to a certain extent the "jumpy" nature of cinema. The screenwriter doesn't know how the fabula will develop, what the plot will be, and neither does the director prior to viewing the unedited footage. And here, the distinctive features of a certain style or material can enable the development of the entire fabula as it appears in the screenplay; this screenplay-fabula could be included "whole hog" in the movie. Or these features could fail to enable it, and in the course of production the fabula could change imperceptibly, bit by bit, its direction determined by the development of the plot.

An "ironclad screenplay" is only possible in cases where there are standardized styles of directing and acting; in other words, when the script was written with an established cinematic style in mind.[33]

14

Theory improperly understood can lead to still more substantial errors in practice.

This is the problem with cinematic genres.

The genres that emerged in literature and theatre often migrate into cinema ready-made, wholesale. And what do we get? The most unexpected results.

Consider the *historical newsreel*. Having migrated ready-made into cinema from literature, it makes a film, more than anything else, a reproduction of a *moving portrait gallery*. This is because in literature, the basic premise (authenticity) is just given through the historical names, dates, and so on, while in cinema that uses this type of documentary approach, authenticity itself is in question. "Is that what he really looked like?" will be the first thing the viewer asks.

When we read a novel about Alexander I, his actions in the novel, whatever they may be, will be the actions of "Alexander I." If they seem implausible, then "they didn't get Alexander I right"; nevertheless, "Alexander I" is still the initial premise. At the movies, a naïve viewer will say: "That actor really looks like (or doesn't look like) Alexander I!" and he will be right; and by being right, even if he means well, he will undermine the very premise of the genre—its authenticity.

That's how closely tied the question of genre is to the question of specific material, and to that of style.

In effect, cinema has continued to exist in parasitic genres: "the novel," "comedy," etc.

In this regard, the primitivism of the "comic film" was more honest, and theoretically contained more of a foundation for resolving the question of cinematic genres than the fence-straddling "cine-novel."[34]

In the "comic film," plot developed outside of fabula; or rather, there was a primitive storyline, and the plot developed on the basis of arbitrary material (arbitrary from the fabula-perspective, but actually highly specific).

---

33 "Ironclad screenplay" is a term from early cinema referring to tightly controlled moviemaking, where everything is planned ahead of time.

34 In Tynianov's time, the "comic film" was a circus-like slapstick comedy reminiscent of Charlie Chaplin movies; the "cine-novel" refers to narrative-driven stories and film versions of existing works of literature.

Here we come to the heart of the matter, which is not in the extrinsic, secondary attributes of genres borrowed from neighboring art forms, but in *the relationship between the specific cinematic plot and the fabula.*

Maximum orientation toward plot = minimal orientation toward fabula, and vice versa.

The "comic film" was not reminiscent of comedy; it was more like a humorous poem, since its plot developed in an overt way out of its semantic-stylistic devices.

Timidity is the only thing keeping us from discovering both the cinematic narrative poem and the cinematic lyric poem among contemporary cinematic genres. Only timidity prevents us from indicating directly on the film poster that a historical newsreel is a moving portrait gallery from this or that era.[35]

Let me repeat: the question of the link between plot and style in cinema, and of their role in determining cinematic genres, requires extensive research. I have limited myself here to merely posing that question.

---

35 See the genre Tynianov calls a "cinematic ode," in "On FEX" (292)—*MC.*

On Literary Evolution (1927)[1]

For Boris Eikhenbaum

1

Among the disciplines that study culture, literary history continues to languish in the position of a colonial territory. On the one hand, it is ruled to a large extent by an individualist psychological approach (particularly in the West), whereby the question of authorial psychology unjustifiably supplants the question of literature per se, and the problem of literary evolution is supplanted by that of the genesis of literature. On the other hand, an oversimplified, causal approach to the literary series[T] brings about a rift between the viewpoint from which literature is being analyzed (and this is always the primary social series, as well as those more remote) and the literary series itself. But attempts to construct a closed literary series, and to examine evolution within it, are constantly running up against neighboring cultural, social, and "real-life" series, and are therefore doomed to remain incomplete. The theory of value in literary scholarship fueled the temptation to study major (but also isolated) phenomena and has turned literary history into a "history of generals." Blind opposition to this focus on a few leading figures in turn fueled an interest in popular, mass-produced literature, but without a clear theoretical awareness of the methods for studying it or the nature of its significance.

Finally, the connection between literary history and living, contemporary literature—a connection fruitful and necessary for scholarship—is not always as necessary and fruitful for actively developing literature. The latter's representatives readily accept literary history for its establishment of various traditional norms and laws, and tend to mix up the "historicity" of a literary phenomenon with "historicism" in relation to it. This conflict has led to attempts at

---

1 First published as "The Question of Literary Evolution" [Vopros o literaturnoi evoliutsii] in the journal *Eyes on Literature* [Na literaturnom postu] no. 10 (1927), 42–48. Translation from "O literaturnoi evoliutsii," *PILK*, 270–281. Selected notes by Alexander Chudakov, Marietta Chudakova, and Evgenii Toddes [*CCT*], 518–530. Additional notes by Yuri Tynianov [*YT*] and the translators [unmarked].

studying individual works and the laws of their construction in extra-historical terms (the abolishment of literary history).

2

In order to finally become a true scholarly discipline, literary history must make a claim for authenticity. All of its terms must be reevaluated, beginning with the term "literary history" itself. This is an extremely broad term, covering both the material history of literary art and the history of verbal art as such. It is also presumptuous, since "literary history" is presumed to be a discipline that is ready to be incorporated into "cultural history" as a series with a well-established scholarly foundation. It does not yet have this right.

Meanwhile, historical studies of literature can be broken down into at least two main types, based on their points of observation: the study of the *genesis* of literary phenomena, and the study of the *evolution* of literary series, that is, of literary changeability.

The point of view determines not only the meaning, but also the character of the phenomenon being studied. In the study of literary evolution, the fact of genesis has a distinct meaning and character, and these are, of course, different from those within the study of genesis itself.[2] Furthermore, the study of literary evolution—or changeability—must break with naïve theories of value, which result from confounding the points of observation: the values of one cultural-historical system are used in evaluating another. Evaluation itself must shed its subjective overtones, and the "value" of a given literary phenomenon must be viewed in terms of its evolutionary meaning and distinctive character.

The same thing needs to happen with value-based concepts like "imitation," "dilettantism," and "mass-produced literature."[3]

---

2 For more on the distinction between evolution and genesis (one extraordinarily important for Tynianov and many of his colleagues), see "Tyutchev and Heine" (especially 70–74)—*CCT*.

3 One need only analyze the "mass-produced" literature of the 1820s and 30s to see the colossal evolutionary difference between them. In the 1830s, when the previous traditions were becoming automatized and when writers were working with stagnant literary material, "dilettantism" suddenly acquired colossal evolutionary significance. Dilettantism, the ambience of "poetic jottings in the margins of books," gave rise to a new phenomenon—Tyutchev—who transfigured the language and genres of poetry with his intimate intonations. *A casual, mundane* [bytovoe] *attitude toward literature*, while seeming, from an evaluative point of view, to signal its dissolution, *transfigures the literary system*. In the 1820s, an age of literary "masters" and new poetic genres, "dilettantism" and "large-scale literature" were declared to be "graphomania." While in the 1830s, "first-rate" poets (from the

"Tradition," the fundamental concept of the old literary history, proves to be an unjustified abstraction of one or more literary elements from a specific system—in which they play a specific role and are typecast in a certain way—which are then converged with identical elements of another system in which they play a different role, to make a falsely unified and seemingly cohesive series.

The most important concept for literary evolution is, in fact, the *shift*[T] between systems; the question of "traditions" is relegated to another level.

3

To properly analyze this fundamental question, we have to begin by agreeing that a literary work is a system, and that literature is also a system. This agreement serves as a crucial premise for the construction of a literary science that does not merely observe but *studies* the chaos of various phenomena and series. This does not downplay the question of the role of neighboring series in literary evolution; on the contrary, it allows for that question to be properly posed.

Having analyzed individual elements of a work, such as the plot[T] or style, rhythm and syntax in prose, rhythm and semantics in poetry, etc., we are convinced that these elements can be abstracted to a certain extent *as a working hypothesis*, but that they are all *interrelated*[T] *with one another* and exist in interaction. Studying rhythm in verse and in prose necessarily reveals that the role of one and the same element within different systems is different.

I use the term constructive *function* (of a given element) to refer to the interdependence of each element of a literary work (a system) with its other elements and, it follows, with the system as a whole.

---

perspective of evolutionary significance) took up the mantle of dilettantism (Tyutchev,[N] Polezhaev) or "imitation and apprenticeship" (Lermontov)[N] in their struggle against preceding norms, in the 1820s even "second-rate" poets went around in the trappings of first-rate masters. See, for instance, the "universalist" and "grandiose" genres in the work of such mass-producing poets as Olin. Obviously, the evolutionary significance of phenomena like dilettantism, imitation, etc., varies from period to period, and a condescending, judgmental attitude toward these phenomena is a legacy of the literary history of old—*YT*. Note that when speaking of "mass-produced literature" Tynianov has in mind authors who produced on a large scale. Alexander Polezhaev (1804–1838) and Valerian Olin (1788–1841) were poets and contemporaries of Alexander Pushkin.[N] For Lermontov, see also "Interlude" (179; 201–202); "Literary Evolution" (269–272); "On Parody" (299–302)'; On Parody (309); Composition (114–150).

On close examination, this function turns out to be a complicated concept. A given element is simultaneously interrelated with a number of similar elements in other works/systems, and even other series; as well as with other elements in its own system (the auto-function and syn-function).

Thus, the lexicon of a given work is immediately interrelated with the literary lexicon and the general lexicon of everyday speech, as well as with other elements of the work. These two components, or more precisely, these two equivalent functions, do not carry the same weight.

For example, the function of archaisms depends wholly on the *system* in which they are used. In Lomonosov's system their function was that of so-called "high-style" usage, since in this system lexical coloring played a dominant role (archaisms were used for their lexical associations with liturgical language). In Tyutchev's system, archaisms have different functions: in many cases they are abstract, e.g. "waterworks" in place of "fountain."[4] There are interesting cases of archaisms used in an ironic function:

> Пушек гром и *мусикия!*—[5]
> [The thunder and *musick* of cannons!]

This is in the work of a poet who used words like "musickal" [*musikiiskii*][6] in an entirely different function in other contexts. The auto-function is not decisive: it merely presents possibilities that the syn-function proceeds to realize. (Thus, prior to Tyutchev, there was already an extensive parodic literature in the eighteenth and nineteenth centuries, in which archaisms had a parodic function.) But the decisive element in this case is, of course, the semantic and intonational system of the work, which allows us to relate the given expression to "ironic" rather than "high-style" usage; that is, which determines its function.

It is wrong to pluck individual elements out of their systems and, outside of it (i.e. without their constructive function), interrelate them with similar series of other systems.

---

4 The Russian is *fontan—vodomet.*

5 From the poem "Something Modern" [Sovremennoe] (1869)—*CCT*. F. I. Tiutchev, *Complete Works* [Polnoe sobranie sochinenii] (St. Petersburg: Izd-vo A.F. Marks, 1913), 330.

6 Compare the unmarked, non-archaic "musical" [*muzykal'nyi*].

4

Is it possible to approach a work of literature "immanently," to study it as a system without reference to its interdependence with the system of literature? Studying a work of literature in isolation is the same kind of abstraction as when the individual elements of a work are abstracted from the whole. This approach is used successfully all the time by critics of contemporary literature, because the interdependence of a contemporary work with contemporary literature is a foregone conclusion, a fact that remains unspoken. (The same is also true of the interdependence between a work of literature and other works by the same author, between a work and its genre, etc.)

But this isolated approach is no longer possible even for contemporary literature.

The existence of a fact *as a literary fact* depends on its differential quality (i.e., on its interdependence with either the literary or extra-literary series); in other words, on its function.

What counts as a literary fact in one historical period will be a ubiquitous phenomenon of everyday speech in another; and vice versa, depending on the entire literary system in which the given fact circulates.

Thus a letter by Derzhavin[N] to a friend is a fact of everyday life [*byt*],[T] while such a letter in the age of Karamzin[N] or Pushkin is a literary fact.[7]

Consider also the literary significance of memoirs and diaries in one literary system, and their extra-literary significance in another. When we study a literary work in isolation, we cannot be sure that we are doing justice to its structure, the structure of the work itself.

Another point to consider is that the auto-function (that is, the interdependence of an element with the series of similar elements in other systems and other series) is a prerequisite for the syn-function—the constructive function of the element in question.

This is why it matters when a particular element is "hackneyed" or "worn-out." What makes a verse line, meter, or plot "hackneyed" or "worn-out"? In other words, what is meant by the "automatization" of a particular element?

In linguistics, for example, when a given definition "gets worn out," the word expressing that definition comes to express a connection or relation; it becomes an auxiliary word. In other words, its function changes. The same goes

7 For everyday life [*byt*], see also section ten of this article and "Literary Fact" (156, 164 and 169). For Karamzin, see "The Ode as an Oratorical Genre" (109–112).

for automatization, for the "exhaustion" of any literary element. The element does not disappear; only its function changes into an auxiliary one. If the meter in a poem is "hackneyed," the significance will shift to other poetic features and elements of the poem, while the meter will assume other functions.

Thus the "little verse feuilletons" published in newspapers tend to use hackneyed, banal meters, which real poetry has long since left behind. No one reads them as "poems," as something related to "poetry." In cases like this, the hackneyed meter is a means of *attaching* the topical, mundane "feuilleton" material to the literary series. Its function is entirely different than it would be in a poetic work; it is auxiliary. "Parody" in verse feuilletons belongs to the same series of facts. Parody can exist as literature as long as that which is parodied remains relevant to literature. What possible literary significance could there be in an umpteenth parody of Lermontov's "When the yellowing field stirs ... " or Pushkin's "Prophet?"[8] Yet the verse feuilletons can't get enough of them. This is just another example of the same thing: the parodic function has become auxiliary, serving to *attach* extra-literary facts to a literary series.

When so-called plot-centered prose becomes "worn out," the fabula[T] performs different functions in the work than it would if plot-centered prose were not "worn out" in relation to its literary system.[9] The fabula can serve as a mere motivation for style, or as a means of setting up the material.

To generalize, when we are within our particular literary system, we are inclined to relegate descriptions of nature in old novels to an auxiliary role, that of a joining or a braking device (and thus to all but skip over them). But in a different literary system, we might see them as the most important, indeed dominant, element, because it is conceivable that the fabula is merely a motive or pretext for setting up "static descriptions."

5

The question of literary genres, which is one of the most difficult and least studied, can be resolved in a similar way. The novel, which had seemed for centuries to be a self-sufficient genre with internal development, proved to be variable rather than constant: its material changed from one literary system to the next, as did its method of introducing extra-literary speech material into literature. Even the characteristics of the genre evolved. In the system of the 1820s–1840s,

8 Tynianov refers to two extremely well-known poems. For more on parody, see "On Parody."

9 See also "The Foundations of Film" and "On Plot and Fabula in Film".

the genres of "story" and "tale" were defined by different characteristics than in our time (as is clear from the designations themselves).[10] We are inclined to name genres *according to secondary resultative characteristics,* in other words, according to size. For us, the words "story," "tale," or "novel" are equivalent to a specific quantity of printed pages. This is proved less by genres being "automatized" for our literary system than by the fact that for us, genres are defined by other characteristics. The size of a work, its verbal space, is a meaningful characteristic. But when a work is isolated from its system, we are simply incapable of determining its genre, since that which was called an ode in the 1820s—or, for that matter, Fet[N]—simply has different characteristics from what was called an ode in Lomonosov's time.

10 Cf. the usage of "story" [*rasskaz*] in an 1825 *Moscow Telegraph* review of [Pushkin's] *Eugene Onegin*: "What poet had as his aim a *story*, i.e. *the performance of a long poem*, and even, what prose writer in his more expansive writings? In *Tristram Shandy*, where the whole point, evidently, lies in the *story*, the *story* is not at all the aim of the composition" (*Moscow Telegraph*, 1825, no. 15. Special supplement, 5) [emphasis *YT*]. That is, the word *story* here appears to be close in meaning to our term *skaz*.[T] This terminology is quite specific and persisted for a long time. Cf. the definition of genres in Druzhinin in 1849: "The author himself [Zagoskin—*YT*] called this work [*The Russians at the Beginning of the Eighteenth Century* [Russkie v nachalo os'minadtsatogo stoletiia]—*YT*] a *story*; but in the title it is called a *novel*; what it actually is, is now difficult to determine, because it has yet to be finished [...] In my opinion, it is neither a story nor a novel. It is *not a story* because it is *narrated neither by the author* nor by some *secondary figure*; on the contrary, it is dramatized (or dialogized); such that scenes and conversations succeed one another without cease; finally, the narrative itself is relegated a very minor role. It is *not a novel* because this word entails a demand for poetic creation and artistry *in the depiction of the characters and situations* of the cast of characters [...] I will henceforth call it a novel because that is exactly what it claims to be" (A. V. Druzhinin, "Letters from an Out-of-town Subscriber" [Pis'mo inogorodnego podpischika], in *Collected Works* [*Polnoe sobranie sochinenii*], vol. 6 [St. Petersburg: Tip. Imp. Akademii nauk, 1865], 41). I will take this opportunity to pose an interesting question.

Various different historical periods and national literatures have demonstrated a type of "story" in which the very first lines present a narrator who subsequently plays no role in the plot whatsoever, though the story is told in his voice (Maupassant, Turgenev[N]). It is difficult to explain the plot function of this narrator. Nothing changes in the plot if the first lines, in which he is sketched out, are erased. (The usual opening cliché in these stories: "N. N. lit up a cigar and began his story.") I think that this is a phenomenon of genre rather than plot. The "narrator" here is a marker for the genre, a signal of the "story" genre—within a certain literary system.

This signaling indicates that the genre with which the author interrelates his work has stabilized. For this reason, the "narrator" here is actually a rudiment of an old genre. In this case Leskov's[N] *skaz* could have arisen at first out of an orientation [*ustanovka*][T] toward an old genre, as a means of "resurrecting," renewing an old genre, and only subsequently outgrew its genre function. This question clearly demands separate investigation—*YT*. For more on the concept of orientation [*ustanovka*] see "The Ode as Oratorical Genre" (especially 77–79).

On these grounds, we conclude that the study of isolated genres, without the signifiers of the genre system with which they are interrelated, is impossible. A historical novel by Tolstoy is not interrelated with a historical novel by Zagoskin, but rather with the prose of Tolstoy's time.[11]

6

Strictly speaking, there can be no study of literary phenomena outside of their interrelations.[T] Consider the question of prose and poetry. We tacitly think of metrical prose as prose, and of non-metrical free verse as poetry, without realizing that in another literary system, this would land us in a difficult position. The fact is, prose and poetry are interrelated; there is a reciprocal function between prose and poetry. (Compare the interrelations in the development of prose and poetry—their interdependence—as established by Boris Eikhenbaum.[N])[12]

In one kind of literary system, the function of poetry was performed by the formal element of meter.

But just as prose becomes differentiated and evolves, so poetry evolves at the same time. The differentiation of one interrelated type brings about—or better yet, is linked to—the differentiation of the other interrelated type. Metrical prose appears (for example, Andrei Bely[N]).[13] In poetry, this is caused by the transferral of the poetic function from meter to other characteristics, which are to some extent secondary and resultative; for example, the function can transfer to rhythm as a signpost of verse units, or to a distinctive syntax or lexicon. The function of prose in relation to poetry remains, but the formal elements carrying out this function are different.

The ongoing evolution of forms could either anchor this function of poetry to prose, extending it to a number of other characteristics; or disrupt it and render it irrelevant. Just as in contemporary literature the interrelation of *genres* (in terms of their secondary, resultative characteristics) is of little importance,

---

11 Mikhail Zagoskin (1789–1852) was celebrated in the 1830s as Russia's first author of historical novels.

12 Tynianov has in mind works such as Eikhenbaum's 1922 essay "Pushkin's Path to Prose" [Put' Pushkina k proze], in Eikhenbaum, *O proze*, ed. I. Iampol'skii (Leningrad: Khudozhestvennaia literatura, 1969), 214–230], his 1921 "Problems of Pushkin's Poetics" [Problemy poetiki Pushkina] in Eikhenbaum, *Skvoz' literaturu (sbornik statei)* (Leningrad: Academia, 1924], 157–170)], and a 1920 talk on poetry and prose—*CCT*.

13 Tynianov has in mind Bely's "Symphonies"—*CCT.* See Andrei Bely, *Simfonii* (Leningrad: Khudozhestvennaia literatura, 1991).

so there could come a time when it will be irrelevant whether a work is written in poetry or prose.[14]

7

The question of the evolutionary relationship between the formal element and its function remains unexplored by scholarship. I offered an example of how the evolution of forms gives rise to changes in function. We can also find many examples of how a form with indeterminate function can give rise to new functions and determine them. Additionally, there are examples of function seeking form.

Here is an example that combines both phenomena.

In the 1820s, among the Archaists,[T] there arose a verse epic whose function was simultaneously high style and folkloric. *Literature's interrelations with the social series led the Archaists to this large verse form.* But there were no formal elements to work with; the "mandate" of the social series was incommensurate with the literary "mandate," and was left hanging. The search for formal elements was on. In 1822, Katenin[N] suggested the *ottava rima* as a formal element of the verse epic.[15] The passion of the debates around the seemingly innocent *ottava rima* was matched only by the tragic orphanhood of a function without form. The Archaists' epic was not successful. Eight years later, Shevyryov[N] and Pushkin used the epic form in a different function—one that completely destroyed the epic in iambic tetrameter and created a new, lower (rather than "high-style") prose epic ("The Little House in Kolomna").[16]

The connection between function and form is not incidental. Neither is the combination of a certain kind of lexicon with a certain kind of meter that we see in Katenin, and in Nekrasov[N] twenty to thirty years hence (the latter probably had no idea who Katenin was).

The variability of the functions of a given formal element; the emergence of a function in a formal element; the formal element's attachment to a function—these are all important questions of literary evolution that cannot be solved or pursued further in the present article.

---

14 See also "On the Composition of *Eugene Onegin*" (114–150) in this volume.

15 *Ottava rima* is a kind of rhyming stanza that dates back to Boccaccio and has been used in European (including Russian) poetic tradition for long narrative poems on heroic or mock-heroic themes (for example, Byron's "Don Juan").

16 "The Little House in Kolomna" [Domik v Kolomne] (1830) is one of Pushkin's humorous narrative (long) poems.

I will say only that the whole question of literature as a series and a system depends on these future investigations.

8

There is a notion that the interrelations of literary phenomena take place in the following way: a literary work enters a synchronic literary system and "accumulates" functions. This is not entirely accurate. The very notion of a perpetually evolving synchronic system is contradictory. The system of a literary series is, first and foremost, *a system of the functions of a literary series, in perpetual interdependence with other series*. The content of these series changes, but the differential quality of human activities remains constant. As with all cultural series, the evolution of literature does not coincide, either in tempo or character (given the specificity of the material it is working with), with its various interrelated series. The constructive function evolves quickly. The literary function evolves from one historical period to another, while the functions of the entire literary series relative to its many neighboring series evolve over centuries.

9

A system is not the egalitarian cooperation of all its elements, but instead assumes that some groups of elements ("the dominant") will be foregrounded and the others deformed. It is through this dominant[T] that a work enters literature and acquires its literary function. This is why we interrelate a poem with the poetry series (and not the prose series) in terms of some of its features, but not all of them. The same is true for interrelation by genre. We currently see the novel as interrelated with "the novel" according to its size, or the way the plot is developed, while at one time it was defined according to the presence of a love story.

This brings up another fact of interest in connection to evolution. A work is interrelated with a given literary series on the basis of its "divergence" or "differentiation" from the literary series to which it has been assigned. Thus, for example, the question of the genre of Pushkin's long poems[T]—which was extremely fraught in 1820s criticism—arose because Pushkin's genre was mixed, composite, new; it lacked a ready "designation."[17] The more acute the divergences from a given literary series, the greater the emphasis on the system

---

17 Tynianov discusses this same case in "Literary Fact" (especially 153–154).

from which it diverges and differentiates itself. Thus, free verse emphasized the poetic principle through *extra-metrical* characteristics, and Sterne's novel emphasized the plot principle through characteristics *external to the fabula* (Shklovsky[N]).[18] A parallel in linguistics: "the inconstancy of the stem necessitates a concentration of the greatest possible expressiveness upon it and takes it out of the network of prefixes, which remain constant" (Vendryes).[19]

10

In what way is literature interrelated with its neighboring series?

Furthermore, what are these neighboring series?

Everyone has a ready answer to this: everyday life [*byt*].

But in order to work out how literary series are interrelated with everyday life, we must pose another question: *how, by what means,* is everyday life interrelated with literature? After all, everyday life is multifaceted and multifarious; only the function of all its many aspects has any specificity. *Everyday life is interrelated with literature primarily through its speech aspect.* The same goes for the interrelations of literary series with everyday life. These interrelations of a literary series with the everyday series take place through speech; literature's function in relation to everyday life is a *speech* function.

We have used the term "orientation" elsewhere.[20] It means something like "the author's creative intention." And yet it often happens that, as Pushkin said, "the intentions were great, but the results are second-rate."[21] To this we will add that authorial intent can only serve as a catalyst. In handling specific literary material, the author retreats from his original intention, submitting to the material. "Woe from Wit" was meant to be "high style" and even "magnificent" [*velikolepnyi*] (in the author's sense of the word, which does not correspond to our own); but it ended up being a political, "Archaist" pamphlet comedy.[22] Similarly, *Eugene Onegin* was originally meant to be a "satirical narrative poem,"

---

18 Shklovsky, "Sterne's *Tristram Shandy* and the Theory of the Novel" (Petrograd: Opoiaz, 1921)—*CCT*.

19 J. Vendryes, *Le langage* (Paris, 1921), 95—*CCT*.

20 See also "The Ode as an Oratorical Genre".

21 Tynianov quotes a letter from Pushkin to Vyazemsky[N] (1 September 1828). See Alexander Pushkin, *Sobranie sochinenii v 10-i tomakh* (Moscow: GIKhL, 1959–1962), 9:282. All quotations from Pushkin are from this publication, unless otherwise specified.

22 "Woe from Wit" [Gore ot uma] (1823) was a seminal satire by Alexander Griboedov.[N]

in which its author would "spew bile" [9:84].[23] But by the time he was working on the fourth chapter, Pushkin could already write: "Where is my satire? There isn't a trace of it in *Eugene Onegin*" [9:144].[24]

The constructive function, the interrelations of elements within a literary work, converts "authorial intention" into a catalyst, nothing more. "Creative freedom" is an optimistic slogan, but it does not correspond to reality, and ultimately yields to "creative necessity."

The literary function—the interrelations of an individual work with various literary series—makes this process final.

Let's remove the teleological, goal-oriented connotation—the "intention"—from the word "orientation." What do we get? The "orientation" of a literary work (or of a series) is actually its *speech* function, its interrelations with everyday life.[25]

The orientation of Lomonosov's odes—their speech function—is *oratorical*. Their language is "oriented" toward *recitation*. Its further, real-life associations are with *recitation in large palace rooms*. By Karamzin's time, the ode had "run its course" as literature. Its orientation had expired, or become attenuated in its meaning, and moved on to other, everyday forms. Congratulatory odes, among other types, became "overcoat poems,"[T] an exclusively quotidian, non-literary phenomenon.[26] There were no ready-made literary genres on hand, and so their place was occupied by *everyday speech* phenomena. The speech function—orientation—was seeking a form, and located it in "romances," jokes, rhyming games, *bouts-rimés*, charades, etc. And this is where the moment of *genesis* acquires its evolutionary significance: in *the availability of various everyday speech forms*. In Karamzin's time, the ultimate real-life series for these speech phenomena was the salon. Otherwise a fact of everyday life, during this period the salon became a literary fact. This is an example of how everyday forms get attached to the literary function.

Similarly, there have always been domestic, intimate, "club" semantics, but in certain historical periods such semantics acquire a literary function. Such is the consolidation of *incidental results* in literature: Pushkin's brief outlines for his poems and draft "scenarios" evolved into his polished *prose*. This kind of

23 Letter from Pushkin to A. Turgenev, 1 December 1823—*CCT*. See Pushkin, *Sobranie sochinenii*, 9:84l. *Eugene Onegin* (1834) is Pushkin's novel in verse. For more on this work, see "On the Composition of *Eugene Onegin*" (114–150).

24 Letter from Pushkin to A. Bestuzhev, 24 March 1825—*CCT*.

25 The following paragraph reprises some of the ideas Tynianov first raised in "The Ode as an Oratorical Genre" (1922).

26 For "overcoat odes," see also "Literary Fact" (165) and "Interlude" (186).

thing is possible only in the context of the evolution of an entire series, *the evolution of its orientation.*

An analogous struggle between two orientations in our own time can be found in the rally-oriented poetry of Mayakovsky[N] ("the ode") struggling with the intimate, song-oriented poetry of Esenin ("the elegy").[27]

11

The speech function should also be taken into account when considering the reverse *expansion of literature into everyday life.* At various times, the "literary personality," "authorial personality," or "protagonist" constitutes a *speech* orientation on the part of literature, and from there can make its way into everyday life [*byt*]. This is the case with Byron's lyric protagonists, who are interrelated with his "literary personality"—the personality that came to life for the readers of his poetry and thus transitioned into everyday life. Heine's "literary personality" was likewise quite removed from the biographical, authentic Heine.[28] At certain times, biography can function as oral, apocryphal literature. This is carried out consistently, in keeping with the speech orientation of a given system: compare Pushkin, Tolstoy, Blok,[N] Mayakovsky, or Esenin[N] with the absence of a literary personality in Leskov, Turgenev,[N] Fet,[N] Maikov, Gumilyov, et al., resulting from the absence of a speech orientation toward the "literary personality."[29] It goes without saying that in order for literature to expand into everyday life, specific conditions of everyday life have to be in evidence.

12

For literature, this is the *social function* closest at hand. We can only determine what this function is and properly explore it by studying the series closest to it. The only way this can be done is by examining the conditions closest at hand, not by forcibly enlisting more distant, causal series, no matter how crucial they may be.

I should also mention that the concept of "orientation" (speech function) pertains to the literary series or the system of literature, but not to an individual

27 For more on Mayakovsky, see "On Mayakovsky" (293) and "Interlude" (185–190).

28 For Heine, see also "Tyutchev and Heine" (64–76).

29 Apollon Maikov (1821–1897) was a poet and scholar; Nikolai Gumilyov (1886–1921) was founder of the Acmeists, an early twentieth-century group of Modernist poets. For more on literary personality and contemporary poetry, see "Interlude."

literary work. An individual work must be interrelated with its literary series before anything can be said about its orientation. The law of large numbers does not apply to small ones. When we try right away to determine the most distant causal series for individual works of literature and individual authors, we are studying not the evolution of literature but its modification; not how literature changes and evolves in relation to other series, but how it is deformed by neighboring series. This question is worthy of study as well, but on a completely different level.

A particularly unreliable approach is the straightforward study of authorial psychology, whereby a causal bridge is drawn between the *author's* milieu, everyday life, class, etc.—and his works. Batyushkov's[N] erotic poetry came out of his engagement with poetic language (see his essay "On the Influence of Light Verse on Language"), and Vyazemsky refused to seek its genesis in Batyushkov's psychology.[30] The poet Polonsky, who was never a theorist, nevertheless grasped the situation as a poet and master of his craft; regarding Benediktov, he wrote: "It is entirely possible that stern nature—forests, stones, [etc.]—left their mark on the child's impressionable soul, the soul of the future poet; but in what way? It is a difficult question, one that cannot be resolved without straining credulity. Nature, which is the same for everyone, is not the deciding factor here ..."[31] Artists often experience creative turning points that cannot be explained by turning points in their personal lives. There is the kind of turning point experienced by both Derzhavin and Nekrasov; in their youth, "high-style" poetry and "low," satirical poetry went side by side, and under objective conditions the two flowed together, engendering new phenomena. This obviously has less to do with individual psychological conditions than with objective ones—with the evolution of the functions of the literary series in relation to the social series closest at hand.

13

This is why we must reevaluate one of the thorniest evolutionary questions of literature: the question of "influence." There are profound psychological and

---

30 Tynianov refers to a passage from Vyazemsky's correspondence, quoted in the article "Literary Fact" (159–160).

31 Vladimir Benediktov (1807–1873) was a minor poet who became famous shortly after Pushkin's death; Yakov Polonsky (1819–1898) was a poet who sought to continue the "Pushkin line" in the later nineteenth century (a somewhat thankless task due to the dominance of prose at that time).

real-life personal influences that are not reflected on the literary level at all (Chaadaev and Pushkin).[32] There are influences that modify and deform literature without being evolutionarily significant (Mikhailovsky and Gleb Uspensky).[33] Most striking of all, though, is the fact that external data can be found for drawing conclusions about influence—in cases where there is actually no influence. I offered the example of Katenin and Nekrasov earlier. The list of these examples goes on. South American tribes came up with the Prometheus myth without the influence of Greco-Roman antiquity. These are facts of *convergence,* coincidence. These facts prove to be so massively significant that they completely blot out the psychological approach to the question of influence, and the chronological question—"who said it first?"—proves inconsequential. "Influence" happens at the time and in the way allowed for by the appropriate literary conditions. Given a coincidence of function, influence provides the artist with the formal elements for developing and consolidating that function. If this "influence" is absent, a similar function can lead to the appearance of similar formal elements anyway.[34]

14

And here, at last, we come to the principal term of literary history—"tradition." If we agree that evolution is a change in the interrelations of a system's parts—i.e., a change in its functions and formal elements—it follows that evolution is a "shift" of systems. These shifts can be slower or more abrupt depending on the historical period, and they do not presume a sudden and total renewal and replacement of formal elements; however, they do presume a *new function for these formal elements.* This is why these various literary phenomena should be matched up according to their functions, and not just their forms. Phenomena from different functional systems that are completely dissimilar in appearance may have similar functions, and vice versa. This issue is obscured by the fact that every literary trend in a given period seeks to root itself in preceding systems—for example, "traditionalism."

Thus the functions of Pushkin's prose may be closer to those of Tolstoy's prose than the functions of Pushkin's poetry are to the functions of his imitators in the 1830s, or to Apollon Maikov.

---

32 Pyotr Chaadaev (1794–1856) was a Russian philosopher and the author of an influential series of "Philosophical Letters" on Russia, long banned for their critical viewpoint.

33 Nikolai Mikhailovsky (1842–1904) was a writer and critic, and Gleb Uspensky (1844–1902) a writer; both were closely associated with the Narodnik nationalist movement.

34 Compare thesis five in "Problems of the Study of Literature and Language" (287)—*CCT.*

15

In conclusion: studying literary evolution is only possible when literature is treated as a series, a system interrelated with other series and systems and conditioned by them. This investigation should proceed from the constructive function to the literary function, from the literary function to the speech function. It should clarify the evolutionary interaction of forms and functions. The study of evolution should proceed from the literary series to the closest interrelated series, not to more distant ones, though the latter may be of major significance. This does not deny the overarching significance of major social factors; in fact, this significance becomes clearest when considering the *evolution* of literature. The unmediated diagnosis of the "influence" of major social factors, meanwhile, substitutes the study of the *modification* and deformation of literary works for the study of the *evolution* of literature.

Part Four

EPILOGUE

Problems of the Study of Literature and Language (1928)[1]

CO-AUTHORED WITH ROMAN JAKOBSON[N]

Translators'/Editors' Note:

These lapidary points were first published in the journal New LEF. The journal editors prefaced the article with a brief description of the Formalists' gains against older methods of scholarship, claiming that the new science replaced the old question "Why?" with "What for?"—i.e., emphasizing the question of functionality and (social) context. For Tynianov, the collaboration with Jakobson was a breath of new life into the edifice of the Formalist method, which by 1928 had become somewhat deflated and scattered (not least because of pressures from both old-guard academics and radical Marxist critics). The reemergence of Formalist analysis was envisioned as the comprehensive structural engagement of language and literature alike; among other ideas, Shklovsky[N] and Tynianov planned a collective history of Russian literature on a Formalist theoretical basis. Although well received, the Jakobson-Tynianov theses did not ultimately lead to the reestablishment of OPOYAZ[T] or further collaborative scholarship; for Tynianov, in fact, they effectively marked the end of his literary-theoretical publications. From 1929 on, the ideological pressures from above became too much to bear, and the movement collapsed under their weight.

1

Tackling the latest problems in Russian literary and linguistic scholarship requires a clearly defined theoretical platform, as well as a complete break

1 First published in *New LEF* [Novyi LEF] 12 (1928): 35–37. Translation from "Problemy izucheniia literatury i iazyka," *PILK*, 282–283. Selected notes by A. Chudakov, M. Chudakova, and E. Toddes [*CCT*], 530–536. Additional notes by Yuri Tynianov [*YT*] and the translators [unmarked].

with the increasingly frequent practice of mechanically sticking new methodologies onto obsolete methods, and of smuggling in a naïve psychological approach and other methodological detritus under the mantle of new terminology.

There must be a break with academic eclecticism (Zhirmunsky et al.);[2] with the scholastic "formalism" that offers in place of analysis the mere naming and classifying of phenomena; and a rejection of repeated attempts to turn literary and linguistic scholarship from a systemic discipline into a hodgepodge of episodic and anecdotal approaches.

2

Insofar as it is linked to other historical series, the history of literature (and likewise of art) is characterized (as is each of these other series) by an elaborate complex of specific structural laws. Only by elucidating these laws will it be possible to scientifically establish the interrelations between the literary series and other historical series.

3

We cannot understand the evolution of literature as long as the evolutionary problem remains obscured by questions of episodic, extra-systemic genesis, whether literary (so-called literary influences) or extra-literary. Only when the literary and extra-literary material used in literature is viewed from a functional standpoint will it be brought into the fold of serious scientific research.

4

The sharp opposition between the synchronic (static) and diachronic viewpoints has lately become a productive working hypothesis for both linguistics and the history of literature, since it demonstrates the systemic character of language (and of literature) at each individual moment of its life. At present, gains on the part of the synchronic conception are forcing a reappraisal of the

---

2 Viktor Zhirmunsky (1891–1971) was a literary critic with views that often coincided with those of the Formalist critics, but which differed from Tynianov's on key points. He was known for analyzing formal elements as such, not as a part of the functioning construction of the text; unlike the Formalists, Zhirmunsky also held to more traditional academic labels such as Classicism and Romanticism, and grounded his literary criticism in philosophy and Zeitgeist.

principles of diachrony as well. Synchronic studies replaced the notion of a mechanical agglomeration of phenomena with the notion of a system or structure; and diachronic studies has followed suit. The history of a system is, in turn, itself a system. Pure synchronism is now revealed to be an illusion: each synchronic system has its own past and future as integral structural elements of the system. (For example: A. Archaism[T] as a fact of style; the linguistic and literary background recognized as an old-fashioned style that is on its way out; and B. innovative tendencies in language and literature recognized as an innovation of the system).[3]

The opposition of synchrony and diachrony entailed opposing the concept of a system to the concept of evolution; this opposition loses its relevance when we acknowledge that every system necessarily exists in evolution, and that evolution inevitably has a systemic character.

5

The notion of a synchronic literary system is incompatible with that of a naïvely conceived chronological period, since the former comprises not only works of art that are chronologically close to one another, but also works from foreign literatures and earlier periods that have been pulled into its orbit. An indifferent classification of concurrent phenomena is not enough; their hierarchical significance for the given literary-historical period must also be accounted for.

6

The assertion of *parole* and *langue* as distinct concepts and the analysis of the relations between them (the Geneva School) was extraordinarily productive for the science of language.[4] A basic elaboration of the problem of the relation

---

3 The authors refer to the early nineteenth-century Archaist movement in Russian poetry, a favorite example of Tynianov's in several articles in this volume (See "Literary Fact", "On Literary Evolution", "On Parody", and others).

4 Tynianov and Jakobson refer to the Geneva School of Linguistics, and to the linguistic and semiotic concepts developed in the first decade of the twentieth century by the school's most famous representative, Ferdinand de Saussure. The Formalists were particularly taken with Saussure's insistence on viewing language as a system of signs, and on distinguishing between abstract "language" (*langue*) and speech in an individual and concrete communicative context (*parole*).

between these two categories (i.e. the existing norm and individual utterances) should now be applied to literature. Here, too, the individual utterance cannot be examined without reference to the existing complex of norms (the scholar who abstracts the first from the second will inevitably deform the system of artistic values under investigation, and will eliminate the possibility of establishing its immanent laws).

7

The analysis of the structural laws of language and literature, and of their evolution, inevitably leads to the identification of a limited series of attested structural types (and likewise types of structural evolution).

8

The disclosure of the immanent laws of the history of literature (and of language) lets us describe each specific shift of literary (and linguistic) systems, but does not help to explain the tempo of evolution, or the choice of an evolutionary path given several theoretically possible ones. This is because the immanent laws of literary (and linguistic) evolution are only an indeterminate equation, one that leaves open the possibility of an admittedly limited number of solutions, but not necessarily a single correct one.

The question of a specific choice of path, or at least of a dominant,[T] can only be solved by analyzing the interrelations between the literary series and other historical series. These interrelations (a system of systems) have their own structural laws, also subject to study. It would be methodologically disastrous to examine this interdependence of systems without considering the immanent laws of each individual system.

9

Given the importance of further collective research into the aforementioned theoretical problems, as well as the specific directions of study implied by these principles (a history of Russian literature, a history of Russian language, a typology of linguistic and literary structures, etc.), it is vital that OPOYAZ be reinstated under the leadership of Viktor Shklovsky.

On FEX (1929)[1]

It would seem that besides us, no one in the whole world has any doubt that we make marvelous films. We have a great deal of naïve respect for Western cinema. The people who run breathless to every single Western film and only deign to watch their own out of obligation are wrong. Western viewers in turn watch the majority of these same Western films out of condescension and run just as breathlessly to see our films. Our cinema has nothing to apologize for. The irritability, peevishness and arrogance of our criticism, which piles on the praise and then falls into panic and shrieks about a "crisis," bears witness to nothing more than its own crisis. The critics demand that every film be, at the very least, a work of genius, while forgetting that works of genius are, of necessity, rare.

The revolution created a marvelous cinema and hasn't had time to notice it. We already have people working in our cinema who have earned the right to make mistakes. Something must be said about two of these people—Kozintsev and Trauberg, or more succinctly—FEX.[2] What does this term mean, FEX, the "Eccentric Actors Factory"? One thing is clear: something experimental is going on here. Before turning to cinema, the FEX artists spent a while doing something very youthful, jolly, and unintelligible in theater, painting, and elsewhere. I met them after their second production, *The Sailor from the Aurora.* Their first production, which few people likely remember, but which FEX loves with the kind of love people reserve for their own childhood, was *The Adventures of Octobrina.*[3] This minor film, shot who knows where and how, does not belong to any serious film genre. The most unostentatious shots that I remember were of people riding bicycles around on rooftops. The *Adventures* are a no-holds-

1 First published in the newspaper *Soviet Screen* [Sovetskii ekran], no. 14 (1929): 10. Translation from "O FEKSakh," in Iurii Tynianov, *PILK*, 346–348. Selected notes to this publication by Marietta Chudakova [*MC*], 557. Additional notes by Yuri Tynianov [*YT*] and the translators [unmarked].

2 Grigorii Kozintsev (1905–1973) and Leonid Trauberg (1902–1990) were filmmakers who, along with Sergei Yutkevich, founded FEX in 1921. Their artistic principles were declared in the manifesto "Cinema as Unmasker" (in the collection *Eccentrism* [Petrograd, 1922])—*MC*. FEX stands for *Fabrika ekstsentricheskogo aktera*; note that in the 1920s the term "eccentric" had specific associations with circus-like tricks and stunts.

3 [Pokhozhdeniia Oktiabriny], (Grigorii Kozintsev and Leonid Trauberg, dirs.; 1924; Lenfilm).

barred collection of all the tricks that these ravenous, film-starved directors could cook up. And still, the FEX artists have reason to love their *Adventures.* They didn't cut their teeth on monumental epics, but rather on simple comic films that still bear the traces of cinema as a new invention, with cinematic elements that allow one to observe, sample, and touch with their own hands, and without excess timidity or deference, that which the more respectable but less perceptive consider taboo: the very essence of cinema as an art. FEX thus gained something that remains to this day their most valuable quality: freedom of genre, a sense of tradition as non-obligatory, and the ability to see paradoxes.

I met the FEX crew after their *The Sailor from the Aurora.* Though youthful, *Sailor* was a good film. Actually, it went through several name-changes and was eventually released as *The Devil's Wheel.*[4] It was under this name that it met with the approval of experts and gave FEX their first commercial success, as well as their first taste of abuse from the Leningrad critics.

FEX decided to shoot *The Overcoat* using my screenplay.[5] *The Overcoat* was a polemical piece: its target was the easy and pointless success of *The Stationmaster.*[6] *The Overcoat* once more raised the issue of "literary classics" in the cinema. Dispensing with the big names of theater, FEX gave the lead role to a young actor in their group, and they did the right thing: Rychalovian cinematic tours, while still quite frequent, are a provincial and dilettante-ish phenomenon.[7] *The Overcoat* was hastily edited. Nevertheless, the film was a marvelous experiment. This time, the Leningrad critics' ecstatic witch hunt went beyond anything the average reader could have imagined. One critic called me an impertinent, illiterate troublemaker, and suggested, if I'm not mistaken, that FEX be cleared out with an iron broom.[8] This seems to have been a student at the university where I was teaching at the time. Now he's full of praise. Another one reasoned that, since the classics are the property of the people, when the

---

4 [Chortovo koleso], (Grigorii Kozintsev and Leonid Trauberg, dirs.; 1926; Leningradkino).

5 The film *The Overcoat* [Shinel'] (Grigorii Kozintsev and Leonid Trauberg, dirs.; 1926; Sevzapkino) was based on Gogol's[N] eponymous story and several other stories from the "Petersburg Tales" cycle. For Gogol, see "Dostoyevsky and Gogol" (27–63).

6 *The Stationmaster* [Kollezhskii registrator] (1925; Mezhradprom), based on Pushkin's story "Stantsionnyi smotritel'," was directed by Yu. Zheliabuzhsky and I. Moskvin—MC.

7 Tynianov refers to a satirical play by Mikhail Bolkonsky (1860–1917), a well-known writer and playwright of the late imperial period. In *Rychalov's Tour* [Gastrol' Rychalova] (1911), the title character is a famous actor from the big city who descends upon a small-town theatre.

8 This is a modern (iron!) variation on a standard Russian idiom, "to clear out with an outhouse broom."

screenwriter and directors mangle a classic, they ought to be dragged in by the public prosecutor for misappropriation of public property. I don't know where this critic is now, but I fear that he is alive and well and still at it.

While FEX was working on *The Overcoat,* I would drop by the studio and lecture the actors on Gogol. I understood why they were so cheerful: theirs was a close-knit, disciplined, and focused group. Moskvin, the cinematographer, was a master of "inventions" and "tricks"; the artistic director, Yenei, was cinematically economical, and the actors were well trained and serious.[9]

The critics' heavy artillery fire had its desired effect, and the FEX ship began to list: they made a dull and unnecessary film which set out to prove, if I remember correctly, that an old and bad automobile is better than a new one.[10] After that they rallied and made *S.V.D.* (1927).[11] When Yulian Oksman and I were working on the screenplay for this film, we wanted to highlight the extreme leftism of the Decembrist movement, as a counterweight to the pompous uniforms, bad taste, and parades portrayed in *The Decembrists.*[12] The FEX artists were captivated by the romance of the 1820s, and they managed to achieve something beyond the chronological and historical side of things: cinematic pathos. The image of the uprising, in which every situation is used to the strongest possible effect, is among the best things they have done. In this film, they mastered one of the most difficult things of all: a gradually building and authentic ambience. At the same time, their attraction to picturesque material is also on display. But one thing distinguishes them from "photogenicists," that is, people in constant pursuit of beautiful material per se: with FEX, this material is always tied to some kind of plot twist, and this twist is colored in some way or other by the material.

I saw their most recent work, *The New Babylon,* when it was still in a rough cut. With the courage of people who have not lost their appetite for hard work, FEX is having a crack at working with foreign historical material (the film deals with the 1871 Paris Commune). They were able to take on this difficult task

---

9 Andrei Moskvin (1901–1961) also worked on S. V. D. and *The New Babylon,* along with Evgenii Yenei (1890–1971)—MC.

10 Tynianov has in mind the film *Little Brother* [Bratishka] (Grigorii Kozintsev and Leonid Trauberg, dirs.; 1927; Sovkino)—MC.

11 *Soiuz velikogo dela* [S. V. D., "The Union of the Great Deed" (Grigorii Kozintsev and Leonid Trauberg, dirs.; Lenfilm; 1927)].

12 *The Decembrists* [Dekabristy] (Alexander Ivanovsky, dir.; Lenfilm), screenplay by Ivanovsky and P. Shchegolev, was released in 1927—MC. Yulian G. Oksman (1895–1970) was an historian of Russian literature who had been close with Tynianov since the Vengerov seminars.

thanks to their "poetic," rather than "prosaic," interpretation of the cinematic construction of material. I think that historicity is not what will make this film important, but rather, its purely poetic images, and metaphors. Such are the new methods of this cinematic ode: these images and metaphors, which are rooted in the "comic film" but here, in this different genre, take on the role of hyperbole.

I don't think it's accurate to say that the FEX artists are people working in a "historical genre." To begin with, this genre simply does not exist, in the cinema or anywhere else. But if we are talking about historical material, then the urgency and contemporaneity of this material can hardly be denied. Viewers need this material, because it makes the genesis of their own era clearer, closer and more contemporary, and in this way helps them to orient themselves within it. Artists need it, because it forces them to work outside of "ready-made" fabulas[T],[13] with their eternal "triangles" and heroes and tempters, and instead establish precise conditions for the fabula that have been verified not just by some artists' bureau, but by history itself.

13 For the concept of fabula, also see "On Plot and Fabula in Film" (240–241).

On Mayakovsky. In Memory of the Poet (1930)[1]

For the generation born at the end of the nineteenth century, Mayakovsky[N] was not a new way of seeing—he was a new form of free will.[2] For the stay-at-home types of his time, Mayakovsky was a public incident. He didn't make himself felt through books. His poems were a phenomenon of an entirely different order. He was quietly working away at some kind of difficult labor; initially invisible to those on the sidelines, it would later reveal itself through a change in the pace of verse or even poetry itself, in the new, revolutionary commitments of poetic language [*slovo*].[T] In some of his writings, and especially in his final long poem, it is clear that he himself viewed this difficult labor with conscious detachment. He fought for a socially conscious poetic framework, against the elegy; this was an outward struggle but also a muted one, fought from inside his poetry, "stepping on the throat of his own song."[3] This willful, charismatic consciousness was not limited to his work with verse: it could be found in the very framework of his poetry, in lines that were more like units of muscular willpower than of speech—and always spoke directly to the will.

---

1 First published in "Vladimir Mayakovsky" (one-time newspaper), 24 April 1930. Translation from "O Maiakovskom. Pamiati poeta," *PILK*, 196. Notes by the translators.

2 Tynianov thus contrasts Mayakovsky to Velimir Khlebnikov,[N] who *was*, in his view, a "new way of seeing." See "On Khlebnikov" (217–229). For more on Mayakovsky in the context of contemporary poetry, see the 1924 essay "Interlude".

3 Tynianov refers to a well-known phrase from the first introduction to Mayakovsky's long poem "At the Top of My Voice" [Vo ves' golos] (1930), "But I/tamed/myself,/stepping/on the throat/of my own song" [No ia/sebia/smirial,/stanovias'/na gorlo/sobstvennoi pesne]." See V. V. Maiakovskii, *Polnoe sobranie sochinenii v 13–i tomakh.* (Moscow: Gos. izd. khud. literatury, 1955–1961), 10:280.

On Parody (1929)[1]

1

The existing definition of parody, as it was conclusively established by the mid-nineteenth century, can be quoted from Bouillet's dictionary (to take one example):[2] "Parody is a composition, in verse or prose, made after the manner of one or another serious work, rendering the latter humorous through changes or diversions away from its original designation, toward an amusing end" (I quote from the 1859 translation—*YT*).[3]

But it is curious that this definition did not stand up to the facts, and that one of its essential components fell apart that very same year of 1859. This happened when the definition was cited by the publisher of K. S. Aksakov's dramatic parody "Oleg at Constantinople."[4] The publisher cited it with the intention of settling the matter, but suddenly stopped short, struck by how the definition did not fit the work he had published:

> Oleg's spectacular [...] feat is dramatically presented in colors so full of freshness, clothed in such exquisite speech, accompanied by such lovely images, that the reader is unwillingly captivated: by the relative richness of the ideas and the imaginative playfulness and the music of the verses; even by a sense of attachment to the fate of the characters, as if this were a most serious dramatic work. [...] That this is a parody, of course, is

---

1 "O parodii" remained partly in draft form and was published in full for the first time in *PILK*, 284–310. Selected notes to this publication by A. P. Chudakov [*AC*], 536–544. Additional notes by Yuri Tynianov [*YT*] and the translators [unmarked].

2 Marie-Nicholas Bouillet, *Dictionnaire de sciences, des lettres et des arts* (Paris: Librairie De L. Hachette et Cie, 1854)—*YT*.

3 Tynianov quotes the 1859 Russian translation, but cites the original in Bouillet's dictionary, which is slightly different: "sorte d'ouvrage en vers, ou même en prose, fait sur une oeuvre sérieuse que l'on rend comique au moyen de quelques changements ou que l'on détourne de sa destination primitive en l'applicant à un sujet ridicule." M. -N. Bouillet, *Dictionnaire universel de sciences, des lettres et des arts* (Paris: Hachette, 1859), 1217.

4 "Oleg at Constantinople, a dramatic parody with epilogue, in three acts, in verse" [Oleg pod Konstantinopolem, dramaticheskaia parodiia, s epilogom, v 3-kh deistviiakh, v stikhakh] by K. S. Aksakov (St. Petersburg: Izdanie liubitelia, 1858)—*AC*. Konstantin Aksakov (1817–1860) was a writer and literary critic affiliated with the Slavophile movement in mid-nineteenth-century Russia.

> beyond dispute. But consider carefully the definition of parody given above, which is based on existing examples of this type. Does it actually fit Mr. Aksakov's work?

Citing Aksakov's own statement that the exaggerated depiction of Oleg "as a sovereign of an advanced and enlightened age is also a parody of the idealized histories in verse that appeared in certain patriotic dramas of the 1830s, and more generally, of the sonorous verses that even today are taken by some to be poetry,"[5] the publisher (namely, the author of the article cited) points to some verses from Aksakov's parody that indeed make one reconsider the definition of parody as a comic literary genre. He had in mind the parodic "Song of the Kievans" [Pesnia Kievlian] which the publisher comments on as follows: "Although the author [K. Aksakov], in his own words, indicated *parody* as his aim, when you read these verses you feel only enchantment and forget about their parodic aim":

Над рекою,	Above the river,
Над родною	Above the river
Да над быстрою,	Dear and clear,
Я заботой	Through care
Да работой	And work I'll
Хату выстрою;	Build a homestead;
Разукрашу,	I'll carve
Да окрашу	And paint it
Краской белою;	White as snow;
Где дорожка,	By the path,
Три окошка	Three windows
Там проделаю	Will open
Против ясна,	To the bright,
Против красна,	To the red
Против солнышка;	Red sun;
А на ловлю	And for fishing
Изготовлю	I will build us
Я три челнышка.	Three canoes.
Всем богата	Riches full
Будет хата,	Will be our homestead,
Чаша полная.	Overflowing.

5 Quotation modified, from K. S. Aksakov's preface to the 1858 publication—*AC*.

С светом встану,
Утром рано
  Кинусь в волны я.
< … >
Раз в народе,
В хороводе
  Он пошел плясать,
Да покой свой
Со поры той
  Он не мог сыскать.
Свет девица,
Белолица!
  Ты взяла покой.
Так поди же
Принеси же
  Мне его с собой.

At first light,
I will rise
  And jump in the waves.
[…]
Once with people,
In the ring-dance
  He went dancing,
No peace since then
For ever more
  No peace he'll find.
O lady light,
Face of white!
  You took his peace.
So go on then
Bring it to me
  Bring me back my peace.

In citing the "Song of the Kievans," the publisher openly admits: "And so the definition we provided here [the theoretical one given above—*YT*] is inadequate. And this demonstrates that Mr. Aksakov's work has extended the limits of parody and elevated it, lending it a more important aim and significance."[6]

The point, however, is not limited to Aksakov or his parody alone. The notion of parody as a comic genre, which was current in the nineteenth century and has become firmly entrenched in our day, renders the question too narrow and simply does not apply to the overwhelming majority of parodies. For instance, it doesn't fit N. Polevoi's remarkable parodies, or the equally remarkable and equally non-comic parodies of his evolutionary successor, Panaev[N] (the New Poet).[7] Here is an example: in 1830, Polevoi published a parody section in his journal *The New Painter*, entitled "Poetic Balderdash, or Excerpts from a New Almanac, 'The Literary Mirror.'" The first piece in the section was "Russian Song" ("Oh you curls, black curls!") which appeared

---

6 *The Open Briefcase: excerpts from the "Sewn Notebooks" of an author who prefers to remain anonymous* [Raskrytyi portfel': Vyderzhki iz "Sshitykh tetradei avtora, ne zhelaiushchego ob''iavliat' svoego imeni]. First solo edition (St. Petersburg: Izdanie liubitelia [Ia.V. Pisarev], 1839). The article "A Publisher's View of the First Work of K. S. Aksakov to be Published by Amateur's Publishing House [Izdanie liubitelia] …," 7–12. This rather eccentric writer was I. E. Velikopolsky, whose dramatic experiments were doubtless useful to Kozma Prutkov for his famous ballet—*YT*.

7 Nikolai Polevoi (1796–1846) was a writer, journalist, and historian.

under the parodic byline of Feokritov (a transparent reference to Delvig,[N] who wrote idylls).[8] Then 1831 saw the appearance of *Euterpe*, an almanac which in both its aims and content had nothing in common with parody. In issue number thirty-three, the poem "Oh you curls, black curls!" appeared on pages sixty-seven to sixty-eight, alongside poems by Shevyrov,[N] Yazykov,[N] et al.; it was signed by Feokritov, which at this point was, if not a real last name, then at least a serious pseudonym. The reasons behind this curious instance lie primarily in the specific role played by the almanac in literature of the 1830s. Author-publishers from the mixed and merchant classes (usually dilettantes) flocked to the almanacs. A whole swath of these publications (those put out by M. A. Bestuzhev-Riumin, F. Solovyov, A. Pugovoshnikov, and P. Sobolev, et al.) not only took an antagonistic stance vis-à-vis the domineering role of the "aristocratic group" of writers; they also consciously employed some of that group's genres in a different function. Take, for instance, the wholesale transfer of elegies and "poetic songs" into the ranks of "romances"[T] (meaning not so much concrete musical works as verbal material for potential improvisations). At the same time, the style and poetic language of the works published in the "democratic" almanacs of the 1830s were such that it was generally quite simple for parody to shift[T] into "romance."[9] And the fact that the parody in question was not comic (like all of Polevoi's other parodies) was actually a necessary literary condition for this particular case. Aksakov's poem, with its virtuoso rhymes and rhythmic pacing, is no exception. Recall Karolina Pavlova's[N] poetic parody ("Meditation." "Where have I not wandered with heavy heart …"). Not so long ago, during the final days of Symbolism[T] and its obsession with the exotic, this poem could have been read seriously and been well received in some poetic circle or other.

In fact, both Aksakov's and Pavlova's poems parody *virtuosity* itself. Meticulous, microscopic literary vision is needed to fully appreciate these poems' gradual transformation of virtuosity into sophistication, and sophistication into affectation. (Consider the rich rhymes in both poems; and Aksakov's elegantly stylized, excessively Russian phrasing: "for ever more";[10] or the overly "conversational" syntax in an intricate metaphorical construction such as: "so go on then, bring it to me" ("it" being "peace"); also Pavlova's exotic vocabulary and

---

8 The pseudonym "Feokritov" refers to Theocritus, author of the *Idylls* and founder of bucolic poetry (third century BCE).

9 For more on the concept of "shift," also see "On Literary Evolution" (267–282).

10 The syntax in the original Russian is a permissible but odd-sounding reversal: *so pory toi* in place of the standard *s toi pory.*

exotic phonetics.) The case of Polevoi and Panaev is even more complicated. Polevoi used the following lines as an epigraph to his "Poetic Balderdash":

> Они, как пол лощеный, гладки:
> На мысли не споткнешься в них!
> [They, like a polished floor, are smooth: / You won't stumble over any thoughts in them!]

In his "programmatic" preface he declares: "We dearly hope for another thing as well: our wish to please readers accounts for our faithful adherence to the fundamental rule of our literature, imitation. We will not think about the beauty or the elegance of poems and prose. No, we will present precise imitations of the most fashionable, most famous poets, in such genres as were found pleasing to others and made them famous [...]."[11] Polevoi thus parodies the *smoothness* of the verse itself. Similarly, the New Poet's parodies are directed against the "smoothness, *melodiousness,* external finish, and gloss, which for several years now have been mixed up with poetry" (preface to the 1855 publication).[12] And just as Polevoi's parody found itself in the company of serious and even highly regarded poetic works, Panaev himself attests to the fact that his "parodies printed in periodicals were actually received by some as serious works. One of these parodies, which begins with the line:

> Густолиственных кленов аллея ...
> [An alley of thick-leafed maples ...]

was even set to some beautiful music by Mr. Dmitriev in Moscow."[13]

And while the faint theatrics in Aksakov's and Pavlova's parodies could, at a stretch, be ascribed to "implicit" or "imperceptible" comic phenomena, Polevoi and Panaev's parodies do not exhibit even the slightest comic element. And so we can either keep the comic characteristic in the definition of parody and declare Polevoi and Panaev's parodies to be inconsequential or even non-

---

11 *The New Painter of Society and Literature* [Novyi zhivopisets obshchestva i literatury], edited by Nikolai Polevoi, pt. 2 (Moscow: Izdanie knigoprodavtsa V. Logonova, 1832), 181–184—*YT*.

12 *Collected Poems of the New Poet* [Sobranie stikhotvorenii Novogo poeta] (St. Petersburg: V tip. glav. shtaba ego imp. Velichestva po voenno-ucheb. zavedeniiam, 1855)—*AC*.

13 I. Panaev, *Collected Works* [Sobranie sochinenii], vol. 5 (Moscow: Izd. V.M. Sablina, 1912), 722–723—*YT*.

existent, or discard this characteristic. But if we take the former stance, we have to acknowledge that, even in comic parodies, the comic is not really the point. Recall the story of one of the most famous parodies in world history, which played a significant role in the ideological struggle of the sixteenth century: the story of the *Epistolæ Obscurorum Virorum*, or "Letters of Obscure Men."[14] The enormous success and excitement around this parody lay entirely in the fact that it was *deceptive*, that it managed to hoodwink its readers, that opponents took it to be an authentic and serious work and only afterwards were *forced* to recognize their mistake. We are thus dealing here with the same fact of *non-recognition*, the fact of deceptiveness.[15] It follows that the existing definition ("rendering it humorous") is in part inaccurate, even if you replace the word "humorous" with the term "comic," and it is inaccurate even with respect to comic parodies. Because it raises questions like: comic in what circumstances, under what conditions, comic for whom? These questions take us away from the "general" meaning of "comic" and force us to subject the concept to clarifying structural analysis. And on that knife's edge where the comic essence of

14 The *Epistolæ Obscurorum Virorum*, or "Letters of Obscure Men," was a sharply satirical literary prank carried out in sixteenth-century Germany, reflecting disputes between humanist scholars and the Catholic church. The resulting furore is thought to have contributed to the burgeoning Protestant Reformation.

15 The chronological aspect is not, however, enough to go on with regard to this interrelation: to say that Pushkin or Lermontov or some other old poet is being parodied means that the parody is no longer relevant, and therefore doesn't help with our argument here. We must not forget that certain old phenomena enter into the system of literature in a contemporary capacity. This is connected to the fascinating phenomenon of the *readdressed parody*: a parody of an old work or old author that meanwhile serves as the foundation for one or another contemporary trend in literature. This, in turn, demolishes a host of *formal* analogies on the basis of which works are joined into a forced and false unity, and suggests instead that works should necessarily be brought together according to their *functional* characteristic. For instance, it would have seemed quite natural to pair Blumauer's travestied *Aeneid* with his direct followers in Russia, Osipov and Kotliarevsky: but the *Aeneid* of Aloys Blumauer, the Viennese Jesuit, was simultaneously a political satire against the Pope and Rome and a reply to Schiller and Goethe and the "resurrection of antiquity." It is thus more of a parody of the "eighteenth-century Aeneid" than of Virgil's *Aeneid*, and "directed" toward Schiller and Goethe rather than Virgil. For more on this see: *E. Grisebach*. "Die Parodie in Oesterreich," in his book: *German Literature* [Die deutsche Litteratur] (Vienna: F. & P. Lehman, 1876), 175–213. Similarly, Pushkin readdressed his parody of the resurrecters of the ode (mostly Küchelbecker)[N] by parodying Khvostov. More recently, the parodist Izmailov parodied Trediakovsky by directing his parody toward Vyacheslav Ivanov—*YT*. Tynianov refers to Wilhelm Küchelbecker, a friend and colleague of Pushkin's, and Alexander Izmailov (1873–1921), an early twentieth-century essayist and parodist; for more on (Count) Khvostov and Vasily Trediakovsky,[N] see part four of this article.

the parodic genre and the comedic elements of the work being parodied both disappear, we can ask: is the point really in the comic?

The first half of Bouillet's definition is thus all the more important: "directed toward some work." This *directedness* is, of course, an important characteristic, and careful treatment of it immediately resolves a very important question.

But first, two preliminary observations: we will understand directedness to mean both the interdependence of one work with another, and a particular emphasis on this interdependence; we will subsequently go on to explain the particular character of this interdependence. And at this point we note that "*directedness toward some specific work*" once again defines the concept too narrowly. This is because the directedness can relate not only to a specific work, but also to a specific set of works unified by the characteristic of genre, author, or even literary movement.

When we analyze phenomena in terms of their directedness, we are immediately confronted with the very diverse nature of this directedness.

As a case in point, the political feuilleton in verse makes abundant use of old poetic models. Outside topics are inserted into the rhythmic-intonational template of Pushkin's or Lermontov's[N] "Prophet," or Derzhavin's[N] odes, that is, everything goes along as if the "parody" were directed toward these poems by Pushkin[N] or Lermontov, et al.[16] And if we limit ourselves to examining the work from within, in an isolated way, if we fail to take into account the interrelations of the work (as well as the work being parodied) with the literary system and, further, with speech and other more distant social series, then we cannot make sense of the specific nature of its directedness. Another complicating factor is that, given the firmly entrenched layman's definition of parody as a comic literary phenomenon, this kind of verse feuilleton with formally parodic elements (as an invariably comic genre) can appear to be a type of parody. But as soon as we analyze this work in all of its interrelations, it becomes clear that it is not *functionally parodic*, that consciously parodying a Pushkin or Lermontov poem for the thousandth time has a *different* kind of directedness.[17]

16 Alexander Pushkin (in 1826) and Mikhail Lermontov (in 1841) both wrote programmatic poems entitled "The Prophet," subsequently very well known by the Russian reading public. For Pushkin, see also "On the Composition of *Eugene Onegin*" (114–150).

17 This is the sense in which we should understand the title of the *Apparent Poetry* [Mnimaia poeziia] collection, which was taken from a historic old collection (*The Pocket Library of the Aonides, compiled from a few of the best writers of our day and laid out according to a new method* [...] [Karmannaia biblioteka Aonid ...] by Ivan Georgievsky (St. Petersburg: Tip. imperatorskogo vospitatel'nogo doma, 1821). The word "apparent" in the title did not have the negative

2

We should clarify our terms regarding an important point—the problem of the *formally parodic* and the *functionally parodic*; in other words—the problem of parodic form and parodic function.[18] Formal parody, or the formally parodic, is the application of parodic form to serve a non-parodic function. Using an existing work as a model for a new one is a very common phenomenon. But if the given works belong to different (say, thematic and lexical) environments, then something emerges that is formally close to parody while having nothing functionally in common with parody at all. A topical verse satire "directed" toward, say, a Pushkin or Lermontov poem, only *seems* directed: Pushkin and Lermontov are both equally irrelevant for the satirist, as are their poems, but the model they provide is a very convenient indicator of literariness, a sign of being anchored to literature in general. Furthermore, the manipulation of two semantic systems at once, conveyed through a single sign, produces an effect that Heine[N] (using a technical term from painting) called "underpainting," and considered to be a prerequisite for humor.[19]

And so we end up with the absence of *any directedness toward any work.*

This was already obvious to the angry reviewer of "The Twelve Sleeping Coppers,"[20] which was just such a non-parodic parody: "'The Twelve Sleeping

connotation that it has in contemporary language. In the *Pocket Library* this title refers to a section of verse quotations, verse maxims and "apothegms"; the word "apparent" in this case did not mean "not real," but rather "illusory." The editor of the collection probably had in mind the dissimilitude between verse quotations and the whole poems from which they were taken, and the possibility of "non-recognition"; illusory in this sense. This *illusory* quality is one of the distinctive conditions of parody. The connection between parody and citation will be treated in what follows—*YT*.

18 Tynianov has been using these terms since in the opening section of the article, but here he explains the difference as he sees it. He uses two slightly different Russian adjectives: *parodiinyi*, meaning functionally parodic, and *parodicheskii*, meaning formally parodic. In the absence of more than one English adjective, we have opted to retain the distinguishing adverbs (functionally / formally) in cases where the distinction is important; where no adverb is given, the less-marked term *parodicheskii* [formally parodic] can be assumed, sometimes in a meaning closer to "[neutrally] parodic."

19 For Heine, see also "Tyutchev and Heine."

20 "The Twelve Sleeping Coppers" [Dvenadtsat' spiashchikh butoshnikov] composed by Elistrat Fityulkin (Moscow, 1832). The author was V. A. Protashinsky, the Protasovs' stepbrother and a comrade of Nikolai Turgenev; thus this formally parodic work came out of a circle close to Zhukovsky[N]; evidently, it already existed in 1819. Cf. Vyazemsky's 1819 letter to A. I. Turgenev: "Zhukovsky is using Schiller and Goethe to wean us from the saccharine foodstuffs of the French table, but using his *coppers* and their ilk will ensure that our stomachs are unable to digest the Germans' brave and harsh vittles for some time to come" [Ostaf'evo

Coppers cannot be called a parody. It's just a bunch of malarkey in verse [...] mocking the tone of Zhukovsky's[N] lovely ballad for the sake of some laughs."[21]

(This example actually helps to prove that the functionally parodic and the formally parodic are systemic concepts, and cannot be conceived of outside the literary system: the application of the exact same formally parodic methods can have varying functions depending on the systemic (or extra-systemic) position of both the work being parodied and the work doing the parodying. As we have seen, the function of the "coppers" in the literature of the 1820s was not only formally parodic (auxiliary) but also functionally parodic; in the literature of the 1830s its position changed, and thus the functional parody was ousted from the structure of the work due to a preponderance of other elements.)

In fact, there is a more or less stable connection between parodic form and parodic function; there are conditions in place ensuring that this function does not change or turn into an auxiliary function. According to these conditions, the parodying and parodied works can be connected both through similar elements (rhythm, syntax, rhymes, etc.) and dissimilar ones—through opposition. In other words, a parody can be not only directed *toward* another work, but also *against* it.

There is yet another side to this deliberate, genre-based connection between the topical verse satire, political and social satires and parodic form.

For instance, let's look at the various formally parodic uses of Zhukovsky's "Bard in the Camp of the Russian Warriors" [Pevets vo stane russkikh voinov] (1812). There is a staggering number of parodies of this famous poem—including one by the young Pushkin,[22] as well as Batyushkov's literary satire ("Bard in the Colloquy of Slavo-Russians" [Pevets v Besede slavianorossov]),[23] which became no less famous than the original. This abundance cannot be explained by the poem's fame alone. Meanwhile, the character of the parodies (the fact that they are directed *toward,* not *against*) is best explained by Zhukovsky's

archive]. V. Saitov believes that "coppers" is a short, parodic name for "The Twelve Sleeping Maidens" [Dvenadtsat' spiashchikh dev]. Ostaf'evo archive: 1, 274, 616—*YT*. Zhukovsky's popular verse tale "The Twelve Sleeping Maidens" was published in 1811.

21 *Molva* 11 (1832): 41–43—*YT*.

22 Pushkin, "Students Feasting" [Piruiushchie studenty] (1814)—*AC*.

23 See A. I. Pisarev's literary satire "Bard Bivouacking at the Foot of Parnassus" [Pevets na bivakakh u podoshvy Parnasa] (1825), V. Maslovich's satire "Bard in the Epicures' Camp" [*Pevets vo stane Epikureitsev*] (1816), etc., all the way to D. D. Minaev's "Bard in the Russian Politicians' Camp" [*Pevets vo stane rossiskikh deiatelei*] and A. N. Apukhtin's[N] "Bard in the Russian Composers' Camp" [Pevets vo stane russkikh kompozitorov] (1875)—*YT*.

relationship to his own work. He seems to have had a hard time letting go of his poem, writing "Bard in the Kremlin" in 1814, which, according to the author's own explanation, presents "the bard of the Russian warriors after he has returned home, singing a song of liberation at the Kremlin." This is a highly typical phenomenon. The poem is modified, supplemented, brought to greater completion. And thus others modify it as well: for instance, in 1823 M. A. Bestuzhev-Riumin released just such a variation with an undisguised title, which was enough to signal that this was an intentional variation: "Bard Among the Russian Warriors Returned to their Fatherland in 1816" [Pevets sredi russkikh voinov, vozvrativshikhsia v otechestvo v 1816 godu]. And in the same year (1814) that he wrote "Bard in the Kremlin," Zhukovsky "sang his song again," this time in a parodic manner: a family event was the occasion for the poem "Carousel of Love, or the Five-year-old Melancholic Husks of Heartful Loving. A Tula Ballad" [Liubovnaia karusel' ...] (seven stanzas), the first line of which,

> В трактире тульском тишина
> [In a Tula tavern silence reigns]

serves as a kind of sign of parody (other parodies of the "Bard" also use the first line to set the parodic tone of the whole piece).[24]

If we inquire into the origins of this abundance of non-functionally parodic parodies, if we ask why this one poem proved so useful as an underlying parodic structure, we find our answer in the very process of the formally parodic manipulation of a work. This process not only involves taking the work out of the literary system (replacing it with something else), but also taking apart the work itself as a system. This process brings different aspects of the work into focus, aspects which were previously just elements of the system. Thus, a plot was discovered in the new "lyric-epic" genre of the "Bard," both in Zhukovsky's variations and the parodies; once stripped of its stylistic trappings, this plot turned out to be capacious and useful, even outside of its systemic form. The work yielded distinct formulas that could be used in a variety of thematic dimensions. This explains the peculiar phenomenon of "parodic selection": some works and some authors are subject to parodic use more often and more intensively than others.

---

24 V. A. Zhukovskii, *Collected Works in 4 vols.* [Sobranie sochinenii v chetyrekh tomakh], vol. 1 (Moscow/Leningrad: Gos. izd-vo khud. literatury, 1959–1960), 237. Zhukovsky's original "Bard in the Camp of Russian Warriors" begins with the line "On the field of battle silence reigns" [Na pole brannom tishina] (Zhukovsky, *Collected Works*, 1:149).

Here, when analyzing parody as a working process and taking into account the working aspects of parody, we can start to comprehend its connection with *imitation* and *variation*. When encountering *individual* facts, it is quite difficult to decide each time whether one is dealing with an imitation or a parody. On the one hand, as we saw in the example of Polevoi and Panaev, there is non-comic parody, and in many cases the line separating the parody from the parodied objects is very thin. On the other hand, an imitation can be very close, the connection to its work of origin can be obvious, while in its differentiating features it comes close to parody.

At the end of the 1820s, when both parodies and countless variations of Pushkin's long poems were being written, this was less a theoretical question than an entirely concrete phenomenon that critics had to contend with. For instance, this is how O. Somov responded to the imitations:

> And by the way, on parodies: the last year has seen not only dear departed Virgil subjected to them, but also the living Pushkin; for what, other than parodies of Pushkin's long poems, could you call the following works of poetry: "Eugene Velsky," "Confession on One's Thirtieth Year," "Prisoner of the Kyrgyz," "Love in Prison," "The Bandit," etc., etc.?[25] Calling them imitations does not do justice to the true quality of these poetic effusions, for they often *parody* Pushkin's lines: that is, either mutilate them, or take them wholesale and put them where they don't belong. But for the sake of argument, let's say these were pure parodies: then, when we encountered the poet's dreams and feelings in a new, humorous form, perhaps Pushkin himself might have a laugh along with us. But his so-called imitators, entirely humorless and untroubled by conscience, are just living off of his thoughts and ideas, characters and verses.[26]

The word "parody" has been translated as *re-singing* [Russian: *perepesn'*]. This old word comes to us from the early nineteenth-century literary theorist, poet, and parodist Ostolopov.[27] But the word didn't stick; it couldn't be applied as a term because "singing" was an excessively precise and literal translation of the "Greek" component. Still, this word takes us away from the stale and misleadingly

---

25 The titles listed by Somov are extremely close to those of major works by Pushkin, including *Eugene Onegin*, "Prisoner of the Caucasus," etc.

26 O. Somov, "A Survey of Russian Literature in 1828" [Obzor rossiiskoi slovesnosti za 1828 god] in *Northern Flowers* [Severnye tsvety] (1829), 53–54—*YT*.

27 Nikolai Ostolopov (1783–1833), a poet and literary critic, author of the *Dictionary of Ancient and New Poetry* [Slovar' drevnei i novoi poezii] (St. Petersburg: Tip. Imp. ros. akad., 1821).

precise word "parody" and, even more importantly, brings the concepts of parody and imitation or variations ("re-singing"—"reworking") nearer to each other.

The variations on poems—both one's own and others'—that occur in parody constitute an evolutionary phenomenon of tremendous significance, and include both reworked texts and self-parodies, which are found much more frequently than one might think. For instance, Ogaryov[N] returned to his poems time and time again. He has a variation on his own famous "Old House" ("Old house, old friend, I visited you …") entitled "Imitation of the Distant Past":

> Белый снег, старый друг, увидал я
> Наконец на чужбине тебя …
> [White snow, old friend, I saw / You in a strange land, at last]

He wrote similar variations of the poem "The Tavern." Interestingly, when drawing up these "imitations," Ogaryov's editor Gershenzon continued: "We also present here Ogaryov's other *parodies*."[28] This is followed by the parodies "Song of the Russian Nanny by her Noble Charge's Bedside" [Pesnia russkoi nian'ki u posteli barskogo rebenka] (subtitled by Ogaryov himself as "an imitation of Lermontov"), "Once there Lived a Stylish Knight" [Zhil na svete rytsar' modnyi] "But Reading Krayevsky is Not Worth the Trouble" [Chitat' zhe Kraevskogo ne stoit truda]; and two "Imitations of Pushkin" in a row:

1. Люблю народ, любовь моя не может Прийти в испуг отнюдь ни перед кем …	1. I love the people, my love cannot Be frightened off by anyone at all …
2. Я всех любил, любовь еще, быть может, В моей крови угасла не совсем …	2. I loved everyone, love still, perhaps, In my blood has yet to be snuffed out …[29]

I think the editor's slip, in using the word "parody" for variations on the poet's own poems and the chaotic distribution of the material, is entirely correct, because for Ogaryov the functions of both were very close.

The evolution of literature, and of poetry in particular, takes place both through the invention of new forms and—most often—through the applica-

28 N. P. Ogarev, *Poems* [Stikhotvoreniia], vol. 1 (Moscow: M. i S. Sabashnikovy, 1904), 383, 385—*YT.*

29 Ibid., 387. The two poems parody a famous love lyric by Alexander Pushkin: "I loved you, and love may still be …" [Ia vas liubil, liubov' eshche byt' mozhet …] (1829). In the previous paragraph, the "stylish knight" poem parodies Pushkin's "poor knight" [*rytsar' bednyi*], while the "Kraevsky" and "nanny" poems transparently refer to Lermontov.

tion of old forms to serve a new function. Both imitation and parody play a role in this, an instructive and experimental role. For instance, the role of parodies in Nekrasov's[N] work lies in the translation of old forms into new functions, and in this sense his school of parody is close to the way he himself appropriates old forms through imitation in his first collection; it is a sort of next level of study—an experiment. Nor does this exclude the functionally parodic meaning of these works, the way they are directed not only *toward* old phenomena, but in part, *against* them.

Thus, the difference between the formally parodic and the functionally parodic is a functional difference.

It is clear, meanwhile, that the fact of a work being directed toward another one (and even more so, *against* another one), i.e., its functionally parodic nature, is intimately connected with the significance of the other work in the literary system. (Only, one should not mix up significance with magnitude, overall value, etc.—a work can be of negligible value and at the same time be characteristic and even significant within a given system.) This is why functionally parodic works are usually directed toward phenomena of contemporary literature, or toward contemporary attitudes to old phenomena; a functionally parodic relationship to half-forgotten phenomena is hardly feasible. Consider a contemporary reviewer's remarks on parody in *The Contemporary* [Sovremennik]:[30]

> The "Greek Philosophers' Debate over Elegance" is written well enough, but we simply cannot find anything in our literature that serves as a motivation or original for this caricature: have you perhaps read, over the last thirty years, any "Wise Men's Conversations" or "Conversations on the Elegant and Beautiful" or anything else like that? None of these parodies [...] have a point, they have no topicality or life to them. Now that they have been written, we can soon expect to see parodies of Lomonosov's[N] odes, Sumarokov's[N] tragedies, Bogdanovich's "*Dushen'ka*," Kheraskov's "Rossiad" and M. N. Muravyov's[N] "Conversations in the Kingdom of the Dead."[31] The motto of parody should be: lively and modern.

30 *St. Petersburg Gazette* [Vedomosti], 1854, no. 80—*YT*.

31 The reviewer refers to major eighteenth-century poets Mikhail Lomonosov, Alexander Sumarokov, Ippolit Bogdanovich, Mikhail Kheraskov, and M. N. Muravyov. For Lomonosov and Sumarokov, see also "The Ode as an Oratorical Genre" (77–113).

But the formally parodic is a very widespread phenomenon and quite broad with regard to the works it uses as material. In our day, we are far more likely to see a formally parodic verse satire using material from Pushkin or Lermontov than from Blok.[N] While popular mainstream poets are a customary and rewarding object of functional parody, they are never used as the material for formal parody. And finally, while the functionally parodic is not necessarily tied to the comic, the formally parodic constitutes both a method and a characteristic of comic genres.

All the different methods of parodying consist, without exception, in changing a literary work, or an element that unites a series of works (an author, journal, almanac), or a series of literary works (a genre), as a system; in transferring them into a different system.

Properly speaking, each time a word is used in a new environment or context, there is a partial change in its meaning (Roswadowski).[32] Each time a literary fact is withdrawn from one system and introduced into another, we see the same partial change of meaning.[33] Consider the following two curious examples of the translation of elements from one system into another, with the second system actually being opposed to the first. The main actors in this unusual systemic interchange are, in the first camp, Karamzin[N] and Vyazemsky,[N] and in the second—Derzhavin.[34] Karamzin's literary system (Vyazemsky was his disciple) was essentially antagonistic toward Derzhavin's.

And then we have the following interchange.

Derzhavin wrote an ode, "The Spring," dedicated to Kheraskov. Vyazemsky writes, quoting the ode:

32 J. Roswadowski, *Wortbildung und Wortbedeutung. Eine Untersuchung ihrer Grundgesetze* (Heidelberg: Indogermanische Forschungen, 1904), 20, 25—*AC*.

33 It is hoped that the word "system" here will not be replaced by "reader reception." Dividing up literature between reader and writer is basically impossible, because neither writers nor readers are fundamentally different things. The writer is also a reader, and the reader, in constructing a literary work, follows the writer in doing exactly the same work. The opposition of reader to writer is furthermore incorrect because there are different readers and different writers. The writer in one cultural and social system is closer to the reader of the same system than he is to a writer from a different system. The question of "reader reception" comes up only when these questions are being addressed from a subjective-psychological point of view, instead of being examined in terms of system and function—*YT*.

34 For more on Karamzin, see also "On Literary Evolution" (especially 278) and "The Ode as an Oratorical Genre" (especially 109–112).

35 Derzhavin, *Sochineniia*, vol. 1, 48.

> Священный Гребеневский ключ!
> Певца бессмертной Россияды
> Поил водой ты стихотворства, —
>
> The sacred spring of Grebenevo!
> Him who sang the Immortal Rossiad
> You gave to drink of your poetic waters,—[35]

> A splendid epigram about Kheraskov […] When talking about his poetry, poetic waters is an exceptionally apt and funny expression![36]

Karamzin "found humorous a certain line" in Derzhavin's ode "On the Demise of a Benefactor." According to Grot and Pekarsky's well-founded conjecture, the lines are:[37]

> Как огнь лампады ароматный,
> Погас, распространил приятный
> Вкруг запах ты < … >[38]
>
> Like the flame of aromatic lamp
> Gone dark, a pleasant
> Smell you spread around […]

Derzhavin's metaphoric style was based on the bold juxtaposition of different semantic series; neither of the two examples mentioned would appear at all comical in his system. But when these lines were taken out of the whole of their respective works and transferred into the system of Karamzin and his followers—with their demands for "clarity," prosaic "precision," proximity of the concepts under comparison, and overall wittiness—Derzhavin's style changed: the meaning of the words changed, and Derzhavin became a parody of himself.

But the opposite also took place.

Consider, for instance, Derzhavin's response to Karamzin's poem "Epistle to Women." This epistle is autobiographical; its theme, fully in line with the Karamzinian system, is friendship with women. The epistle ends with the following lines:

> Что истина своей рукою
> Напишет над моей могилой? Он любил:

---

36 P. A. Vyazemsky, *Collected Works* (Sobranie sochinenii), vol. 8 (St. Petersburg: Izd. grafa S.D. Sheremet'eva, 1883), 15—*YT*.

37 Nikolai Karamzin, *The Letters of N. M. Karamzin to I. I. Dmitriev* (St. Petersburg: Tip. Imperatorskoi akademii nauk, 1866), 141—*YT*.

38 "On the Demise of a Benefactor, Which Took Place August 31 1795 in Saint Petersburg," *Aonides*, book 2 (Moscow: V universitetskoi tip., u Ridigera i Klaudiia, 1797), 152—*AC*.

Он нежной женщины нежнейшим другом был![39]
[What will Truth in her own hand / Write above my grave? He loved: / He was a tender friend to a tender woman!]

Already old, Derzhavin wrote in response to this poem: "I received the *Aonidy* from Nikolai Mikhailovich [Karamzin], a book with many beautiful poems. His epistle to women is particularly lovely, though I do not care for the ending, that is, the last line, which immediately makes one think:

Что с таковыми жен друзьями
Мужья с рогами.[40]
[That when wives have such friends / Their husbands wear horns.]"

This shows why personal correspondence was such a breeding ground for parody. The correspondence of Batyushkov, A. Turgenev,[N] Vyazemsky, and Pushkin is brimming with tiny, microscopic parodies, parodic verses, words, nicknames, etc.[41] The letter-writers were unrestrained, and this would quite naturally transfer the literary work under discussion—and really, all of literature—into everyday usage, provoking shifts in the system.

Here is one example of this kind of functionally parodic approach. Fyodor Glinka published two poems in the 1831 *Northern Flowers* that seemed predestined for parody. One should not think that all of Glinka's work is like this, or that he is of trifling significance. Pushkin acknowledged his significance in the 1830s; Glinka's natural-philosophical poems left a mark on Tyutchev. He is a complicated poet, and the following example is characteristic not of all of his poetry, but only the spiritual genres in which he worked most frequently, and which earned him Pushkin's nicknames: Kuteikin and Sexton F.[42]

---

39 "Poslanie k zhenshchinam," N. M. Karamzin, *Complete Poems* [Polnoe sobranie stikhotvorenii] (Leningrad: Sovetskii pisatel', 1966), 179.

40 Karamzin, *Letters*, 39—*YT*.

41 For more on the literary significance of Pushkin-era correspondence, also see the articles "Literary Fact" (especially 166–168) and "On Literary Evolution" (especially 271).

42 Kuteikin is a seminary student in eighteenth-century playwright Denis Fonvizin's comedy "The Minor" (1782). Fyodor Glinka (1786–1880) was a poet affiliated with the Decembrists in his youth.

These, then, are the poems published in *Northern Flowers*:

1. *Непонятная вещь*
Странная вещь!
Непонятная вещь!
Отчего человек так мятежен?
Отчего он грустит,
И душою болит,
Отчего так уныл, безнадежен?
Странная вещь!
Непонятная вещь!
и т.д.

1. *Incomprehensible Thing*
Strange thing!
Incomprehensible thing!
Why is man so troubled?
Why is he sad,
And his soul in pain,
Why is he despondent and hopeless?
Strange thing!
Incomprehensible thing!
etc.

2. *Бедность и утешение*
Не плачь, жена! мы здесь земные постояльцы;
Я верю: где-то есть и нам приютный дом!
Подчас вздохну я, сидя за пером;
Слезу роняешь ты на пяльцы:
Ты все о будущем полна заботных дум:
Бог даст детей? … Ну что ж?—пусть Он наш будет Кум!

2. *Poverty and Comfort*
Do not weep, my wife! We are but guests on this earth;
I believe: a sheltering home awaits us somewhere!
At times I sigh, seated with my quill;
You drop a tear onto your embroidery:
Engulfed by anxious thoughts about the future:
Will God grant us children? … Well then! Let Him be their Godfather!

The refrain "Strange thing! Incomprehensible thing!" is repeated at the end of each stanza; this exclamation, perhaps common in writing of a religious nature, along with the idea of "god as godfather," provoked a barrage of parody on Pushkin's part. He wrote to Pletnyov:[N]

> My dear, I saw the *Flowers*. Strange thing, incomprehensible thing! Delvig didn't put in a single line. He treated us like a landowner treats his serfs. We slave away and he sits there on his stool and scolds us. Neither nice nor prudent. He opens up our eyes, and we see that we've been duped. Strange thing, incomprehensible thing! Poor Glinka is working away like a mule and nothing comes of it. I think he's gone round the bend out of grief. Just look at who he's inviting to be his godfather! Imagine what he'd do to the priest, and the sexton, and the godmother and the midwife, and the godfather himself—he'd force him to swear off the devil and spitting,

> blowing, matchmaking and other such hanky-panky. Nashchokin insists that the dear departed tsar spoiled everyone by christening their kids. I still haven't gotten over Glinka's audacity. A strange thing, an incomprehensible thing![43]

Examining the conditions for parodic genesis can help us sort out several important questions.

For instance, the methods of parody can seem excessively *trivial*. After all, eighteenth- and early nineteenth-century theorists largely accepted the ancient theory that changing *one* letter (or sound) constituted a parodic method. Cf. Ostolopov: "Sometimes changing a single letter results in a parody. Cato, in speaking of Marcus Fulvius, changed his sobriquet from *Nobilior*, the most noble, to *Mobilior*, the most mercurial and changeable."[44] Of course, the point here is not the changing of a letter (or sound), but the pun that results. But the fact alone that a speech construction as minor as a pun counts as parody is characteristic; we see the same thing with parodies of single verse lines. Cf. Ostolopov again: "Citing a few well-known lines of verse, or just one line, without any changes, made up the third type of parody." (He proceeds to cite Lomonosov's well-known punning epigram directed toward a single line, or actually, a single expression, from Sumarokov's tragedy "Hamlet." This epigram is thus classified as a parody.)

The formally parodic methods used by the greatest writers of the nineteenth century were strikingly trivial. Pushkin, for instance, uses orthography to parody Kachenovsky.[45] Kachenovsky adhered to his own orthographic system, in which the Old Church Slavonic letter "*V*" and the "dotted i" played a prominent role. This is the orthography Pushkin uses in his epigram directed at Kachenovsky. Ultimately, the *Old Church Slavonic V* became the sign of Kachenovsky, his parodic designation. For instance, in Pushkin's "Journey to Arzrum," he writes of a certain abusive critic: "The review was overflowing with the usual flourishes of our criticism: it was a conversation between a sexton, a church-wafer baker, and a copy editor [...]."[46] Pushkin doesn't

---

43 Alexander Pushkin, *Pushkin's Writings* [Sochineniia Pushkina], vol. 2, *Letters*, ed. V. I. Saitov (St. Petersburg: Tip. Imperatorskoi Akademii nauk, 1908), 210–211—*YT*.

44 Ostolopov, *Dictionary of Ancient and New Poetry* [Slovar' drevnei i novoi poezii], 334—*AC*.

45 Mikhail Kachenovsky (1775–1842) was a historian and publisher known for his skepticism and the dullness of his lectures. His antagonism with the Karamzinists made him a favorite target for their epigrams.

46 Pushkin's "Journey to Arzrum" (1829) is a travelogue documenting the poet's adventures as he accompanies the Russian army through various locations in the Caucasus during the Russo-Turkish war.

mention either the journal that published the review or its author. But the manuscript has the word "copy editor" written with the Old Church Slavonic letter. In this way, without losing its parodic directedness, the instrument of parody became a sign, a marker, a brand,[47] whereby a given phenomenon could be recognized.[48]

Herzen can seem even more trivial.[49] His parodies deserve a closer look: *The Travel Notes of Mr. Vyodrin* (1843), which parodies Pogodin (Vyodrin is transparently a substitute for Pogodin), is a truly exceptional parody for the subtlety of its stylistic devices.[50] But this subtlety can, in some cases, qualify as triviality.

For instance, Herzen parodies both the stylistic particulars of Pogodin's style (his short, intentionally compact phrases, which had provoked jabs in the press and reviews that veered into parody) as well as the visual features of his writing, the punctuation of his short paratactic constructions.

In the parodic article "*The Muscovite* on Copernicus" (published in *Notes of the Fatherland*, 1843, book nine), Herzen copies out an obvious typo from an article published in *The Muscovite* (and edited by Pogodin): "'Tycho Brahe wrote poetry in honor of his instrument; known as a *paralacticum*, its abilities in painting are proved by his portrait, taken by himself.' What a surprise follows that semicolon!"[51]

---

47 The triviality of its speech signs renders Pushkin's language a completely conventional system, a sort of argot or secret language. For instance, Pushkin's circle used the word "küchelbeckerish," based on their friend's name and onomatopoeically indicating rather unpleasant sensations. And in a letter (to Gnedich, in 1822) Pushkin writes: "Things here are *moldovish* and nauseating, my God, something's happening with him—his fate troubles me in the extreme—tell me about him if you answer this." In this way the very method of producing a word became a marker, a representative of the whole word (referent); using the same kind of word production in "moldovish" made it possible to ask a question about Küchelbecker without naming him, just having pronouns refer to "him" [*Collected Works*, 9:42]—*YT.*

48 From this point on the text is reproduced from Tynianov's drafts—*AC.*

49 Alexander Herzen (1812–1870) was an émigré writer and political figure, known for his radically anti-tsarist, free-thinking and pro-democratic views. He has been called the "father of Russian socialism."

50 Herzen parodies Pogodin's *A Year in Foreign Lands* [God v chuzhikh kraiakh (Moscow: Univ. tip, 1844)]. Mikhail Pogodin (1800–1875) was a historian and journalist known for pan-Slavism. His last name derives from *pogoda*, "weather," while Herzen's parodic *Vyodrin* [Putevye zapiski g. Vyodrina], *Otechestvennye zapiski*, no 11 (1843) comes from *vyodro*, "good weather."

51 A. I. Herzen, *Complete Works and Letters* [Polnoe sobranie sochinenii i pisem], ed. M. Lemke. Vol. 3 (Petrograd: Literaturno-izdatel'skii otdel Narkomprosa, 1915), 273—*YT.*

Subsequently, in the *Travel Notes of Mr. Vyodrin*, Herzen uses the semicolon to emphasize how Pogodin's short sentences are formed from forcibly chopped up speech intervals:

> I run home ... about five versts—got hungry, my stomach was grumbling: but here civilization; had so appetizingly tossed liver into open shops; I took out a penny; they hacked me off a huge chunk, two handfuls, salt for free—of course, they have their own considerations. I noted that when one's chewing the road seems shorter. A gastrical illusion! A ragged little urchin came along selling boot tops, stolen somewhere; I had a look, German manufacture, I'd have haggled some—he wanted too much—let him go!"[52]

This triviality, however, seems entirely legitimate if we acknowledge that different types of speech, the individual difference between them, is actually most evident in the structural minutiae that act as markers for one or another type. But the roots of this phenomenon may be deeper still.

This reliance on speech phenomena may explain yet another fact: the unusual vivacity and popularity of parody, which at times crosses over into a peculiar kind of folkloric material.

In the early twentieth century, schoolkids in provincial grammar schools were fond not only of the famous recursive verse game "The priest had a dog ...," but also of the following:

Странная вещь,	Strange thing,
Непонятная вещь,	Incomprehensible thing,
Отчего человек потеет,	Why do people sweat,
И, потея, кряхтит,	And when they sweat, they wheeze,
И, кряхтя, говорит:	And when they wheeze, say:
«Странная вещь,	"Strange thing,
Непонятная вещь ... »	Incomprehensible thing ..."
и т.д.	etc.

Of course, the schoolkids had no idea that they were playing with a fragment from a parody of Fyodor Glinka's aforementioned poem, which had inspired even Pushkin to parody:

---

52 Ibid., 274—*YT*.

Странная вещь!	Strange thing!
Непонятная вещь!	Incomprehensible thing!
Отчего человек так мятежен? <...>	Why is man so rebellious? [...]

In the 1870s–1880s, people used to *sing* verse parodies of elegies in the Baratynskian vein: "Get your oranges 'n lemons ..."[53]

Thus parody can be isolated from the functionally parodic but still preserve, in its structure, the sense of a comical shift [*sdvig*] of systems, and so reveal itself to be valuable and stable material.

We will soon see the enormous influence humorous poems had on Trediakovsky's[N] posthumous literary fate: linked with his name through formal parody, these poems almost completely replaced all of Trediakovsky's own works in readers' imagination for two centuries.

The point is that, while laying bare the different speech series that are interrelated with various genres or trends, parody is itself interrelated with and dependent on specific speech phenomena.[54]

Imitative speech phenomena—*speech* parodies—have yet to be properly studied.

Tolstoy and Turgenev each left us with famous examples of speech parody—from one national system to another (see *War and Peace,* vol. four, part five, chapter eight; see *Rudin,* chapter two).[55] Zaletayev and Pigasov both parody songs and poems.[56] Zaletayev uses the *melody* as a kind of axis for stringing together physical-articulatory substitutes for the sounds of singing in French (also note Zaletayev's gestures: "exaggeratedly pursing his lips," "waving his hands").

We should also note that this was only perceived as parody after the fact, as a result of the juxtaposition of two language systems; here, the functionally parodic

---

53 Tynianov refers to a parody of Evgeny Baratynsky's mournful elegy "To Delvig" (1821), entitled "Elegy" [Elegiia] and signed "S-v." The parody shifts the focus from emotional matters to gastronomic concerns. See V. S. Morozova, O.N. Tsvigun, eds., *Apparent Poetry: Materials from the History of* 18th-19th*-century Poetic Parody* [Mnimaia poeziia] (Moscow: Academia, 1934). Tynianov's preface to this volume reprises many of his observations in this article.

54 For more on the interrelations between literature and extra-literary speech phenomena, also see "On Literary Evolution" (especially 277–279).

55 Tynianov refers to Zaletayev, a minor character (a captive soldier) in [Leo] Tolstoy's *War and Peace.* Pigasov is a minor character (a buffoon and a nobody) in [Ivan] Turgenev's *Rudin.*

56 Pigasov is, across the board, Turgenev's inveterate speech parodist. See a spot later cut by Turgenev (I. S. Turgenev, *Polnoe sobranie sochinenii v 28 t.* (Moscow/Leningrad: Izd. Akademii nauk SSSR, 1960–68), 6:468—*YT.*

came down to 1) the melodic and physical-articulatory resemblance; 2) following that, the phonetic differences, moving closer to the Russian language system (cf. in particular the word *detravagala*); 3) when French speech is translated into the Russian language system, the meaning of the song was eliminated.[57]

Of course, Pigasov's parodying is much more complex and more literary, although his now-famous phrase[58] contains the very same speech mimicry.[59]

The facts of speech parody, like the facts of speech fashion, are naturally more complicated and intriguing when examined within the context of a national language system.

Cf. the mimicking of the speech of the intelligentsia and nobility that Zoshchenko takes as literary material.[60]

3

When elements from one system of poetic language, which are interrelated with certain speech series, are entered into a different system interrelated with different series, a change of dimensions takes place. Suppose that elements of low style, which are interrelated with everyday speech series, are entered into the ode, which is in turn interrelated with oratorical speech. The speech that was attributed to an abstract "orator," a mouthpiece of odic speech, becomes the speech of a concrete public speaker; the height of the oratorical podium is lowered. This is an example of genre parody.

---

57 Any given language system allows for the possibility of a type of literary parody, similar to the one described above, in which phonetic intensity devolves into speech mimicry. Cf., for example, a rare parody by Otto Erich Hartleben of the famous German Modernist Richard Dehmel:

> Du,
> Die du da dem da
> Der dich dort am ehbruchsschwülln,
> Dich in Brünsten gabst,
> Du - - - - —*YT.*

58 Pigasov's phrase depends on his mangling of Russian spelling norms, in the direction of Ukrainian—see Turgenev, *Polnoe sobranie*, 6:255—*AC.*

59 The speech parodying of Ukrainian literary phenomena appears in Russian literature as early as the 1830s–1840s, when the role and participation of Ukrainians in Russian literature and culture was tremendous. See the 1830s parodic collection *The Thistle* [Chertopolokh] (St. Petersburg, 1830) [...]—*YT*

60 Tynianov refers to Mikhail Zoshchenko (1894–1958), a major prose writer popular in the 1920s for his satirical miniatures that foregrounded the speech habits of various (often clashing) class groups.

If we decide to go after the precise definition of a given poetic genre according to theme, or style, or some other element derived from a set of works, we will find ourselves retreating before that phenomenon's instability. Genres differ as *systems*, along two axes at once: first, they are interrelated with each other within the literary system; second, they are interrelated with various speech tendencies. For instance, the ode is interrelated with the elegy, the epistle, etc. within the literary system, while at the same time, the ode is oriented toward oratorical speech, the elegy is oriented toward singing, and the epistle (of a certain kind) is oriented toward dialogic speech, etc.

The evolution of genres depends on changes in the interrelations between members of a system (e.g. the "struggle" between the ode and the elegy, the "victory" of the elegy), which are changes in the interrelations between various tendencies of speech activity. This usually results in either the combination of genres or even the complete disappearance of some of them, i.e., the transformation of the genre system.[61]

Different speech tendencies constitute a fact that is interrelated with a given society's social structure and its changes and is determined by them.

Of course, the prevalence of the oratorical tendency over the melodic-romantic, of the grandiose style of the ode over the intimate style of the elegy, is very closely tied to both the social conditions governing the genesis or emergence of a particular literary genre, and to the process by which the genre will continue to exist, change, and exert influence.

Parody, therefore, does not entail replacing grandiose *themes* with minor ones, or substituting corresponding stylistic elements. Since every work constitutes a systemic interaction and correlation [*korreliatsiia*] of elements, there are no unmarked elements; if one element is replaced by another, it means that a sign from another system has been introduced into the system; this introduction results in the destruction of the systemic quality (or actually, makes clear its provisional nature).

The simplest and most powerful method of verse parody is intonational or melodic parody. Try reading a poem using intonations borrowed from a different speech series, say, those of a stuffy business conversation: what you get is parody. The same is true of melodies. I once heard the poem "Glory to you,

---

61 Both these possibilities tend to significantly complicate the study of genre evolution, which makes it all the more necessary to conduct wide-reaching research into every case of genre definition, studying not only the interrelations between genres of a literary system, but also the more distant series on which these genres depend—*YT*.

inescapable pain" sung to the tune of "To the fair, to the fair, a rakish merchant went ..." (I think this was Mayakovsky's[N] parody).[62] Since the melody fit perfectly with all the variations of the "To market ..." song and was colored by them, the resulting parody was rude and harsh.

But changing some stylistic devices, while leaving others intact, leads to the same phenomena, with all of their attendant consequences.

And these consequences are enormous.

Authorial speech, when it is violated and displaced, becomes the *speech of the author.*

The provisional nature of the system is laid bare, and authorial manipulation of speech is replaced by the *author's speech behavior*; the *speech position* is replaced by a *speech pose*. The fate of the author is like that of the protagonists of Romantic-era dramatic parodies: for example, Tieck's play "Puss in Boots."[63]

Prince Nathaniel arrives from distant lands to woo the princess. Her father, the king, asks the prince where his country is located. The prince answers that it is very far away:

> O great king, if you were to leave from here, you would need to go down the big road, then take a right, and keep riding, bearing right all the while, and when you get to the mountain—take another left, and that way you'll get to the lake, and keep riding north (if, of course, there's a good wind), and then, if everything goes well, in about a year and a half you will make it to my realm.

(Both characters' speech is pointedly casual and even recognizably that of a "Berliner").

Following these interrogations, the king is entirely satisfied, but at the end asks:

> Yes, just one more question: please tell me, if you live so far away, how is it that you speak our language so fluently?

---

62 Tynianov refers to Anna Akhmatova's[N] "Glory to you, inescapable pain!" (the first line in "The Grey-eyed King," Akhmatova, *Poems and Long Poems* [Stikhotvoreniia i poemy] 44; and the well-known Russian folksong "Ekhal na iarmarku ukhar'-kupets ..." (verses by I. S. Nikitin). For more on Akhmatova and Mayakovsky, see also "Interlude" (183–184 and 185–190, respectively).

63 Ludwig Tieck (1773–1853) was a major figure in early German Romanticism. His "Puss in Boots" [Der gestiefelte Kater] (1797) is a dramatic satire presented as a fairy-tale for children.

NATHANIEL. Shh!

THE KING. What?

NATHANIEL. Shh! Quiet!

THE KING. I don't understand.

NATHANIEL, *whispering*. Please, don't say anything about that, or else the audience, which is down there, will notice that this is, in fact, very unnatural.

Tieck expanded the space of the stage to include the space of the theater, and introduced extra-systemic elements into the system of his protagonist's speech—everyday elements that were not consistent with the conventions and conventionality of speech relations in the drama. As a result, what was exposed was not the protagonist's manipulation of speech, but the actor's speech *behavior*.

Much as an *actor* replaces a *protagonist* in theatrical-dramatic parody, an authorial personality, using ordinary everyday gestures, replaces the character of the author in verse parody.

4

This brings us to the curious phenomenon of the *parodic personality*.

Historically, parody has appeared not only in functionally parodic genres, that is, as full-fledged parodies—parody can also be a process. A functionally parodic relationship to the literary system draws out a host of amorphous, not yet crystallized literary phenomena (cf. my earlier comments on Pushkin and Vyazemsky's correspondence). These phenomena can then attach themselves to a literary personality, are strung onto it and cycle around it. There may be only a few fully crystallized parodies, but the literary personality itself becomes *parodic*.

Meanwhile, the living personality of the writer, the flesh-and-blood writer, can either become slightly deformed or distorted to the point of being unrecognizable, or—in rare cases—can be entirely absent.

Such was the role played by Count Khvostov and Prince Shalikov in early nineteenth-century literature (we can even delimit the period more precisely: in the 1820s).[64] An analysis of their literary personalities helps to clarify a great deal about the unusual phenomenon of the literary personality Kozma Prutkov,

64 (Count) Dmitri Khvostov (1757–1835) was a statesman and famous graphomaniac of the late eighteenth / early nineteenth century. Pyotr Shalikov (1767–1852) was a poet and journalist of a sentimentalist,[T] Karamzinian bent.

and likewise of the figure of General Dityatin.[65] First and foremost, certain aspects of literary structure shape the way a parodic personality is constructed: a necessary condition for this personality is that it be brought out of its original system and integrated into a different one.

Both Khvostov and Shalikov were more than just Pylyaev's eccentrics and Burnashev's miracle workers.[66] It is utterly impossible to understand both men's fame, the deafening literary boom and bluff that surrounded both of these literary names, if we forget that both of them were functionally parodic representatives of literary systems.

Count Khvostov is not quite the same person as the Grafov, Svistov, Khlystov, or Oslov known from parodies and epigrams.[67]

For the mostly invented, anecdotal tradition with which these names are associated, we can turn to Burnashev, a notorious inveterate liar and author of memoirs diligently cobbled together from low-quality and fantastical material and scattered among various journals. Not only because Khvostov's parodic image does not include, say, his bibliographic works; but mostly because this flesh-and-blood Khvostov turned out to be an ideal whetstone for honing a particular kind of formally parodic style—and ultimately even became its victim (this occasionally befell those who parodied him as well).

Khvostov was a poet of the "Colloquy of Lovers of the Russian Word" group, clearly a third-rate poet even in the context of his literary movement and time; a poet of mistakes and anomalies.[68] But not all mistakes and

65 Kozma Prutkov (1803–1863) was an imaginary writer created by Aleksei Tolstoy and the brothers Aleksei, Vladimir, and Alexander Zhemchuzhnikov in the 1850s. A fatuous bureaucrat devoted to his service, Prutkov became famous for his glaringly tautological, yet memorable, aphorisms and sharply satirical poems. General Dityatin (whose last name suggests a word for "child") was a character created by the writer and actor Ivan Gorbunov (1831–1896); Dityatin was known for expressing a humorously outdated view of the world. For more on both, see section five of this article.

66 Tynianov refers to M. I. Pylyaev and V. P. Burnashev, authors, respectively, of *Remarkable Eccentrics and Originals* (St. Petersburg, Izdanie Suvorina, 1898) and *Our Miracle-workers. A Chronicle of All Manner of Weirdness and Eccentricity* (Nashi chudodei. Letopis' chudachestv i ektsentrichnostei vsiakogo roda, ed. Kas'ian Kas'ianov [St. Petersburg: Tip. V. Tushnova, 1875]).

67 The name "Khvostov," while ordinary sounding in Russian, features the root word "tail" [*khvost*]. The other last names listed, which refer to him, sound more openly ridiculous: Grafov (*graf* is count, thus "Count Countson"), Svistov (*svist*, whistle), Khlystov (*khlyst*, whip or flagellant) or Oslov (*osel*, donkey).

68 For the early nineteenth-century, aesthetically conservative ("Archaist"[T]) "Colloquy of Lovers of the Russian Word" [*Beseda liubitelei russkogo slova*], see also "The Ode as an Oratorical Genre" (112).

anomalies are alike, after all: and indeed, Khvostov's mistakes and anomalies belonged to the same category as the ones Derzhavin made, which were discussed earlier. One could say he was picking up the tab for Derzhavin's eighteenth century.

If we analyze the polemics against "Lovers of the Russian Word," we can see that Khvostov was just one of several candidates—though one of the most obvious—for the position of parodic personality. Similar attacks and mockery were aimed at Bobrov, Shatrov, Nikolev, and a few others.

Cf. Karamzin's comments: "You must have read Nikolev's odes [...] and Khvostov's ode, published as a *poem*, in the 'Academic Journal.' What poetry! what taste! what language! My God! have mercy upon us!" (1791).[69]

Also cf. Pushkin's "proscription list": *And Nikolev, departed poet ...* [70]

It is of no small significance that Khvostov was associated with the "Colloquy" group. Attitudes toward him as a poet tended to reflect one's attitude toward the "Colloquy." And one way to ridicule the group was to make Khvostov its representative.

But the choice had been made. First of all, Count Khvostov did not wish to die (he lived until 1835 and wrote until the very end of his life). His time had long since passed on, but he persisted, displaying remarkable vitality. One might say that the longer he lived, the more his activity expanded. The features of a third-rate poet confident in his talent were blown up to incredible proportions. The eighteenth-century poetic custom of responding to societal and political events was exaggerated to the point that Count Khvostov would respond to any and every possible event. The custom of sending one's books to acquaintances, also typical of eighteenth-century aristocratic dilettantes, began to resemble an egregious flood. But it should be added that these features didn't appear on their own; they were supported by the literature in which Khvostov had gone so astray. Like the protagonist of a parody, he had been transferred from one literary system into another. These features were encouraged. It was as if Khvostov had been placed into a special literary incubator. For Khvostov's obnoxiousness alone is not enough to explain the hyperbolic style that accompanied the praise and commendations written to him.

---

69 Karamzin, *Letters*, 19—*YT*.

70 Tynianov refers to a humorous poem embedded in an April 1816 letter from Pushkin to his uncle, V. L. Pushkin. The poem calls for the resurrection of reason and decency in matters of state, but then lists a number of writers "who would better stay forgotten," including Khvostov. See Alexander Pushkin, *Sobranie sochinenii v 10–i tomakh*. Moscow: GIKhL, 1959–1962), 1:356.

Khvostov was needed as a fulcrum, as a protagonist in the development of a specific system of formally parodic style.

Due to his important position in high society and at court (he was a favorite and close relative by marriage to Field Marshal Suvorov), as well as the appointments he held, Khvostov was influential, a member of the aristocracy.[71] Attacks on the talentless poet might be punished by the grand nobleman. And so a specific system of speech behavior took shape around Khvostov.

First came the art of the *evasive* and ambiguous compliment (cf. Karamzin's letter to Dmitriev). Then evasiveness was combined with hyperbole, and finally the prevailing style in relation to Khvostov ultimately became that of pure hyperbole (cf. Pushkin: "Count Khvostov, a poet beloved by the heavens").[72]

Accordingly, the primary function of this style was ambiguity. The protagonist of letters and epistles was assigned one stylistic function, while all the others had a different one. This was something like a secret language with its own rules, to be used with only one personality. And the personality in question managed his role superbly, for his part almost never allowing the real, flesh-and-blood Khvostov into the game. We have reason to believe that Count Khvostov *the senator* understood the style of the works in which he was the protagonist. There was an unspoken understanding between the authors and their protagonist, who was reluctant to break up a game that had been taken this far. At any rate, we see proof of this in an episode that is the high point of all Khvostoviana.

The pinnacle of this development was Dashkov's famous speech.[73] But this speech also reveals certain finer points in the connection between a specific function and a specific form. The hyperbolic style of the compliments had become too unrestrained, had outstripped its function—that of ambiguity, the seesawing between two opposite crests of meaning—and its openly ironic nature was revealed to all, including the protagonist himself.

---

71 Suvorov was a key figure in the 1812 campaign against Napoleon and remains one of the most illustrious military leaders in Russian collective memory.

72 The line comes from Pushkin's long poem "The Bronze Horseman" (1833). Ibid., 3:295.

73 The reference is to a speech read by D. V. Dashkov to the "Free Society of Lovers of Literature, Science and the Arts" [Vol'noe obshchestvo liubitelei slovesnosti, nauk i khudozhestv] group on 14 March 1812. *Readings in the Imperial Society of History and Russian Antiquities at Moscow University* [Chteniia v imp. Ob-ve. istorii drevnikh i rossiiskikh pri Moskovskom u-te], book 4, section 5 (Moscow: Universitetskaia tipografiia, 1861), 183–186—*AC*. In a speech dripping with irony, Dashkov solemnly "welcomed" Khvostov as a new honored member of the Society—scandal erupted and Dashkov himself was compelled to quit the society.

Balance was crucial here, and it was tipped to such a degree that the protagonist could not go on pretending and playing along. For a split second, the literary personality became a private individual. Still, the art of ambiguous speech was very difficult, even with the protagonist's consent. The form had a double function—hyperbolic speech was not only latently ironic, but also openly hyperbolic.

One and the same form could have opposite functions, and this form was often used specifically in a complimentary function. Khvostov had special audiences living in his house (cf. Shchedritsky, et al.),[74] and he gave critics who studied and praised his works well-paid university appointments.

Secondly, the protagonist himself could be quite clever: for instance, he brought younger and less experienced poets into this ambiguous game, and they did not always find honorable ways out of this predicament. Cf., for instance, what Katenin wrote about Yazykov[N] and Delvig.[75]

Yazykov, too, was pulled into Khvostov's circle on somewhat false pretenses, and found himself in an uncomfortable position.

Some of Pushkin's poems are almost impossible to understand without grasping their relationship toward the secret rules of Khvostoviana (and even more so outside of their ironic context); Yazykov, too, takes a slight, barely noticeable jab at Khvostov in the ironic wording of the first stanza of his second epistle:

Младых поэтов Петрограда
Серебровласый корифей,[76]
[The silver-tressed luminary/Of Petrograd's fledgling poets,]

Yazykov's first epistle to Khvostov, meanwhile, could be shown freely by its addressee to any and all.

---

74 Tynianov refers to Izmail Alekseevich Shchedritsky (1792–1869), a professor at Moscow University remembered for a few flattering verses to Khvostov.

75 "Count Khvostov's correspondence on his seventy-first year is laughably pathetic: how is the senator, an old man, not ashamed to be publishing ridiculous epistles to youths like Yazykov and Delvig? How can he not see that they are making a fool of him?"—from *Letters of P. A. Katenin to N. I. Bakhtin* [Pis'ma P.A. Katenina k N. I. Bakhtinu] (St. Petersburg: Elektrotip N. Ia. Stoikovoi, 1911), 116; Katenin refers to Khvostov's brochure "A Correspondence in Verse. On the Author's 71st Year" (St. Petersburg, 1828); the epistle to Delvig is not included in this publication—*AC*.

76 Nikolai Iazykov, *Collected Poems* [Sobranie stikhotvorenii] (Moscow: Sovetskii pisatel', 1948), 166.

Yazykov defended himself in a letter to his family: "Here's the story. We got word that the fifth volume of his poems, recently published, contains some of his most ridiculous work yet; the desire to own this volume—and for free—inspired me to write my epistle to Khvostov: in return I received both an epistle and the fifth volume."[77]

In any event, the phenomenon of the *formally parodic personality* is essentially the same phenomenon found in the functionally parodic genres: the line that separates parody from serious literature is very fine. If Delvig's parody was presented to readers of the 1820s as a melancholy song, those same readers would doubtless have read Yazykov's epistle to Khvostov with straight faces as well.

As the game dragged on, its scope became ever more grandiose; the hyperbole of the style seemed to infect the protagonist himself, and push him to ever greater lengths. Khvostov sent his own marble bust to the sailors of Kronstadt. A ship was named after Khvostov, and the naval minister inquired into the reasons behind this strange occurrence. Khvostov had agents watching Izmailov, his literary nemesis. Khvostov distributed copies of his portrait to posting stations. At the same time, an illustration for Izmailov's fable "The Versifier and the Devil," which featured a tiresome versifier and made obvious allusions to Khvostov, became a popular woodcut [*lubok*]. To judge the extent of its dissemination, cf. the following account of a traveler […][78]

The game took on Homeric dimensions. And yet Khvostov was a member of academies. Critics who doubled as panegyrists of Khvostov enjoyed his special support and received professorships. He squandered his fortune through this gamble on literature and fame. He achieved that *sublime de bêtise* [French, "sublime stupidity"—*YT*] that Küchelbecker wrote about. There wasn't even room for him in Voeykov's "Madhouse":

> Ты дурак, не сумасшедший,
> Не с чего тебе сходить.
> [You haven't lost your mind, you fool, / You haven't anything to lose.][79]

---

77 Letter from 14 September 1827—Yazykov archive, Issue 1: *Letters from N.M. Yazykov to his Family during his Derpt Period (1822–1829)* [*Pis'ma N.M. Iazykova k rodnym za derptskii period ego zhizni*] (St. Petersburg: Izd. Otd-niia russkago iazyka i slovesnosti Imp. Akademii nauk, 1913), 342. It should be noted that both Katenin and Polevoi used the ambivalence of the evasive and hyperbolic style to their advantage—*YT*.

78 The traveler in question is Vyazemsky. At this point there is a gap in Tynianov's manuscript—*AC*.

79 The poet and journalist Alexander Voeykov (1778–1839) wrote his poem "The Madhouse,"

Having begun with subtleties and sneers, the Khvostov game (Karamzin suggested that every home should have a Khvostov room, while Vyazemsky recommended a museum) outgrew itself and crossed over into an open conflict between living literature and official life.

The elderly Khvostov's complaints at having been excluded from the eighteen-volume *Collection of Exemplary Works* [*Sobranie obraztsovykh sochinenii*] (which included some poets who were in no way better, or even downright worse, than he), at the conspiracy of silence and the vacuum forming around him—these complaints, when accompanied by the stubborn pose of a misunderstood genius which he assumed at the parodists' prompting, were no longer comical.

The scope of this article does not include a detailed analysis of the literary fate of the people and poets who served as material for functionally parodic personalities.

I will just note that, much as Khvostov was ejected from the eighteenth-century system and inserted into the first quarter of the nineteenth as a representative of the Colloquy group, with its "lyricists" and "ode-writers," Shalikov was the scapegoat of the Karamzin school. As a writer, Shalikov cannot be compared to Khvostov. If we were to quote one or two of his poems, it would be easy to mistake him for Karamzin or even Batyushkov. His literary and publishing activity was very lively. But as a poet and a man of letters, Shalikov possessed certain qualities that presented potential material for parody. The journalist's pugnacious temperament was not a natural match for delicate subjects and refined style. In the 1820s, he belonged to the generation which Pushkin described as follows:

Тут был в душистых сединах	And that old man … with scented hair
Старик, по-старому шутивший:	Who joked both cleverly and wryly
Отменно тонко и умно,	In quite a keen old-fashioned way,
Что нынче несколько смешно.[80]	Which seems a touch absurd today.[81]

a searing satire of contemporary letters, between 1814 and 1831 (he constantly updated the poem with portraits of new poets and writers as they appeared in the literary scene). Alexander Voeykov, *Poety 1790–1810-kh godov* (Leningrad: Sovetskii pisatel', 1971), 292–302.

80 Quoted from Pushkin, *Eugene Onegin*, chapter 8, 24—*AC*. Pushkin, *Sobranie sochinenii*, 4:165.

81 Alexander Pushkin, *Eugene Onegin: A Novel in Verse*, trans. James Falen (Oxford: Oxford University Press, 1995), 246. Translation slightly modified.

There are almost no parodies of Shalikov's poetry, and his work from the 1820s has been forgotten—but Shalikov himself became the parodic Vzdykhalov and the "mournful newspaperman," the protagonist of epigrams and jokes.[82]

The study of Shalikov should focus on how the parodied individual's actual literary activity and his living personality are not equivalent to the phenomenon of his functionally parodic personality.

In this respect, the history of someone like Trediakovsky can be an instructive example. He too became a functionally parodic personality, a target of sorts for humorous verse of various periods and systems. This verse was not even Trediakovsky's own work, and was not intended as parody, even though it became parody in a practical sense.[83]

Likewise, some of Trediakovsky's own poems fulfill the same function: poems that have been wrenched from their system, from the system of Trediakovsky's poetry and time—and outside of it they indeed seem strange or funny.

We have already mentioned that this separation or withdrawal from the system, as a partial alteration of meaning, is a typical element of literary parody.

In this way citation, its functionally parodic directedness notwithstanding, can, under certain conditions, play a functionally parodic role—and, in any event, can characterize the attitude toward a poet more than it characterizes the poet himself.

Consider the following excerpts:

1) Частая сеча меча	1) The frequent slashing of the sword
Сильна могуща плеча.	Makes mighty the strong-armed.
Стали о плиты стуча,	Clanging steel against the slabs,
Ночью блеща, как свеча,	Shining candle-bright in night,
Эхо за эхами мча,	Speeding echo after echoes,
Гулы сугубит, звуча.	Doubling rumbling as it sounds.
2) Се — ярый мученик, в ночи скитаясь, воет;	2) Behold—a raging martyr, wand'ring by night, howls;
Стопами тяжкими вершину Эты роет.	With heavy tread rends down the peak of Oite.

82 For Vzdykhalov (the name is patently humorous, something like "Mr. Sigh-a-lot"—*trans.*), see P. A. Vyazemsky, "Vzdykhalov's Departure," etc.—*AC*. The "mournful newspaperman" comes from a Pushkin epigram ("Prince Shalikov, our mournful newspaperman …").

83 It is curious that Trediakovsky's own parodies of paeonic verse were attributed to him as actual serious work—*YT*.

3) Преславный Град, что Петр наш основал,	3) Most glorious City, which our Peter founded,
И на красе построил толь полезно:	And built with such a beauty and a use:
Уж древним всем он ныне равен стал;	Has now become the equal of all ancients;
И обитать в нем всякому любезно.	And every man does love to dwell there.

The first excerpt is from Derzhavin, the second from Pushkin and the third from Trediakovsky.[84]

The quotation from Pushkin is perhaps the most curious. Reading the whole poem, "A cloak suffused with caustic blood …" ("From A. Chenier," 1835) leaves one convinced that poetic language is a complex and extensive network, and not merely a point on the tracks running between the "good" and "bad" stations. In this poetic translation, Pushkin attempts to enter the system of archaic style.[85]

The excerpted lines from this poem, meanwhile, could even be attributed to the functionally parodic Trediakovsky. And this folkloric Trediakovsky is a phenomenon with unusually deep roots, one that almost completely overshadows the concrete literary facts.

The functionally parodic personality is extremely influential: when the conditions are right, different phenomena in free variation will attach themselves to it. The personality thus constitutes a substitute fact, its double.

All the more important that we study it.

5

The Kozma Prutkov phenomenon is closely tied to both the formally and functionally parodic genres.

Of course, this phenomenon deserves further study, and will not be treated here in full. The Prutkov phenomenon is intriguing because of the complete and full character of the functionally parodic personality, which is not actually tied to any flesh-and-blood literary biography. The poetry of Prutkov's joint creators—Aleksei Tolstoy and the Zhemchuzhnikov brothers—is distinct from Prutkov's style.

The functionally parodic pseudonym is a frequently encountered phenomenon of the specific culture around thick literary journals in the 1850s.

---

84 Derzhavin, "Perseus and Andromeda"; Trediakovsky, "In Praise of the Izherian Land …"—AC. Derzhavin, *Sochineniia*, 2:391; V. K. Trediakovskii, *Selected Works* [Izbrannye proizvedeniia] (Moscow/Leningrad: Sovetskii pisatel', 1963), 178.

85 Pushkin, *Sobranie sochinenii*, 2:433.

On the pages of the journal *Entertainment,* the name Kozma Prutkov looks like just another pseudonym among many. And his transformation into a formally parodic personality with a biography was preceded by a proliferation of pseudonyms in the journals—the "Follower of Kuzma Prutkov" appeared practically at the same time as [...] and Kuzma Prutkov.[86]

The pseudonym accrued associations in the journal and was gradually concretized. This process of concretization was completed through the alternation of *functionally parodic* poems with humorous, formally parodic poems, as well as formally parodic prose. At one point S.A. Vengerov was at a loss trying to find the connection between brilliant and subtle literary parodies like "Quietly above the Alhambra ..." and the bureaucrat from the Assay Office. There is no direct, self-evident connection—and this, more than anything else, is why K. Prutkov was more than just the pseudonym of parodists, why he became a formally parodic personality in his own right.

Of course, the crucial thing in the work of this pseudonymous *parodist* was the orientation[T] toward the works being parodied, the interrelations[T] with them;[87] but the unity of the formally parodic style is not a simple or straightforward matter. The alternation of parodies with humorous verse featuring a concrete speaker lends a certain speech tonality to these parodies as well.

The formally parodic personality of Kozma Prutkov was created through a stylistic approach. The concreteness of this personality depends neithetr on the "biography" of its collective creators nor even on Prutkov's imaginary biography (since that biography is very straightforward and short).

This article will not include an examination of General Dityatin, a functionally parodic personality of the theater created by Gorbunov.

It should be mentioned, however, that this theatricalized parody was in part created using formally parodic literary materials as a base. Cf. the general's romances:

Тучи черные
Мой гарнизон покрыли.
[Black stormclouds / Have covered my garrison.[88]]

86 The ellipsis marks a blank in the manuscript—*AC.*

87 For orientation [*ustanovka*], see also "On Literary Evolution" (277–279) and "The Ode as Oratorical Genre" (throughout, but especially 77–79).

88 "Garrison" in place of "horizon" [the word in Russian, *gorizont,* more closely resembles "garrison"]—*YT.*

Cf. the general's famous speech at a luncheon in honor of "Ivan Turgenev, collegiate secretary," etc.[89]

The laws for the creation of this literary personality are essentially the same as those governing the fundamental parodic devices: General Dityatin was a man of the old Nicholas I-era "society," who was withdrawn from his own system and entered into another one as a formally parodic fulcrum.

The history of Russian parody awaits further study.

Russian parody has hidden layers (for instance, the parodic layers of the groups vying with Pushkin in the 1830s). The history of parody is intimately tied to the evolution of literature.

The baring of convention and the unmasking of speech behavior and speech poses are part of the enormous evolutionary work done by parody.

The process of mastering any literary phenomenon is the process of mastering it as a structure, as a system connected and interrelated with the social structure. This process of mastering hastens the evolutionary succession of aesthetic movements.

---

89 I. F. Gorbunov, *Collected Works* [*Sobranie sochinenii*], vol. 1 (St. Petersburg: A.F. Marksa, 1904), 304–305—*AC.*

APPENDIX

Names and Terms

Names

Note that names are given, as in the text of the articles, according to common pronunciation rather than LOC transcription.

Anna AKHMATOVA (1889–1966) (real name: Anna Gorenko), a seminal twentieth-century poet affiliated with the Acmeist group in pre-revolutionary St. Petersburg. Her work is marked by brevity, a simple but refined lexicon, and a restrained exploration of powerful emotions. [Interlude, Parody]

Sergei AKSAKOV (1791–1859), father of Konstantin and Ivan Aksakov; a writer and memoirist known particularly for his evocations of noble country life. [Ode, D&G]

Ivan AKSAKOV (1823–1886), son of Sergei and brother of Konstantin (see "Parody"); a journalist and prominent ideologue of the Slavophile movement. [T&H, D&G]

Aleksei APUKHTIN (1840–1893), a poet of the later nineteenth-century known for writing melodious "ROMANCES" and other forms of love poetry. [Parody, Interlude]

Evgeny BARATYNSKY (1800–1844), a major poet, master of the elegy and the "philosophical lyric." With TYUTCHEV, he came to be associated with the "metaphysical strain" in Russian poetry. [Interlude, Parody, Khlebnikov, EO]

Konstantin BATYUSHKOV (1787–1855), a celebrated early nineteenth-century lyric poet (known for his elegies) and translator, and an advocate of euphony. He was associated with PUSHKIN and the Arzamas group. [Fact, Ode, Parody, Evolution, Interlude, EO]

Vissarion BELINSKY (1811–1848), an influential critic of the mid-nineteenth century, was known particularly for his radically liberal, populist views. An early advocate of Gogol and the young Dostoyevsky, he worked alongside Nikolai NEKRASOV to promote the realist, socially engaged "Natural School" of writing. [D&G, Interlude]

Andrei BELY (1880–1934) (real name: Boris Bugaev), a poet, prose writer, critic and theorist, was a prominent representative of Russian SYMBOLISM. His poetry, and particularly his prose, experimented with sound orchestration and synesthesia; he was also interested in forms of mysticism. [Evolution, Foundations]

Alexander BLOK (1880–1921), a major poet and playwright affiliated with Russian SYMBOLISM. Despite the Modernist leanings of his work, he has been called "the last Romantic poet," in part because of his self-conscious presentation of himself as melancholic lyric protagonist. Note that Tynianov devotes several other articles to Blok, including "Blok and Heine" and "Blok" (both 1921). [Parody, Interlude, Khlebnikov, Evolution]

Anton DELVIG (1798–1831), a poet and close friend and associate of Alexander PUSHKIN and Evgeny BARATYNSKY, was known for publishing contemporary literary almanacs, including *Northern Flowers* [Severnye tsvety]. [Parody, Fact]

Gavrila DERZHAVIN (1743–1816), a poet and statesman, particularly under Catherine the Great. Seen as a transitional figure, Derzhavin worked mostly with the poetic form of the eighteenth century (first and foremost, the ode), but his lexical and formal innovations paved the way for the very different poetry of the early nineteenth-century "Golden Age." [Ode, Fact, Evolution, Parody, Interlude, Khlebnikov, T&H, EO]

Boris EIKHENBAUM (1886–1959), a theorist and literary historian, was affiliated early on with OPOYAZ and the Formalists. In addition to contributing important work on poetic and prose style, he articulated the concept of *SKAZ*. [D&G, Evolution, Ode, Interlude, EO]

Sergei ESENIN (1895–1925), a lyric poet who worked extensively with a number of different styles. He is known for emotional evocations of idyllic country life through his persona of the "peasant poet" and "sentimental hooligan"—a sweet peasant boy gone astray in the big city. Esenin's later years were tempestuous and alcohol soaked. He remains one of Russia's best-loved poets today. [Interlude, Ode, Evolution]

Afanasy FET (1820–1892), a major lyric poet of the latter half of the nineteenth century. His preference for writing poems only about nature and love drew the ire of the leading, civic-minded radical critics, and Fet was better received only in the final years of his life. [Fact, Interlude, Evolution, Khlebnikov]

Nikolai GOGOL (1809–1852), a master of the grotesque and the comic, was one of Russia's greatest nineteenth-century writers of prose and drama. He is remembered for his short story cycles (including *Evenings on a Farm near Dikanka* and *Petersburg Tales*), his great novel *Dead Souls*, and plays like *The Government Inspector* and *The Marriage*. [Parody, D&G, Foundations, FEX, EO, Interlude, Ode]

Alexander GRIBOEDOV (1795–1829), a diplomat and playwright literarily affiliated with the Young Archaist movement. His best-known work is the play "Woe from Wit" [*Gore ot uma*], a brilliant satire of contemporary mores in Moscow. Tynianov was fascinated by Griboedov and made him the subject of one of his historical novels, *The Death of Vazir-Mukhtar* (1928). [Ode, Evolution]

Heinrich HEINE (1797–1856), a critical inheritor of the German Romantic tradition, essayist and politically radical journalist. He is known best for his early lyric poetry (the *Lieder*), prose, and later satirical work; his poetry enjoyed great popularity in Russia. In addition to a longer version of "Tyutchev and Heine," Tynianov also wrote on Blok and Heine, and translated the latter's work from German. [Fact, T&H, Parody, Interlude, Evolution, D&G, EO]

Roman JAKOBSON (1896–1982), a literary scholar and linguist, one of the founding members of the Moscow Linguistic Circle (Moscow's answer to Petrograd/Leningrad's OPOYAZ). Jakobson left Russia in 1920 and lived in Prague until the late 1930s, making a significant contribution to the development of European structuralism (in linguistics and literary theory). He subsequently went on to continue his academic career in the United States. [Problems]

Nikolai KARAMZIN (1766–1826), a poet, prose writer, literary critic, travel writer, and historian; his work actively bridged the eighteenth and nineteenth centuries. In innovative prose, he introduced Russians to SENTIMENTALISM and other literary trends from Western Europe, and actively promoted new work in various journals and almanacs. His last work was the monumental twelve-volume *History of the Russian State* (1818–1826). [Ode, Parody, EO, D&G, Fact, Evolution]

Pavel KATENIN (1792–1853), a poet and translator with both Neo-Classical and Romantic-nationalist leanings, pushed for a more authentically Russian poetic language. Accordingly, he was affiliated with the ARCHAISTS and their Colloquy of Lovers of the Russian Word. [Ode, Evolution]

Velimir (Viktor) KHLEBNIKOV (1885–1922), a groundbreaking poet, theorist of language and literature, and self-styled "Futurian" [*budetlianin*], was associated with the origins of Russian FUTURISM. He is remembered for his experimental, primitivist, and yet innovative ideas about poetry and language, as well as for his biography, filled with adventure and a tragic early demise. Considered peculiar by some of his contemporaries, Khlebnikov was adored by younger writers such as Mandelstam and the OBERIU poets, as well as the Formalist critics themselves. [Ode, Khlebnikov, Interlude, Mayakovsky]

Wilhelm KÜCHELBECKER [**Vil'gel'm Kiukhel'beker**] (1797–1846), a poet, critic, and political activist, was also a school friend of PUSHKIN and DELVIG. Through contact with GRIBOEDOV, Küchelbecker came to align himself with the Young Archaists, who opposed excessive softness and euphony in poetic language. Tynianov's first literary-historical novel, *Kiukhlia* (1925), was based on the life of Küchelbecker. [Ode, Parody]

Mikhail LERMONTOV (1814–1841), a celebrated and innovative lyric poet, dramatist, and novelist, embodied the Romantic ideal in his life and work, seeking adventure through travel and political radicalism. He died in a duel at the age of twenty-seven. [Ode, Fact, Evolution, Parody]

Nikolai LESKOV (1831–1895), a prose writer and journalist of nonconformist political views. He is best known for his tales of provincial and village life, including that of the clergy, and his remarkable use of *SKAZ* in evoking convincing speech of rural characters. [Evolution, D&G]

Mikhail LOMONOSOV (1711–1765), a poet, orator, scholar, and polymath, revolutionized Russian literary language in a series of seminal works on rhetoric, grammar, and poetry. His many scientific and literary accomplishments include an influential articulation of the notion of "three styles" (high, middle, and low). [Ode, Fact, Evolution, Interlude, Khlebnikov]

Vladimir MAYAKOVSKY (1893–1930), an artist, innovative poet, dramatist, and theorist of Russian Cubo-Futurism, was a major figure in twentieth-century verse. Renowned for his larger-than-life poetic persona and dramatic performance style, he became the leading Bolshevik poet after the 1917 Revolution. Like many of his Formalist colleagues, Tynianov knew Mayakovsky personally. [Mayakovsky, Interlude, Ode, Fact]

Aleksei MERZLYAKOV (1778–1830), a poet, critic, and professor of literature, was known for his stylized "folk songs" and stubbornly classicist views. His students at Moscow University included LERMONTOV, Polezhaev, TYUTCHEV, and VYAZEMSKY. [Ode, T&H]

Mikhail MURAVYOV (1757–1807), a poet and theorist whose work exemplified the transition from the formal, courtly style of the eighteenth-century ode to the emotionally charged work of Sentimentalist small forms. [Ode, Parody]

Nikolai NEKRASOV (1821–1878), a poet and publisher, was known for his radically liberal political views and contributions to the realist tradition. His lyric poetry, which he called "civic," sought to reflect and critique contemporary social and political reality, through the prism of the poet's feelings. Tynianov acknowledged Nekrasov's important stature in nineteenth-century poetry, and his significance for literary evolution, in the article "Nekrasov's Verse Forms" (1921). [Fact, Evolution, Interlude, Khlebnikov]

Nikolai OGARYOV (1813–1877), a poet, essayist, and publisher, was known best for his lyric poetry with Romantic and idealist leanings. He was a close literary and political associate of Alexander Herzen and, after 1856, an active figure in émigré Russian literature. [Ode, D&G, Parody]

Ivan PANAEV (1812–1862), writer and co-editor (with poet Nikolai NEKRASOV) of the influential journal *The Contemporary* (founded by PUSHKIN). Among his other activities, Panaev published topical verse feuilletons under the pseudonym "New Poet." [Parody, EO]

Karolina PAVLOVA (1807–1893), a poet and translator, was one of the few women to forge a literary career in the nineteenth century. She had a lukewarm reception from her contemporaries, but was rediscovered and praised by the fin-de-siècle SYMBOLISTS. [Parody, EO]

Aleksey PISEMSKY (1821–1881), a novelist and playwright of the Realist mode dominant in the mid-nineteenth century, although he was antagonistic toward the 1860s radical critics. [Fact, D&G, Khlebnikov]

Pyotr PLETNYOV (1792–1865), a poet, literary critic and teacher who belonged to the circle around Pushkin and published him (hence *Eugene Onegin*'s dedication "to Pletnyov"). Pletnyov was also close personally and aesthetically to BARATYNSKY, DELVIG, KÜCHELBECKER, and VYAZEMSKY. [D&G, EO, Parody, Interlude]

Alexander POTEBNYA (1835–1891), a Ukrainian-Russian linguist and philosopher of language and aesthetics. His ideas were a favorite target of the Formalists, beginning with Viktor SHKLOVSKY'S polemical opening to the article "Art as Device" (1916). Tynianov refers obliquely to some of these positions of Potebnya at the beginning of "Literary Fact," when he refutes the notion that poetry is "thinking in images." [Fact, Ode]

Alexander PUSHKIN (1799–1837), Russia's foremost poet of the nineteenth century, is considered by many to be the national poet. His innovations in poetry were crucial for its further development, and he continues to be cited by poets writing in Russian today. In addition to poetry, Pushkin also produced literary and historical prose, criticism and drama, and was a controversial political figure. Tynianov made Pushkin the subject of multiple critical articles, a separate volume (*Pushkin and his Contemporaries*), and an unfinished multiple-part biographical novel (*Pushkin*). [Fact, Evolution, Ode, EO, Foundations, Parody, Interlude, Khlebnikov]

Semyon RAYICH (1792–1855), a poet, translator, and teacher of literature (his students included TYUTCHEV and LERMONTOV). He founded several important almanacs, including the "Northern Lyre" [*Severnaia lira*]. [Ode, T&H]

Vasily ROZANOV (1856–1919), a writer, critic and philosopher, was known for his controversial views on literature, religion, and society, and his idiosyncratic, aphoristic writings. His reading of Dostoyevsky's "The Grand Inquisitor" (in *The Brothers Karamazov*) proved convincing and influential in later interpretations of the writer's work. [Foundations, Interlude]

Osip SENKOVSKY [**Baron Brambeus**] (1800–1858), a writer, critic, and scholar of Asian cultures, was known for his fantastic tales written under the pen name Baron Brambeus [Parody, Fact]

Stepan SHEVYRYOV (1806–1864), a poet, critic and prominent member of the ARCHAIST, nationalist Slavophile movement, is remembered best for his essays on GOGOL and PUSHKIN. [Ode, Parody, Evolution]

Alexander SHISHKOV (1754–1841), a writer and early Slavophile with strongly conservative views on politics and language. Attacking KARAMZIN and the SENTIMENTALIST school, he advocated purifying Russian literary language and style from excessive European influences. [Ode, Parody, Interlude]

Viktor SHKLOVSKY (1893–1984), a writer, critic, and literary theorist, was one of the founders of OPOYAZ and, by extension, the Formalist method in literary scholarship. He is known for articulating concepts like "art as device," "making strange" or "defamiliarization" [*ostranenie*], and the distinction between FABULA and PLOT in literature. Shklovsky and Tynianov worked closely together and corresponded extensively. In 1930, Shklovsky publicly recanted his Formalist views in a notorious newspaper article, "Monument to a Scientific Mistake," but in later decades returned to this approach in writings on literature and film. [Fact, Evolution, Interlude, Foundations, D&G, EO, Fabula and Plot, Problems]

Nikolai STRAKHOV (1828–1896), a critic and philosopher closely associated with Dostoyevsky and the nationalist *pochvennik* ["native soil"] movement, as well as with Tolstoy in the 1870s. [Khlebnikov, D&G]

Alexander SUMAROKOV (1718–1777), a poet, playwright, and critic who sought to establish a modern, secular, European-oriented literary culture in Russia. He was immensely prolific and used satire to lampoon his opponents (such as LOMONOSOV and TREDYAKOVSKY), who advocated for the ongoing use of Church Slavonic language in poetry. [Ode, Interlude, Khlebnikov, Parody]

Vasily TREDYAKOVSKY (1703–1769), a poet, translator, playwright, and scholar of Russian versification, was frequently at odds with the two other giants of eighteenth-century Russian letters, LOMONOSOV and SUMAROKOV. Tredyakovsky is generally acknowledged as the loser in these disputes, since his innovations in versification were eclipsed by those of Lomonosov and his style remained, for the most part, unreadably cumbersome. [Ode, Parody]

Alexander TURGENEV (1784–1846), a Russian statesman, historian, and friend of the literary circles around KARAMZIN, ZHUKOVSKY, and PUSHKIN (Arzamas). [Fact, Parody, Evolution]

Ivan TURGENEV (1818–1883), one of the premier prose writers of the nineteenth century in Russia, is remembered particularly for his story cycles (like *Notes of a Hunter*, 1852) and the novel *Fathers and Children* (1862). Late in life, as an émigré writer in Paris, he experimented with the genre of "little poems in prose." [D&G, Parody, Khlebnikov]

Fyodor TYUTCHEV (1803–1873), a poet and diplomat, spent half of his life in Germany and conducted much of his day-to-day business in French. As a Russian-language poet, meanwhile, he (with BARATYNSKY) represented the "philosophical lyric" and metaphysical element in Russian nineteenth-century poetry; he also had an ARCHAIST streak. Tyutchev only became widely acclaimed as a poet when his work was rediscovered by the fin-de-siècle SYMBOLISTS [T&H, Fact, Ode, D&G, Parody, EO, Evolution, Interlude, Khlebnikov]

Paul VERLAINE (1844–1896), a celebrated French poet, coined the term *poète maudit* [accursed poet] to describe his circle of French Symbolists and Decadents. [Interlude, Khlebnikov]

Prince Pyotr VYAZEMSKY (1792–1878), an early nineteenth-century poet, critic, passionate letter writer, archivist, and older contemporary of PUSHKIN and the Arzamas poets, was known for his quick wit and sharp tongue. By the end of his long life, he had become a compendium of knowledge about the Golden Age of Russian poetry. [Parody, EO, Fact, Evolution, Interlude, Ode]

Nikolai YAZYKOV (1803–1846), an innovative lyric poet, was known particularly for his song-like lyrics. After a conservative turn, later in life he was affiliated with the Slavophile movement. [D&G, Parody]

Vasily ZHUKOVSKY (1783–1852), a major poet and translator of the early nineteenth century, was a representative of early Romanticism and a popularizer of various trends in Western European poetry. He is particularly remembered for his work with the elegy and the Romantic ballad, but his prolific output covers a variety of poetic genres. [D&G, EO, Parody, Ode, T&H, Foundations, Fact].

Terms

ARCHAISM / ARCHAISTS: in historical terms, the Archaists were an early nineteenth-century movement of poets and writers initially associated with the conservative Colloquy of Lovers of the Russian Word [Beseda liubitelei russkogo slova] (led by DERZHAVIN and SHISHKOV), later on with the group of radical "Young Archaists" such as KÜCHELBECKER. The Archaists were involved in harsh literary polemics with the Arzamas society (to which PUSHKIN, VYAZEMSKY, et al. belonged), who touted Neo-Classical values such as "taste" and "clarity." For Tynianov theoretically, meanwhile, "archaism" primarily meant advocacy of the specificity and conspicuousness of the Russian (or any native) language as a driving force of literary evolution as opposed to the idea of literary language as a mere means of expression. Tynianov's groundbreaking revision of the history of early nineteenth-century Russian poetry (still known as the Golden Age in Russia) was laid out in his "Pushkin and the Archaists" [Arkhaisty i Pushkin] (1924). Proceeding from the Formalist premise that literary evolution pivots on the problem of language and style, Tynianov began to apply the concept of "archaism" to other historical periods as well, and arrived at a universal model of literary struggle between language-conscious "Archaists" striving for "cumbersome," "deformed" verbal form, and "innovators" with their agenda of "smoothing" the conspicuousness [Tynianov calls them "smoothers," *sglazhivateli*] (hence the title of the collection *Archaists and Innovators*). Tynianov thus problematized the notion of "Classicist" and "Romantic" writers in Russian literature. In Tynianov's view, the Archaist agenda consistently proved more productive for literary evolution than that of the "innovators": such, for instance, was the role of LOMONOSOV in his struggle against the clarity-driven SUMAROKOV; in a very different way from each other, of TYUTCHEV and NEKRASOV in the mid-nineteenth century; and of the FUTURISTS in the twentieth century. [Ode, Problems, EO, Evolution, T&H, Interlude, D&G, Fact]

BYT: derived from the Russian verb "to be" [*byt'*], the concept of *byt* covers everyday, day-to-day, or "real" life phenomena, with connotations of the mundane and trivial, but also the practical and down-to-earth. Thus, "peasant *byt*" refers to peasant ways of life and everyday practices, while MAYAKOVSKY could write passionate verse in the 1920s about the struggle of uncompromising revolutionary values against bourgeois *byt*. Indeed, this concept was squarely in the public and artistic eye during the early Soviet period, which sought to create new forms of everyday life and to reject the old, pre-revolutionary ones. [Fact, Evolution, EO, Interlude, Khlebnikov, Foundations; Parody, Ode]

DOMINANT: Formalist term denoting the primary or most important factor in a given work of art, to which all of the other elements are subordinated and which actively shapes or "deforms" those elements accordingly. For Tynianov, the concept of the dominant is linked to the concept—crucial for his thought—of "function" (see section nine of "On Literary Evolution"). Used by other Formalists and contemporary thinkers including EIKHENBAUM, JAKOBSON, Tomashevsky, and Bakhtin (the last found the concept particularly useful in his book on Dostoyevsky). Looking back, Jakobson called the dominant "one of the most fundamental, well-developed, and productive concepts developed by Russian Formalist theory" (Jakobson, "The Dominant" (1935), in *Language in Literature*, Translated by Krystyna Pomorska [Boston: Belknap Press, 1990], 41). [Ode, Evolution, Problems]

FABULA: Formalist term (cf. French/Latin *fabula / fable*) first articulated by Viktor SHKLOVSKY in his *Theory of Prose* (1925), in opposition to *siuzhet* (cf. French *sujet*), or plot. Fabula is understood as the linear and chronological summary of the narrative events of the work (its "semantic blueprint") and "plot" as its actual, not necessarily linear or chronological, trajectory ("dynamics"). [Fact, Evolution, Ode, EO, Plot & Fabula, Screenplay, Foundations, FEX]

FUTURISM (RUSSIAN): a movement in Russian literature and visual art that began in the second decade of the twentieth century and encompassed many diverse groups, including the Ego-Futurists, the Cubo-Futurists and Centrifuge. These groups had in common a demonstrative break with literary traditions both recent and distant and a commitment to experimentation with poetic language. The Formalists were advocates of Futurist poetry and found confirmation of their theories in some of its experiments. Among the writers Tynianov discusses, Aseev, KHLEBNIKOV, MAYAKOVSKY, Pasternak, and Selvinsky were all in one way or another connected with Futurism or its descendants. [Fact, Ode, Interlude, Khlebnikov]

INTERRELATION: Tynianov uses the verb "correlate" [*sootnosit'sia*] and related nouns "correlation" [*sootnoshenie*], "correlatedness" [*sootnesennost'*], and "correlativity" [*sootnositel'nost'*] to describe the complex, interdependent, and mutually responsive nature of the elements that make up a literary work (and which link that work to elements of the outside, "real" world—or "social SERIES," in Tynianov's terms). We have opted to substitute "interrelate" and "interrelation(s)," and occasionally, the related words "interdependence" and "relate" / "relation" because of the distracting causal associations attached to the word "correlation" in English. Note, however, that "interrelation" lacks the sense of things being (neatly) matched up with one another, which is present in the Russian. [Fact, Ode, Foundations, Evolution, Parody, EO, Problems]

LEF: the "Left Front of the Arts" [Levyi front iskusstv] was the journal for an eponymous group of politically engaged, experimentally inclined artists, writers, and theoreticians in the 1920s, including Vladimir MAYAKOVSKY. [Problems, Interlude]

LONG POEM [*POEMA*]: a Russian literary genre with its origins in the verse epic, understood in the classical sense. (It was in this sense, for instance, that Nikolai GOGOL subtitled his picaresque (prose) novel *Dead Souls* "a *poema*.") Starting in the early 1820s, PUSHKIN and others were writing long poems with adventure plots and entertaining, exotic details; this shift toward the long poem made possible *Eugene Onegin*, a "novel in verse." By the end of the nineteenth century there was a shift to the lyric long poem, a form that enjoyed some popularity among early twentieth-century poets, including MAYAKOVSKY. [Fact, Evolution, Parody, EO, Interlude, Foundations, Khlebnikov, Mayakovsky]

OPOYAZ: (the "Society for the Study of Poetic Language" [Obshchestvo izucheniia poeticheskogo iazyka]): a group of early Formalist scholars (including Eikhenbaum, Shklovsky, Boris Tomashevsky, and Tynianov) based in Petrograd/Leningrad between 1916–1922. In the early twenties, the scholars of OPOYAZ were engaged in dialogue with the Moscow Linguistic Circle and, later, with LEF.

ORIENTATION [*USTANOVKA*]: the rather open-ended word *ustanovka* [standpoint, viewpoint, orientation—cf. German *Einstellung*] plays a crucial role in Tynianov's whole conception of literature as a *functional* system. "Orientation refers not just to the dominant [factor] of a literary work (or genre), which functionally colors the subordinated factors, but also to the function of a work (or genre) vis-à-vis the closest extra-literary series" ("Ode"); in "On Literary Evolution," Tynianov emphasizes the orientation toward the closest *speech* series. On the one hand, the idea of a work (or genre) having a fundamental orientation resolves the problem of "authorial intention"; on the other hand, the orientation of a work also situates it vis-à-vis its historical and social context and illuminates the different functions a work can have at different times. [Fact, Evolution, Ode, Parody, EO, Foundations]

OVERCOAT ODES [*SHINEL'NYE ODY*]: servile compositions aimed at currying favor and flattering one's Superiors. The destitute functionaries who authored them would allegedly read their odes directly from the doorstep, without taking off their overcoats (a typical clerk's item of clothing—cf. Gogol's "The Overcoat"). The term originates with Prince VYAZEMSKY, who accused ZHUKOVSKY of writing them. [Fact, Evolution, Interlude]

PAUZNIK: (cf. "pause"): a kind of poetic meter with a fixed number of stressed syllables and a variable number of unstressed syllables between them. The term "dol'nik" is sometimes used interchangeably with "pauznik," the main difference being that the term "pauznik" was in use much earlier. [Interlude, T&H]

PLOT [*SIUZHET*]: see **FABULA**

POEMA: see **LONG POEM**

ROMANCE (also **SONG**)**:** like the "song," the "romance" (which originated as a narrative ballad in Spain) is a poetic genre associated with sentimental emotion and actual or suggested musical components. [Interlude, Parody, Evolution, Fact, Ode, T&H]

SENTIMENTALISM: a pre-Romantic literary tendency in Russian poetry and prose during the final decades of the eighteenth century (1770s–1800s). Characteristic of the transition from the late eighteenth to the early nineteenth century, the general movement of this mode was away from high-style language and courtly themes, toward "trivial" genres and intimate subjects that hybridized classical and Western European genres (the ode, elegy, idyll, epistle). As Tynianov writes (in "The Ode"), it was a "movement that fostered the development of the elegy, the didactic and friendly epistle, and small forms such as the rondo, charade, etc." Meanwhile, Tynianov cautioned against the common practice of treating Sentimentalism as primarily associated with "teary" emotions. [Interlude, Ode]

SERIES [*RIAD*]: The notion of "series" is central to Tynianov's thought: a partly visual, partly mathematical, metaphor, it expresses the notion of various spheres of cultural, social, economic, and political activity ("the historical series," "the literary series") existing in parallel states of evolution and frequently intersecting / interacting. The interactions (correlations or interrelations) between series occur when one series approaches exhaustion (cf. automatization) and needs to be revitalized, through new material (as when the literary series draws on that of everyday life), new devices (when history borrows a metaphor from literature, for instance), etc. [Ode, Foundations, T&H, Evolution, Fact, Problems, Parody, EO, Interlude, Khlebnikov]

SHIFT: The concept of "shift" is significant for Tynianov, who uses it to illustrate his view of different kinds of INTERRELATIONS within literary works, literary systems, and literary evolution overall (he applies the same concepts to film as well). The notion of shift is polemical with regard to prevailing conceptions of literature and art developing in a smooth, linear succession: evolution through shift is instead nonlinear, with each new shift reconfiguring the entire system of interrelations. In Russian, these words (covered by the noun *smena*—meaning both a change or alteration and a length of time, e.g. "the night shift"—and the verb *smeshchat'* / *smestit'* and its intransitive reflexive form *smeshchat'sia* / *smestit'sia*) can also mean to "displace" or "supplant"; the idea of "succession" is also present. Of the available options, "shift" is the most open-ended and capacious; we occasionally substitute one of the other options for clarity's sake. Note too that Tynianov occasionally uses another word that could be translated as "shift," *sdvig*, beloved by the Russian Futurists; in accordance with their harsh aesthetics, it suggests a more abrupt, even violent shift. [Fact, Evolution, D&G, Parody, EO, Interlude, Foundations, Khlebnikov]

***SLOVO* [WORD / LANGUAGE]:** The word "slovo" in Russian has a primary meaning of "word," with derivative adjective "verbal" [*slovesnyi*] and noun "verbal art" (or "literature") [*slovesnost'*]. Tynianov uses it in the primary meaning, as in, for instance, "the word 'seeking'" ("On Khlebnikov"), or in the following passage from "Tyutchev & Heine": "The word does not exist in a vacuum, but as part of a familiar series with its own particular coloring; it is a *verbal element*. Seen this way, the words 'winged' and 'wingèd' have nothing in common as poetic elements" (64). But *slovo* in the Russian tradition also has a much broader and more general meaning that can evoke both the religious depth of "the Word [*Logos*] and the experiments with the "self-sufficient word" [*samovitoe slovo*] of Tynianov's contemporaries the Futurists. In these contexts, *slovo* comes much closer to standard English-language use of "language," and we have translated it accordingly in a number of instances. Readers should bear in mind, however, that by emphasizing the "word" itself, Tynianov is advocating a more precise and scientific approach to literary studies: instead of speaking broadly of "types" or "themes," the "literary science" envisioned by the Formalists looks at how words, even individual words, function within literary series. [Khlebnikov, Interlude, Film—Word—Music, Ode, EO, Mayakovsky, Foundations, T&H]

SKAZ: (cf. *skazat'*, "to say"): a narrative device first identified by the Formalists (EIKHENBAUM, SHKLOVSKY, TYNIANOV) whereby some or all of a given work of literature is narrated in a way distinctively oriented toward oral speech rather than written (literary) language. In the Russian tradition, skaz has often been associated with non-standard (peasant, regional, uneducated) speech, understood to be distinct from that of the author. For Tynianov, skaz was particularly important for signaling the need for a performative response from the reader. [Fact, Evolution, Interlude]

SYMBOLISM RUSSIAN: in Russia, a fin-de-siècle literary and artistic movement that particularly flourished during the first decade of the twentieth century. Drawing on Symbolist predecessors in Western Europe (France and Germany), as well as on nineteenth-century Russian writers like Dostoyevsky, most of the Russian Symbolists were interested in philosophy, religion, mysticism, the occult, and aesthetics. Symbolist poets advocated techniques including evocation instead of naming and describing; the search for mystical correspondences between observable reality and the world of the invisible eternal, as well as the coupling of the mystical and the grotesque. Prominent Symbolists include Valery Briusov, Vyacheslav Ivanov, Alexander BLOK, and Andrei BELY. [Ode, Fact, Parody, Interlude, Khlebnikov]

VERSE / POETRY: Tynianov uses the word *stikh* [verse line, line of poetry] far more often than *poeziia* [poetry]; cf. the plural *stikhi* [verses or poem/poems] vs. *stikhotvorenie* [a poem]. This is a polemical point for him; as he wrote, "I reject the fuzzy concept of 'poetry' [*poeziia*], which as a term has taken on an evaluative coloring and lost its actual contours and content; instead, I choose one of the basic constructive categories of verbal art—[the] verse [line] [*stikh*]."[1] The concepts of *verse* and *poetry* are, however, much closer to one another in Russian than they are in English, where the former term is used primarily in technical discussions of versification, and, in some contexts, sounds archaic ("As a youth, Byron scribbled verses"). *Poeziia* in Russian is likewise rather more vague ("fuzzy") and flowery than the more neutral "poetry" in English. Still, Tynianov's preference for *stikh* reflects his aim of specificity and precision: he really does want the word to be a technical term. For this reason, we have chosen to vary the terms in English, using *poetry* and *poems* throughout when Tynianov writes more generally, and *verse* when his discussion is more technical.

ZAUM: (literally, "beyond the mind"—cf. "beyonsense," in Paul Schmidt's excellent translation]: term for the abstract "sound poetry" that was most fully articulated by Velimir KHLEBNIKOV and Aleksei Kruchonykh, another early Futurist. For Khlebnikov, *zaum* was a tool for reconstructing a universally comprehensible language (both ancient and utopian) governed by ultimately logical laws; for Kruchonykh, *zaum* was "self-sufficient," spontaneous and lawless sound-speech, the source of unexpected, ultimately indeterminate meanings. [Fact, EO, Khlebnikov, Interlude]

---

1 "Predislovie k knige *Problema stikhovoi semantiki*," *PILK*, 253. *Problems of Verse Semantics* was the original title of the book that eventually came out at *Problems of Verse Language* [Problema stikhotvornogo iazyka]; Tynianov wrote that the change came at the insistence of an editor "spooked by the word 'semantics'" (note that the adjective for "verse" is also tellingly different).

Yuri Tynianov: Biographical Note

Yuri Nikolayevich [Nasonovich] Tynianov (1894–1943) was a writer and literary theorist, and a central figure among the scholars who came to be known as the Russian Formalists. Born into a Jewish doctor's family in the small town of Rēzekne (in what is now Latvia, then the Pale of Settlement), Tynianov began his career as a student in pre-revolutionary Petrograd (he studied at Petersburg University between 1912–1919). There, he began working around 1918 with the other innovative thinkers of the OPOYAZ (*Obshchestvo izucheniia poeticheskogo iazyka* [Society for the Study of Poetic Language] group. From 1921, Tynianov taught literary history at the Institute for Art History in Petrograd/Leningrad; in 1930, the institute was "reorganized" and Tynianov was among the many instructors purged for being ideologically untenable.

The OPOYAZ scholars (Eikhenbaum, Shklovsky, Tynianov), along with their contemporaries in the Moscow Linguistic Circle, would (despite substantial differences and even occasional animosity) come to comprise the Formalist movement. As contemporaries and advocates of the Russian Futurists, their ideas about how to talk about literature were similarly radical and stark in comparison to the mystical impressionism of pre-revolutionary writers and critics; they were also explicitly opposed to the traditionalist academicism of most of their predecessors and, later in the 1920s, to the increasingly dogmatic Marxist literary criticism. Also like the Futurists, the Formalists found themselves in step with the revolutionary times; for instance, Viktor Shklovsky's interpretation of a work of literature as a machine (though it harks back to his pre-revolutionary military service) seems tailor-made for the early Soviet cult of new technology. Some of Tynianov's thoughts on literature (such as his rejection of the idea of "literary genius") likewise seem to reflect the radical democratization of society carried out in his formative years. Yet, the Formalists as a whole (including Tynianov) were largely apolitical, a stance that would cause most of them no end of problems in their highly politicized time.

Tynianov's thought can be condensed into a number of key concepts. His notion of "literary fact" expresses the Formalists' conviction that the proper object of literary study has to be that which distinguishes it from other areas of intellectual activity—its unique *literariness*—in contradistinction to the psychological, biographical, socio-political, and other extra-literary phenomena often treated in contemporary literary criticism. While acknowledging the importance of the interrelations of literature with other phenomena, Tynianov insists on understanding the specificity of these interrelations and warns against taking shortcuts (say, from political context to literary) that elide the significance of intermediary "series" like that of speech. The literary fact is itself, meanwhile, a dynamic entity—at different times and in different contexts, the same material can hold much literary significance or none, i.e. its status as literary fact is mutable.

This takes us to another central topic of interest for Tynianov: literary evolution. The Formalists' initial efforts had focused on an immanent study of literature (cf. Shklovsky's 1916 "Art as Device"); by the mid-1920s, most of them were trying to articulate how, in terms of evolution, extra-literary material is transformed in literature. In his discussion of literary evolution, Tynianov develops a conception of literature as a complex system, the elements of which are constantly interacting (and changing through interaction) with those of other systems: the internal system of a given work, the system of a genre, the system of a literary movement, of a national literature, etc. Change in literature comes about through intra-literary interactions (such as parody, a topic to which Tynianov devotes special attention), but also through the absorption of extra-literary elements. This consideration also helps Tynianov shore up the distinction—crucial for him—between evolution and genesis, since for Tynianov the point of origin cannot be nearly as relevant (or revelatory) as the process of development and change.

Another focus for Tynianov—first and foremost a scholar of poetry—was getting to the bottom of "poetic language" and, crucially, developing a coherent scholarly vocabulary for such investigations. Tynianov argued for the need to treat poetic language as a specific entity, but not because of any innate features of individual words or collocations; what distinguishes poetry from other uses of language (such as prose or everyday speech) is context, form, and function. As elsewhere, he emphasizes the dynamism of all the component parts of a poem: "The form of the literary work must be recognized as a dynamic phenomenon." Tynianov also emphasized that the rhythm of poetry is fundamental to its essence and meaning (rather than a superficial formal garnish to the separate "meaning" or content of the poem). In articles including "The Ode as an Oratorical Genre," "Tyutchev and Heine," and "The Composition of *Eugene Onegin*," Tynianov's explication of the immanent structural functioning of verse texts provides a highly serviceable method for parsing and discussing poetry.

In the mid-1920s, Tynianov began writing screenplays and was involved with the experimental filmmaking group FEX (the "Eccentric Actor Factory"), members of which were making some of the early classics of Soviet film (see "On FEX" in this volume). This experience gave rise to Tynianov's theoretical articles on film, such as "Film—Word—Music" and "The Foundations of Film." These articles should be read as part of the lively polemics around the emergence of film in the 1920s as a relatively new and unprecedentedly powerful art form; Tynianov insists adamantly on film's fundamentally different means of expression, particularly the ways in which it diverges from theater. At the same time, some of Tynianov's insights into the functions of poetry (itself essentially different from prose or ordinary speech) proved applicable to understanding film. And vice versa: "The Foundations of Film," for instance, contains brilliant insights into literature proper, regardless of the article's title.

After the dismantling of the Formalist school in 1930, Tynianov largely withdrew from theoretical work and devoted his efforts to writing literary history and historical fiction. He had been diagnosed as early as 1928 with multiple sclerosis and suffered from resulting complications for the remaining decades of his life; nevertheless, his literary and scholarly productivity remained impressive. He had published several novels in parallel to his scholarly work in the later 1920s (*Kiukhlia*, a novel about Wilhelm Küchelbecker, came out in 1925; 1927 saw *The Death of Vazir-Mukhtar*, about the playwright and diplomat Alexander Griboedov, and the novella *Lieutenant Kije*, set at the very end of the eighteenth century). In the 1930s, Tynianov produced *The Wax Figure* (a novella set at the end of Peter the Great's reign) and a multiple-part novel about the life of Pushkin (the first two parts were published to great acclaim in 1937; part three remained unfinished). From 1931 he worked as an editor of the authoritative "Poet's Library" [*Biblioteka poeta*] series at the Soviet Writer [*Sovetskii pisatel'*] publishing house. Tynianov's family was evacuated from besieged Leningrad in 1941; he died, of complications from multiple sclerosis, in Moscow in 1943.

Works cited

Akhmatova, Anna. *Stikhotvoreniia i poemy*. Leningrad: Sovetskii pisatel', 1977.

Aksakov, Konstantin. *Oleg pod Konstantinopolem, dramaticheskaia parodiia, s epilogom, v 3-kh deistviiakh, v stikhakh*. St. Petersburg: Izdanie liubitelia, 1858.

———. *Long Poems* [Poemy] (1925)

Aseev, Nikolai. *Stikhotvoreniia i poemy*. Leningrad: Sovetskii pisatel', 1967.

Baratynskii, Evgenii. *Polnoe sobranie sochinenii*. St. Petersburg: Akademproekt, 2000.

———. (Yevgeny Baratynsky.) *A Science Not for the Earth*. Translated by Rawley Grau. Brooklyn, NY: Ugly Duckling Presse, 2015.

Batiushkov, Konstantin. *Sochineniia*. St. Petersburg: Tip. B. S. Balasheva, 1885–1887.

Blok, Alexander. *Polnoe sobranie stikhotvorenii v dvukh tomakh*. Leningrad: Sovetskii pisatel', 1946.

Bliumbaum, Arkadii. *Konstruktsiia mnimosti: k poetike "Voskovoi persony" Yuriia Tynianova*. St. Petersburg: Giperion, 2002.

Chudakova, M. O. "Sotsial'naia praktika, filologicheskaia refleksiia i literature v nauchnoi biografii Tynianova i Eikhenbauma." In *Tynianovskii sbornik: Vtoryie Tynianovskie Chteniia*. Riga: Zinatne, 1986.

Chukovskaia, L. K. *Dom poeta*. Moscow: Vremia, 2012.

Derzhavin, Gavrila. *Sochineniia*. 7 vols. Edited Ia. Grot. St. Petersburg: Tip. Imperatorskoi Akademii nauk, 1866–1878.

———. *Stikhotvoreniia*. Leningrad: Sovetskii pisatel', 1957.

Dostoevskii, F. M. *Complete Letters of Fyodor Dostoyevsky*. Translated by David Lowe and Ronald Meyer. Ann Arbor, MI: Ardis, 1988.

———. *The Double*. Translated by George Bird. Bloomington, IN: Indiana University Press, 1958.

———. *The House of the Dead*. Translated by David McDuff. New York/London: Penguin, 1985.

———. *The Idiot*. Translated by Alan Myers. Oxford: Oxford University Press, 1992.

———. *Netochka Nezvanova*. Translated by Jane Kentish. New York/London: Penguin, 1985.

———. *Poor Folk & A Little Hero*. Translated by David Magarshack. New York: Doubleday, 1968.

———. *Poor Folk and Other Stories*. Translated by David McDuff. New York: Penguin, 1988.

———. *Polnoe sobranie sochinenii*. St. Petersburg: Tip. A. S. Suvorina, 1883.

———. *Uncle's Dream and Other Stories*. Translated by David McDuff. New York/London: Penguin, 1989.

———. *The Village of Stepanchikovo and its Inhabitants*. Translated by Ignat Avsey. Ithaca, NY: Cornell University Press, 1987.

———. *Writer's Diary*. Translated by Kenneth Lantz. Evanston, IL: Northwestern University Press, 1993.

Eikhenbaum, Boris. *Lermontov: Opyt istoriko-literaturnoi otsenki*. Leningrad: Gosudarstvennoe izdatel'stvo, 1924.

———. *O literature*. Moscow: Sovetskii pisatel', 1987.

———. *Lev Tolstoi: Issledovaniia. Stat'I*. St. Petersburg: Fakul'tet filologii i iskusstv Sankt-Peterburgskogo Gosudarstvennogo Universiteta, 2009.

Erlich, Viktor. *Russian Formalism: History—Doctrine*. The Hague: Mouton, 1955.

Esenin, Sergei. *V stikhakh i zhizni*. 2 vols. Moscow: Respublika, 1997.

Galushkin, Aleksandr. "'I tak, stavshi na kostiakh, budem trubit' sbor …,' K istorii nesostoiavshegosia vozrozhdeniia Opoiaza v 1928–1930 gg." *Novoe Literaturnoe Obozrenie* 44 (2000): 136–153.

Gogol', N. V. *The Complete Tales of Nikolai Gogol*. Edited by Leonard J. Kent. Translated by Constance Garnett. Chicago: University of Chicago Press, 1985.

———. *Dead Souls*. Translated by Bernard Guilbert Guerney. Edited by Susanne Fusso. New Haven, CT: Yale University Press, 1996

———. *Mirgorod*. Translated by David Magarshack. New York: Noonday, 1962.

———. *Polnoe sobranie sochinenii*. Vols. 1–14. Moscow: Izd. Akademii nauk, 1937–1952.

———. *The Overcoat and Other Tales of Good and Evil*. Translated by David Magarshack. New York: Norton, 1965.

———. *Selected Passages from Correspondence with Friends*. Translated by Jesse Zeldin. Nashville, TN: Vanderbilt University Press, 1969.

Gorbunov, I. F. *Sobranie sochinenii*. St. Petersburg: Izd. A. F. Marksa, 1904.

Grigor'ieva, G. G., ed. "'Razzhimaiu ladoni, vypuskaiu Vazira': iz pisem Iu. N. Tynianova V. B. Shklovskomu." *Soglasie* 30 (1995).

Hansen-Loeve, Aage. *Russkii formalizm. Metodologicheskaia rekostruktsiia razvitiia na osnove printsipa ostraneniia*. Moscow: Iazyki russkoi kul'tury, 2001.

Heine, Heinrich. *Buch der Lieder, Lyrisches Intermezzo*. Hamburg: Hoffmann und Campe, 1827.

———. *H. Heines sämtliche Werke*. Vol. 7. Leipzig and Vienna: Prof. E. Elster, 1890.

———. *The Poems of Heine, Translated into the Original Metres with a Sketch of His Life*. Translated by Edgar Alfred Bowring, C. B. London, 1866.

———. *Polnoe sobranie sochinenii*. Edited by Petr Veinberg. St. Petersburg: Izd. A. F. Marksa, 1904.

———. *Werke und Briefe*. Berlin: Akademie Verlag, 1961.

———. *The Works of Heinrich Heine*. Vol. 3. Translated by Charles Godfrey Leland. London: William Heineman, 1891.

Herzen, A. I. *Complete Works and Letters* [*Polnoe sobranie sochinenii i pisem*]. Vol. 3. Edited by M. Lemke. Prague, 1915

Iazykov, N. A. *Pis'ma N. M. Iazykova k rodnym za derptskii period ego zhizni*. St. Petersburg: Izd. Otd-niia russkago iazyka i slovesnosti Imp. Akademii nauk, 1913.

———. *Sobranie stikhotvorenii*. Moscow: Sovetskii pisatel', 1948.

Jakobson, R. O. "Iurii Tynianov v Prage." In *Selected Writings*. Vol. 5. The Hague, 1979.

Kak my pishem. Moscow: Kniga, 1989.

Kalinin, Ilya. "Istoriia literatury mezhdu parodiei i dramoi. K voprosu o metaistorii russkogo formalizma." *Novoe Literaturnoe Obozrenie* 50 (2001).

———. "Istoriia literatury kak Familienroman (russkii formalizm mezhdu Edipom i Gamletom)." *Novoe Literaturnoe Obozrenie* 80 (2006).

Karamzin, N. M. *Izbrannye proizvedeniia*. Moscow/Leningrad: Khudozhestvennaia literatura, 1964.

———. *Pis'ma N. M. Karamzina k I. I. Dmitrievu*. St. Petersburg: V tip. Imperatorskoi Akademii nauk, 1866.

———. *Polnoe sobranie stikhotvorenii*. Leningrad: Sovetskii pisatel', 1966.

Kaverin, Veniamin, and Vladimir Novikov. *Novoe zrenie*. Moscow: Kniga, 1988.

Kaverin, V. A. *"Zdravstvui, brat, pisat' ochen' trudno ..." Portrety, pis'ma o literature, vospominaniia*. Moscow: Sovetskii pisatel', 1965.

———. *Sobesednik (vospominaniia i portrety)*. Moscow: Sovetskii pisatel', 1973.

———. *Osveshchennye okna (Trilogiia)*. Moscow: Russkaia kniga, 2002.

———. *Epilog*. Moscow: Vagrius, 2006.

Khlebnikov, Velimir. *Collected Works of Velimir Khlebnikov (3 vols.)*. Translated by Paul Schmidt. Cambridge, MA: Harvard University Press, 1997.

———. *Tvoreniia*. Moscow: Sovetskii pisatel', 1986.

Khodasevich, Vladislav. *Sobranie sochinenii v 4–kh tomakh*. Moscow: Soglasie, 1996.

Khmel'nitskaia, Tamara. "Emkost' slova." In *Vospominaniia o Iu. N. Tynianove. Portrety i vstrechi*, edited by V. A. Kaverin, 121–137. Moscow: Sovetskii pisatel', 1983.

Kumpan, K. A. "Institut istorii iskusstv na rubezhe 1920–1930-kh gg." In *Konets institutsii kul'tury dvadtsatykh godov v Leningrade*, 8–129. Moscow: Novoe Literaturnoe Obozrenie.

Lee T. Lemon and Marion J. Reis, eds. *Russian Formalist Criticism: Four Essays*. Lincoln, NE: University of Nebraska Press, 1965.

Levchenko, Ian. *Drugaia nauka: russkie formalisty v poiskakh biografii*. Moscow, NIU VshE, 2012.

Levchenko, Ian, and Igor Pil'shchikov, eds. *Epokha "ostraneniia": russkii formalizm i sovremennoe gumanitarnoe znanie*. Moscow: Novoe Literaturnoe Obozrenie, 2017.

Lomonosov, M. V. *Polnoe sobranie sochinenii*. 11 vols. Moscow/Leningrad: Izd. Akademii nauk SSSR, 1952.

———. *Sochineniia: v 8–mi tomakh*. St. Petersburg/Leningrad: Akademiia nauk, 1891–1948.

Maguire, Robert, ed., *Gogol From the Twentieth Century: Eleven Essays*. Princeton, NJ: Princeton University Press, 1974.

Mandel'shtam, *Osip. Slovo i kul'tura*. Moscow: Sovetskii pisatel', 1987.

———. *The Selected Poems of Osip Mandelstam*. Translated by Clarence Brown and W. S. Merwin. New York: NYRB, 2004.

———. *Stikhotvoreniia.* Leningrad: Khudozhestvennaia literatura, 1973.

Mayakovsky, V. V. *Polnoe sobranie sochinenii v 13–i tomakh.* Moscow: GIKhL, 1955–61.

Morozova, V. S. and O. N. Tsvigun, eds. *Mnimaia poeziia: Materialy iz istorii poeticheskoi parodii 18–24 vv.* Moscow: Academia, 1934.

Ogarev, N. A. *Stikhotvoreniia.* Moscow: M. i S. Sabashnikovy, 1904.

Panaev, Ivan. *Sobranie sochinenii.* Moscow: Izd. V. M. Sablina, 1912.

———. *Sobranie stikhotvorenii Novogo poeta.* St. Petersburg: V tip. glav. shtaba ego Imp. Velichestva po voenno-ucheb. zavedeniiam, 1855.

Pasternak, Boris. *Stikhotvoreniia i poemy.* Leningrad: Khudozhestvennaia literatura, 1990.

———. *My Sister Life and the Zhivago Poems.* Translated by James Falen. Evanston, IL: Northwestern University press, 2012.

Pletnev, P. A. *Sochineniia i perepiska P. A. Pletneva,* vol. 1. St. Petersburg: Tip. Imperatorskoi Akademii nauk, 1885.

Polevoi, Nikolai, ed., *Novyi zhivopisets obshchestva i literatury.* Moscow: Izdanie knigoprodavtsa V. Logonova, 1832.

Poety 1790–1810-kh godov. Leningrad: Sovetskii pisatel', 1971.

Potebnya, A. A. *Iz zapisok po russkoi grammatike.* Kharkov: D.N. Poluekhtov, 1899.

———. *Mysl' i iazyk.* Kharkov: Zhurnal ministerstva narodnogo prosveshcheniia, 1913.

Pushkin, Alexander. *Eugene Onegin: A Novel in Verse.* Translated by James Falen. Oxford: Oxford University Press, 1995.

———. *Sobranie sochinenii v 10–i tomakh.* Moscow: GIKhL, 1959–1962.

———. *Sochineniia Pushkina.* Edited by V. I. Saitov. St. Petersburg: Tip. Imp. Akademii nauk, 1908.

Pushkin i ego sovremenniki (periodical), issues 33–335. Petersburg: Tip. Imp. Akademii nauk, 1922.

Sel'vinskii, Il'ia. *Sobranie sochinenii v 6–i tomakh.* Moscow: Khudozhestvennaia literatura, 1971.

Shishkov, Aleksandr. *Sobranie sochinenii i perevodov admirala Shishkova.* St. Petersburg: V. tip. Imperatorskoi rossiiskoi akademii, 1824.

Shklovskii, Viktor. *Literatura i kinematograf.* Berlin, 1923.

———. *Gamburgskii schet: Stat'i, vospominaniia, esse.* Moscow: Sovetskii pisatel', 1990.

Shubin, V. F., ed. *Yuri Tynianov. Bio-bibliographic Chronicle.* St. Petersburg: Arsis, 1994.

Sumarokov, A. P. *Polnoe sobranie vsekh sochinenii v stikhakh i proze.* Moscow: V univ. tip. N. Novikova, 1787.

———. *Stikhotvoreniia.* Moscow: Sovetskii pisatel', 1935.

Svetlikova, Ilona. *Istoki russkogo formalizma: traditsiia psikhologizma i formal'naia shkola.* Moscow: Novoe Literaturnoe Obozrenie, 2005.

Tikhonov, Nikolai. *Sobranie sochinenii.* Moscow: GIKhL, 1958.

Tomashevskii, B. V. "Darovanie literaturoveda." In *Vospominaniia o Iu. N. Tynianove. Portrety i vstrechi,* edited by V. A. Kaverin, 224–230. Moscow: Sovetskii pisatel', 1983.

Trediakovskii, V. K. *Izbrannye proizvedeniia.* Moscow/Leningrad: Sovetskii pisatel', 1963.

Tsiv'ian, Yuri. *Na podstupakh k karpalistike: Dvizhenie i zhest v literature, iskusstve i kino*. Moscow: NLO, 2010.

Turgenev, I. S. *Polnoe sobranie sochinenii v 28 t.* Moscow/Leningrad: Izd-vo Akademii nauk SSSR, 1960–68.

Tynianov, Iurii. *Arkhaisty i novatory*. Leningrad: Priboi, 1929.

———. "Predislovie ." In *Dnevnik V. K. Kiukhel'bekera*. Leningrad: Priboi, 1929.

———. *Sobranie sochinenii v trekh tomakh*. Moscow/Leningrad: GIKhL, 1959.

———. *Poetika. Istoriia literatury. Kino*. Moscow: Nauka, 1977.

———. *Problema stikhotvornogo iazyka*. Moscow: Sovetskii pisatel', 1965.

———. *Pushkin i ego sovremenniki*. Moscow: Nauka, 1968.

Tiutchev, F. I. Ostaf'evskii arkhiv kniazei Viazemskikh. St. Petersburg: Tip. M. M. Stasiulevicha, 1899–1913.

———. *Polnoe sobranie sochinenii*. St. Petersburg: Izd. grafa S. D. Sheremet'eva, 1878–1896.

———. *Polnoe sobranie sochinenii*. 4 vols. St. Petersburg: A. F. Marks, 1913.

———. *Mikhail Zoshchenko, Stat'i i materialy*. Leningrad: Academia, 1928.

Ustinov, Denis. "Materialy disputa 'Marksizm i formal'nyi metod' 6 marta 1927." *Novoe Literaturnoe Obozrenie* 50 (2001).

Zhukovskii, V. A. *Sobranie sochinenii v chetyrekh tomakh*. Moscow/Leningrad: GIKhL, 1959–1960.

Index

www.ingramcontent.com/pod-product-compliance
Lightning Source LLC
LaVergne TN
LVHW020503100826
845148LV00003B/693